The
Rise and Fall
of the
People's Century

The Rise and Fall of the People's Century:

Henry A. Wallace
and American Liberalism,
1941–1948

Norman D. Markowitz

The Free Press, New York
Collier-Macmillan Publishers, London

Copyright © 1973 by Norman D. Markowitz

Printed in the United States of America

The Free Press
A Division of The Macmillan Company
866 Third Avenue, New York, New York 10022

Collier–Macmillan Canada Ltd., Toronto, Ontario

Library of Congress Catalog Card Number: 72–86508

printing number

1   2   3   4   5   6   7   8   9   10

*For my mother and father, Julia and Charles
Markowitz, and for my uncle, Isaac Markowitz,
whose world also changed in 1945.*

Contents

Preface

Lost causes, especially when the events in question concern the recent past, are usually the preserve of polemicists and poets rather than serious scholars. In writing about Henry Wallace, whose cause, the New Deal, supposedly triumphed as he strayed from it, historians especially have shown themselves to be captives of the present and its stereotypes when they have sought to write about the recent past. To Arthur Schlesinger, Jr., for example, it was the personal eccentricities of Wallace that largely explained his opposition to the postwar Truman administration and to the Democratic party in 1948. Taking a more sympathetic view of Wallace, Eric Goldman in the early 1950s did not follow the Communist dupe image to which Schlesinger was so attached. Goldman portrayed Wallace and his followers as unsophisticated liberal isolationists, blind to both the real danger of the Soviet Union and to the shift within postwar American liberalism from an almost exclusive emphasis upon economic problems to a concern with "liberty, opportunity and security—all vital and all vitally equal."

As the cold-war stereotypes were modified in the 1960s it became fashionable to accept Goldman's interpretation and to view Wallace as a tragic figure who had served well as Secretary of Agriculture and as Vice President but had thrown away his career and reputation in a wrong-headed and futile crusade against American foreign policy. In this tradition, Edward L. and Frederick H. Schapsmeier, the most recent biographers of Wallace, have warned their readers that "to try to understand his [Wallace's] ideas when viewing them entirely through the maze of events taking place since 1940 is tantamount to gazing through a telescope from the wrong end."

Like the Wallace family and many of the late Vice President's friends, the Schapsmeiers contend that "the agrarian years represent the finest hour of Wallace's presence upon the stage of history."

In the 1940s Wallace's "presence on the stage of history" was set against the national and international events that shaped the postwar world. In responding to those events, his abilities as a thinker of and spokesman for American liberalism, and as a practical politician and public servant were sorely tested. I have sought in this book to describe in depth the wartime liberal program for a world New Deal and an American social service state and to contrast that program with the anti-Communist liberalism of postwar America. I have sought also to analyze the strengths and weaknesses of Henry Wallace the political theorist and Henry Wallace the political actor and to deal in a scholarly fashion with the controversial events surrounding Wallace's career in the 1940s.

A great many people have contributed to the development of this work from its inception in Sidney Fine's seminar at the University of Michigan five years ago. Although the number of librarians who have made my work less difficult is too great to mention, a few deserve special commendation: Earl Rogers of Special Collections of the University of Iowa Library; Harry Clark and Philip Lagerquist at the Harry S Truman Library; Robert Parks and Joseph Marshall at the Franklin D. Roosevelt Library; Josephine Harper of the Wisconsin State Historical Collections, and Herbert Davis of the Library of Congress.

The members of my doctoral committee at the University of Michigan, John Higham, Shaw Livermore and Harold Jacobson, contributed valuable criticism to the work. To a considerable extent, my own intellectual growth was largely the product of contact with the gifted men and women who were my colleagues in a remarkable history department at Northern Illinois University at DeKalb, Illinois. To all of them, and especially to one of them, Martin J. Sklar, goes substantial credit for the changes in my own thinking that are reflected in the present manuscript.

My colleague at Livingston College, Gerald Grob, provided truly invaluable assistance and support. The critical comments of Charles Smith of the Free Press were also very helpful. Susan Harrow performed the difficult task of typing the final manuscript with dexterity. Donna Walcavage assisted with the proofreading and in other important ways. Without the generous aid of Professor Edward L. Schapsmeier and Gladys L. Baker, who gave me access to their private correspondence, my knowledge of Henry Wallace's personality would have been much poorer.

Above and before anyone else, Sidney Fine, my major Professor and mentor at the University of Michigan, is responsible for this book. His diligent and patient criticism, his tolerance for interpretations at variance with his own, and his high professional standards guided this study and helped to turn a student into an historian. In 1967 I knew Wallace only as a much misunderstood figure, one of the cast of thousands who blew trumpets and carried spears in Arthur Schlesinger, Jr.'s *Age of Roosevelt*. When Sidney Fine suggested that I write a paper on the thought of Henry Agard Wallace, neither of us knew where the work would eventually lead.

NORMAN D. MARKOWITZ
NEW BRUNSWICK

1
Prelude to the People's Century

"The day will come," prophesied Henry A. Wallace in 1935, "when this world will be more secure, when people who ask only to live a good life here and make a living will not be driven to meanness and to littleness, to a calculated denial of their highest capacities, and to hate. We live by these ancient standards of withdrawal and denial in a world bursting with potential abundance. The fears, coupled with the narrowness and hatred of our forefathers, are embodied in our political and educational institutions and bred in our bones. It will only be a little at a time that we can work ourselves free." [1]

In these words Henry Wallace captured the essential reform vision of twentieth-century social liberals—the vision of a society evolving toward higher levels of material security and spiritual freedom, gradually overcoming the vestiges of competitive institutions and values. For Wallace, as for most American reformers, this vision centered around the creation of a vaguely defined cooperative commonwealth, a society in which use and need would replace profit and the personal relationships and ethical values of preindustrial America would be united with the material advantages of industrial civilization.

Defining the cooperative commonwealth as a middle path between capitalism and socialism, Wallace accepted capitalism in the present in the belief that the development of science and technology would modify its competitive and debasing aspects and thereby give rise to a new and more humane society in the future. Thus he could spend a lifetime denouncing imperialism while advocating trade expansion and condemning a materialist culture while making social relationships dependent upon economic relationships between the groups within the economy and between the nation and the world.

That there were contradictions between the needs of society and the needs of the individual, between order and freedom, Wallace readily admitted. Indeed, much of his intellectual life was spent in search for mechanisms to overcome those contradictions. Yet in reality he ignored the contradictions. He believed instead that new social machinery would create the new man, while he simultaneously believed that substantive social change could be brought about only when the people freely and voluntarily changed their minds.

In this regard, his dilemma mirrored that of twentieth-century social liberals. Believing in progress through the march of science and technology, Wallace—like most liberals—could accept elite manipulation without accepting the class nature of political power, for such an acceptance was not compatible with the liberal belief in a competitive society threatened by vested interests rather than a clearly defined ruling class. If there were no ruling class, capitalism might kill itself (euthanasia might be a better word) when its competitive aspects were shown to be irrational and obsolete. Were there a ruling class, of course, the technology and the abundance might be turned to ends quite different than those of the cooperative commonwealth.

In the life and career of Henry Wallace, in his journey through the twentieth century, the gap between social liberal ideology and the realities of American political and economic life were powerfully expressed. The grandson of a Presbyterian minister, Wallace moved from a farm family representing agriculture in the struggle with industry to the worlds of science, journalism, and national politics. A Progressive and a New Dealer, he was a part of and bridged the two central movements of reform in twentieth-century America. At his best, he could sing out the democratic promise of America and thrill men with the quality of his ideas. Yet, Wallace's career also displayed the poverty and ultimate emptiness of social liberalism—its failure to deal realistically with the American political economy and thus to make a difference in the real world.

In the 1940s, Henry Wallace the man and social liberalism the movement came together at a time of great conflict and change for America and the world. By studying both Wallace and social liberal thought in the 1940s and by relating one to the other, one can gain powerful insights into America's contemporary domestic and international problems. Before doing that, however, one must say something about the liberal heritage and its meaning for America.

I

In an advanced capitalist society, the history of liberal ideology becomes an inevitable journey into false consciousness, a perpetually frustrating attempt to strike a balance between order and freedom while preserving a market society that produces disorder and denies freedom. A look at the diverse histories of European and American liberalism will support this contention. Emerging triumphant in the seventeenth and eighteenth centuries against the system of special privileges and private rights that had nurtured it, the European bourgeoisie evolved the doctrines of common rights, equality before the law, and individual freedom—ideas that were most suited to its consolidation and expansion.[2]

Each class, Marx observed, perceives its own values as universally applicable, the means of its own ascendancy as the means for the liberation of humanity.[3] So it was with the apostles of bourgeois liberalism. The citizen–soldiers of the French Revolution spread the doctrines of common rights and individual freedom through Europe by the sword, encouraging the rise of the republican nation-state. The industrializing nations of Europe used the prevailing liberal ideology as a rationale to create a world market governed by the principles of cash and contract, a universe in which progress and freedom were united with each other and hinged ultimately upon the freedom to trade.[4]

These achievements were prodigious, but hardly suited to the attainment of freedom through liberal means, that is, to what R. G. Collingwood called "A life of discipline and moral progress." [5] The creation of the free citizen, self-disciplined and governed by individual initiative, had been the revolutionary aspect of liberal thought. Confronted with the problems created by nineteenth-century capitalist expansion, specifically with the industrial city and the struggles for world empire, liberal ideology was increasingly threatened.

In Europe, the liberals could no longer safely tilt against the old regime. On the left, socialists arose from and pointed to the contradiction between the liberal ideas of individual freedom and progress and the effects of industrial capitalism on the new urban proletariat. Conservatism, with the granting of the franchise to the middle and lower classes, accepted the old liberal program of equality before the law and open opportunity to provide for entry into the marketplace. As socialists appealed to comradeship, loyalty to one's class and humanity over citizenship, and conservatives manipulated the mystique of national duty and honor and imperial adventure over the self-disciplined, self-defining individual, European liberalism moved in the direction of its most familiar modern posture—that of standing between two closed and well-differentiated systems.[6]

Faced with the grim realities of industrial society, European liberals in the late nineteenth century veered toward what Guido Ruggiero has called *social liberalism.*[7] With great dexterity, social liberalism rejected laissez faire in favor of state intervention in the economy to protect the general welfare and rationalized the rise of labor unions as a check upon unrestrained corporate power. The historical school of economics in the German Empire provided an anti-laissez-faire rationale for social liberalism in Europe and America while the early welfare state policies of an authoritarian Bismarck in Germany and of the early twentieth-century leaders of British Liberalism, Herbert Asquith and David Lloyd-George, represented the model programs through which liberal parties sought to win over the newly enfranchised workers.[8]

Beneath the social–liberal rhetoric proclaiming the death of the economic man and hailing class cooperation and social reform, there were, as Ruggiero has noted, economic arguments for the new policies that stressed competition and efficiency.[9] Social liberals looked to competition from labor and the modernization of industry to continuously lower the cost of goods and services and saw a new age in which the extremes of great wealth and poverty would forever be reduced. Thus, the rough equality of competitors within the marketplace, regulated by the state, would eliminate the class conflict and imperialist expansion created by modern industrialism and would produce an increasingly complex and interdependent world system.[10]

In Europe, where a sense of class had developed out of feudalism, liberal parties in the twentieth century failed either to regain their old middle class base or win over the workers from the socialists. Further shattered by the world wars, the political remnant of European liberalism took its stand in the center with those parties (reflecting middle-class and agricultural interests and often called conservative or Christian) who advocated a managed capitalism as an alternative to socialism.[11]

But what of America, the land where ideology had presumably been exorcised by practical experience and where social classes feared to tread? Was not America, as Louis Hartz has wryly observed and most scholars and citizens have always assumed, born free? [12] The absence of an hereditary aristocracy, abundant natural resources, and Yankee ingenuity had all combined to make the new world the opposite of the old, egalitarian and individualistic, free from both the tyranny of rulers and the mob. At least, so went the public ideology, and the public ideology was Locke in a coonskin cap. By maximizing individual freedom and equality of opportunity one would free men to pursue wealth so that they might obtain independence and mastery over their own lives. Independence, the union of self-discipline and moral progress, was ultimately more important than wealth itself, which was only a means to an end.[13] Was this not the bourgeois idealism that had receded with the consolidation of industrial capitalism in Europe? Even in the depression-haunted 1930s, Harold Laski, a socialist student of the rise of liberalism, noted that the "American civilization of the last hundred years may not illegitimately be regarded as the fulfillment of the liberal ideal." [14]

But then the machine, or more broadly industrialization, entered the garden of the farmers and mechanics in search of wealth, and the old world crossed the ocean to frighten the new. A Civil War was fought between Northern capitalists and farmers and Southern slaveholders and farmers, primarily for control of the West as an area of expansion and secondarily over the principle that each man must control his own labor to compete with others for a chance at the good life. The triumph of the North coincided with, and ultimately accelerated, rapid industrialization.[15] Corporations, treated as self-defining individuals under laissez-faire law, used freedom and the competitive means of the marketplace to strive for monopoly. The factory system inexorably robbed men of mobility and independence. Above all, the revolutionary creation of a national market wreaked havoc with the livelihoods and thus the lives of farmers, workers, and small businessmen. To many, the corporate revolution threatened to destroy the calculus of equality of opportunity and individual freedom that had been both the liberal ideology and the American dream. In the late nineteenth century, the lines of battle were drawn between the defenders of the old liberalism and the builders of industrial America.[16]

Believing that the public ideology had been perverted by criminal Trusts and an alien Money Power, the America of the towns and the farmsteads called upon the government to restore the marketplace, fought for credit and currency inflation and antimonopoly legislation, and threw up a myriad of William Jennings Bryans to lead countless poorly defined crusades of the righteous people against the vested interests. Coherent and largely irrelevant, the preindustrial liberal ideology lived on through the twentieth century, commanding the loyalty of a large minority of the population who grudgingly accepted the corporation and in prosperous times concentrated its energies against the expansion of both government power and the institutions of urban life.[17]

Others sought to transform liberalism into a new public ideology. Specifically, the new class of salaried experts—managers, administrators, social scientists—thrown up by the corporate revolution sought to use the methods of that revolution—bureaucratic organization and control—to solve the problems created by the process of industrialization. Rising through confidence in the organizational revolution, rather than in angry rebellion against it, the advocates of the American version of European social liberalism sought the familiar middle path of American reform, rejecting laissez faire as anachronistic and ignoring socialism save as a specter with which to haunt those who were unsympathetic to specific reform proposals. Ideology, with an assist from both scientific management and a vulgarized pragmatism,[18] gradually gave way to techniques of administration; and the competitive individuals of the old liberal ideology were transformed into cooperative functional groups (business, agriculture, labor). Above all, the state was redefined as a mediator between these groups, with vaguely defined powers to protect an even more vaguely defined General Welfare.[19]

In practice, social liberalism always represented a tenuous type of popular front joining corporate reformers and humanitarian reformers—those interested primarily in adjusting people to an efficient business culture, and those interested in social welfare and democratic procedures—who were united only in their rejection of the negative state and their antipathy toward socialism. On the one hand, the guiding vision of twentieth-century social liberals, the secure, managed society, reflected the corporate world view; on the other hand, the unending search of so many social liberals for *mechanisms* to provide for popular participation in government and to safeguard individual rights represented the constant tension between the corporate world view and the older assumptions of an America born free and equal.[20]

Viewing state power primarily as a vehicle to rationalize and expand the existing economic system, corporate reformers sought to reorganize municipalities for the benefit of business interests and to use the regulatory powers of the state to encourage business consolidation and aid in the procurement of domestic and foreign markets. (Herbert Hoover's attempt in the 1920s to turn the Department of Commerce into a "clearinghouse" to provide informational services to business, assist in the creation of restrictive trade associations, and lead the aggressive search for foreign markets cut through to the core of corporate reform.) [21] The end product of corporate reform, very visible by the 1920s, was the socially controlled consumer society. In the aftermath of World War II, that society would be enshrined as the American Way of Life.

For the humanitarian reformers, the social workers, intellectuals, trade unionists, *et al.*, the question of means and ends was more complex. Advocates of everything from slum clearance and workman's compensation to national economic planning and vigorous antitrust campaigns, the humanitarian reformers were caught in the paradox of condemning social injustice while upholding capitalism as a system. This paradox was overcome by an act of philosophical transubstantiation, i.e., the belief that capitalism would evolve organically into something other than itself, that the force of technological innovation and the growing spirit of cooperation would induce capitalists to de-emphasize profits and manage industry in the public interest.[22] A government of the people, administering the society for the workers and the consumers rather than the owners, became for the humanitarian social liberals the grand mechanism for making industry serve man; thus, democratic procedures, individual consent, and education for citizenship became all important for the humanitarian social liberals. Only an educated and secure populace could discipline itself and its leaders, interpret and enforce the General Welfare.[23]

Accepting capitalism as a system in the present in order to transform capitalism in the future, the humanitarian social liberals assured that they would be subservient to and eventually subsumed under corporate social liberalism. Thus, the humanitarian reformers were condemned to dwell in a world of perpetual fantasy, supporting governments that bowed to big business in the name of fighting big business, eschewing the need to create a new public ideology while blaming the absence of such an ideology on an unenlightened public opinion, and veering between a utopian glorification of the common man and a conservative fear of mass action and popular Philistinism.[24]

In retrospect, one may contend that the contradictions within twentieth-century social liberalism were most dramatically expressed in the crisis years between Pearl Harbor and the inauguration of the Marshall Plan. Henry Agard Wallace, scientist, devout Christian, and progressive capitalist, acted as the leading liberal philosopher and politician of the time. Summing up liberal hopes through the vision of a people's century, Wallace, during the war, also delineated liberal false consciousness by defining that vision in capitalist terms, muddling conceptions of an international people's revolution and a world mixed economy with images of reformed capitalists bringing prosperity to America and the world through expanded trade and nonimperialist investments.

In the early postwar years, Wallace had the courage of his very contradictory convictions and fought against men who offered the nation something far worse. Yet, his ideas and career, when studied closely and related to the transformation of liberal thought in the 1940s, gives one insight into the central failure and irony of twentieth-century social liberalism. Committed to a faith that an expanding capitalist system would evolve into a cooperative commonwealth, liberals first failed to overcome and then became disciples of a conservative politics rooted in a pervasive fear of communism, distrust of "populistic" democracy, and identification with the rule of the benevolent open elites, manipulating opinion and compromising all differences.[25]

II

Henry A. Wallace was the scion of a middle-western farm family whose history was a monument to the America of piety, practicality, and luck. John Wallace, a descendant of

Scottish Protestants who had settled in Ireland in 1690, left the Old Sod and arrived penniless in the frontier country of western Pennsylvania in 1823. Gradually, the immigrant Wallace moved from the status of pioneer to prosperous farmer. His first son, Henry Wallace (later known as Uncle Henry) prepared for a career in the ministry before the Civil War, took his first pulpit in the Presbyterian Church for Davenport, Iowa, and Rock Island, Illinois, in 1862, and later served as a Union Army chaplain. After ill health compelled him to leave the ministry, Uncle Henry settled down to the life of a farmer and landlord in Winterset, Iowa, in 1877, engaging in business ventures, writing for local farm newspapers, and standing fast as a local booster and a pillar of the Presbyterian Church and the Republican party.[26]

Henry Cantwell Wallace, Uncle Henry's studious son, was destined eventually for a career of teaching, journalism, and government service. First, he tried the hard life of a dirt farmer, leaving Iowa State College at Ames in 1887 to marry and become a tenant on one of his father's farms in Adair County, Iowa. In October of 1888, Henry C.'s first son, Henry Agard Wallace, was born on the tenant farm. According to an old family legend, his middle name had come from Arthur Agard, an ancestor of his mother who was rumored to have been an English knight.[27]

The 1890s were years of crisis and change for both the Wallaces and the nation. Hit hard by the depression of the early nineties, Uncle Henry settled with his sons, John and Henry C., in Des Moines and started a farm newspaper. Taking the name of *Wallace's Farmer* in 1896, the paper eventually became the most influential farm journal in the Middle West. Like so many later leaders of the Progressive Movement, the Wallaces opposed the Bryan–Populist alliance of 1896 as a financial heresy and a threat to the social order. Still, they were keenly aware of the problems highlighted by the farmer–labor protest against the new industrialism.[28]

In 1899, Uncle Henry wrote that the trusts, hitherto considered the agents of economic progress, had corrupted government and compelled labor to "meet organization with organization." Fearing both state power and labor unions, the Iowa editor called upon an aroused public opinion to reform government and restrain corporate power. In themselves, Wallace mused, the trusts might prove to be harbingers of the cooperative commonwealth, "the halfway house between competition and cooperation which we believe is the only way in which general business can square itself with the Sermon on the Mount." [29] One should note, as a hint of later difficulties, that the cooperative commonwealth was not for the Wallaces separable from the producer interest of agriculture, which in turn was identical with the general welfare. In Uncle Henry's mind, the moral and ethical problems posed by the trusts were given focus by the fact that city-based monopolies threatened farm prosperity by closing off the *industrial and railroad expansion* upon which such prosperity had been based and by forcing farmers to act as sellers in a competitive market and buyers in a noncompetitive market.[30]

Uncle Henry defended the proprietary interest of agriculture as a member of Theodore Roosevelt's County Life Commission, as a champion of the agrarian insurgent wing of the Republican party, and as a follower of the Progressive party of 1912.[31] His influence on his precocious grandson was substantial. From Uncle Henry, Henry A. Wallace imbibed a passion for the Old Testament, a faith in the Main Chance (what was called, in the Middle West of his youth, practical idealism), and the memory of revivalist rhetoric against the trusts and for the Christian cooperative commonwealth and the common man—a rhetoric that Wallace would one day combine with the ideas of John Maynard Keynes to provide American liberalism, in the middle of World War II, with a program and a style.[32]

The Henry Wallace who entered Iowa State College at Ames in 1906 was a long way from the national power he would enjoy during World War II. Although he wrote glowingly for the school newspaper about the movement for rural reform and followed his family in support of the Progressive wing of the Republican party, his interest in plant genetics, agricultural economics, and quantitative analysis in science greatly outweighed his concern for contemporary political matters. After reading Henry L. Moore's pioneering study on the relationship of climate to agricultural prices, Wallace in 1909 launched independent statistical analyses of the problem. From this work he developed correlation techniques that emerged in pioneering corn–hog ratio studies in 1915 and were continued in his work on price and commodity ratios for Herbert Hoover's Food Administration during World War I. At the same time, young Henry Wallace continued the cross-breeding experiments with corn that were later to bring him fame and wealth.[33]

Out of his experiences as an economist and a plant geneticist, Wallace developed a view of science as a process, as the interrelationship of different elements and forces over time, and as a method for obtaining truth from conflicting hypotheses. Beginning at the age of twenty to study the works of William James (whose version of pragmatic philosophy contained a sense of mystery and rejection of final solutions that conformed closely to Wallace's own state of mind), the young economist launched his lifelong quest to relate the approaches of science to spiritual life and to contemporary social problems.[34]

Unhappy with the parochial nature of scholarship within agricultural economics, Wallace first learned of Thorstein Veblen's business-cycle studies in 1915. Recovering from a touch of tuberculosis in the Colorado Rockies in 1916, the young economist carefully read Veblen's *Theory of the Leisure Class* and *Theory of Business Enterprise*. A year later, Wallace met Veblen in the offices of the Food Administration in Washington and was impressed with the fact that the famous economist had also once believed in the statistical solution to all problems.[35]

From Veblen, himself the product of rural isolation in Minnesota, Wallace took the idea of cultural lag, of the inability of economic and social institutions to keep pace with advancing technology (this was to become such a powerful rationale for social liberal reform programs as to make Veblen appear to many to be the patron saint of the New Deal). Also,

1. *The three Henry Wallaces—Henry A. (left), his father, Henry C. (center), and his grandfather, Uncle Henry (right). (Courtesy of James W. Wallace.)*

Veblen's emphasis upon the instinct for workmanship as a prime human motive and his later stress upon the removal of profit-seeking businessmen in favor of an engineering elite provided the young Wallace with the rudimentary framework for the society his grandfather had searched for in religion and in an inspired public opinion: a workable cooperative commonwealth. In *Agricultural Prices* (1920), his first book and a major work in early agricultural economics, Henry Wallace displayed his debt to Thorstein Veblen.[36]

Placing his faith in government-supported programs to study business cycles and price and production variables, Wallace hoped that contemporary business civilization would soon give way to the rule of "production engineers" and "statistical economists." [37] Although this view may appear rather sanguine (not to say utopian), it is indicative of a central strand of liberal thought in the western world: evolutionary positivism. For the evolutionary positivist, progressive social change occurs naturally as more information becomes available, enabling men to use their reason more effectively to control environment. Eventually, the *data* become the mechanism of social change, their mastery and administration the solution to social problems. The development of science and the growing complexity of society, Wallace maintained in *Agricultural Prices* (which later critics would allude to as an example of his radicalism), militated against the continuation of a system "whereby the bulk of the people get just enough to keep them going." Veblen's concept of an *instinct for workmanship*, Wallace believed, was stronger than the profit motive. Together, the people and the engineers would build a cooperative society.[38]

In his years of national eminence Wallace would invoke the gods of technology in the name of New Deal economic planners, antimonopolists, and new socially conscious businessmen (progressive capitalists) to create the cooperative commonwealth. Always, he would search for specific mechanisms and techniques to avoid popular coercion, to retain individual freedom by permitting man to accept voluntarily the new social discipline of a cooperative society. For Wallace, as for most twentieth-century social liberals, the grand mechanism to achieve the cooperative commonwealth, the union of reason and technology through a people's government, was assumed rather than analyzed. This assumption provided for a comfortable defense against a workable definition of the general welfare and a serious examination of what the division of society into functional groups, i.e., business, agriculture, and labor, meant for both individual freedom and popular democracy. Finally, the evolutionary positivist world view behind such assumptions led Wallace and most social liberals to the dubious and ultimately self-defeating assumption that an expanding capitalist economy would produce an essentially noncapitalist cooperative commonwealth.[39]

In Wallace's specific case, faith in a cooperative commonwealth was strongly reinforced by a deep commitment to revealed religion. In this regard, one may note that the commonwealth idea had roots in medieval Christianity and the English Puritan revolution and had served in colonial America as a possible alternative to and check upon the entrepreneurial spirit. Social Gospel ministers of all political hues had in the Progressive Era raised the hope of a Christian Cooperative Commonwealth, and influential secular leaders of Progressive thought such as the New Economists Richard T. Ely and Simon Nelson Patten were lay leaders of the Social Gospel movement. Connecting the values of the Social Gospel with his own adoration of a God that lived in and through all things, Wallace in the early 1930s took Max Weber's famous correlation of the Protestant ethic with the entrepreneurial spirit to argue that the old Protestantism, whose doctrine of individual salvation had provided the rationale for an expanding frontier America, had died with the depression. The Social Gospel, he maintained, must go forth to regenerate religion as the New Deal strove to revive and reform capitalism.[40]

Although Wallace's all-too-visible piety made him somewhat out of place among the more secular New Dealers and encouraged distorted and malicious charges of mysticism by his enemies, colleagues like Frances Perkins and perceptive scholars like Ralph Gabriel and Sidney Fine have long noted his con-

nection with the Social Gospel.[41] Whereas the Social Gos-
pelers above all else sought to interpret religion in terms of
contemporary social problems, Wallace in *Statesmanship and
Religion*, the most extensive public expression of his religious
views, freely returned to the political stereotypes of his youth
by portraying Amos as a farmer angry at a corrupt and reactionary commercial civilization, David as a politician who had
betrayed the downtrodden debtor classes, and the worshippers
of Baal as the "Standpatters" of the Bible. Also, he affirmed
the basic idea of the Social Gospel with the contention that
religion must reveal itself "not merely by way of giving a
mystical glow to the individual worshipper, but also by way
of bringing about the kingdom of heaven on earth." [42]

In 1938, Wallace wrote to Henry C. Taylor of his hope that
an American religion was in the process of evolution, a religion of the whole people that would unite the best of
capitalism, democracy, and revealed religion. As in the world
of nature and affairs, organic evolution and synthesis would
bring harmony and unity to apparently diverse and contradictory forces.[43] In the 1940s, Wallace would unite a Social
Gospel evangelism with populistic rhetoric and Keynesian
economic policies to preach the doctrine of a people's century.

The agricultural depression of the 1920s produced serious
strains in the thought of Henry Wallace. Replacing his father
as editor of *Wallace's Farmer*, when the latter became Warren
Harding's Secretary of Agriculture in 1921, young Wallace
watched the forces of industrial progress and general prosperity crash head on into the proprietary interest of agriculture. Even labor, agriculture's old ally in the cooperative
commonwealth of the Greenbackers and the Populists, appeared to be growing rich while farmers became poor. In
the early 1920s, Wallace directed his sharpest attacks against
labor. In April, 1921, he wrote that capital and labor were
both enemies of agriculture and that the city worker was
profiting at the farmer's expense. Later, he suggested that
agriculture might be better off if labor were "more fully
employed at a somewhat lower wage." Returning to his family's
faith in the moral and ethical superiority of the farmer over

the city worker, Wallace conceded that his early belief in a farmer–labor alliance might have been wrong and warned farmers to "stay clear of entangling alliances with both labor and capital." [44]

Wallace's fascination with cycles in nature led him in the 1920s to seek similar developments in history. With the enthusiasm and lack of discrimination that was so characteristic of him, he explored the work of the Egyptologist Sir Flinders Petrie and Gugliemo Ferrero, the historian of the Roman Empire, both of whom stressed the corrupting force of urbanization and wealth upon society and the inevitable fall of civilizations after the removal of the self-reliant peasant. Oswald Spengler, who in *Decline of the West* presented similar ideas in a more compelling and blatantly racialist manner, encouraged Wallace's fears that an independent rural civilization was being engulfed by cities, immigrants, and "soulless" laborers. Responding to the Spengler vogue, the young farm editor wrote in 1923 that cities were the "lethal chambers of civilization," the harbingers of racial suicide. Observing the manners and complexions of Italian and Slavic immigrants with uneasiness through most of the decade, Wallace told farmers to support immigration restriction out of a sense of patriotic duty, even if this meant a reduction of agricultural markets (perhaps the only time in his long career that he consciously advocated the reduction of markets that were not already lost). Visiting New York in the last year of the boom, he proclaimed in mock-heroic fashion, "your standards of money and wealth are not our standards . . . you shall not have our best sons and daughters to add brilliancy to your flaming civilization." [45]

But the standards of money and wealth that were operative in the urban world were what farmers aspired to; and Wallace, seeking ways to preserve a unique rural civilization, returned to the ways of the industrial society, organization and expansion, to achieve these ends. In 1921, *Wallace's Farmer* began to preach the doctrine of production control with the slogan "Less Corn, Less Clover, More Money." With Irving Fisher, James Rogers, and other important economists, the young farm editor became a leader of the Stable Money League, an organization that stressed increased purchasing power through a managed currency. Joining with other farm leaders to lobby for the passage of the McNary–Haugen bill, which was advertised as a tariff for agriculture, Wallace worked for a political alliance of all agricultural producers, a "marriage of cotton and corn," and began to look more sympathetically on the idea of united action with labor.[46]

In 1924, these considerations led the young farm editor to vote for Robert M. La Follette, the candidate of a partial farmer–labor alliance. By 1927, Wallace was speaking publicly of a possible third party that would unite the farmers of the South and the West with Eastern workers and the liberal middle classes. Contemptuous of Herbert Hoover, whom he saw as his late father's and agriculture's worst enemy in the Harding and Coolidge cabinets, Wallace sought to convince Frank O. Lowden, the former governor of Illinois, to lead a farm-oriented third party in the wake of the 1928 Republican convention. Failing that, he joined other disgruntled farm leaders to support a presidential candidate from the sidewalks of New York.[47]

Wallace's not-so-enthusiastic advocacy of Al Smith was neither surprising nor ironic, for in the Jazz Age economic issues took precedence over cultural ones for the leaders of depressed agriculture, if not necessarily for their followers. Traveling widely as a farm spokesman during the 1920s,[48] Wallace had little reason then to identify with the service capitalism preached by Herbert Hoover and the trade associations. Throughout the decade, he expressed hostility to business consolidation and to the propaganda of an ordained business leadership. Retaining his personal affection for Veblen and his belief that advancing technology would still solve the problems of a business civilization, Wallace had come to accept in principle what John Dewey had called by the end of the 1920s the *new individualism:* the realization that men would need security before they could obtain true freedom. The conformity of the twenties, Wallace argued, had been a response to organized society's refusal to grant security to the people. New plans, he maintained, even utopian ones, were needed as "the blueprints of our future." [49]

Throughout the twenties, Wallace looked to the farm cooperative (especially to the educational and cultural activities of the Scandinavian cooperatives) to provide the focal point for the reorganization of rural life. Perhaps, he reasoned, the cooperative idea might be expanded to other sectors of the economy. Even though he believed that cooperatives proved that the profit motive and competition were not inevitable parts of human nature, Wallace's interest in farm cooperatives highlighted his and social liberalism's dubious attempt to make capitalist means serve noncapitalist ends.[50]

The farm cooperative was, when looked at objectively, an attempt to provide farmers with control over their production and marketing comparable to that already held by large corporations in industry—a goal that Wallace deferred to while he talked airily about a cooperative rural civilization springing forth in the Mississippi Valley. Consistently warning farmers through the decade to reduce production, Wallace also called for reduced tariffs in order to permit European debtors to pay American creditors with industrial imports (and thus revive trade generally and agricultural exports especially). Indeed, the fact that America had become a creditor nation at the end of World War I was to become his perennial stock explanation of the need to adopt new national and international economic policies. Despite his constant attacks on competition and materialism, coupled often with allusions drawn from Veblen and the Bible, Wallace remained committed to a cooperative commonwealth defined in terms of and subordinate to a marketplace society.[51]

Wallace's standing between two worlds, competition and cooperation or capitalism and socialism, made him at times an insightful and prophetic thinker, even if it did turn him into a quixotic politician. In a letter written in January, 1922, that included the recommendation of Thorstein Veblen as an advisor to President Harding's Conference on Agriculture, Henry A. Wallace wrote to his father that "it would seem that the United States has before her two rather clearcut paths. The

one leads to economic self-sufficiency and aloofness from
Europe and the other leads to taking a very active interest in
Europe, reorganizing Europe financially, investing liberally
in European industries and eventually taking a very vital interest in Europe's military and political affairs." Although he
expressed no direct commitment to either path, his way of
framing the proposals (identifying the latter proposal with the
interests of agriculture) displayed where his own sympathies
were.[52] In the second solution, Wallace had seen the outline
of the American Century nearly two decades before Henry
Luce, who was to become his philosophical antagonist in
World War II, had given to that program of unilateral
American expansion its name. The energies released by the
depression and the hopes for economic planning and social
justice on a world scale brought forward by World War II
would provide Wallace and American social liberalism with
a fleeting alternative to the American Century.

III

The early 1930s, Henry Wallace remembered in the last
years of his life, "were days of great despair." From the misery,
there came intellectual ferment and political upheaval that
brought liberals to power and compelled social liberalism to
test its stress upon concrete action, organization, and administrative technique against the realities of a shattered economic
system.[53] Roosevelt and his minions went forward to save
capitalism from the capitalists. In retrospect, few in the New
Deal truly tested the tenets of social liberalism more completely than Henry Wallace and the legion of liberal intellectuals, social scientists, and planners who followed him into
the Department of Agriculture.

By 1929, Wallace had largely rejected McNary–Haugenism
for the domestic allotment plan for agriculture, a program of
production control through voluntary acreage reduction contracts between the producers and the government (domestic
allotment eventually served as the basis of the first Agri-

cultural Adjustment Act). Advocating both public works legislation and the old agricultural panaceas of currency and credit inflation to fight the depression in the early 1930s, Wallace campaigned for Franklin Roosevelt in 1932 and was instrumental in persuading the New York governor to accept the domestic allotment plan. After his appointment as Secretary of Agriculture, the Iowa editor quickly became one of the administration's foremost advocates of national economic planning. In *New Frontiers* (1934), the best of his many books, he portrayed the New Deal as an adventure in planning and popular participation—a movement toward economic democracy—by the government and ordinary citizens. Rexford Guy Tugwell, the administration's most significant advocate of national economic planning and humanitarian social reform, became his first Undersecretary of Agriculture. From the outset, Wallace looked toward the production–planning committees of the Agricultural Adjustment Administration as a step toward "a new democratic process at work in this country, a process of economic self-government." [54]

As the depression continued, Wallace defined the New Deal as an attempt to mediate between the extremes of total security and total freedom. Striking at the strawman of laissez faire, he spoke endlessly about the need to construct new social machinery, to create an economic democracy that would permit farmers to control the centralized economic system of the day as political democracy had enabled citizens to control the decentralized economy of nineteenth-century America. For the nation as a whole, he advocated planning to provide for industrial expansion that would maintain increased farm prices, stressing, as did most of the New Dealers, the need to increase mass purchasing power and develop high levels of consumption in order to achieve recovery. Preaching the gospel of crop control through land-use planning and an Ever–Normal Granary, Wallace found himself portrayed by administration supporters and much of the mass media during the 1930s as an idealist and philosopher, a dreamer who epitomized the best hopes of the New Deal. [55]

Another caricature of Wallace, employed in the early New

*2. Secretary of Agriculture Henry Wallace (right) looks on as
President Roosevelt presents the first AAA acreage-reduction
check to a Texas cotton farmer, July, 1933. (Courtesy of the
Franklin D. Roosevelt Library.)*

Deal by both the Right and the Left, was cruder but perhaps
more to the point. It concerned the Secretary of Agriculture's
involvement in 1933 in the destruction of ten million acres of
cotton and the slaughter of six million little pigs.[56] These acts,
Wallace conceded, were a shocking commentary on contemporary civilization; nevertheless he presided over a farm
program that differed in form rather than in substance from
the AAA's first brutal acts of emergency production control.
Denouncing throughout the depression the continuation of

scarcity principles in an economy of abundance, Wallace administered a program designed primarily to inflate prices by limiting production. For the most part, the attempts at production control outside of cotton were haphazard; Wallace would later admit that the dustbowl had contributed far more than the AAA to reduced production in wheat. Also, the principal beneficiaries of AAA acreage-reduction payments were the large farmers. Tenants and sharecroppers, especially in the South, were usually defrauded of benefit payments and taken out of production with the acreage.[57]

In practice, the AAA committees that were supposed to act as the vanguard of decentralized, democratic planning for agriculture were controlled by the county agents of the extension service and the large farmers, both of whom were usually connected with the American Farm Bureau Federation. The Farm Bureau, gaining enormous power through its cooperation with the New Deal, ignored the plight of tenants and croppers and often collaborated with local authorities in terrorizing tenant and farm-labor organizers. Theirs were hardly the policies to uphold human rights over property rights, erect new social machinery for agriculture, or light the way to either economic democracy or the kingdom of God on Earth. They were, however, moderately successful in maintaining agricultural prices and providing relief for a hard-pressed agricultural establishment. Economic recovery, Wallace maintained, as did all who understood the workings of capitalism, must precede institutional reform if the reforms were to endure. "Social reform by publicity is one thing," Wallace would note years later in commenting on the conflicts within the Department of Agriculture, "social reform through Congress has to be approached in another way." [58]

Unfortunately, social reform—more significant after 1934 as the administration found itself deluged with support from urban workers and the rural poor, who often appeared ready to take things into their own hands—did not flow effortlessly from an agricultural program designed to strengthen the bargaining power of large producer groups. The Farm Bureau, weaned by the AAA, was unsympathetic and obstructionist

3. Secretary of Agriculture Henry Wallace (seated) with his Undersecretary, Rexford Guy Tugwell. (Courtesy of the United States Department of Agriculture.)

in regard to the department's long-postponed plans to aid the rural poor, modifying and diluting those programs where it could not block them outright.[59] Administration attempts at counterorganization in agriculture, that is, support for alternative groups like the National Farmers Union and the Southern Tenant Farmers Union to organize the rural poor and thus balance the Farm Bureau in negotiations with the government, were half-hearted and eventually shattered by the war. Even had they succeeded, the achievement would have been dubious, for counterorganization evades problems rather than solving them.[60]

The modern liberal state, as Theodore Lowi has noted, can neither plan nor govern for "liberalism replaces planning with bargaining." This tendency to avoid clear programs in favor of compromise and administration—implicit in twentieth-century social liberalism—was erected into a system by the New Deal. Committed above all else to recovery through the private sector of the economy, the New Deal sought to act as a broker, intervening in the economy to the advantage of organized groups on the basis of their power (although this approach was explained as an attempt to balance interest groups against one another and thus restore an economy that was obviously out of balance). In essence, the belief that government could balance interest groups against one another and remain free of the contending groups to serve the public welfare was utopian; some groups, the large corporations and commercial agriculture, remained so much stronger than the others that they could make any attempt by government to organize the powerless into competing interest groups largely impossible. Through their ability to manipulate the state, the large groups would ultimately be strengthened by the distribution of corporate rights and responsibilities to new groups (the great example being organized labor).[61]

For the New Deal as a whole, the shift to counterorganization in the late 1930s, as Ellis W. Hawley has noted, was less purposeful than resigned, a *fait accompli* emerging from the frustration of attempts at national economic planning and market revival, and the growth of a lower-class New Deal political base.[62] Most scholars agree that, after the fall of the NRA, most administration attempts at economic planning were lodged in the Department of Agriculture. From the mid-thirties, attempts at economic planning and counterorganization corresponded with department programs for social reform. The Bankhead–Jones Farm Tenancy Act of 1937 provided for loans to tenants and farmers and created the Farm Security Administration to administer a program of relief and rehabilitation for the rural poor. With the reorganization of the Department of Agriculture and the enactment of the AAA of 1938, the Bureau of Agricultural Economics was elevated and expanded to serve as a coordinating agency for the production-planning program and a clearinghouse for general agricultural planning. The Ever–Normal Granary, the Secretary's fondest wish for agriculture, became a partial reality with the establishment of crop insurance and grain storage programs under the AAA of 1938. In his last report as Secretary of Agriculture, Henry Wallace could write with some justice that "agriculture has laid the basis in production planning which other branches of the economy may have to copy. It is pioneering in social and economic readjustments and all the signs to date indicate that it is moving in the right direction." [63]

As both Sidney Baldwin and Richard Kirkendall have shown, the achievements of economic planning and social reform in agriculture were largely casualties of World War II. After Wallace left the department, the planning program disintegrated under Claude Wickard's leadership. The Food Stamp Plan, the department's last achievement of social reform before the war, was liquidated by the conservative coalition in Congress in 1943 (to return two decades later under John Kennedy). While the Farm Bureau worked with congressional conservatives to greatly reduce funds for the Farm Security Administration and force the resignation of its director, C. B. Baldwin, farmers demanded and got prices that were 110 percent of parity. As a sad reminder of what the farm program had really been about, the New Deal was still paying farmers to take land out of production after rationing had begun in World War II. [64]

Henry Wallace continued to talk about economic planning and social justice long after the New Deal had lost its congressional majorities, to call for world Ever–Normal Granaries and TVA's abroad at a time when the war crisis seemed to endanger the survival of New Deal programs in the United States. In his emergence into national politics, one can grasp the problems that would haunt his political career and that reflected the failures of the New Deal.

IV

It is difficult to date the beginning of Wallace's interest and involvement in the quest for national office in 1940. In retrospect, it appears that he received the 1940 vice-presidential nomination as he would lose that nomination four years later, a stranger to the central events as others fought passionately both for and against him, chosen at last by Roosevelt through a devious process of elimination.

A maverick Republican since the days of Theodore Roosevelt, Wallace became a registered Democrat in the 1936 presidential campaign and vigorously attacked Alf Landon as an agent of the Liberty League, suggesting to Roosevelt that the Democrats "strip the mask off the National Republican party and show up Landon as an amiable tool." After the election, the Secretary of Agriculture continued to call for industrial expansion and to stress the natural solidarity of agriculture and labor in a cooperative economy.[65] On the most controversial public issues of the second Roosevelt administration, however, one must note that Wallace moved to the right.

Although he had indignantly attacked the Supreme Court for its invalidation of the first Agricultural Adjustment Act, Wallace resisted administration pressure and staunchly refused to take sides in the court reorganization controversy. When Senator Guy Gillette of Iowa was placed on the White House's purge list of conservative Democrats for the 1938 primaries, the Secretary of Agriculture openly backed Gillette. Through Gillette's victory, he gained a powerful lever against fellow Iowan Harry Hopkins, a leader of the purge drive, who was widely rumored to be a potential successor to Roosevelt. Paul Appleby, Wallace's chief administrative aide in the department, in 1938 began to work for a Wallace candidacy in

1940, using his field trips for the department to meet with state and county Democratic leaders and to keep lists of potential Wallace supporters. Against the private wishes of Senator Clyde Herring, an Iowa Democrat who apparently harbored vice-presidential ambitions himself, Appleby maneuvered for a pro-Wallace Iowa delegation to the 1940 national convention, writing to a local Wallace supporter that the strategy must be "if not Roosevelt—Wallace." [66]

Following the outbreak of the European war, Wallace became an early and enthusiastic supporter of the third term, even after White House press secretary Steve Early stated publicly that "he should have told the victim before he spoke." As the third-term nomination movement entered the spring of 1940, Roosevelt's advisors wished to make certain that Iowa's first-ballot presidential votes would not go to Wallace. With his usual aplomb in these matters, the President permitted stories to circulate that he felt Wallace lacked political "It" and then patiently informed Iowa Democrats that the Secretary of Agriculture, fine fellow though he was, had no chance for the nomination.[67]

To the anger of many party regulars and the surprise of both friends and foes, Roosevelt chose Wallace to be his runningmate. Although there is evidence that the President had thought about his choice for a number of days, the final decision came at the last moment. Paul Appleby, who represented Wallace's interests at the convention, was greeted by Harry Hopkins in pajamas at 7:30 a.m. of the day that the vice-presidential balloting was scheduled to commence. Roosevelt, Hopkins told Appleby, had called at 2:30 a.m. to announce that Wallace was the nominee and arrangements had been made to break the news to the other candidates.[68]

Acting with surprising forcefulness, the President then compelled the convention to accept Wallace or face the possibility that he would refuse his own renomination. On the convention floor, delegates of all political colors attacked the Wallace candidacy, although the bulk of the opposition came from party organization men and Southerners. Jimmy Byrnes, acting on Hopkins' instructions, informed delegates of Roosevelt's threat to withdraw if Wallace were not nominated, but the opposition continued. The President's tactics finally resulted in the withdrawal of most of the candidates for the nomination, especially in that of Paul McNutt of Indiana, the leading contender. Faced with limited opposition, Wallace won a decisive though unpopular first-ballot victory over his only serious challenger, William Bankhead of Alabama. Although many observers hailed the nomination as a vindication of liberalism and the New Deal, a closer look at the President's actions cast some doubt on that assumption.[69]

Initially, Roosevelt had expressed great interest in Secretary of State Cordell Hull, a white-haired symbol of conservatism and internationalism and the perfect candidate to balance a risky third-term ticket, but Hull had adamantly refused to run. Roosevelt then suggested a possible candidacy to Jimmy Byrnes, a Southerner and a moderate conservative with very strong influence in the Senate and a record of general loyalty to the administration. When Byrnes showed little interest in the nomination, Roosevelt turned to Wallace.[70]

The President, as was his custom, gave different reasons for his choice to different people, stressing political considerations in conversations with politicians and ideological reasons in discussions with New Deal stalwarts. Cordell Hull and Alben Barkley both remembered Roosevelt's prenomination comments that Wallace would help him in the farm states. Edward J. Flynn, Bronx political boss and successor to James Farley as national chairman, privately supported the nomination. Indeed, the press noted in early July that the Willkie–McNary Republican ticket made a Wallace nomination more likely. With an ex-liberal Democrat and an old farm hero running for the GOP, who could balance the Democratic ticket more effectively than an ex-Progressive Republican who was both Secretary of Agriculture and the scion of one of the most famous farm families in the Middle West? [71]

To those more sympathetic to New Deal aspirations, Roosevelt generally explained his choice of Wallace as a reaffirmation of his administration's domestic and foreign policies. Wallace, he told Frances Perkins, "would be a good man if something happened to the President. He is no isolationist. He knows what we are up against in this war that is rapidly engulfing the world." Judge Samuel Rosenman remembered that Roosevelt believed that he had chosen a man "in whose hands the program of the New Deal—both domestic and foreign—would be safe." Eleanor Roosevelt, who had flown to the convention to calm rebellious delegates, believed that her husband "felt that Wallace at that time could be trusted to carry out our policies in foreign affairs if by any means, he, Wallace, found himself hurled into the Presidency." As Ilo Wallace, Henry's wife, sat next to Mrs. Roosevelt at the hostile convention and bewilderedly asked the First Lady, "Why do you suppose they are so opposed to Henry?" the President, according to Judge Rosenman, had a letter drafted formally declining the nomination if Wallace were defeated.[72]

In his letter, Roosevelt saw the nomination fight as crucial to the future of the Democratic party. In part, the letter read "until the Democratic party makes clear its overwhelming stand in favor of liberalism and shakes off all the shackles of conservatism and reaction it will not continue its march to victory. . . . It would be best not to straddle ideals. It would be best to have the fight out." [73]

Behind the President's brave words, the Democratic party's condition was in itself evidence of what had happened to the New Deal. Roosevelt had not solved the problem of mass unemployment short of war, and he had not, despite the purge attempts of 1938, created a responsible liberal–labor party. Indeed, in 1940 the President was without a domestic program for the future, as the foreign-policy crisis began to shift the initiative in the country to the corporate establishment. New Deal politics had crystallized into an uneasy interest-group coalition and a personality cult. If the 1940 Democratic convention was any evidence, only Roosevelt could unite the coalition and then only out of its fascination with his political magic and its fear of being dislodged by the Republicans.[74]

In many ways, Henry Wallace had been a measure of both the strengths and weaknesses of the New Deal. Committed to reviving the existing economic system so that a better one might emerge from it, he had dealt in broad generalities and concrete programs for action, limiting both the scope of his ideas and the nature of his experiments by the need to defer to the groups and the values that make up a market society. In so doing, he had followed Roosevelt in avoiding a true pragmatic approach to the depression, standing with the President as the prophet and prisoner of slogans that might win the people's votes but were not connected to programs that could change their lives. His election to the Vice-Presidency in 1940 increased his opportunities and audience without solving his problems as a political leader.

Possessed of a keener intellect than Roosevelt, Wallace lacked the charm and cunning with which to build a career of his own in a politics increasingly dominated by personality. His vision, however, remained large and his imagination open. The nation, as he had written in *New Frontiers*, was on the threshold of great adventures. For Wallace, the greatest adventures would come as he sought to make sense of the New Deal for a generation lost in a world war and an emerging cold war. The people's century was in the offing, the people's revolution would soon be on the march.

NOTES

1. Henry A. Wallace, "America: Recluse or Trader?" *Colliers*, XCV (February 2, 1935), p. 35.
2. The best studies of the development of European liberalism remain Harold Laski, *The Rise of European Liberalism* (London, 1936), and Guido Ruggiero, *The History of European Liberalism* (London, 1927).
3. Karl Marx and Friedrich Engels, "The German Ideology," pp. 246–261 in Lewis Feuer, ed., *Marx and Engels* (Garden City, N.Y., 1959).
4. For a lucid and subtle expression of the relationship between free trade, progress, and freedom, see L.T. Hobhouse, *Liberalism* (London, 1911), pp. 78–101.
5. Ruggiero, *European Liberalism*, p. vii.
6. For the rivalry with socialism, see Hobhouse, *Liberalism*, pp. 167–213.
7. Ruggiero, *European Liberalism*, p. 269. J. Salwyn Schapiro uses the term *social liberalism* as synonymous with the twentieth-century wel-

fare state. J. Salwyn Schapiro, *Liberalism: Its Meaning and History* (Princeton, N.J., 1956).

8. Hobhouse, *Liberalism*, pp. 214–251. For the effects on America, see Sidney Fine, *Laissez-Faire and the General Welfare State* (Ann Arbor, 1956), Chapter VI.

9. Ruggiero, *European Liberalism*, pp. 269–270.

10. *Ibid.*

11. Of course, one may also argue that the major socialist parties of Western Europe have abandoned socialism for a de facto form of state capitalism that is more akin to the politics of Lloyd–George than the principles of Karl Marx.

12. Louis Hartz, *The Liberal Tradition in America* (New York, 1955), pp. 3–32.

13. *Ibid.*

14. Laski, *Liberalism*, p. 238.

15. For a different view of the Civil War's effects on American industry, see Thomas Cochran, "Did the Civil War Retard Industrialization?" *Mississippi Valley Historical Review*, XLVIII (September, 1961), pp. 197–210.

16. For a brilliant evocation of late nineteenth-century American life, see Ray Ginger, *Age of Excess* (New York, 1965).

17. The old public ideology, as Theodore Lowi notes, could not come to terms with the facts of twentieth-century economic life. Theodore Lowi, *The End of Liberalism* (New York, 1969), pp. 26–28.

18. Robert H. Wiebe, *The Search for Order* (New York, 1967), Chapters 5–6.

19. *Ibid.*, pp. 159–193.

20. *Ibid.*, Chapters 7–8.

21. Although he deals narrowly with the National Civic Federation, James Weinstein uses his research to interpret corporate liberalism as a public philosophy in early twentieth-century America. See James Weinstein, *The Corporate Ideal in the Liberal State. 1900–1918* (Boston, 1968).

22. Cf. David Noble, *The Paradox of Progressive Thought* (Minneapolis, 1958). Noble's perspective is both different from and essentially complementary to this study.

23. For the problems of using corporate means to attain humanitarian ends, see Wiebe, *Search for Order*, pp. 161–163.

24. For a more optimistic and traditional appraisal of twentieth-century American liberalism, see Eric F. Goldman, *Rendezvous with Destiny* (New York, 1952).

25. For post-World-War-II liberal intellectual fear of the people, see Michael Rogin, *The Intellectuals and McCarthy* (Cambridge, Mass., 1967).

26. Henry Wallace, *Uncle Henry's Own Story* (Des Moines, 1917), I, 22–24, 91–98; II, 84–90, 110–111, 120–123; III, 36–56, 71–80.

27. "Henry C. Wallace of Wallace's Farmer," *W.F.*, October 31, 1924, p. 1415; Russell Lord, *The Wallaces of Iowa* (Boston, 1947), pp. 104–107.

28. Wallace, *Uncle Henry's Own Story*, III.

29. Henry Wallace, *Trusts and How to Deal With Them* (Des Moines, 1899), pp. 51-52.

30. *Ibid.*, pp. 17-25.

31. For insight into Uncle Henry's private views on national questions during the Progressive era, see his correspondence with Walter Hines Page in the Henry Wallace (Uncle Henry) Papers, University of Iowa, Iowa City, Iowa. The Papers are listed by item number.

32. For Wallace's own memories of his family and the Iowa of his youth, see Henry A. Wallace, "Reminiscing and a Look Into the Future," Address, Pioneer Club of Des Moines, September 18, 1962, Henry A. Wallace Files, United States Department of Agriculture Library, Washington, D.C.

33. For example, see Henry A. Wallace, "The National Grange," *Iowa Agriculturalist*, XI (January 10, 1910), pp. 196-198; HAW to Dr. L. H. Parmel, July 16, 1924, HAW Folders, Iowa State Historical Collections, Iowa State University, Ames, Iowa. For an excellent summary of Wallace's early scientific work see Mordecai Ezekiel, "Henry A. Wallace, Agricultural Economist," *Journal of Farm Economics*, XLVIII (November, 1966), pp. 789-93.

34. HAW to Lynn Eley, June 23, 1951, HAW Papers, University of Iowa.

35. Ezekiel, "Henry A. Wallace," p. 790; Lord, *Wallaces of Iowa*, p. 189.

36. Henry A. Wallace, "Odds and Ends," *W.F.*, August 30, 1929, pp. 1167 (hereafter, Wallace's "Odds and Ends" column, which was a regular feature in the paper from the early 1920s, will be cited as HAW, "OE," and the appropriate issue).

37. Henry A. Wallace, *Agricultural Prices* (Des Moines, 1920), pp. 109-27.

38. Wallace, *Agricultural Prices*, p. 110.

39. The search for mechanisms to reconcile absolute order with absolute freedom has been the great quest of the progressive mind in the twentieth century. See Noble, *Paradox of Progressive Thought*, p. viii.

40. HAW, "The Challenge to Protestantism," Address, December 7, 1934, in Addresses of the Secretary of Agriculture, Record Group 16 National Archives (hereafter cited as RG 16, NA). For the role of the social gospel in the American reform tradition, see Sidney Fine, *Laissez-Faire and the General Welfare State* (Ann Arbor, 1956), Chapter 6.

41. *Ibid.*, p. 381; Ralph Gabriel, *The Course of American Democratic Thought* (New York, 1940), p. 306.

42. Henry A. Wallace, *Statesmanship and Religion* (New York, 1934), pp. 18-37, 91-92.

43. HAW to Henry C. Taylor, December 30, 1938, Henry C. Taylor Papers, Box 23, Wisconsin State Historical Society, Madison, Wisconsin (henceforth called WSHS).

44. *W.F.*, April 22, 1921, p. 664; *W.F.*, May 13, 1921; HAW, "OE," *W.F.*, April 26, 1926, p. 623.

45. "The Lethal Chambers of Civilization," *W.F.*, November 2, 1923, p. 1472; HAW, "OE," *W.F.*, November 5, 1926, p. 1441; HAW, "OE," *W.F.*, January 25, 1929, p. 173.

46. *W.F.*, May 13, 1921, p. 744; "A Stable Price Level," *W.F.*, September 19, 1924, p. 1221; "McNary–Haugen History," *W.F.*, February 25, 1927, p. 302. The McNary–Haugen bill sought to solve the problem of low farm prices by using a two-price system. The government would guarantee a domestic price above the world price for a staple crop (with farmers themselves paying part of the cost through an equalization fee). No production controls were planned, however, and surpluses were to be dumped on world markets.

47. Donald Murphy to the Author, November 22, 1968; HAW, "OE," *W.F.*, April 23, 1926, p. 623; HAW, "Party Changes Needed," St. Louis, November 2, 1927, in Chester Davis Papers, Box 11, Western Historical Collections, University of Missouri, Columbia, Mo. (henceforth cited as WHC).

48. For Wallace's lukewarm endorsement of Smith, see "Helping The Doubtful Voter," *W.F.*, October 19, 1928, p. 1427.

49. "We Want to Be Safe," *W.F.*, May 8, 1925, p. 675; "The Making of Utopia," *W.F.*, February 23, 1923, p. 299.

50. HAW to Frank O. Lowden, December 26, 1926, Frank O. Lowden Papers, Series I, Box 39, University of Chicago, Chicago, Illinois; "Farm Community Halls," *W.F.*, May 1, 1924, p. 643; "The Love of Money," *W.F.*, May 14, 1924, p. 4420.

51. Writing as late as 1951 to a student preparing a masters thesis on his thought, Wallace noted "a great nation which has suddenly changed from a debtor nation to a creditor nation must act in accordance with her new position" as an example of the kind of truism regularly violated by the press and the politicians. HAW to Lynn Eley, June 23, 1951, HAW Papers, University of Iowa.

52. HAW to Henry C. Wallace, January 3, 1922, in Taylor Papers, Box 23, WSHS.

53. HAW to Edward L. Schapsmeier, March 11, 1964, in the private possession of Professor Schapsmeier.

54. HAW to William Hirth, February 17, 1932, HAW to Hirth, August 30, 1932, Hirth Papers, Box 10, WHC; Henry A. Wallace, *New Frontiers* (New York, 1934); HAW, "Economic Democracy in the Corn Belt," Address, October 5, 1935, p. 6, RG 16, NA.

55. For an early example of this essentially favorable image of Wallace, see Felix Belair in the *New York Times*, April 2, 1933.

56. Wallace attempted to laugh off the charges about the little pigs, but they followed him for the rest of his career, returning to haunt him even in 1948.

57. For the difference between the rhetoric and the reality of New Deal farm policies, Broadus Mitchell's old study, *Depression Decade* (New York, 1947) remains the most honest account.

58. HAW to Mr. Conrad, June 13, 1959, HAW Papers, University of Iowa.

59. For an analysis of the Farm Bureau's estrangement from the USDA, see Christiana Campbell, *The Farm Bureau and the New Deal* (Urbana, 1962).

60. For the administration's general shift to counterorganization in the

late 1930s, see Ellis W. Hawley, *The New Deal and the Problem of Monopoly* (Princeton, N.J., 1966).

61. Lowi, *End of Liberalism*, p. 101.
62. Hawley, *New Deal*, pp. 12–14.
63. For the reorganization in the USDA, see Richard S. Kirkendall, *Social Scientists and Farm Politics in the Age of Roosevelt* (Columbia, Mo., 1966), pp. 150–164; Henry A. Wallace, *Report of the Secretary of Agriculture, 1940* (Washington, 1940), p. 21.
64. Kirkendall, *Social Scientists*, pp. 195–254; Sidney Baldwin, *Poverty and Politics* (Chapel Hill, N.C., 1968), pp. 365–404.
65. HAW to FDR, July 15, 1936, FDR Papers, PSF, Agriculture, Box 22. For the farmer–labor theme, see HAW, "The Community of Interest Between Labor, Capital and Agriculture," Address, January 3, 1938, RG 16, NA.
66. Bernard F. Donahoe, *Private Plans and Public Dangers* (South Bend, 1965), pp. 69–72; Appleby, Notes for Columbia Oral History Project, undated, Appleby Papers, Carnegie Library, Syracuse University; Appleby to William Riley, September 25, 1939, Appleby Papers.
67. *San Francisco Chronicle*, October 26, 1939; *St. Louis Post-Dispatch*, October 27, 1939. Roosevelt purportedly made his statement about Wallace to Guy Gillette. *Des Moines Register*, January 10, 1940.
68. Paul Appleby Interview, *COHC*, p. 194.
69. James F. Byrnes, *All In One Lifetime* (New York, 1958), p. 125. Appleby, *COHC*, pp. 222–229.
70. Cordell Hull, *The Memoirs of Cordell Hull* (New York, 1948), I, p. 861; Byrnes, *All In One Lifetime*, p. 118.
71. Hull, *Memoirs*, p. 861; Transcripts, Sidney Shalett's Interview with Alben Barkley, p. 24, HSTL; Edward J. Flynn, *You're The Boss* (New York, 1947), p. 117; *Des Moines Register*, July 7, 1940.
72. Frances Perkins, *The Roosevelt I Knew* (New York, 1946), p. 130; Samuel Rosenman, *Working with Roosevelt* (New York, 1952), p. 206; Eleanor Roosevelt, *This I Remember* (New York, 1949), pp. 216–218; Rosenman, *Roosevelt*, p. 217.
73. *Ibid.*
74. Although writing from a different perspective than the present author, Bernard Donahoe has noted that the convention was as much an example of liberal failure as of liberal success. Donahoe, *Private Plans*, pp. 191–196.

2

Keeper of the Flame

. . . there must be genuine democracy in approaching problems of the human soul and access to raw materials.

Henry A. Wallace
to William F. Riley
September 30, 1941 *

World War II ended the depression in America, but the ending was hardly happy at the outset. When Henry Wallace entered the Vice Presidency in January, 1941, German and Japanese domination of most of Europe and Asia offered the grim prospect of a barbaric new order committed to a world of force without law and without justice. The war crisis led Roosevelt to give Wallace powers and responsibilities well beyond the usual ceremonial role of the Vice President—new authority as chairman of the Board of Economic Warfare, member of the War Production Board and other important agencies, and the President's special emissary on missions to Latin America and China.

Yet, Wallace's most important wartime role was to serve as the leading spokesman for a revived and confident social–liberal movement. Opposed to both Adolf Hitler's New Order and Henry Luce's American Century, social liberals developed ambitious plans during the war for a postwar New Deal for the world and for the creation of a full-employment mixed economy in the United States. These hopes gained their most vivid expression in Henry Wallace's advocacy of a postwar Century of the Common Man. But the war had heightened nationalist feeling and increased corporate and conservative power just as it expanded government control over the economy and raised liberal hopes about the use of the state's planning and spending powers to transform America and the world. In his struggle to retain control of the Board of Economic Warfare from the assaults of administration and congressional conservatives, Wallace highlighted both the strengths and the weaknesses of the liberal attempt to identify the war crisis with plans for thoroughgoing reform in America and the world.

4. *President Roosevelt and Vice President Wallace on Inauguration Day, January, 1941. (Courtesy of the Franklin D. Roosevelt Library.)*

I

Was the New Deal dead? Malcolm Cowley asked this familiar wartime question with dismay as he noted the New Dealers' flight from their own administration. The businessmen, the hated economic royalists of another era, appeared to be taking over. On the surface, Cowley's pessimism seemed to be both justified and typical. Throughout the war, it was apparent that anti-New Deal forces were effectively combining war-induced appeals to patriotism and national unity with more familiar arguments about economy in government and opposition to radicalism in order to strike at administration programs and personnel.[1]

Strengthened by wartime inflation, the shortages of consumer goods and the loss of millions of young voters from the electoral scene, the conservative coalition in Congress fought a guerrilla war against executive power and prerogatives while the authority of the federal government as a whole expanded enormously. In the years after Pearl Harbor, Congress acted to abolish the Works Progress Administration, the National Youth Administration, and the National Resources Planning Board; conservative congressmen had successfully rebelled against New Deal tax measures and thus compelled the war to be financed through massive deficit spending; and everywhere, New Dealers faced such special harassments as an "anti-professor amendment" to bar those without business experience from OPA, attempts by Congress to secure veto power over the appointment to war agencies of all officials with salaries above $4,500, and a tireless struggle to reduce funds for New Deal social programs and agencies.[2]

These were hardly the conditions one would expect for a renaissance of social liberalism. In looking at the wartime liberal movement from the perspective of the cold war, some scholars have portrayed the period as a time of rampant irrationality, of both an intense fear among liberals of incipient American Fascism and a boundless hope in a millennial world order aborning in the aftermath of the war. Other writers,

harking back to Sidney Hook's 1943 polemic against the failure of nerve, have simply portrayed wartime liberalism in terms
of a growing disillusionment with mass movements and an increasingly uneasy search for ways to defend individual freedom
in an organized society.[3]

Yet, a careful study of liberal thought will unearth very
different tendencies. For most social liberals, the government-
financed growth of the economy and the realities of wartime
production planning and full employment revived confidence
in man's ability to create and control his environment and set
precedents for a planned economy and a welfare state that
were unheard of in the 1930s. Furthermore, social liberals came
to enthusiastically define the war as a revolutionary struggle
and to look to America to redeem her own revolutionary heritage by uniting with the forces that sought the destruction of
colonialism and by working to construct international organizations to eliminate the social and economic inequalities that
produce war. As in 1917, when Herbert Croly, Walter Lippmann, et al., rose to fulfill the Progressive Movement by
making the world safe for Wilsonian Democracy, so in 1941
humanitarian social liberals proclaimed a two-front war to expand the New Deal at home and create what Freda Kirchwey
later called a "New Deal for the World." [4]

In the months before Pearl Harbor, the idea of a two-front
war emerged as a major theme for liberal interventionists. The
Union for Democratic Action, founded in 1941 to support the
administration's foreign policy, made the two-front war its
motto, its aim being to relate militant opposition to Fascism in
the name of freedom to the domestic programs of the New
Deal. UDA's purpose, Reinhold Niebuhr wrote to David Dubinsky, was to connect "the fight for democracy on the foreign front with the domestic issues" of the New Deal. Herbert
Agar echoed this contention with the warning that America,
if she were to survive, must "carry on two struggles at once;
a struggle at home to show that we mean democracy and a
struggle abroad against the murderers of freedom." Even
Archibald MacLeish, in a famous polemic that struck savagely
at all rationales for isolationism, called upon young men to

resist Fascism with the faith that society could be organized for both freedom and security.[5]

The two-front war concept provided social liberals with an answer to the wartime riddle of how to fight Fascism without either succumbing to Fascist repression or being molded into the image of Henry Luce's imperialist American Century. Max Lerner was among the first to reply to Luce in 1941 with the call for a postwar people's century, an era in which America would achieve prominence by merging her wealth and skills with the energies of underdeveloped nations to create a genuinely pluralist and progressive world order. If, as Stanley High insisted, it was the liberals' war, they were determined to transform the conflict into a struggle for a welfare state in America and a world New Deal abroad.[6]

Flushed with confidence in America's ability to plan for and reform the world, social liberals repudiated the New Deal's interest-group approach to politics and capacity for compromise as appeasement. Indeed, as *Common Sense* noted, Hitler and Roosevelt had come to represent the contending forces in the world. The compromises and support for the status quo embodied in much of State Department policy was futile in a world revolutionized by Hitler's strategy of terror. Only Roosevelt's support for a strategy of freedom, of opposition to Fascism and colonialism in spite of the British Empire, could produce a new international order that would give meaning to the sacrifice and misery created by the war.[7]

While Cordell Hull privately fumed at the "vociferous persons" who condemned State Department support for colonialism and the Franco and Petain regimes, social liberals responded by raising the Munich analogy to argue that the policies that had caused the war would certainly not win the peace. Perhaps, the *New Republic* suggested in the early months of the war, an investigation of the department's relations with France, Spain, and even Japan was needed. The *Nation*'s Freda Kirchwey's comment that the only difference between State Department policy in Latin America and Hitler's was that "the puppets we pick are Hitler's, not ours" represented the social–liberal perspective that saw appeasement and Realpolitik as interconnected and conservative, that looked at Munich as the central failure of the old order in the West.[8]

George Soule's argument that the State Department could not win both a war and a social revolution (for the one ultimately depended on the other) with the policies that had produced the war represented the other side of the social–liberal argument. America could not defend the status quo or move to the right in the face of a world social revolution; any such attempt would eventually produce a new war. The United States, Alfred Bingham wrote in a review of Walter Lippmann's popular explication of balance-of-power politics, *U.S. Foreign Policy*, could not ignore "social revolution, communism, imperialism, racial consciousness, and the incalculable forces that were raising Asia [and by inference the world] to action."[9]

The world people's revolution would in itself become the mechanism for social change, defeating Fascism abroad and reaction (often equated with American Fascism) at home; yet the revolution would have to be controlled, made to conform to social liberal definitions of order and progress if it were not to degenerate into anarchy and terror. For social liberals, this could be achieved by internationalizing the planning and social welfare policies that had been the best of the New Deal. As an example of this hope, Stuart Chase, prophet and popularizer of a planned economy in the 1930s, saw in plans such as the Tennessee Valley Authority (TVA) "the cathedrals of the twentieth century" and echoed many social–liberal writers in freely applying the TVA principle (with appropriate assistance from international Reconstruction Finance Corporations—RFC's) to the great river valleys of the world. Regional planning of the type represented by TVA would create the rise in living standards and productivity that would both control and fulfill the people's revolution. For Chase, as for social liberals during the war, democracy became again economic democracy, measurable in TVA's, medical care, housing, standards of wage and hours, and employment. Unlike those who would still call themselves liberals in the Truman–McCarthy era, the wartime advocates of a world New Deal saw revolution and democracy as complementary rather than antithetical concepts.[10]

Indeed, social liberals saw conservative attacks against the world New Deal as evidence that the wartime debate merely rehashed the depression struggle between old and New Dealers over the ideas of planning and popular democracy. After Henry Wallace gave the idea of a people's revolution national attention in the Century of the Common Man speech, Samuel Grafton noted privately that "Wallace is the international Tugwell, the state department is the international Farley." If the New Deal, *Common Sense* argued, had been part of an international revolution against laissez faire, then a return to the old system after the war would only reproduce the conditions that had bred chaos. In its place, the liberal magazine advocated a long range policy for world abundance, with a world bank, an international RFC, and a world trade commission as initial mechanisms to maintain the peace.[11]

For George Soule, a "world economic state" appeared to be the only alternative to postwar collapse and war. Along with international TVA's, Soule saw the need for international investment and developmental agencies to fund interregional public works projects. An international labor standards commission would also be needed to protect workers' rights and to assist in increasing living standards and purchasing power through the world. To Abba Lerner, a rising young economist, postwar American prosperity and peace were related to international planning for economic growth and social welfare. The world WPA that Lerner envisioned would appropriate one half of the world total increase in per capita income to raise the per capita income of the poorest nations.[12]

In the establishment of such programs, social liberals portrayed Americans in the postwar world as missionaries of progress, using their sophisticated skills to eliminate disease, illiteracy, and hunger (while Henry Luce, who envisioned a very different postwar world, used these same images). Poverty and incipient Fascism, Hubert Herring wrote, were cause and effect in Latin America; only American assistance to remove the economic feudalism of the continent could achieve democracy and peace. As the left New Dealers had advocated an economy of abundance through purposeful planning for expanded production and increased purchasing power, so the adherents of a world New Deal looked primarily to world economic expansion to provide for prosperity, finance social reform, and thus eliminate the conditions that had produced the depression and the war. Commenting on the Hot Springs Conference of 1943, which laid the groundwork for the Food and Agricultural Organization of the United Nations, a writer for *Common Sense* expressed this standard social–liberal argument with the remark that the conference's program was but a beginning "to an expansion of the whole world economy to provide for the purchasing power sufficient to maintain an adequate diet for all." [13]

Humanitarian social liberals had a powerful program to produce real change abroad, a world situation that appeared to cry out for the program, and an American economy that apparently would require a united and prosperous world if it were to maintain full employment in peacetime. Yet, certain problems arose. Expanded trade, social liberals argued, would arise from industrial development in the poor countries; still, could one expect the industrialists who were the prime beneficiaries and masters of the wartime expansion to relax their monopolistic controls over existing markets for the benefits of future world peace and prosperity? If capitalist cooperation had eluded the New Deal in the depths of the depression, was corporate statesmanship anything more than a pipedream in a period of economic expansion? Social liberals responded to this dilemma with denunciations of prewar cartels, attacks on American monopolies fostered by the war, and calls for vigorous use of the antitrust laws to limit corporate power. In the context of the world New Deal program, opposition to American or international monopoly power was both progressive and complementary to any program of international economic planning. Yet, America's own experience with the antitrust laws was not something to encourage those who fought for regulated competition on a world scale.

The world people's revolution would be the agency of

social change; the programs of the world New Deal would become the means for channeling social change for constructive purposes. Between the two stood the mechanisms for change, the international organizations—capped by a United Nations—that would unite the people's revolution against poverty and oppression with the modernizing world New Deal to produce the Century of the Common Man.

It almost went without saying that one could not, as Stuart Chase noted, bomb democracy into one's enemies (although this view eventually lost support among postwar American leaders). Without an international organization to enforce peace, the world New Deal would be the hostage of the power politics that it sought to eliminate. Furthermore, the subsidiary organizations of such an agency—the United Nations Relief and Rehabilitation Agency, for example—provided the best framework for programs of the world New Deal, making those programs truly international and not subject to the direct influence of American or any other form of capitalism or imperialism.[14]

Social liberals were no more precise about the form of such a world organization than the Roosevelt administration; still, the idea of regional organizations within a greater world organization, with the model of a Good Neighbor version of Pan-America, remained the most common vision. The regional organizations would for social liberals serve less as spheres of influence—which they were in practice in Roosevelt's plan to base the peace on the "police power" of the principal Allied nations—than a device to assure local freedom and flexibility against central power. The world organization would represent unity, the regional organizations would represent diversity. Both would interact to preserve the rights of small nations and to permit the great powers to cooperate to maintain the peace.[15]

For Professor Frederick Schuman, an influential partisan of social liberalism and popular-front politics, writing in the forties, regional organizations must lead to new political entities, the federation of Europe for example, that would remove the national rivalries that stimulate wars. European federation,

Schuman argued, served the national interests of the coalition fighting the war and the oppressed masses in whose name the war was being fought.[16]

If Schuman's hopes of a federated Europe were to prove operational—indeed, if the whole social–liberal conception of the United Nations as the organizing mechanism of the world New Deal were to have any relevance—a genuine harmony of interests between the great powers, a real commitment to co-existence within a world mixed economy, was essential. Schuman's assumption that the reality of the war in the midst of a world people's revolution made such organizations both practical and necessary avoided the problem. Self-fulfilling prophecies usually fall to those who have power, and wartime planning and economic expansion managed by and for the large corporations and defined in terms of patriotic duty was a dubious foundation for a world New Deal. Political power remained with Franklin Roosevelt, to whom social liberals were one group within a diverse interest-group coalition.[17]

In 1942, Henry Wallace had given the idea of a people's revolution its most eloquent wartime expression in his Century of the Common Man speech. During the war, Wallace was to serve as social liberalism's leading spokesman in the administration and in the country at large, identifying himself with the programs for a world New Deal and a postwar American welfare state and with the liberal–labor alliance within the Democratic party. Combining the rhetoric of Populism and Progressivism with the tangible programs of the New Deal, Wallace fashioned a progressive capitalist alternative to the benevolent imperialism of Henry Luce's American Century. His vision had power and foresight; its chance of realization within an expanding corporate economy was quite another matter.[18]

II

Wallace was no stranger to the internationalist cause. During and after the debate over American ratification of the Versailles Treaty, he had served as a director of the Iowa Non-Partisan Association for the League of Nations. An opponent of the Fordney–McCumber and Smoot–Hawley tariffs, he had championed the cause of lower tariffs in the 1920s and of reciprocity during the depression. When war came to Europe, Wallace began to define the conflict as a struggle for the survival of freedom and for world reconstruction. As the Wehrmacht swept through the low countries into France, he told a national radio audience that "civilization is burning" and that America would have to defend herself against Nazi arms and Hitlerite racial ideas. During the 1940 presidential campaign, the future Vice President attacked Republican isolationists for giving aid and comfort to the Nazis.[19]

Shortly after his inauguration as Vice President, Wallace wrote to publisher John Cowles that he feared an American return to economic nationalism after the war. Confident that worldwide chaos would ensue upon the fall of Hitler, Wallace told a radio audience in February, 1941, that "the wisdom of our actions in the first three years of peace will determine the course of world history for half a century. . . ." Writing to his uncle, John Wallace, he maintained that postwar defense would present a greater problem than the present rearmament controversy, because it would be with the people longer.[20] From the outset, Wallace thought primarily of a postwar settlement that would remove the economic rivalries that had led to war. Yet, his goals in the pre-Pearl Harbor period merely echoed the fourteen points and the four freedoms—programs which were ultimately dependent upon increased trade and expanded investment for reconstruction and development. This point came through with unconscious irony when he wrote to a friend in September, 1941, that in the postwar world "there must be genuine democracy in approaching problems of the human soul and access to raw materials." [21]

In the months after his inauguration, Wallace revived memories of Woodrow Wilson and the blasted dream of a League of Nations by calling for a second chance for America. In what he apparently considered to be his most important address of the period, the Vice President told the American

5. Vice President Henry Wallace signing the Senate's resolution declaring war upon Japan, January 8, 1941. (Courtesy of the Franklin D. Roosevelt Library.)

Foreign Policy Association in April, 1941, that America would have to assume world leadership to construct a peace free forever from the menaces of Hitlerism and Prussian militarism. A few weeks later, Wallace returned to his theme of a second chance for America, a chance to organize the postwar world around "the eradication of human suffering and poverty." In a passionate outburst, he set the stage for much of his wartime oratory (and for the rhetoric of the cold warriors who eventually ended his political career) with the contention that "Nazism is a deadly disease . . . creeping across the world, moving in on one free nation after another, first by psychological poison, lies and discord. Then by storm and steel." The idea of an inevitable struggle between freedom and slavery, the theme that introduced the Century of the Common Man speech, also thundered through the frightened years of the cold war.[22]

Like Woodrow Wilson a generation before, Henry Wallace had defined the war as a struggle between human reason and intolerable evil and as a cauldron out of which the greater good of social reconstruction must come. These themes were well established in his public statements when Mrs. Borden Harriman asked him to address a meeting of the Free World Association scheduled for New York City on May 8, 1942. America's entry into the war, however, while Axis forces were advancing on all fronts made the situation quite different than in the previous two years. In clearing the speech with Roosevelt, Wallace informed the President that his purpose was to show the captive peoples of the world that the United States would accept nothing less than complete victory.[23] In restating his prewar arguments, the Vice President gave them clarity and force through the unifying themes of a people's revolution and a people's century.

In brief, Wallace saw the war as a climactic moment in a 150-year-old people's revolution, a revolution that would produce in the postwar world a people's century. Much of the speech was replete with the religious imagery that always made the Vice President stand out in the tough-talking, secular world of the New Deal; yet, contemporary scholars who portray the address as an outgrowth of either populism or revivalism are deluded perhaps by surface meanings and by later stereotypes that were effectively used to picture Wallace as a dreamy agrarian and a religious mystic. Taken as a whole, the speech reflects a combination of the radical democratic and evolutionary positivist views of social progress, of linear development in history, punctuated by revolutionary epochs (the American and Russian revolutions and the Second World War) in which the people triumph over the forces of demagoguery and exploitation that seek to keep them in bondage. The war thus becomes a struggle between the revolutionary Common Man and the "Nazi Counter-revolution." Although Hitler remains the embodiment of Satanic forces, this is less important than the realization that he is at war with science and history.[24]

If God, to Wallace, had ordained the people's revolution and the people's century, the secular standards of twentieth-century society—literacy, national income, industrialization, and employment—were its commandments. The people's revolution, Wallace argued implicitly, must be defined through the standards of modernization and order, of increasing levels of security, equality, and abundance. Through the march toward modern society, the individual would be liberated and genuine community would be achieved. If some revolutions had gone to excess, Wallace maintained, it was more important to retain faith in the process of social revolution, the pattern by which "the people groped their way to the light . . . learned to think and work together."[25]

Rhetorically, Wallace had reclaimed America's revolutionary heritage for a world convulsed by war. America, the Vice President argued, had inaugurated the people's revolution at Lexington and Concord. Now America must use her wealth and power to teach the world the meanings of abundance and peace. In that sense, as Wallace jokingly told Madame Litvinoff, the war was being fought to make sure that every child in the world had at least a pint of milk a day. Security and abundance, which the Vice President believed had reached higher levels in America than in any other nation, provided the only answers to war. "Some," Wallace said, "have spoken of the American Century. I say that the century upon which we are now entering, the century that will come out of this war, can and must be the century of the common man."[26]

There were problems posed by Wallace's vision of a people's century. Beyond advocating complete dedication to war production, he offered no means to fulfill the people's revolution. Nor did he acknowledge the possibility that American abundance was war-induced and that the corporations who reaped the benefits of that abundance would hardly sacrifice their new advantages to cooperate in the creation of a postwar people's century (indeed, Wallace's later attacks against monopolistic business leaders as "American Fascists" would be a desperate attempt to overcome this contradiction). As a piece of oratory, though, the Century of the Common Man speech was a significant event of the war and a major attempt to redefine the conflict in radical democratic as against conservative balance-of-power terms. By Americanizing the people's revolution, Wallace had provided social liberals with a concept and a leader to identify with and a dynamic reply to Henry Luce's self-heralded American Century.[27]

Beginning with an essay in *Life* in February, 1941, Luce had propagated his program for a postwar peace based consciously on opposition to any social change inconsistent with American free enterprise and on the expansion of the American private enterprise system and its benefits throughout the world. New Deal policies, the publisher argued, had weakened the nation before the onslaught of war in much the same way that Leon Blum's *Front Populaire* had prepared France to collapse before the Nazis. In what may have been a special allusion to Wallace, Luce called for the repudiation of demagogues who preached the doctrine of economic abundance (presumably through public control over economic planning) in favor of a revival of unrestrained enterprise at home and trade and investment abroad. In the American Century to come after the war, U.S. power and ideals (which Luce defined in simple conservative terms as law, truth, charity, and freedom) would be imposed on the world as a kind of dispensation. Pursuing their private interests and the interests of humanity, legions of capitalists, teachers, doctors, agronomists, and engineers, would take up the White Man's Burden and bring American-style stability and progress to the world. With great dexterity, Luce had combined the Invisible Hand of Adam Smith with the benevolent imperialism of Rudyard Kipling to create the American Century.[28]

For both Luce and Wallace, the war became an extension of the political conflicts of the depression. The people's century, with its doctrine of social revolution to obtain economic abundance, would extend the best of the New Deal to the world (and as social liberals and Wallace himself would later argue, provide conditions abroad that would encourage the expansion of the New Deal at home). On the other hand, the American Century would subordinate, if not liquidate entirely, the New Deal as a movement for humanitarian social reform by committing the United States to oppose revolutionary social movements disruptive to American capitalism. For the American Century to succeed, the war crisis, and with it the ascendance of patriotic and national as against populist and class appeals, would have to be maintained indefinitely. Luce, who saw the postwar world as a perpetual struggle between nations for wealth and power, accepted the permanent division of the world into hostile power blocs after the war. In a clever reversal of Hitler's idea, the publisher concluded that "freedom would require more living space than tyranny" (a concept that leads explicitly to John Foster Dulles' verbal doctrine of Liberation and implicitly to the actual postwar American policy of containment of Communism). [29] Rejecting the New Deal model with contempt, Luce chose a blunt and benevolent imperialism over isolationism and took up the old idea of a succession of empires to justify his position (in the postwar world, those who would make the American Century a partial reality would speak always of the international responsibilities of great nations, defining greatness implicitly as imperial mission to maintain a world balance of power by inhibiting social revolutions). [30]

For Wallace, a faith in the revolutionary rise of the Common Man permitted one to escape from isolationism without descending into imperialism. The *free world*, a concept used widely by Wallace and wartime social liberals, was one world free from Fascism, one world that included the Soviet Union because of that state's adherence to the ideals of equality, justice, and security (the people's century's answer to what Henry Luce considered to be the central American ideals, as just discussed). Genuine diversity within a broader framework of cooperation and unity among nations would permit the United States to lead in the transformation of the postwar world from scarcity to abundance while keeping that world free from the domination of American business. [31]

To his great surprise, Wallace was overwhelmed with praise

for his speech, which quickly became a rallying cry for social liberals everywhere and a target for the isolationist–nationalist Right (the Vice President soon found himself condemned by conservatives as an advocate of Milk for Hottentots and TVA's on the Danube). Edward R. Murrow, writing to a young colleague from war-ravaged London in August, 1942, expressed a common view among wartime social liberals when he remarked that the fate of Europe and of the postwar world depended on whether the ideas of Henry Wallace or Henry Luce proved to be "the forerunner of the American policy of tomorrow." [32]

As the war went on, Wallace found himself increasingly a prisoner of the old social liberal paradox of using capitalist means to obtain noncapitalist ends, of arguing that American free enterprise (which, as the Vice President's own oratory shows, again reigned supreme as a political slogan) would be invigorated through its connection with a world social revolution. Wallace carried this paradox out further by speaking out publicly for international Rural Electrification Administrations, World Ever–Normal Granaries, and world decentralization of population as mechanisms to attain a lasting peace. A new type of American businessman, the Vice President argued, would spring forth to work with the new international authorities. Indeed, the new businessman, combining the desire for profits with a commitment to social service (à la Herbert Hoover and the popular business rhetoric of the 1920s) was to play a crucial role in the creation of the people's century, providing through United Nations agencies a good deal of the capital and skill for developmental projects that in principle were to aid the areas in which they were to be undertaken rather than any private or imperial interest. The agencies themselves, reinforced by the vigilance of the people in the regions of development, would guard against predatory capitalists. The difficulties of this position were expressed unconsciously by Wallace when the Vice President pointed with pride to the activities of the United Fruit Company in Central America as an example of the new social responsibility that American business would have to accept in response to the militant anti-imperialist climate growing in the underdeveloped countries.[33]

Dwight MacDonald after the war and New Left historians in the 1960s maintained that there was no essential difference between the programs of Luce and Wallace.[34] Narrowly stated, this view is an extreme distortion of recent history, positing a false consensus to explain the creation of America's postwar policy. Capitalists, one might argue, are no more monolithic than socialists, and within the framework of capitalism there is

6. *Winston Churchill in Washington as Guest of Honor after his address to a Joint Session of Congress. Senator Tom Connally (Senate Foreign Relations Committee), Henry Wallace, Senator Alben Barkley (Senate Majority Leader), and John McCormack (House Majority Leader).*

room for radically different strategies to obtain such universal goals as world stability and prosperity. The different strategies produce or may produce qualitatively different views concerning the type of world system to be created: The old vision of corporate reformers was born anew in the idea of an American Century achieving American world hegemony through containment of revolution and organization of the world into power blocs in the name of fighting communism. The vision of the humanitarian social reformers, that is, technology as the mechanism to free people and make them increasingly equal, was revived in the idea of a people's century born of a marriage between American economic power and a world people's revolution, to be reared by the agencies of a United Nations organization based on American–Soviet cooperation. In calling for developmental agencies and investments in programs to directly raise living standards—international REA's and Ever–Normal Granaries—Wallace called for programs that were fundamentally different from the direct foreign ownership of railroads and mines, that had characterized previous imperialist investment. The public nature of the programs of the people's century and the heavy reliance upon international public agencies of control such as world trade and labor standards commissions made the world New Deal program fundamentally different from the American–private-enterprise-dominated international system envisioned by Henry Luce.

Yet, the dynamics of an expanding American capitalist system within the context of a world war greatly favored the triumph of the American Century over the people's century. That this unprecedented expansion—an increase in the gross national product of 67 percent between 1940 and 1945—had been achieved through government deficit financing, production planning, and rationing mattered little to the corporate leaders who controlled the war-production program and clamored only for government tax credits and the restoration of foreign markets after the war without sacrifices of America's tariff advantages or limitations upon profitable investment opportunities at home.[35] If humanitarian social liberalism had

failed to transform capitalism into a cooperative commonwealth in the midst of a depression, could it really hope that
an American corporate establishment grown rich through war
could be either cajoled or coerced into taking the lead to
create a people's century? By its connection with a mythical
progressive capitalism, the world New Deal was greatly handi-
capped from the outset in competition with an American Century program that accepted American capitalism as it really
was and sought to impose it upon the world.

As long as the war lasted, the continuation of the Soviet–
American alliance and the direct relevance of anti-Fascism provided a healthy climate for advocacy of a world New Deal.
Wallace, acting as both a sounding board and a safety valve
for the Left during the war, continued to delight social liberals
with appeals for a strong international organization and an
international air force to maintain the peace. In December,
1942, his address before the annual Woodrow Wilson birthday
dinner sponsored by the Woodrow Wilson Foundation was
hailed by the liberal journals, who had grown accustomed
since the Century of the Common Man speech to using the
Vice President as a model to contrast with the "pettifogging
legalisms" of the State Department and the compromises of the
President. In his address, Wallace called for a world organization to outlaw political and economic warfare and to "establish a world court that presupposes some kind of world council." [36]

Along with a restatement of the familiar theme of regional
organizations within a world organization, Wallace emphasized continued cooperation between the great powers, postwar economic reconstruction, and the creation of an international air force as the principal mechanisms to attain peace. As
if to answer the arguments of Henry Luce, the Vice President
told Raymond Clapper in an interview after the Wilson dinner
speech that "force without justice would make us sooner or
later into the image of that which we have hated in the Nazis."
In reviewing the speech and Wallace's ideas on postwar planning, the *Nation* warned the administration that "where there
is no vision, the people perish." [37]

When a vision is divided against itself, frustration and defeat only can follow. For most social liberals and for Wallace himself during the war, this division was expressed not only in a faith in the union of an expanding progressive American capitalism with a world social revolution, but in adherence to the Democratic party coalition and the Roosevelt personality cult as guardians of the people's century. Most typically, Wallace was portrayed by the liberal journals as representative of Roosevelt's better nature, of the reformist side of the New Deal that would finally reemerge (it had existed, some thought, in the rhetoric against economic royalists in 1936) once the familiar vested interests—the Big Money men, the Southern Bourbons, and the urban machine bosses—had been laid low by the CIO, the New Deal loyalists, and the common people of America.[38]

If Wilson had lost the peace after World War I by being too rigid, the *New Republic* hinted, then Roosevelt might lose the coming peace by being too opportunistic. The country would have been much better off, the *Nation* contended, if Roosevelt had had the courage to say to Congress what Wallace had said to a pro-United Nations group in Chicago: that world democracy must be the goal of American foreign policy. The foreign policy that the State Department openly advocated and the President appeared to accept, *Common Sense* concluded (in a phrase that embodied the world view of the wartime liberal movement), could only produce a sterile defense of a "a rotten past against the future." [39]

Wartime social liberals had seen the future, but they didn't quite know how to make it work. The wartime liberal movement had not blindly succumbed to a failure of nerve, as Sidney Hook contended in 1943. Nor was it afflicted with a naive and sentimental view of world politics, as the "crackpot realists" of cold-war liberalism, the Schlesingers and the Rostows, would later maintain. Its vision of a people's century gave men the courage to fight Fascist barbarism in the present while preparing to eradicate the causes of Fascism and war in the future. In retrospect, its understanding of what the war meant to the world and its attempt to commit America to a world New Deal was the highest form of realism. It had come close to achieving the radical vision that John Dewey had demanded for liberalism in 1935; yet it would fail the instrumental test, Dewey's test of experience. Dependent upon the Roosevelt personality cult, the Democratic party, and the maintenance of friendly relations between the United States and the Soviet Union, it was subject to forces that it could not control and ultimately lacked the independence or power to make a difference in the real world.[40]

III

During the war, social liberals turned to a welfare-state domestic program that combined the compensatory fiscal theory of John Maynard Keynes with methods of planning and social welfare that had begun in the depression. Ironically, Keynesian economic ideas and policies achieved predominant influence in government circles and spectacular success in the economy during World War II, when production planning and deficit spending for economic expansion produced a warfare rather than a welfare state. Still, the growth of state planning power and the reality of full employment during the war led social liberals to go well beyond the confusion of the depression in developing programs to guarantee full employment in peacetime through compensatory public spending for social-welfare purposes.[41]

Such programs usually looked toward a postwar mixed economy. Here, the old social–liberal idea of cooperation between the government and the functional groups within the economy was often adopted for welfare–state purposes in proposals for public and private enterprise to coexist with one another and with semiprivate enterprise. A postwar federal commitment to full employment was seen as the foundation for a permanent mixed economy. Such a commitment, Harry Hopkins told his aides, Oscar Cox and Isadore Lubin, must serve as the basis for any American security program; Americans would never accept a program predicated on failure. To

Stuart Chase, a federal commitment to full employment would permit the society both to be prosperous and to begin long overdue expenditures for housing, public health care, and the development of natural resources. Eventually, Chase maintained, a full employment economy, compensating for lapses in private investment with thermostat-like efficiency, would lead to major modification of capitalism, to control of the economy by "a super duper planning agency." After all, he concluded, "this is not only a war but a people's revolution (see Henry Wallace)." [42]

While the world New Deal looked to the Danube and the Yangtse for the TVA's of the future, the New Deal at home saw the Missouri and the Columbia as the new frontiers for regional planning and public power. Preaching the gospel of decentralized, democratic planning, TVA director David Lilienthal called for the expansion of the TVA principle to the other great river valleys of America and for a full program of reforestation, soil and mineral conservation, and river-systems development that would both conserve and improve America's natural resources. Democratic planning, Lilienthal hoped, reflecting the renewed confidence of the social liberals, would "awaken in the whole people . . . a sense of common purpose" and fulfill the promise of the New Deal. [43]

Defense of the rights of small business in an expanding economy and rigorous opposition to monopoly were also significant parts of the wartime social liberal program. Stringent public regulation and renewed antimonopoly activity, Thurman Arnold argued, would be needed to protect the consumer from a Broker State that encouraged "irreconcilable pressure groups, each seeking a larger share of the diminishing national income, each destroying purchasing power in order to maintain artificial prices for itself while the increasing number of the unorganized and insecure compel the government to provide subsidies out of the same diminishing national income." [44]

Of course, the Broker State had been the essence of New Deal politics and Arnold's own remarkable career as director of the antitrust division of the Justice Department had been cut short by the war. Although many social liberals refused as in the past to attack bigness in business as an evil in itself, all were publicly committed to the idea of government's responsibility to protect the people from concentrations of private economic power and to somehow obtain a true harmony of interests or General Welfare above the specific interests of business, agriculture, and labor. For most social liberals, economic planning for full employment and a revival of antitrust prosecutions were not seen as antithetical programs but as components of the same policy.[45]

During the war, planning for a social–welfare state became most closely identified with the National Resources Planning Board. Attached to the newly created executive office of the president in 1939, the NRPB was responsible for advising the White House on the use and development of natural resources, trends in employment, and long-range programs for public works. In 1940, the board was commissioned by the President to undertake studies into postwar planning. Reflecting after 1940 the substantial influence of Alvin Hansen, the Harvard economist whom many considered to be the American Keynes, the board sought in its reports to develop both programs and a rationale for postwar economic planning and social welfare.[46]

First, the NRPB sought to redefine democracy. In a report that called for the expansion of local planning agencies and public health, recreation, and welfare services, the NRPB defined democracy as self-imposed discipline in defense of the common good and the rights of other individuals. "To permit anyone to be stunted, impaired, wasted, humiliated, degraded or exploited" was to threaten the foundation of democratic government, for "anyone so treated is less capable of the conduct necessary to maintain a democratic social order. . . ." Professor Charles Merriam, distinguished University of Chicago political scientist and a permanent member of the board, advocated a public acceptance of peaceful social change through the establishment of national and international planning mechanisms. In the western world, Merriam confidently concluded, public responsibility for "the full development of natural resources, full employment, and a fair share of advancing income is now coming to be accepted by the Democracies."[47]

Beginning with the pamphlet "After the War–Full Employment," Alvin Hansen transformed the NRPB's search for a social definition of democracy into a specific postwar program. Far less confident than corporate spokesmen that the magical power of deferred demand plus expanded trade would in itself insure long-range economic expansion after the war, Hansen advocated a sweeping program of planned expansion of private and public capital investment in physical and human resources and in the expansion of goods and services for the domestic market. In Hansen's model, urban planning and development would represent one of the major areas of domestic expansion. Expansion and modernization of the transportation system would facilitate distribution. Increased spending on all levels of government for public welfare would both raise the quality of American life and increase lower-class consumption levels. Finally, Hansen sought to finance this expansion of the public sector of the economy through relatively high yet flexible rates of taxation (which had become a reality with the broadening of the tax base and the imposition of withholding taxes during the war); thus, oversaving and underconsumption, and with them economic stagnation and the resulting crisis of employment, could be avoided.[48] Alvin Hansen's program for a mixed economy played a major role in the controversial NRPB report for 1943.

A three-part study, the bulk of which was in the form of a previously prepared analysis of welfare expenditures and programs of the 1930s, the NRPB report gained fame because of its popular identification with Britain's wartime "cradle to the grave" Beveridge Plan for social welfare, its release at a time when the board was caught in a hopeless struggle for survival against attacks by the conservative coalition in Congress, and above all its call for a "new bill of rights" that would commit the government to maintain employment and security for the people. Prepared by a committee directed by William Haber of the University of Michigan, *Security, Work and Relief Policies*, the study upon which the social-welfare recommendations of the report were based, called for expanded public and private health services rather than compulsory national health insurance (of the kind advocated in the Beveridge

Plan), increased unemployment–insurance coverage and benefits and provisions for general public assistance where such insurance proved to be inadequate, and public expenditures to provide for greatly extended education and welfare services.[49]

In its recommendations, the final NRPB report for 1943 called for federal guarantees for "full employment for the employables" and for "equal access" to food, health care, education, and housing. The specific parts of Hansen's program were represented by the board call for a postwar Federal Transportation Agency and Federal Development Corporation, both of which would work with private enterprise to facilitate expansion of the transportation system and urban development, respectively. At all levels of the economy, the report called for public and private institutions to join, finance, and direct projects for the public welfare, to seek to evolve administrative mechanisms that would maintain security without crippling private initiative.[50]

The social–liberal goals of a mixed economy and a welfare state gained their most effective expression during the war in the NRPB report for 1943. In essence, the report attempted to glean the best of New Deal planning and welfare programs and apply them more extensively to a permanent peacetime cooperative economy. Decentralized planning on the model of the TVA was, for example, to be applied through the economy. The Federal Employment Service was to be strengthened to become a major agent of the full employment policy, and a permanent WPA was to be created for the unemployed. In its advocacy of antimonopoly programs to prevent the "rise of new industrial oligarchies," the report represented less an old fashioned antitrust revival than a reflection of the social–liberal refusal to have the great economic expansion created by the war benefit private economic power. In its call for means to provide for the "participation of both public and private investment and representation by business and government in management" in programs for housing, health, transportation, and natural resources, the report provided a possible beginning for the creation of a cooperative American economy. In its central emphasis upon a national commitment to maintain full employment and extend social-welfare programs, the report reflected the old quest of humanitarian social liberalism to create public standards and means to protect the people from the inequities produced by modern capitalism.[51]

The report also recapitulated the past errors of social liberalism in avoiding any precise definition or division between public and private power or any answer to the question of who would regulate the regulators in the new economy. Although monopolies were condemned, an underlying harmony of interest between the public and private sectors of the economy was assumed. Differences, it was implied, could be settled through compromise and administration. In summary, both a greatly expanded public commitment to and investment in the economy and in social-welfare programs were the essential parts of the NRPB's plan for postwar America. Domestic events in the war highlighted the difficulty in obtaining support from corporate and political leaders for such a program.[52]

The fate of the NRPB itself was an omen of what awaited the advocates of a postwar welfare state. After Roosevelt released the report in March, 1943, Congress carried out its previous threat to liquidate the board and went to the extreme of prohibiting the President from transferring any of the board's activities to other agencies. To the Right during the war, planning was synonymous with dictatorship. The National Association of Manufacturers, for example, condemned the "statism" associated with planning programs and hailed the "American Individual Enterprise system," which it credited with becoming "the world's arsenal for victory . . ." in spite of New Deal abuse. The United States Chamber of Commerce was fond of using such nonsequiturs as "individual planning" to avoid any serious discussion of the issue. Although postwar planning, as John Kenneth Galbraith has wryly noted, "acquired the status of a modest industry during World War II," the strength of the conservative coalition in Congress and the renewed prestige of business in the direction of the war production program produced a countertrend, a business-sponsored revival of faith in the market and in the power of

KEEPER OF THE FLAME

restored business confidence and unfettered consumer demand to solve all the problems of the postwar American economy. The success of Friedrich von Hayek's bitterly antiplanning scholarly treatise, *Road to Serfdom,* was evidence of the free-market revival that was at war with a postwar welfare state.[53]

As congressional conservatives struck out wildly at any mention of planning or social welfare and many of the nation's leading business spokesmen grew nostalgic about the law of supply and demand, corporate social liberalism developed its own postwar program. The Committee for Economic Development (CED) founded in 1942 with the blessings of Commerce Secretary Jesse Jones and the active participation of Jones' undersecretary, Will Clayton, advocated a program of expanded markets at home and abroad for business through cooperative planning with government and through greatly reduced federal taxes on corporations and consumption to stimulate investment.[54] Primarily a research organization, CED reflected big business interests and generally ignored any proposals for welfare-state fiscal policies; yet Studebaker's Paul Hoffman, one of the organization's early leaders, publicly accepted the contention that government fiscal and monetary policies were essential to maintaining business confidence and thus the high levels of employment (with the emphasis upon business confidence, which as the CED developed its program came to mean government planning to encourage private investment and absorb private losses).[55]

In a more subtle way, CED represented in its proposals the domestic equivalent of the American Century. Attempting to organize and bring its research services to small and medium-sized business in an attempt to convert the antiplanning Right to its proposals, CED was probably closest in its views to the big businessmen who directed the war production program; supporting government fiscal and monetary policies as legitimate devices to prevent either postwar depression or postwar inflation, it remained entranced by the vision of a New Deal killed painlessly by flowing private capital and consumer goods. "Jobs and Markets," the title of a collection of its wartime pamphlets, showed the expectations of the CED and the most powerful sections of the American business community.[56]

If the antiplanning conservatives who crusaded against the New Deal had no program, the welfare-state liberals who sought to revive the New Deal had no real congressional base of power. In the struggle over reconversion, these facts were all too apparent. Although there was a great deal of division over what to do with the government-financed war plants, all social liberals opposed any hasty sale of the plants to private industry in order to prevent either monopolistic concentration or an inflationary spiral. In the liberal journals, some toyed with the idea of using the plants as a base for the postwar public sector of the economy. Yet, this idea was completely absent in the debate between the administration and Congress over reconversion. Private enterprise reaped the profits of the publicly financed expansion of the economy and then received the fruits of public planning and taxation back on very generous terms. Indeed, the pressure for rapid reconversion to private peacetime production at the end of the war was probably checked only by the large corporations themselves, who, as the late C. Wright Mills noted, joined with the military to delay reconversion in order to thwart any incipient depression or any loss of the advantages that the large corporations had gained through the war. For Mills, this wartime alliance saw the birth of the military–industrial complex; at the very least, it was indicative of who held real power in the society and a precursor of what the "compensatory" spending ideas of John Maynard Keynes would be used for in the postwar world.[57]

The "new bill of rights" of the martyred NRPB eventually became Franklin Roosevelt's much heralded Economic Bill of Rights, the remnants of which would be championed by postwar social liberals without any real success until the Lyndon Johnson administration. Privately sympathetic to both the NRPB and the CED—avoiding their contradictions as he had always avoided the contradictions between humanitarian nad corporate social liberalism—Henry Wallace became the most enthusiastic wartime champion of both revived free enterprise and a postwar welfare state. In his struggles over the

7. *The first meeting of the Supply Priorities and Allocations Board, September 2, 1941. Standing left to right: James V. Forrestal, Robert P. Patterson, Leon Henderson, Sidney Hillman. Seated left to right: Harry L. Hopkins, William S. Knudsen, Henry A. Wallace, Donald M. Nelson.*

Board of Economic Warfare, Wallace was compelled to contend with the political forces that made both the welfare state at home and the world New Deal abroad so desperately out of place in wartime America.[58]

IV

During the brief existence of the Board of Economic Warfare, Henry Wallace fought for the world New Deal against

State Department and Congressional opposition and the authority of Jimmy Byrnes and Jesse Jones, two conservative Democrats whose authority in the administration had expanded greatly because of the war.

Wallace formally entered the defense program on July 30, 1941, when President Roosevelt created the Economic Defense Board (EDB) to coordinate government policies in economic defense, advise the President on the interrelationship between defense and postwar reconstruction, and foster the establishment of "stable" economic relations between the United States and the world. EDB, however, did not have control over the administration of foreign economic warfare, which remained with the State Department and the purchasing subsidiaries of the RFC, or over the domestic defense program, which was still under the control of the Office of Production Management (OPM). Faced with mounting criticism of OPM policies, Roosevelt replaced the agency's priorities division with a Supply Priorities Allocation Board (SPAB) in August, 1941, with Wallace as chairman and General Motors' William Knudsen and the CIO's Sidney Hillman, the cochairman of OPM, as the principal members. As the press noted after the creation of SPAB, Wallace now had greater responsibilities than any other Vice President in history.[59]

Placing Donald Nelson, a former Sears Roebuck executive, in charge of the actual administration of the SPAB, Wallace began to transform the EDB from an agency primarily concerned with postwar planning to one involved in economic warfare. Milo Perkins, originator of the Food Stamp Plan and an ardent world New Dealer, was appointed executive director of the EDB. After Pearl Harbor, the agency was rechristened the Board of Economic Warfare and requested by the President to redirect its activities from postwar planning to procurement and control over strategic war materials.[60]

With the assistance of Budget Director Harold Smith, Wallace and Perkins sought in the weeks after Pearl Harbor to consolidate the BEW with Lend-Lease and to gain control over the import of strategic war materials into the United States. In late February, 1942, the three succeeded in convincing the President to request Smith to draft an executive order combining the BEW, Lend-Lease, and the purchasing subsidiaries of the RFC into one board (it was tacitly assumed that Milo Perkins would direct the board). Bureaucratic reform of foreign economic warfare, however, soon came into conflict with entrenched bureaucracies.

Expecting State Department and RFC resistance to the proposed reorganization, Wallace was surprised by Lend–Lease administrator Harry Hopkins' bitter opposition to the plan (Hopkins apparently refused at this time to abandon the agency which served as his power base in the administration). Exempting Lend-Lease from the proposed reorganization, Wallace still had Roosevelt's tentative support for the consolidation of the RFC purchasing subsidiaries with the BEW. At this point, the rather premature Communist issue arose in the form of the Dies committee to cast confusion on the reorganization question. In a public letter to the Vice President in late March, 1942, Dies portrayed the BEW as a refuge for Communist dupes, assorted left-wingers, and a prominent nudist named Maurice Parmelee.[61]

Drafted by Dies' counsel J. B. Matthews (who would return in the early 1950s to crusade against "Communists" among the Protestant clergy at the behest of Joseph McCarthy), the letter accused thirty-five employees of the BEW of having either belonged to or signed petitions for so-called Communist front groups supporting the Loyalist cause in the Spanish Civil War. Matthews, perhaps out of deference to his former occupation as a minister, paid special attention to Maurice Parmelee, a BEW employee whose well-illustrated book, *Nudism in Modern Life*, had been the subject of obscenity trials in the federal courts. The press seized upon the story, vilifying the BEW and satisfying its readers with accounts of and occasional pictures from Parmelee's book. After initially suggesting that Dies' activities made him worthy of inclusion "on the Hitler payroll," Wallace sought to belittle the affair with the comment that the Texas congressman wanted "to create the impression that the Board of Economic Warfare is planning a Nudist postwar world. . . ."[62]

It is possible, although no hard evidence exists on this point, that the Dies letter was timed to assist Jesse Jones in the latter's opposition to the BEW reorganization plan. In reality, Roosevelt's reorganization order of April 13, 1942, contrary to contemporary press accounts, was a defeat for Wallace and Perkins. Though the order required the RFC to approve BEW funding requests automatically, the RFC's subsidiaries were left in the hands of Jesse Jones, giving Jones a position from which to continue his struggles against the BEW. According to Lillian Buller, the author of the unpublished government history of the BEW, Dies' assault on the agency was an important reason for Roosevelt's decision not to challenge Jones and Congress with a strong reorganization order.[63]

Under the provisions of the April 13 order, the BEW had the authority to advise the State Department on the terms to be included in master Lend–Lease agreements and to send representatives abroad to negotiate with the economic warfare agents of foreign governments. Within days, the department evinced displeasure at these provisions. On April 15, Assistant Secretary of State Dean Acheson called Budget Director Smith to complain that the President's order had not been cleared through the department, noting that the effects of the order were such that the department "might as well go out of business." In a letter to Roosevelt, Undersecretary Sumner Welles called the order an attempt to "create a second State Department and a second foreign service. . . ." Faced with unanticipated State Department pressure, Roosevelt retreated. When Wallace on April 20 forwarded to Roosevelt a copy of a request to Welles that all State Department negotiations on foreign procurement and production be sent to the BEW, Roosevelt replied that the administration and funding of all BEW orders on foreign imports remained with the existing agencies, although policy-making powers were with BEW. A day later, Roosevelt wrote to Welles that he believed that all BEW personnel abroad should be registered with local American missions, while still upholding their right to "be responsible to and report to the Board." [64]

Continued State Department opposition forced further compromises in May. Under a new arrangement, BEW personnel were to be responsible to the local chief of mission, who in turn was to report any conflict to both the Secretary of State and the chairman of the Board of Economic Warfare for review. In spite of this sweeping victory, Cordell Hull refused to publicly sign the compromise agreement with Wallace, insisting instead that the new arrangement be put in the form of a presidential clarification to the original order; to the disgust of Wallace and Perkins, Roosevelt complied with Hull's request.[65]

Hull had previously feared that the BEW's powers might be expanded to give the agency the right to negotiate a post-war economic settlement.[66] Indeed, if the administration had seriously considered creating any administrative vehicle for the world New Deal, it might have moved in the direction of giving the BEW such powers (as an attempt at counterorganization, one might even say, against the vested interests of the State Department). But Roosevelt the broker had always dealt on the basis of existing power. From the outset, the BEW's plans to combine the war emergency with model programs for economic development and improved labor and welfare standards abroad became subordinate to the superior power of the State Department and the President's need to retain the appearance of unity within his administration.

Jesse Jones soon emerged as the leading opponent of the BEW's attempts both to expand the procurement of strategic war materials and to negotiate contracts that would raise purchasing power and improve labor standards in Latin America. Along with his colleagues in the RFC and the Department of Commerce, Jones was less subtle than the State Department in his assaults on the BEW. In his memoirs, Jones boasted that he had obstructed the plans of "the socialist-minded uplifters and uppity underlings" of the BEW. In memoranda to Jones and Undersecretary of Commerce Will Clayton, RFC staff people constantly referred to the BEW's attempts to negotiate safeguards as to conditions of work, purchasing power in the local economies equivalent to North American workers, and above all to develop new sources for strategic war materials regardless of the effect on American business. The ease with which BEW officials talked about the agency as a starting point for hemispheric TVA's and REA's was enough to provoke Jones and Clayton to blustering rage.[67]

Jones sniped at BEW by deliberately delaying his signature of appropriations requests and by lobbying in Congress to have his veto power over BEW purchases restored. In December, 1942, the BEW with White House support defeated an amendment by Senator John Danaher (Republican of Connecticut) to an RFC appropriations bill that would have restored Jones' veto.[68] Conservative gains in the 1942 Congressional elections, however, greatly strengthened Jones' hand for the coming fight with the BEW.

After attempts to reach a compromise with the RFC proved to be unsuccessful, Wallace, using as his precedent a presidential memorandum to eliminate all duplication and overlapping functions between agencies, issued his own executive order in February, 1943, separating the functions of the BEW and the RFC and placing control over the preparation and negotiation of procurement contracts with the BEW. Fearful that the staffs of the RFC subsidiaries, which had heretofore negotiated procurement contracts, would be transferred to the BEW, Jones proposed instead a transfer of the United States Commercial Company (USCC), the RFC's chief purchasing agent abroad, on the condition that the BEW agree to sell the company's other purchases to the RFC subsidiaries. The subsidiaries would thus remain with RFC; and imports, once in the United States, would return to the control of the RFC.

Although Wallace objected to these conditions, control of the United States Commercial Company now became a major objective of the BEW, and a tentative agreement for the transfer of the company was reached between BEW and RFC representatives in late March, 1943. On May 27, Jones and Wallace reached another tentative agreement to have the USCC, excepting its rubber purchasing facilities, transferred to the BEW. Jones, however, opposed provisions in the agreement to have the Bureau of the Budget pass on the transfer and recommend new appropriations to Congress. Instead, he wanted Congress to provide the RFC with authority to vote funds for the company's purchases after it had been nominally transferred to the BEW, thus preserving RFC power over company purchases. After an acrimonious correspondence between Wallace and Jones, the transfer plans were deadlocked.[69]

On June 10, Wallace complained to Roosevelt of Jones' obstructionism and hoped apparently for presidential support for the transfer; meanwhile, Senator Kenneth McKellar, an ally of Jones and economy-bloc leader Harry Byrd, introduced a new version of the Danaher amendment, and subjected Milo Perkins to sharp questioning over BEW projects. Earlier, Perkins had ordered a group of BEW attorneys to draw up an indictment of RFC practices in the procurement of strategic war materials. Wallace delayed release of the report, but the deadlock in his negotiations with Jones and the fear (later shown to be unjustified) that the McKellar amendment might pass combined to lead him to sign and release the indictment on June 29, 1943. What the press quickly dubbed "the Battle of Washington" then commenced.[70]

Aware of President Roosevelt's August 20, 1942, order to all agency heads requesting that all interagency conflicts be submitted to the President rather than made public, Wallace persisted in his attack, hoping probably that a bold gesture would compel the President to vindicate the embattled BEW. Of Wallace's many charges of RFC procrastination in the procurement of vital war materials, the press focused on Jones' delay in implementing the BEW's quinine project (and thus costing the lives of malaria-ridden American troops in the Pacific) despite the urgent requests of General MacArthur (Wallace privately affirmed and documented these charges in a subsequent letter to Jimmy Byrnes, the director of the Office of War Mobilization).[71]

Jones responded to the incident with an angry denial of the BEW's charges and a demand for a congressional investigation of the entire affair. An attempt by Byrnes to bring Wallace and Jones together on June 30 proved unsuccessful. Although Byrnes makes no mention of this in his memoirs, new material in the Wallace papers affirms that the War Mobilization direc-

tor got Jones and Wallace to make another tentative agreement concerning the transfer of the U.S. Commercial Company. Beyond that, Wallace refused to retract his charges,
claiming only that he did not mean to impugn the patriotism
of Jones. In his memoirs, Byrnes noted that he feared that
Jones might actually assault Wallace during the meeting.[72]

As the crisis developed, the tangible political power of the
conservative coalition made itself felt against the BEW. Senator
Byrd moved toward an investigation of the affair. On July 1,
Wallace, at Roosevelt's behest, met with Senator Harry Truman (a pro-administration moderate whose committee to investigate the national defense effort had wide congressional
support and who it was hoped would protect the administration in any investigation). Truman agreed to do everything
that he could to keep Senator Byrd's economy committee away
from the affair, but demands for an investigation grew. On
July 6, Jones released a letter to Byrd's Virginia colleague,
Carter Glass, in which he renewed his call for a Senate investigation, accused the BEW of "spendthrift" policies in Latin
America, and denounced the Wallace charges as "filled with
malice, innuendo, half-truth, and no truth at all. . . ." Milo
Perkins' reply that Jones was no more than a Rip Van Winkle
did little to reduce the tension.[73]

Encouraged by press references to Roosevelt's August 20
order on interagency disputes and the almost universal media
condemnation of open conflict in the administration in the
midst of a war, the public responded with a torrent of angry
letters calling upon the President to resolve the dispute. On
July 12, Wallace wrote what in retrospect was the decisive
letter of the conflict to Roosevelt, asking the President to
appoint a special committee to investigate the affair (administration representatives were then doing everything they
could in Congress to prevent an investigation). If the BEW's
charges against Jones were proved to be false, Wallace agreed
that Roosevelt should remove him as chairman of the BEW;
if the committee idea was unacceptable, the Vice President
suggested that Roosevelt then go ahead with the transfer of
the U.S. Commercial Company to the BEW. In filing away the
letter at a later date, Wallace noted in pencil that the com-

muniqué had frightened the President's "palace guard" (according to contemporary press accounts, this referred to Hopkins, Byrnes, and Sam Rosenman) who then prevailed upon Roosevelt to issue an executive order abolishing the BEW. According to Wallace, the "palace guard" feared that the letter was to be published.[74]

Roosevelt's July 15 executive order (drafted by Byrnes) abolished both the BEW and the war-procurement functions of the RFC, consolidating both into a new Foreign Economic Administration (FEA was directed by Leo Crowley, a conservative banker and protégé of both Byrnes and Jones). Conservatives were generally jubilant about the resolution of the affair and the public humiliation of the Vice President, while liberals flooded Roosevelt with bitter letters, accusing the President of betraying both the New Deal and Wallace. I. F. Stone summed up these feelings when he compared the BEW executive order with Roosevelt's "plague on both your houses" statement during the Little Steel controversy. "Leon Henderson, Thurman Arnold, Henry Wallace," Stone wrote, "this is the toll in recent months of the men Roosevelt has sacrificed to the right." [75]

In the aftermath of the crisis, it was evident that liberals no less than Wallace himself had remained prisoners of the Roosevelt personality cult, condemning the President for his retreat before conservative pressure and yet trusting him to make amends at another time. Wallace himself noted of the affair that "the danger in the situation is that it may alienate some of the liberals from the President." [76]

In the Battle of Washington, the strength of the conservative coalition in Congress, Jesse Jones' great power within the administration, and above all the appeals to national unity pressed by all and at the end by Byrnes had interacted to destroy the Board of Economic Warfare. Wallace's use of a strategy of confrontation—direct appeals to patriotic and humanitarian sentiments through the quinine charges—could not counterbalance the President's need to maintain the support of Congress and the business community and to protect the semblance of national unity for the war effort.[77]

Writing to Roosevelt at the beginning of the war about the

projected international Ever–Normal Granary, Wallace noted that "we are writing the postwar world as we go along. . . ." [78] The New Deal had written much of its program as it went along, subsuming a tendency toward humanitarian social reform under a commitment to save and expand the capitalist system. During the war, social liberals had formulated, in the plans for a world New Deal and a postwar welfare state, a blueprint for transforming the New Deal into a coherent program and faced powerful enemies who were no longer held in check by mass unemployment. In the aftermath of the BEW affair, social liberals would either have to adapt existing political institutions to the program of a people's century or accept a subordinate position within the New Deal coalition. To a great extent, the future of the people's century would be decided by Henry Wallace's struggle for renomination in 1944. In that struggle, both the strengths and weaknesses of social liberalism as a political force would be dramatically displayed.

Notes

* HAW to William F. Riley, September 30, 1941, HAW Papers, University of Iowa. The Wallace Papers, at the time they were consulted, had not been numbered by box number but by year, with certain years having more than one box, and including special collections donated by prominent persons and friends of HAW.

1. Malcolm Cowley, "The End of the New Deal," *New Republic*, LVIII (May 31, 1943), p. 730.

2. For a brief and gloating summary of conservative victories over the New Deal, see Arthur Sears Henning in the *Washington Times Herald*, July 19, 1943.

3. See Eric F. Goldman, *Rendezvous with Destiny* (New York, 1952), pp. 392–393, and Alonzo Hamby, "Sixty Million Jobs and the People's Revolution," *Historian*, XXX (August, 1968), pp. 578–98. For examples of the work which pictures wartime liberalism as utopian: Sidney Hook, "The New Failure of Nerve," *Partisan Review*, X (January–February, 1943), pp. 2–23. For the disillusionment created by the decade, see Arthur A. Ekirch, Jr., *The Decline of American Liberalism* (New York, 1955) and Chester E. Eisinger, *Fiction of the Forties* (Chicago, 1963).

4. Freda Kirchwey, "Program for Action," *Nation*, CLVIII (March 11, 1944), p. 382. For a stimulating study that provides background for

any analysis of the wartime liberal movement, read Richard Alan Lawson, *The Failure of Independent Liberalism, 1930–1941* (New York, 1971).

5. Reinhold Niebuhr to David Dubinsky, October 7, 1941, Reinhold Niebuhr Papers, Box 4, LC; Herbert Agar, "Who Are the Appeasers?" *Nation*, CLII (March 22, 1941), p. 318; Archibald MacLeish, "To the Class of '41," *Nation* CLII (June 14, 1941), p. 720.

6. Max Lerner, "The People's Century" in Max Lerner, *Ideas For the Ice Age* (New York, 1941), p. 57; Stanley High, "The Liberals' War," *Nation*, CLII (June 14, 1941), p. 692.

7. "Dear Mr. President," *Common Sense*, XI (April, 1942), p. 127.

8. Cordell Hull, *The Memoirs of Cordell Hull* (New York, 1948), II, p. 1599; "The Weak Spots in Our Armor," *New Republic*, CVI (January 12, 1942), p. 38; Freda Kirchwey, "Intervention—Old and New," *Nation*, CLIV (March 7, 1942), p. 274.

9. George Soule, "Liberals and the State Department," *New Republic*, CVII (December 24, 1942), p. 789; Alfred Bingham, "Lippmann's Realpolitik," *Common Sense*, XII (July 1943), p. 262.

10. Stuart Chase, Memorandum on Proposed Pamphlet Series on Postwar Problems, April 18, 1941, Chase Papers, Box 6, LC; Stuart Chase, "A Guidepost for America's Tomorrow," *Progressive*, VIII (February 7, 1944), p. 1.

11. Samuel Grafton, *An American Diary* (Garden City, N.Y., 1942), p. 203; "Have We Lost the War?" *Common Sense*, XI (March, 1942), p. 11; "Daring to Think," *Common Sense*, XII (April, 1943), pp. 126–7.

12. George Soule, "Peacemaking Has Begun," *New Republic*, CVIII (January 4, 1943), p. 76; Abba P. Lerner, "Economic Problems in the Postwar World," pp. 138–39, in Seymour Harris, ed., *Postwar Economic Problems* (New York, 1943).

13. Hubert Herring, "Pan-Americanism—Now or Never," *Common Sense*, XI (March, 1942), pp. 75–76; Walter Waggoner, "Rehearsal at Hot Springs," *Common Sense*, XII (July, 1943), p. 237.

14. Stuart Chase, "What Kind of War?" undated, Chase Papers, Box 11.

15. See Forrest Davis, "Roosevelt's World Blueprint," *SEP*, CCXV (April 10, 1943), pp. 20–21, 109–110.

16. Frederick L. Schuman, "The Need for a Global Strategy," *New Republic*, CVII (August 10, 1942), p. 164.

17. *Ibid.* See Eliot Janeway, *The Struggle for Survival: A Chronicle of Economic Mobilization in World War II* (New Haven, 1951).

18. In retrospect, one might suggest that the wartime liberal program represented the high point of social-liberal thought in twentieth-century America.

19. Henry A. Wallace, "Henry A. Wallace Tells of His Political Odyssey," *Life*, XL (May 14, 1956), p. 183; HAW, "The Defense of Our American Democracy," Radio Address, June 4, 1940, in Records of the Agricultural Adjustment Administration, Record Group 145, NA.

20. HAW to John Cowles, January 18, 1941, HAW Papers, Box 5, LC; HAW, "Road Ahead in the World Crisis," Radio Address, February 22, 1941, RG 145, NA; HAW to John Wallace, February 6, 1941, HAW Papers, University of Iowa.

21. HAW to William F. Riley, September 30, 1941, HAW Papers, Gifts, 1967–1970, University of Iowa.

22. Mary Huss, Wallace's private secretary, informed Lewis Copeland that the Vice President thought that his Second Chance speech should be his contribution to Copeland's anthology of major wartime speeches. Mary Huss to Lewis Copeland, May 31, 1941, HAW Papers, Box 5, LC; HAW, "America's Second Chance," Address, April 8, 1941, reprinted in *Congressional Record*, 77 Congress, 1 Session, pp. A7663–64; HAW, "On a Democracy of Responsibility," *Congressional Record*, 77 Congress, 1 Session, pp. A2084–85.

23. Russell Lord, *The Wallaces of Iowa* (Boston, 1947), p. 492; HAW to FDR, May 4, 1942, FDR Papers, OF 12, Box 5, FDRL.

24. There are countless sources for the Century of the Common Man speech, officially titled "The Price of Free World Victory," which was printed by the Office of War Information in pamphlet form, translated into the languages of the Allies and the occupied nations, and widely disseminated abroad. This analysis is based on the text in Russell Lord, ed., *Democracy Reborn* (New York, 1944), pp. 191–196.

25. *Ibid.*, pp. 192–193.

26. *Ibid.*, p. 193; for a recent view of the speech as a futile attempt to define the war in populist rather than status quo terms, see Paul Seabury, *The Rise and Decline of the Cold War* (New York, 1967), p. 43.

27. Stuart Chase praised Wallace for "Americanizing" the revolution created by the war. See Stuart Chase, "Goals for America," Address, May 19, 1943, Chase Papers, Box 11.

28. Henry Luce, "The American Century," *Life*, X (February 17, 1941), pp. 61–63.

29. *Ibid.*, p. 64.

30. *Ibid.*

31. Lord, ed., *Democracy Reborn*, pp. 191–196.

32. Edward R. Murrow to Eric Severeid, August 26, 1942, Eric Severeid Papers, Box 21, LC.

33. Henry A. Wallace, "What We Will Get Out of the War," *American Magazine* (April, 1943), reprinted in *Congressional Record*, 78 Congress, 1 Session, pp. 546–547; Henry A. Wallace, "The Guts to Win," *Liberty Magazine* (September, 1942), reprinted in *Congressional Record*, 77 Congress, 2 Session, p. A3189; Wallace's comments on the United Fruit Company are in the form of an introduction to the pamphlet, A. A. Pollan, "The United Fruit Company and Middle America" (Washington, 1944), in HAW Papers, Box 2 for 1944, University of Iowa.

34. See Dwight MacDonald, *Henry A. Wallace: The Man and the Myth* (New York, 1948), pp. 70–71, and Ronald Radosh and Leonard

Liggio, "Henry A. Wallace and the Open Door" in Thomas G. Patterson, ed., *Cold War Critics* (Chicago, 1971).

35. See I. F. Stone, *Business as Usual: The First Year of Defense* (New York, 1941); Clifford J. Durr, "The Defense Plant Corporation," pp. 285–311, in Harold Stein, ed., *Public Administration and Policy Development* (New York, 1952), and Bruce Catton, *The War Lords of Washington* (New York, 1948).

36. "Wanted: Political Leadership," *Common Sense*, XI (October, 1942), p. 343; HAW, "America's Part in World Reconstruction," Address, December 28, 1942, in Clapper Papers, Box 246, LC. For State Department opposition to the speech while it was being prepared, see Frederick Henshaw Interview, COHC, p. 153.

37. *Ibid.;* HAW, Interviewed by Raymond Clapper on Mutual Broadcasting Company, December 31, 1942, in Clapper Papers, Box 246; "The Shape of Things," *Nation*, CLVI (January 2, 1943), p. 1.

38. For a simple expression of this liberal faith during the war (one which betrays all of its weaknesses) see Fred Gladstone Bratton, *The Legacy of the Liberal Spirit* (New York, 1942).

39. "FDR and the Postwar World," *New Republic*, LX (January 3, 1944), p. 1; "The Shape of Things," *Nation*, CLVII (September 25, 1943), p. 3; "Lost Victories," *Common Sense*, XII (September, 1943), p. 329.

40. For a truly brilliant analysis of the thinking of the "crackpot realists" or "Bogart liberals" see Gary Wills, *Nixon Agonistes* (Boston, 1970), pp. 456–602. Although Richard Nixon is not a liberal by the definitions of this study, Wills' work nevertheless goes well beyond its dubious protagonist to develop an insightful and scathing critique of contemporary liberal thought.

41. For a stimulating analysis of the influence of World War II on American economic thought, see Herbert Stein, *The Fiscal Revolution* (Chicago, 1969), Chapter 8.

42. Memorandum, Harry L. Hopkins to Isador Lubin and Oscar Cox, April 22, 1943, Harry L. Hopkins Papers, Box 320, FDRL; Stuart Chase, "Toward a Mixed Economy," p. 27, in Leland Chase, ed., *Peace is a Process* (Chicago, 1944); Stuart Chase, "Exploring Full Employment," *Common Sense*, XIII (March, 1944), p. 109; Stuart Chase, "Is the New Deal Lost?" undated, Stuart Chase Papers, Box 1.

43. David E. Lilienthal, "The Grand Job of Our Century," Address, June 18, 1944, pp. 3–9, in George Norris Papers, Misc. III, Box 26, LC; David E. Lilienthal, "The People's Stake in Planning," *Progressive*, VIII (July 10, 1944), p. 2.

44. Thurman Arnold, "The Coming Economic Conflict," *Progressive*, VIII (July 17, 1944), p. 2.

45. For a criticism of Arnold that reflected wartime liberal thought, see Richard Lee Strout, "The Folklore of Thurman Arnold," *New Republic*, CVI (April 27, 1942), p. 571.

46. For a brief summary of the NRPB's history, see Landon G. Rockwell, "The Planning Function of the National Resources Planning Board," *Journal of Politics*, VII (May, 1945), pp. 169–78, and

Charles Merriam, "The National Resources Planning Board: A Chapter in American Planning Experience," *American Political Science Review*, XXXVIII (December, 1944), pp. 1075–88.

47. National Resources Planning Board, *Human Conservation* (Washington, 1943), p. 124; Charles E. Merriam, *On the Agenda of Democracy* (Cambridge, Mass., 1941), pp. 77, 97, 178.

48. Alvin Hansen, "After the War—Full Employment" (Washington, 1942); Alvin Hansen, "The Postwar Economy," p. 19, in Harris, ed., *Postwar Economic Problems*. For a good brief summary of Hansen's ideas on a postwar social-service economy, add Alvin Hansen, "Our Coming Prosperity," *Common Sense*, XI (June, 1942), pp. 186–88, and Alvin Hansen, "Four Outlets for Investment," *Survey Graphic*, XXXII (May, 1943), pp. 198–200, to the full employment article.

49. "A Beveridge Plan for America," *New Republic*, CVII (December 14, 1942), p. 775; National Resources Planning Board, *Security Work and Relief Policies* (Washington, 1942), pp. 1, 445–545 (detailed account of projected postwar program).

50. National Resources Planning Board, *Plan for 1943—Part I: Postwar Plan and Program* (Washington, 1943), pp. 7, 9, 11.

51. *Ibid.,* p. 11.

52. *Ibid.*

53. The Economic Principles Commission of the National Association of Manufacturers, *The American Individual Enterprise System* (New York, 1946), I, p. 29; Walter Wesenburger, "Challenge to the Public," *NAM News*, February 3, 1945; John Kenneth Galbraith, *The New Industrial State* (New York, 1967), p. 38; Daniel Bell, *The End of Ideology* (New York, 1962), p. 80. Like the social liberals, generally, the Board tended to use its reports as policy statements and let them stand on their own. See John D. Millet, *The Process and Organization of Government Planning* (New York, 1947), pp. 21–23.

54. There is no really first-rate study of the CED, an organization which is of crucial importance to any understanding of the ideology and program of big business in the postwar era. Karl Schriftgiesser, *Business Comes of Age: The Story of the Committee for Economic Development and Its Impact Upon the Economic Policies of the United States* (New York, 1960) is usually considered the standard work, even though it only skims the surface of its topic.

55. Herbert Stein is a partisan of the CED position and his study, while in strong disagreement with this one, contains much valuable material for understanding the organization's relationship to the economic thought of the times. See Stein, *Fiscal Revolution*, especially Chapters 8 and 9.

56. William Benton was one of the CED's early leaders, even though he grew disenchanted with its policies. His biography contains a good deal of useful material on the functioning of the organization during the war. See Sidney Hyman, *The Lives of William Benton* (Chicago, 1969); Committee for Economic Development, *Jobs and Markets* (New York, 1946).

57. For a sampling of social liberal plans for reconversion, see Walter

Reuther, "The Freedom from Fear of Abundance," *Progressive*, VIII (June 19, 1944), p. 10; Maury Maverick, "Economic Democracy for Postwar America," *Progressive*, VIII (May 1, 1944), p. 2; and Robert Nation, "A Plan for Free Enterprise," *Common Sense*, XIII (March, 1944), p. 105; C. Wright Mills, *The Power Elite* (New York, 1956), pp. 212-13. See also Barton J. Bernstein, "The Debate on Industrial Reconversion: The Protection of Oligopoly and Military Control of the Economy," *American Journal of Economics and Sociology*, XVI (April, 1967), pp. 159-172.

58. In correspondence with William Benton near the end of the war, Wallace noted that he was "favorably impressed" with the CED. HAW to Benton, February 8, 1945, HAW Papers, Gifts, 1967-1970, University of Iowa.

59. Executive Order 8839, July 30, 1941, FDR Papers, OF 4226, Box 1; *Washington Post*, August 2, 1941; Lillian Buller, "Chronological History of the Board of Economic Warfare" (unpublished manuscript, 1943), p. 40, in Records of the Bureau of the Budget, Record Group 51, File 184, National Archives (henceforth on all BEW materials the abbreviations RG, F for file number and NA will be used); *New York Times*, August 27, 1941; Buller, "Economic Defense Board," p. 46, RG 51, F. 184, NA.

60. *Ibid.*, p. 41; *New York Times*, September 18, October 10, 1941; Memorandum, the President to the Attorney General, December 12, 1941, FDR Papers, OF 426, Box 1.

61. Lillian Buller, "Administrative History of the Board of Economic Warfare" (unpublished manuscript, 1944), pp. 4, 13-18, in RG 51, F. 184, NA; Though in disorganized condition, the notes of BEW official Bernard Gladieux provide an invaluable account of the interdepartmental struggles. They will be cited henceforth in the following manner: Gladieux Notes, March 24, 1942, RG 51, F. 181, NA.

62. Martin Dies to HAW, March 28, 1942, HAW Papers, Box 41, LC; Statement on Dies Charges, March 29, 1942, HAW Papers, Box 41, LC.

63. Executive Order 9128, April 13, 1942, in Jesse Jones Papers, Box 176, LC; Buller, "BEW," p. 19, RG 51, F. 183, NA.

64. Gladieux Notes, April 15, 1942, RG 51, F. 181, NA; Sumner Welles to Franklin D. Roosevelt, April 15, 1942, FDR Papers, OF 4226; HAW to FDR, April 30, 1942, FDR to HAW, April 23, 1942, Memorandum, FDR to Sumner Welles, April 24, 1942, FDR Papers, OF 4226.

65. Gladieux Notes, May 21, 1942, RG 51, F. 181, NA; Clarification and Interpretation of Executive Order 9128, April 13, 1942, FDR Papers, OF 4226.

66. Hull, *Memoirs*, II, pp. 1155-57.

67. Jesse H. Jones, and Edward C. Angly, *Fifty Billion Dollars* (New York, 1951), p. 491; Memorandum, Harvey Gunderson to Will Clayton re: the Goals of the BEW, December 5, 1942, Jones Papers, Box 176.

68. I. F. Stone, "Anti-Wallace Plot," *Nation*, CLV (December 29, 1942), p. 672; *Washington Post*, January 9, 1943.

69. Buller, "BEW: Final Administrative Struggle," pp. 3–6, RG 51, F. 183, NA; HAW to Jesse Jones, March 15, 1943, Jones Papers, Box 176; Memorandum of Agreement Between the Secretary of Commerce and the Chairman of the Board of Economic Warfare, May 27, 1943, Jones Papers, Box 176; Jesse Jones to HAW, June 2, 1943, HAW to Jesse Jones, June 3, 1943, Jones Papers, Box 176.

70. HAW to FDR, June 10, 1943, HAW Papers, University of Iowa; Kenneth McKellar to HAW, June 29, 1943, HAW Papers, University of Iowa; HAW to FDR, June 29, 1943, FDR Papers, OF 4226; Memorandum, George Fort Milton to Dr. Pendleton Herring, June 30, 1943, RG 51, F. 180, NA.

71. *New York Sun*, June 30, 1943; HAW to Byrnes, July 1, 1943. The order was in the form of a letter to all agency heads, reading, "Disagreements either as to fact or policy should not be publicly aired but are to be submitted to me by the appropriate heads of the conflicting agencies. . . ." FDR to HAW, August 20, 1942, FDR Papers, OF 4226.

72. Jesse Jones, Statement on BEW Charges, June 20, 1943, Jones Papers, Box 176; HAW to Byrnes, July 1, 1943, HAW Papers, University of Iowa; James F. Byrnes, *All In One Lifetime* (New York, 1958), p. 192.

73. Jesse Jones to Carter Glass, July 5, 1943; Jones Papers, Box 176; *New York Sun*, July 7, 1943. After Jones' public letter to Glass, Byrnes ordered both Wallace and Jones to remain silent until a congressional inquiry or the President dealt with the affair. James F. Byrnes to Jones, July 6, 1943, Jones Papers, Box 176.

74. For letters to FDR, see FDR Papers, OF 4226, Box 2; HAW to FDR, July 12, 1943, HAW Papers, University of Iowa.

75. *New York Times*, July 16, 1943; Nathan Robertson's Story in *P.M.*, July 17, 1943; I. F. Stone, "Wallace Betrayed," *Nation*, CLVII (July 24, 1943), p. 90.

76. HAW to William F. Riley, July 21, 1943, HAW Papers, University of Iowa.

77. There was speculation that Byrnes, now looming large as a Vice-Presidential candidate for 1944, had been the real winner in the conflict. *Christian Science Monitor*, July 17, 1943, *Baltimore Sun*, July 22, 1943.

78. HAW to FDR, February 24, 1942, FDR Papers, OF 4226.

The Missouri Compromise of 1944

3

One man more than any other in all history has given dynamic power and economic expression to the ageless New Deal. That man is Roosevelt. Roosevelt has never denied the principles of the New Deal and he never will. They are a part of his very being. Roosevelt, God willing, will in the future give the New Deal a firmer foundation than it has ever had before. So on with the New Deal, on with winning the war, and forward march for peace, justice, and jobs.

Henry A. Wallace
January 22, 1944 *

Henry Wallace had fought on the side of the angels in the BEW controversy, but the Broker State politics of the New Deal rarely rewarded angels. After July, 1943, struggling against disparate forces within the Democratic party that sought to dump him as Vice President in 1944, Wallace connected his own political survival with the postwar expansion of the New Deal. As the nomination struggle neared its climax in July, 1944, the Vice President found himself leading an alliance of liberals and CIO labor against a coalition of

Southern conservative and big city and county courthouse machines united only in their opposition to him. Although he thrilled his followers at the convention and terrified the party bosses by being almost renominated on his own, Wallace had in fact been abandoned by Roosevelt in backroom negotiations before the balloting began.

As the victim of the manipulations of National Chairman Robert Hannegan, who had masterfully used every unrepresentative feature of the convention system to force the nomination of his Missouri friend and ally, Senator Harry Truman, Wallace in a broader sense was defeated by Roosevelt's failure to transform the Democratic party into a responsible and representative liberal–labor party. As evidence of the bankruptcy of New Deal Broker State politics, Roosevelt had acquiesced almost indifferently and at the last moment in the nomination of Harry Truman, a border-state Senator who had won some renown as a congressional watchdog over the war-production program. Besides his special relationship with the national chairman, Truman's principal qualification for the nomination was that he was acceptable to all factions of the party. The Truman nomination was hardly an auspicious beginning for those who looked to a postwar expansion of the New Deal at home and to the creation of a world New Deal.

I

Was the New Deal a program of the past or a movement for the future? After the fall of the BEW it appeared to many observers that the President had at last made his choice. Observing the political trends since Pearl Harbor, Roosevelt had reason to suspect that appeals to national unity under a "win–the–war" [1] banner constituted the best hope for political survival in 1944.

Private polls seemed to show that the people were most interested in victory and security (and no longer willing to see either goal as the exclusive domain of the Democratic party). Along with the impressive Republican gains in the

1942 congressional elections, the polls showed that only Roosevelt could win for the Democrats in 1944, and then only on the war issue. Widespread support within the party for a fourth term—a state of affairs quite different from the hostility and confusion that greeted the third-term drive—appeared to show that the politicians agreed with the polls. Given such circumstances, it is little wonder that the President, when asked by reporters to clarify a statement that he was no longer satisfied with the New Deal as a slogan, replied that some people had to be told how to spell cat.[2]

After a press conference in mid-December, 1943, Roosevelt told reporters that the New Deal slogan no longer fitted the times. Asked to explain this statement at a later press conference, the President noted that Dr. New Deal had treated an internally sick nation during the depression. After Pearl Harbor, Dr. Win–the–War had to be consulted to fight the new crisis, an external infection that threatened the country's very survival.

Following his medical analogy, Roosevelt went on at the press conference to describe the New Deal in conservative terms, that is, as a set of accomplished programs that had to be protected from anti-administration forces in Congress. Leaving himself the usual options, Roosevelt defended planning as a concept that would have to play a major part in the postwar world and alluded to the New Deal with the remark that "the program of the past, of course, has got to be carried on after the war in light of what is going on in other countries." What the President meant by planning was left to the imagination of his listeners.[3]

Along with the outraged responses of the leading organs of liberal opinion and the reported dismay of Mrs. Roosevelt, private polls cast some doubt on the wisdom of abandoning the New Deal (even as a slogan). In a confidential report to the President, Hadley Cantril noted that only 54 percent of the population had heard of the Dr. Win–the–War statement and only 22 percent were aware that the statement had been made by Roosevelt. Polls, as Samuel Rosenman informed the President, consistently showed massive support for a federal

BY ANOTHER NAME IT WILL STILL SMELL

8. *A cartoonist's answer to President Roosevelt's Dr. Win–the–War press conference, 1943.* (© *1943*, The Chicago Tribune.)

commitment to full employment and to expanded social security programs. Furthermore, it was felt by many in the administration that the Democrats' significant defeat in the 1942 elections could be attributed to the low turnout of Democratic voters in marginal districts, especially to the apathy of organized labor. The administration's need to appeal to its working-class constituency (the existence of the Political Action Committee of the CIO, committed to Roosevelt,

Wallace, and the "new Bill of Rights" program of the martyred National Resources Planning Board highlighted this need) served as a counterweight to those who called for an accommodation with the much-heralded wartime conservative trend. Also, it encouraged Roosevelt to include an Economic Bill of Rights in his State of the Union address for 1944.[4]

After presenting in his January State of the Union message a five-point program for tax readjustment, price stabilization, and the resolution of labor disputes, the President returned to the left New Deal argument that political democracy had to be transformed into economic democracy in order to survive in the modern world. "Security," Roosevelt stated clearly, "physical, economic, social and moral" constituted the American challenge in the postwar world. With minor differences in phraseology, Roosevelt echoed the NRPB with a call for a "second bill of rights"—a series of federal guarantees for the right to employment, food, clothing, shelter, education, health care, and freedom of enterprise as against monopoly. Congress, the President concluded, should prepare legislation that would give these rights practical expression.[5]

By comparing what the President and the press called the Economic Bill of Rights with the Dr. Win–the–War press conference, one can see that Roosevelt had masterfully avoided a decision as to the future of the New Deal. Just as the President in the Dr. Win–the–War conference had held out the vague possibility of extending the New Deal after the war, so he had placed his plea for an Economic Bill of Rights at the end of a State of the Union message whose specific programs had called for wartime austerity. Whether Roosevelt would commit himself to the programs of the Economic Bill of Rights (he had cheerfully called the message "my blast" in a letter to Henry Wallace) or continue to genially balance Dr. New Deal with Dr. Win–the–War became increasingly connected with the struggle over the Vice Presidency.[6]

Since the fall of the BEW, Henry Wallace had sought to rebuild his political career with impassioned public attacks upon administration opponents and eloquent pleas to create the Century of the Common Man in America after the war. In a well-publicized July, 1943, address in race-riot torn Detroit shortly after the abolition of the BEW, Wallace set the style for his renomination campaign, combining the "people vs. interests" dichotomy of Populism with the programs of a world New Deal and a postwar full employment economy. Condemning the "midget Hitlers" who attacked labor and the "American Fascists" who placed the rights of the people below the prerogatives of property, the Vice President went on to expound upon his major theme, predicting that enormous wealth, power, and the opportunity to achieve social justice would be thrust on America at the end of the war, compelling her to undertake social reconstruction at home before she could fully transfer her programs for a world New Deal to other nations.[7]

In spite of harsh criticism from the press and Republican leaders that his speeches were divisive, Wallace in the fall of 1943 denounced international cartels that created the inequalities of technology, raw materials, and markets that produced wars. Armed with information from the Truman committee reports, the Vice President accused Standard Oil of having conspired with I. G. Farben to prevent American corporations from developing synthetic rubber in the years before the war. In a speech at Dallas in October, 1943, Wallace revived the small-producer attacks against the railroads with a call to save the air freight industry and the newer trucking services from the assaults of monopolistic railroad interests who still exploited regional inequalities. Although a Republican congressman compared his speeches with Don Quixote's fabled and futile adventures, reporters and columnists began to see the addresses as part of a clever campaign for a nomination that had seemed lost forever with the abolition of the BEW.[8]

The second phase of Wallace's early campaign for the renomination began ten days after Roosevelt's Economic Bill of Rights message, when the Vice President captured the publicity of a late January, 1944, Jackson Day dinner meeting in Washington with a rousing defense of the New Deal. "The New Deal," Wallace said in a phrase that summed up his campaign, "is not dead. If it were, the Democratic party would be dead and well dead." The New Deal, the Vice President argued, was the evolving process of human freedom and justice which, from the Old Testament prophets to Franklin Roosevelt, had fought "the paid hirelings of the special interests." In the postwar world, Roosevelt and the New Deal (with the assistance of Henry Wallace, it is fair to assume) would lead the nation to "justice and jobs." [9]

In a speaking tour on the west coast in February, 1944, Wallace completed his early campaign to connect his own renomination with the hopes for a revived New Deal. At Los Angeles on February 4, the Vice President argued that an efficient national economy, based on regional and national planning and guarantees of full employment, was the nation's most pressing need. In San Francisco on February 7, Wallace outlined a five-point economic program that called for prosperity through increased public expenditures for nutritional and health services, hospital construction, housing, education, and rural electrification. In speeches at Milwaukee and Chicago on his way back to Washington, the Vice President called for regional economic planning, federal assistance to small business, and the creation of either a Federal Jobs Authority with compulsory powers to enforce full employment programs or a Jobs Council with advisory powers. In effect, Wallace had used his tour to serve as a lightning rod for the Economic Bill of Rights.[10]

Wherever Wallace went on his tour, he replied to questions about the Vice Presidency with the remark, "I'm in the lap of the gods." The nomination, as the Vice President well knew, depended more on Franklin Roosevelt than the deity, and the President was both bored and somewhat amused by press attacks on the Western tour and increasing speculation concerning Wallace's future. Reminded by reporters in early February of stories that the Vice President had advocated everything from Soviet Communism to the New Deal in his speeches, Roosevelt noted wryly that in some circles the Sermon on the Mount would be considered an inflammatory political statement. Told at a press conference a week later of reports by "young and influential Democrats" that either

Alben Barkley or Sam Rayburn would replace Wallace on the national ticket, the President merely shook his head in mock bewilderment.[11]

Although the press noted after the tour that opponents of the New Deal within the Democratic party had now concentrated their energies on the removal of Wallace, there was general agreement that the Vice President's Western tour had improved his chances for renomination. The large enthusiastic crowds largely brought out by the CIO–PAC, Louis Stark concluded in the *New York Times*, indicated that the Vice President was clearly the candidate of the CIO and that the CIO was a force to be reckoned with in the Democratic party. Even George Creel, an anti-Wallace Democrat with an old and keen sense of public relations, saw the Wallace drive as the great comeback story of 1944.[12]

Wallace's early campaign created both hope and foreboding for the future. On the one hand, the Vice President was not a Don Quixote fighting for the beliefs of a quaint Populism eighteen months before Hiroshima. Nor had he, as a recent student has suggested, abandoned a previously vigorous criticism of laissez faire capitalism for a defense of free enterprise. Rather, he understood that the war had temporarily both solved the problem of employment and freed the forces of monopoly and economic concentration. Given his commitment to a progressive capitalism that wartime expansion had both encouraged and threatened, Wallace could hope only to rouse an outraged public opinion against those whom Franklin Roosevelt had once called economic royalists. In the process, he had perhaps acted as a sounding board for the President and flexed some political muscles through his identification with the CIO. There were, however, disturbing notes in Wallace's early campaign.[13]

Throughout his life, friends had often remarked that Henry Wallace could not attain the long-range discipline, single-mindedness, or clear judgment to capitalize fully on his ability to inspire men with the quality of his ideas. After the tour, Wallace withdrew temporarily to his Vice-Presidential duties, making no serious attempt to develop a substantial campaign staff of his own or to work directly with the CIO–PAC to win popular support and influence the President. Having directly challenged the party leaders on his Western tour with a warning that American Fascists were conspiring to control the nominating conventions of both major parties, Wallace relied on his chief political aide, Harold Young, a less than influential Dallas attorney, to launch a hunt for delegates while he left on a presidential mission to Soviet Asia and China. Charles E. Marsh, a wealthy publisher close to Young and Wallace, provided the Vice President with

9. *Wallace posing with his pilot, Colonel Richard T. Kight, and Soviet war ace Ilya Mazuruk on his Soviet Asian tour.* (*Courtesy of the University of Iowa.*)

political intelligence reports that often appeared to be a cross between Drew Pearson and Alice-in-Wonderland. As the opposition to Wallace's nomination gained cohesion in the spring of 1944, the Vice President's own campaign stood at loose ends, amateurish at best and compromised by its total deference to Franklin Roosevelt. (To uphold Roosevelt and yet bargain with him from a position of strength was Wallace's major problem, just as it had been the general political problem of social liberals through the war.) [14]

Roosevelt often said that Henry Wallace was not, had never been, and would never be a politician. Trusting in the Presi-

10. *Wallace with members of his Soviet Asia mission and Siberian officials on the steps of Communist headquarters, Seimchan, Siberia, May, 1944. (Courtesy of the University of Iowa.)*

dent and an aroused public opinion to vindicate Dr. New Deal, Wallace left for the Orient in the spring of 1944 in the guise of a statesman and world traveler, leaving the liberal journals at home to tremble excitedly over the upcoming renomination struggle and Roosevelt to continue his intricate shadow-boxing with the anti-Wallace forces in the party. In China the Vice President would be called a flower-blessing scholar. At home the regular Democrats, who had waited for so long to avenge the Farleys and the Garners, had other names for him.[15]

II

In the Truman administration, it became fashionable for certain of the President's cronies to boast that they had saved the Republic from Henry Wallace. George E. Allen, a friend whom Truman rewarded with the chairmanship of the RFC, joked about nightmares of a Wallace presidency in a Soviet America; Edwin I. Pauley, a more powerful friend whom Truman tried to reward with an appointment as Undersecretary of the Navy, told everyone in sight forever after that he had conspired with White House aides to block the Wallace nomination. National Chairman Robert E. Hannegan, who had far more to boast about than the rest, liked to tell friends that he wanted one epitaph for his tombstone: Here lies the man who kept Henry Wallace from being President of the United States.[16]

Opposition to Wallace, however, stemmed less from conspiracy than from the increased strength that the war crisis had given anti-administration conservatives and ambitious congressional leaders within the Democratic party. At the 1940 national convention, the Democratic organization had considered Wallace an outsider, a renegade Republican whom it neither understood nor wanted. Following the sweeping Republican victory in the Middle Western agricultural states in 1942, there was speculation that the Vice President had lost his political base. Even before the BEW incident, reports that Roosevelt might drop Wallace from the ticket became so common that Jimmy Byrnes, most often mentioned as the Vice President's successor, issued a public statement in June, 1943, denying any ambitions for national office. After the fall of the BEW, Byrnes and House Speaker Sam Rayburn, whom the press often characterized as an enlightened conservative, were prominently mentioned for the nomination.[17]

Wallace's aloofness, personal eccentricities, and strong identification as the leader of the New Deal left made him unpopular with the Senate establishment and something of a liability to Roosevelt at a time when the President sought to protect executive prerogatives from a hostile Congress. Disliked by powerful Southern Democrats such as Connally of Texas and McKellar of Tennessee, Wallace was of little help to Roosevelt in the behind-the-scenes maneuvering over major pieces of wartime legislation. Even important administration supporters like Senate majority leader Alben Barkley of Kentucky and Senator Harry Truman of Missouri, while protesting their affection for Wallace, often expressed doubts to their colleagues about the Vice President's qualifications for renomination. Indeed, as George Norris noted privately after the convention, prominent administration supporters in the Senate ultimately joined the legion of favorite-son candidates contesting for the Vice-Presidential nomination after a kind of open season had been declared on Henry Wallace. As the approaching convention coincided with the Allied invasion of Europe and the acceleration of attempts to create a United Nations Organization, Wallace's poor relations with the Senate establishment became one more example that he was not a politician in the Rooseveltian sense, one more pressure working against renomination.[18]

Of the major groups opposed to Wallace, the Southern conservatives were the most open. After former Secretary of War Harry Woodring organized the American National Democratic Committee to work against the renomination of Roosevelt in February, 1944, some of the more extreme Southern conservatives began to construct a grassroots movement to nominate Senator Harry Byrd of Virginia for President. Widespread support for the fourth term (even among anti-Wallace conservatives like Melville Broughton of North Carolina and John McClellan of Arkansas) left the Byrd movement without any real hope even in the South. Following a conference of anti-New Deal Southern Democrats in Shreveport, Louisiana, in early June, 1944, Southern conservatives turned their attention to the defeat of Wallace. In late June, the Alabama delegation's chairman to the national convention announced that the Vice President was opposed "by a vast majority of the people of the South. . . ." In early July, Senator John McClellan denounced Wallace and called for his defeat at the convention. Kentucky and North Carolina soon followed suit by pledging their state delegations to favorite sons Alben Barkley and Melville Broughton, respectively. Within a week of the convention, delegates from Tennessee and other Southern states were reported to be suggesting that the removal of Wallace would be the price for an end to the well-publicized Southern rebellion against the administration. To a President encouraged by the war crisis to emphasize national and party unity above all else, the relative ease of disarming Southern opposition by removing Wallace became most apparent as the nomination struggle reached its final stage.[19]

If the opposition to Wallace were to succeed, it needed leadership and control over the machinery of the Democratic party. After 1940, the large urban machines, reflecting the decisive role of the cities in a reduced New Deal coalition, came to have more and more influence with the President. When Bronx boss Ed Flynn replaced Jim Farley as National Chairman, the role of the machine leaders in the party was strengthened. Frank Walker, an old Roosevelt associate who replaced Flynn after the 1942 elections, was known in Washington for his timidity and offered no opposition to the bosses. When Robert E. Hannegan, the former boss of the St. Louis machine, arrived to replace Walker as National Chairman in January, 1944, the National Committee and the city machines forged the alliance that was decisive to the defeat of Wallace.[20]

In retrospect, one can see the Hannegan appointment as providing the Wallace opposition with the leadership necessary to its success. Earlier attempts by Ed Pauley, a prominent California oil man and Treasurer–Secretary of the Democratic National Committee from 1942 to 1944, to undermine the Wallace nomination had not been successful. Although Pauley later claimed to have made an agreement with General Edwin "Pa" Watson, the President's appointments secretary, to fill Roosevelt's schedule with anti-Wallace visitors, there is little evidence that these alleged actions directly influenced the President or that prominent Wallace supporters did not have access to the President through most of the nomination fight. Pauley's further contention that his influence as party treasurer kept Wallace from making speeches before major party organizations and thus contributed to his decline is also highly doubtful. Wallace's speeches before liberal and labor groups in fact improved his chances of nomination and were among the most publicized, albeit occasionally distorted, addresses of the war.[21]

Pauley, who was apparently regarded as an aggressive nuisance by some of the party leaders, displayed his bumbling at the National Committee's Jackson Day Dinner meeting in Washington in January, 1944. After arranging for the featured-speaker's role and the klieg lights to be given to Sam Rayburn, the Californian haplessly watched Vice President Wallace capture the press attention with a short speech proclaiming that the New Deal was not dead. Seeking to counter the effects of Wallace's February western tour, Pauley launched simultaneous boomlets for Sam Rayburn and Harry Truman by inviting both men to speak in California in support of the fourth term. In a speech at San Francisco in March, Truman endorsed Rayburn for the Vice Presidency, and the House Speaker returned the compliment in an address at St. Louis a week later. Soon Rayburn found himself the victim of a pro-Byrd rebellion in Texas. Truman returned to Washington and blissfully denied any interest in the Vice Presidency, and Pauley's self-heralded conspiracy to save the nation from Henry Wallace was a complete shambles. While Pauley chased rainbows, Robert Hannegan was already parrying with Roosevelt over the Vice-Presidential nomination.[22]

Hannegan's terse comment after his appointment, "I am an organization Democrat," summed up his career. Rising through the ranks to lead the St. Louis party machine during the administration of Mayor Bernard Dickmann, Hannegan procured a post as Collector of Internal Revenue for Eastern Missouri after the fall of the scandal-ridden Dickmann administration in 1941 and then rose to the position of United States Internal Revenue Commissioner for Missouri (it was felt by

TOO MUCH OF A LOAD.   By Rube Goldberg.

11. Rube Goldberg's not-so-gentle hint that Wallace would be a liability to the ticket in 1944. (© 1944, Rube Goldberg. Courtesy of King Features Syndicate, Inc.)

many observers that Senator Truman, whom Hannegan had rescued in his own bitter fight to hold his Senate seat against the primary challenge of reform Governor Lloyd Stark, was instrumental in procuring the revenue-department post and then the National Chairmanship for the St. Louis boss). Always pointing to Jim Farley as his model National Chairman, Hannegan had his Roosevelt in Harry Truman, a friend and ally who almost certainly was his personal preference to replace Henry Wallace.[23]

Under Hannegan's command, the movement to defeat Wallace acquired momentum in the spring of 1944. Returning from political scouting trips, both Frank Walker and Ed Flynn told Roosevelt that Wallace was without support in the country except for liberals and organized labor. In large states like Pennsylvania and California, Flynn argued, Wallace's candidacy might spark a rebellion among conservative Democrats that could cost the ticket millions of votes.[24] With Wallace on the ticket, Hannegan added, the party would have difficulty in raising funds from anyone save the liberals and labor, whose votes and money could be counted on in any case. As Paul Porter remembered, the spring meetings of the party leaders to find an alternative to Wallace displayed a more orderly and confident manner. Hannegan had acted as the catalyst for the anti-Wallace forces, and Hannegan would manage the convention in the name of the organization Democrats.[25]

If the conservative and regular party opposition to Wallace resembled a wolf pack, the small but influential group of New Dealers who worked for the nomination of Supreme Court Justice William O. Douglas were rather like a flock of hungry sparrows. Led by Tommy Corcoran, a presidential aide turned lobbyist, the Douglas group included Attorney General Francis Biddle, Harold Ickes, and Undersecretary of the Interior Abe Fortas and in the final stages of the nomination fight had the support of Henry Morgenthau and Eleanor Roosevelt. Beyond a strong identification with Douglas and, in the case of Corcoran, Ickes, and perhaps Morgenthau, a background of hostility to Wallace, the Douglasites saw themselves as contending for the right of succession to the New Deal. After the creation of the War Production Board in January, 1942, it was rumored that Douglas' friends had worked to have him step down from the Court and accept a position as director of the defense program—a position from which a future presidential bid might be made. In January, 1943, Tom Stokes reported that the New Dealers were divided into Wallace and Douglas factions, each jockeying for position in the event that the President did not seek a fourth term. After the fall of the BEW, *Common Sense* remarked that Douglas was "the darling of a small band of New Dealers" who hoped to save the administration at the expense of the Vice President.[26]

In the spring of 1944 the Douglasites repeated party leaders' contentions that Wallace would cost the ticket millions of votes, stressed Douglas' vigor and rugged charm in contrast to the shy, moody Vice President, and suggested that Wallace, should he ever become President, would follow the disastrous path of Andrew Johnson in his relations with Congress.[27]

The analogy to Johnson, subtly playing upon Roosevelt's dissatisfaction with Wallace's work in the Senate, reflected the personality-cult politics that the New Deal had largely become. Only a charismatic leader, the Douglasites appeared to say, could protect the New Deal from the attacks of the Right. Stressing Wallace's weakness and lack of political skills, the Douglas supporters encouraged the climate of opinion that the Vice President could not be renominated at the very time that his foremost backer, CIO–PAC, reached the height of its prestige in its spring primary victories over the Dies committee.[28] Established by the CIO's Executive Board in July, 1943, to mobilize labor's voting strength in the face of growing conservative attacks, the Political Action Committee rapidly emerged as the spearhead of the liberal–labor alliance, becoming for most liberal observers the last great hope of the New Deal. From the outset, the PAC was a revival of the popular front. John Abt, a former attorney for the legal division of the AAA and the National Labor Relations Board, and Lee Pressman, the CIO's General Counsel, were the co-counsels for the organization. The son of a conservative garment manufacturer and the counsel for PAC leader Sidney Hillman's Amalgamated Clothing Workers since 1938, Abt never formally denied his connection with the Communist party. Pressman was later to admit that he had once been a Communist. Beanie Baldwin, whom Murray chose to administer PAC while Hillman acted as its chairman, was an ardent adherent of the popular front and a foe of self-styled anti-Communists.[29]

Seeking to build support for the reelection of Roosevelt and a revived New Deal, PAC, in the words of Sidney Hillman, set out to "educate the entire nation." Under Baldwin's direction, regional offices were established throughout the country, and plans were made to use regular union machinery to mobilize workers and their families for the support of progressive candidates in the coming elections. Millions of pamphlets advocating support for the various programs of the Economic Bill of Rights were distributed to workers. When the PAC forced Martin Dies to withdraw from a primary contest in Texas and contributed to the defeat of Dies committee members Joe Starnes in Alabama and John Costello in California in other spring primaries, liberals hailed the labor committee as the most hopeful development in national politics in years.[30]

Sidney Hillman, however, was primarily interested in reelecting Roosevelt and in maintaining his own high position in administration circles by gaining CIO approval for the President's initiatives. Never optimistic about Wallace's prospects, Hillman sought as flexible a commitment to the Vice President as possible, permitting the PAC's rank-and-file to work for a Roosevelt–Wallace ticket across the country while personally remaining aloof from the struggle.

As the Vice President toured Soviet Asia and China in the spring of 1944 and the party leaders worked behind the scenes to gain Roosevelt's approval for a list of alternative candidates, Hillman made no attempt to apply pressure on Roosevelt for the Wallace candidacy. Indeed, as those close to the union leader remembered, PAC activists had to press Hillman to commit his own union to a Roosevelt–Wallace ticket when the Amalgamated Clothing Workers held their annual convention in May, 1944. Although Hillman stated the CIO's preference for Wallace at a June 7 White House meeting with Roosevelt, Beanie Baldwin remembered that the PAC leader, beyond stating the CIO's opposition to Byrnes, did not rule out alternative candidates. In the spring of 1944, Max Lowenthal, a prominent attorney who had formerly worked with the Amalgamated, acquainted Hillman with the proposed candidacy of Harry Truman. Without a clearly defined position on the Missouri Senator, Hillman would follow Roosevelt down the line of least resistance and acquiesce in the nomination of Senator Truman.[31]

Other than a withdrawal by the Vice President, the most the anti-Wallace forces could hope for was an "open convention," an understanding that the President would not make Wallace's renomination a condition for his own candidacy as he had done in 1940. As early as February, 1944, there were reports that the President had agreed to such an arrangement and had challenged the party leaders to come forth with suitable alternative candidates. In the spring, Hannegan punctuated his attacks on the Vice President with the argument that Wallace could not be renominated without a fight that would split the party on sectional and ideological lines as nothing had done before. After Walker and Flynn returned from their national tours with pessimistic reports to the President about Wallace's support in the country, Hannegan publicly stated on May 23 that the Vice-Presidential contest was "open." Significantly, the National Chairman listed Wallace, Truman, Barkley, Governor Melville Broughton of North Carolina, and Governor Robert Kerr of Oklahoma as the leading candidates for the nomination, rather than Byrnes and Rayburn, who along with Truman remained the press favorites to succeed the Vice President.[32]

With Truman still disinclined to run and Rayburn compromised by the anti-administration rebellion in the Texas Democratic party, Hannegan needed a stronger candidate than either Kerr or Broughton to provide opposition to the absent Wallace. Byrnes possessed the respect of the President, great popularity with the party organizations and enormous prestige in the direction of the war effort; but, as Hannegan well knew, the opposition of organized labor and civil rights groups to the South Carolinian's candidacy—along with the subtle opposition of those who remembered that Byrnes had converted from Catholicism to Protestantism—were almost insurmountable obstacles for a candidate who hoped to be a noncontroversial alternative to the embattled Vice President. With these factors in mind, one can understand why Hannegan expressed his support for Byrnes' candidacy in a conversation with the South Carolinian on June 13, encouraging Byrnes to discuss the subject with the President the following day. Although Roosevelt, with his usual cheerfulness, encouraged Byrnes to run, the entrance of the South Carolinian into the contest gave Hannegan a substantial opponent to use against Wallace, displayed to Roosevelt the seriousness of the anti-Wallace opposition, and permitted the National Chairman to work more effectively behind the scenes for the nomination of a compromise candidate. The events of early July tend to support these contentions.[33]

Although Roosevelt, in a well-publicized meeting with Ellis Arnall, the pro-Wallace Governor of Georgia, had said as late as June 22 that Wallace would be the Vice-Presidential nominee, reports began to spread through Washington in early July that the President had agreed to give the Vice President a perfunctory and thus futile endorsement for renomination. On July 6, Hannegan once more told the press that the nomination was open and added Byrnes and Rayburn to his list of potential nominees. After Hannegan met with Roosevelt to arrange the latter's formal acceptance of a fourth-term nomination, the *New York Times* reported that there was widespread feeling in Washington that Wallace had been dropped by the President and would now have to decide whether or not to withdraw from the contest or continue on his own.[34]

At this point, the Douglas faction may have played a role in further undermining Wallace's position. In the spring, Abe Fortas purportedly went on a scouting trip to the West Coast and succeeded in gaining the mild support of California Attorney General Robert Kenny for the Douglas nomination (National Committeewoman Helen Gahagan Douglas offered Douglas second-choice support). In early July, both Harold Ickes and Henry Morgenthau expressed opposition to Wallace's renomination while the President was polling his official family.[35] Within Roosevelt's inner circle of advisors Judge Samuel Rosenman, a former friend of Wallace, now opposed the nomination because of the Vice President's unpopularity in the Senate. Harry Hopkins, whom illness had prevented from taking an active part in the nomination struggle, returned to be with the President in the last week before the convention and, according to Admiral Leahy, expressed sympathy for Byrnes (Hopkins had initially told Byrnes in December, 1943, that the President was interested in his candidacy).[36]

Faced with these pressures against renomination, Roosevelt in early July apparently agreed not to insist upon the retention of Wallace. In the process the President became irritated with Wallace for his failure to win support from the party's power brokers. In a subsequent conversation with the PAC's Jim Carey, Roosevelt noted with some bitterness that the opposition to the Vice President had increased and that Wallace would never be a good politician. During a similar discussion with Claude Pepper the President expressed confidence in Wallace's ability to carry on with the New Deal but stated that an uncompromising 1940-like endorsement was out of the question. As he had planned from the outset, Hannegan now arranged for Roosevelt to accept the fourth-term nomination without the threat to withdraw if Wallace were not selected as his running mate.[37]

Returning to Washington after his long Asian tour on July 10, Henry Wallace had become an invisible man in a city wildly speculating over his possible successor. The stage was now set for the final meeting on July 11 between the President and the party leaders on the Vice Presidency. When Hannegan asked Paul Porter, the mildly pro-Wallace publicity director of the National Committee to attend, Porter summed up the condition of the Vice President with the reply that he had no intention of becoming part of a lynching party.[38]

III

The tangled and contradictory accounts of the July 11 meeting at the White House poses a problem for the scholar that is as old as recorded history: how to make sense out of limited, biased, and at times palpably false, accounts of events. Yet, a careful sifting and balancing of sources—an intricate counterpointing of lie against lie in order to reach the truth by a process of elimination—enables one to make a number of points about the meeting with some certainty. First of all, the guest list represented a clear triumph for Hannegan. None of the Vice President's supporters or Southern and Congressional opponents were in attendance. Instead, the party insiders, the coalition of National Committee–machine boss elements that Hannegan had molded, were present. Along with John Boettiger (Roosevelt's son-in-law and a figure of no importance), Hannegan, Frank Walker, Ed Pauley, Ed Flynn, Frank Hague, and George E. Allen attended the meeting. Given the guests, it is little wonder that all of the memoirs and unpublished sources of the participants agree that Wallace's name was not even mentioned as a possible nominee.[39]

From all accounts, the President showed little interest when the names of Alben Barkley, John G. Winant, Sam Rayburn, Senator Scott Lucas of Illinois, and Henry Kaiser were discussed. Barkley, Roosevelt noted, was too old to run. When Byrnes' name was mentioned, labor and Negro opposition were cited by Flynn and others. Roosevelt introduced the name of William O. Douglas—noting that the Supreme Court Justice, a good poker player and story teller, possessed the "Boy Scout" quality, that is, a manner that was both straightforward and idealistic, that might appeal to the voters. Except for Mayor Kelly, all of those present were indifferent to Douglas. When Harry Truman's name was mentioned, the President returned to his mood of disinterest, and the party leaders rose to the occasion.[40]

Although each of the party leaders later claimed to have endorsed Truman at the conference, it is reasonable to assume that Hannegan took the lead in stressing the Senator's political attributes. Although Roosevelt initially suggested that Truman, like Barkley, was too old to run, someone mentioned the Senator's approximate age and the conversation continued.[41] As Roosevelt was later to tell Byrnes, the party leaders agreed among themselves that Truman would do the least damage to the ticket. Although a number of sources make the point that Roosevelt concluded the meeting with a remark to the effect that "all right, Bob, it's Truman," George E. Allen's recollection that the President merely noted that everyone in the room was for Truman appears to be more logical, given subsequent events.[42]

After the meeting, Hannegan left Frank Walker and returned to the President, hoping to receive a written endorsement of Truman. Instead, he was given the following handwritten letter:

> Dear Bob:
>   You have written me about Harry Truman and Bill Douglas. I should, of course, be very glad to run with either of them and believe that either one of them would add real strength to the ticket.
>
>   F. R.

Although Grace Tully was later to claim that the letter had originally read "Douglas or Truman" (and that Hannegan's move in convincing Roosevelt to reverse the order in the typed copy had perhaps changed the course of history), the existence of copies of the handwritten letter in the Frank Walker papers (the original is in the possession of Hannegan's widow) makes this view wholly untenable. According to Miss Tully, Hannegan had entered Roosevelt's railway car as it stopped in Chicago on July 15 on its way to a tour of naval installations in California to have the Douglas–or–Truman letter rewritten. According to Mrs. Hannegan, the National Chairman had his last preconvention meeting with Roosevelt on the train in an unsuccessful attempt to persuade the President to alter his letter of endorsement to Henry Wallace. A look at the origins of the Wallace letter will tend to support Mrs. Hannegan's view.[43]

After the July 11 conference, Hannegan had deputized Frank Walker to tell Byrnes of the outcome (the probable "nomination" of Truman) and had given himself the task of breaking the news to Wallace. Without any knowledge that Roosevelt had already given Hannegan the Truman–or–Douglas letter, the Vice President received the National Chairman coldly on July 12 and informed him that he would withdraw only at the request of the President.[44]

After landing in Washington on July 10, Wallace had been met by Sam Rosenman and Harold Ickes who, with Roosevelt's knowledge, sought to convince him to withdraw from the race for the good of the party. Wallace refused and reported to the President on the conduct of his Asian mission on the 10th, failing then and in a subsequent meeting on the following day to gain Roosevelt's support for a strong letter of endorsement. Senator Joseph Guffy, a Wallace supporter, contacted the White House on July 10 to report his own failure to convince the Vice President to withdraw from the race. Right after the crucial July 11 meeting at the White House, Guffy contacted Charles E. Marsh and learned that Wallace still hoped that Roosevelt would "make a statement preferring him but not leaving it to the convention," a position that even a Wallace backer like Guffy realized "was out of the question." [45]

After Hannegan informed him of the White House meeting on the Vice Presidency on the 12th, Wallace worked quickly with Louis Bean to gather an analysis of vice-presidential polls and picked up an advance copy of the Gallup poll for use in his final meeting with Roosevelt on July 13. The polls showed that Wallace would strengthen the ticket in marginal districts where labor votes were crucial, while Gallup recorded that the Vice President was supported for renomination by 65 percent of the enrolled Democrats in the nation (Barkley was a distant second and only 2 percent were tallied for Truman).[46] Wallace also told Roosevelt that Harold Young expected him to have a minimum of 290 delegates on the first ballot. "Well, I'll be damned," the President reportedly said.

In an early draft of his proposed letter of endorsement to

Wallace, Roosevelt had been deliberately ambivalent, praising the Vice President in the first paragraph and injecting the criticisms of the party leaders in the second. The second paragraph of the early draft read as follows:

> The Democratic Party operates under a free convention system and I do not wish in any way to be dictating to the convention. . . . There are two considerations for the nomination in addition to the consideration of experience and ability. Will the nominee strengthen the ticket, and will the nominee meet such opposition as to hurt the ticket by decreasing the number of votes for it? Therefore, as you understand, I am not advocating the choice of any individual but I am asking that consideration be given to the above.[47]

After the meeting with Wallace on the 13th, the President apparently decided to omit these qualifications in the final draft. As Roosevelt saw Hannegan hours *after* his meeting with Wallace, it is probable that the President told the National Chairman of the alterations in the text. The final draft read as follows:

> July 14, 1944
>
> Dear Senator Jackson:
>   The easiest way of putting it is this: I have been associated with Henry Wallace during his past four years as Vice President, for eight years earlier while he was Secretary of Agriculture, and well before that. I like him, and respect him, and he is my personal friend. For these reasons I would personally vote for him if I were a delegate to the convention.
>   At the same time, I do not wish to appear in any way to be dictating to the convention. Obviously, the convention must do the deciding. And it should—and I am sure it will—consider the pros and cons of the situation.[48]

Armed with this letter and the conviction that Roosevelt would not intervene to choose a specific candidate over him, Wallace chose to remain in the race.

Hannegan's plans for Truman were further complicated by

Frank Walker's failure to get Byrnes to withdraw from the contest. After speaking with Walker on the 12th, Byrnes called Roosevelt only to be told that "you are the best man in the whole outfit and you must not get out of the race. If you stay in you are sure to win." After Hannegan, protesting his own sympathy, told Byrnes of the opposition at the July 11 meeting, the former Supreme Court Justice contacted the President's train by radiophone on the 14th and was told by Roosevelt that he had expressed *no preference* for either Truman or Douglas, but had merely told the party leaders that he would not object to either man as his running mate. "After all, Jimmy," the President concluded, "you are close to me personally and Henry is close to me. I hardly know Truman. Douglas is a poker partner. He is good in a poker game and tells funny stories." In what was the masterstroke of his campaign Byrnes then called Truman and received the Missouri Senator's pledge to nominate *him* at the national convention. Hannegan was now in a very difficult situation.[49]

Having carefully maneuvered for both Wallace's defeat and Truman's candidacy, the National Chairman now faced a strengthened Wallace and a Truman committed to Jimmy Byrnes. These problems must have been uppermost in Hannegan's mind when he went with Mayor Kelly to visit the President's railway car as it stopped off in Chicago on July 15. Although Kelly, in his own very scanty account, makes no mention of Byrnes at the meeting, it is likely that Hannegan reiterated the objections to the South Carolinian's candidacy (objections that Sidney Hillman had repeated to Roosevelt on July 13) and was told by the President to discuss Byrnes' candidacy with Hillman. Although, as Frank Walker remembered, Hannegan failed to get Roosevelt to modify his letter to Wallace, it is possible that the National Chairman was able to delay the delivery of the letter, thus compelling an early polarization of forces between Wallace and Byrnes that might have killed the Truman candidacy. As it was, Leslie Biffle, an ally of Hannegan and secretary of the Senate, delivered the letter to Senator Jackson at a time when Byrnes was within hours of knowing that his nomination could not be cleared with Sidney.[50]

When Byrnes reached Chicago on July 16, Hannegan and Mayor Kelly conferred with the former Supreme Court Justice and pledged their support for his nomination. As the meeting concluded, Hannegan said to Kelly, "Ed, there is one thing we forgot. The President said clear it [the nomination] with Sidney." Promising Byrnes to intervene on his behalf with Hillman, Hannegan then contacted both Flynn and Hillman and had both repeat their strong objections to Byrnes' candidacy in radiophone conversations with Roosevelt from his hotel suite on the evening of July 17. Failing to contact Roosevelt himself on the evening of the 17th, Byrnes decided to withdraw after Leo Crowley, who had represented the South Carolinian's interests at the radiophone conversations with Roosevelt, returned with the news that the President had withdrawn his support for Byrnes' candidacy.[51]

Although it is important to remember that Roosevelt had not endorsed Byrnes' candidacy as against the candidacies of Truman, Douglas, or Wallace, it is probable that the President had yielded to the continued labor and black opposition to Byrnes and to Douglas' complete lack of delegate support and had not objected to Hannegan's plans to nominate Truman as the candidate of party unity. Returning from the radiophone conversation, Sidney Hillman told his PAC colleagues that Byrnes had been stopped and that Truman was the likely nominee, only to be greeted with a chorus of "Who the hell is Truman?" [52]

Truman, of course, was the ideal running mate for Dr. Win–the–War, a border-state Democrat with a New Deal voting record, the respect of the Senate establishment, and a reputation as a tireless foe of greed and bureaucratic confusion in the war-production program (even Truman's political origin as a stalwart of Boss Tom Pendergast's infamous Kansas City machine was probably an asset with men like Kelly, Flynn and Hague).[53]

Although Pauley had earlier sought to create a Truman boom and press reports had long pictured him as a likely vice-presidential nominee, the casual way in which Truman agreed to nominate Byrnes on July 14 suggests that he had never taken seriously either the press reports or the pleas of party leaders that he seek the nomination. Arriving in Chicago on July 16, Truman denied any interest in the Vice Presidency, telling reporters that he and his family were happy with his position in the Senate. Although Byrnes claims that Truman came to him on the night of July 17 and asked to be released from his commitment, Truman's own account that he was pledged to Byrnes in principle until July 20 and even then didn't fully believe that he had been endorsed by Roosevelt appears to be closer to the truth. Frank Walker remembered Truman shuttling back and forth between his room in the Hotel Stevens and Hannegan's headquarters in the Blackstone, wondering if he should run. Paul Porter remembered that Truman appeared to be dazed as rumors flew at the convention that he was the President's choice.[54]

At a meeting with Sidney Hillman on July 16, Truman was told that while the PAC would not desert Wallace, Hillman considered both Truman and Douglas to be acceptable candidates. Meeting with the AFL's William Green and the Railroad Brotherhood's A. F. Whitney, Truman learned that both Green and Whitney would support him for the nomination *after* Douglas and *before* Wallace. At a dinner for arriving delegates on the evening of July 18, Kelly and Hannegan began to circulate the story that Roosevelt, in a letter to Hannegan, had specifically endorsed Truman. As a critic of his subsequent administration later wrote, Truman looked like a small boy with a secret as the nomination conflict reached its final stages.[55]

From its headquarters in the Hotel Morrison, the CIO–PAC fought to bring some semblance of order to the chaotic Wallace campaign, using all of its influence to force through pro-Wallace resolutions at state delegation caucuses. Though this strategy was partially successful in states like California and Pennsylvania, most of the delegations, responding to the now openly pro-Truman pressure from Hannegan and the convention managers, either declined to endorse anyone or retreated behind favorite-son candidates. Still, the press reported that the momentum was with Wallace and the CIO as the convention formally opened on July 19.[56]

In response to urgent requests by his leading supporters,

Wallace had flown to Chicago on July 19 to personally direct his renomination fight. At a Wallace rally sponsored by PAC on July 19, Murray and Hillman forcefully reiterated earlier statements that the conflict over the Vice President was really a struggle for the New Deal and that the CIO had no second-choice candidate. Under Beanie Baldwin's direction, Claude Pepper, Ellis Arnall, Oscar Chapman, and Joseph Guffy were pressed into service to act as floor managers for the Vice President. Harold Ickes and Francis Biddle, two errant supporters of William O. Douglas, also joined the CIO on the 19th as the conflict was rapidly transformed into a confrontation between the regular Democratic party and the New Deal. (Douglas, although he was preferred by all of organized labor to Truman, had refused to put himself forward in any way as a candidate and was completely without delegate strength at the convention.) [57]

As the opposition to Truman mounted on the 19th, Hannegan was faced with the prospect that the favorite-son strategy, initially developed as a device to expose Wallace's weakness on the first ballot, could backfire and destroy both Wallace and Truman. Lacking a really firm commitment from Roosevelt and hesitant about releasing the Truman–or–Douglas letter for fear that it might somehow aid Douglas (it was always possible that a deadlock might lead Wallace to throw his support to Douglas or Roosevelt to intervene in Douglas' behalf), Hannegan may have leaked erroneous reports to the newspapers that Roosevelt had called the party leaders on the evening of the 19th and strongly endorsed Truman. While these reports were circulating in the press on the 20th, Hannegan transformed them into a self-fulfilling prophecy by contacting Roosevelt in California, informing him of the conflict raging at the convention and, as Truman and the party leaders filed in to his hotel room, getting the President to finally commit himself to Truman within hours of the scheduled Vice-Presidential nominations.[58]

At a time when Wallace's strength was substantially greater than it had been at the July 11 conference, Roosevelt was in San Diego, speaking only by phone with the party leaders, responding to a climate of opinion in which the Vice President's cause was seen as hopeless before he returned from China. At last Roosevelt chose: a bemused Truman, bouncing on the bed next to Hannegan, heard, as did the other party leaders one by one, the President warn about dividing the Democratic party in the middle of a war and angrily call for Truman's nomination and an end to the convention conflict. In San Diego, James Roosevelt found his father reconciled to the removal of Wallace, indifferent as to who was to receive the Vice-Presidential nomination and irritated with the entire affair. The President's decision, however, had joined him with the party regulars against the liberal–labor alliance that saw itself and the cause of Henry Wallace as representing the New Deal.[59]

Releasing the Truman–or–Douglas letter after his conversation with Roosevelt, Hannegan planned to push through Truman's nomination on the evening of the 20th after the Presidential nominations had been concluded. The National Chairman failed, however, to reckon with the force of Wallace's following and the power of the ideas that had made him a hero to so many during the war. Rising to second Roosevelt's nomination before a crowd composed of Mayor Kelly's stalwarts, the Vice President electrified his audience with a passionate plea for social liberalism. The New Deal lived. Full employment, social welfare, and the spirit of cooperation among groups within the economy and among the United Nations were the foundations of peace and justice in the postwar world. In what Wallace himself and many observers considered to be the statement that lost him all chance for the nomination, the Vice President told a cheering gallery and angry Southern delegates that "in a political, educational and economic sense there must be no inferior races. The poll tax must go." [60]

The ensuing demonstration was the most enthusiastic of the convention—in the opinion of many reporters, of the conventions within their memory. After Roosevelt was easily renominated over Senator Byrd, the chanting for Wallace continued and Hannegan's floor managers were in disarray. Too many delegates, Claude Pepper remembered, were joining in the demonstration. Initially, the Wallace forces had hoped to postpone the balloting in order to have one last night to oppose the steamroller tactics that the convention managers were using to line up support for Truman. After the Wallace speech, the Vice President's supporters, believing that their only hope lay in exploiting the enthusiasm of the moment to start a Wallace bandwagon, desperately sought to place his name in nomination. As Claude Pepper tried to fight his way to the platform to nominate Wallace, Hannegan ordered a reluctant Senator Jackson to adjourn the convention. When Mayor Kelly reported that the Wallace demonstration in the aisles constituted a fire hazard, Jackson accepted a motion to adjourn. As the crowd booed the Mayor's name, Jackson shouted over a loud chorus of nays that the convention was adjourned.[61] To some of the party leaders, many of Wallace's followers, and millions of radio listeners, the heavy-handed adjournment had robbed the Vice President of renomination.[62]

Although Beanie Baldwin, huddled with tally sheets on the convention floor, believed that Wallace had a maximum of only 500 votes short of Presidential intervention (589 were needed for the nomination), Hannegan and his lieutenants took no chances, working through the night to herd support for the Truman candidacy. Paul Porter, who was with Hannegan that evening, remembered that important delegates were just grabbed and offered anything to support Truman. The Wallaceites fought back, condemning both the bosses and the Truman–or–Douglas letter, but they had neither party patronage nor the President on their side.[63]

After Truman announced that he was the President's candidate on the morning of the 21st, the decisive session of the convention began. With the galleries nearly empty (the party leaders feared a repetition of the Wallace demonstration), the nominations commenced. Favorite sons like Governor Prentice Cooper of Tennessee, Paul McNutt of Indiana, Alben Barkley of Kentucky, and Governor Robert Kerr of Oklahoma were nominated. Joseph O'Mahoney of Wyoming and Elbert Thomas of Utah, whose strength could only detract from Wallace's in the Mountain States, were nominated, as was John Bankhead of Alabama, who drew strength from Byrd's Southern following. Senator Harry Truman, by now much more than a favorite son or another border-state candidate, was nominated as the candidate of national unity who, in the words of his Missour colleague, Senator Bennet Champ Clark, "will be an element of possible strength in every part of the United States." As a footnote to the preceding ten days, William O. Douglas' name was not even placed in nomination.[64]

The nominating speeches for the Vice President were filled with allusions to the people as against the interests, to the New Deal as against the forces of monopoly and reaction. The Democratic party, an angry Ellis Arnall proclaimed, would not go to Munich by betraying Henry Wallace. In the most moving of the addresses for Wallace, Claude Pepper argued that "Henry Wallace bears upon his body the scars of many daggers. Those daggers were meant for Franklin Roosevelt." If Wallace were defeated, Pepper told the convention, the "militant democracy" which he had come to represent would also be defeated. When the balloting began the Wallace forces, as Max Lerner would later observe to the Vice President, believed that they were struggling for the future of the nation.[65]

On the first ballot, many states passed and caucused as the delegations, still somewhat unsure of the President's wishes, prolonged the vote and watched for a trend. Pennsylvania, with Phil Murray personally leading the liberal–labor forces, went 46 to 24 for Wallace. Michigan, Minnesota, and Wisconsin went almost entirely for the Vice President, as did states like Connecticut and Iowa. Truman showed scattered strength in the South, the Southwest, New England, and the Northeast and divided the votes with Wallace in Ohio and Massachusetts. At the conclusion of the first ballot it was apparent that the favorite-son strategy had succeeded.

When the balloting ended, Wallace had 429½ votes to Truman's 319½ votes. John Bankhead ran third with 90 votes from the South, Scott Lucas had Illinois' 58 votes, and Alben Barkley had 49 votes from Kentucky and scattered Northern states; the remainder of the vote went to favorite sons whose influence was largely restricted to their own states. Fearful that young Wallace supporters outside the hall might yet upset things if the convention were recessed even briefly between ballots (the CIO had recruited Chicago college and high school students to surround the convention hall with Wallace placards), Hannegan ordered Jackson to go ahead with the second ballot. All that remained was for the favorite sons to fall in line behind Harry Truman.[66]

The ambition of powerful congressional leaders like Barkley and Bankhead, who had lived in the shadow of the Roosevelt presidency for twelve years, became the last obstacle to Truman's nomination. Bankhead, who had run third on the first ballot and whose shift would influence minor favorite sons in the South, held the key to the nomination. The Alabama Senator, however, dashed hopes for a speedy Truman victory when he failed to heed a signal from Ed Pauley to withdraw at the beginning of the second ballot (to Pauley's bewilderment, the initial change in the Alabama vote showed a gain of 2 for Wallace).[67]

With Bankhead still in the race, the round of passing and caucusing resumed as the delegations still waited for someone to start a bandwagon. Colorado's early shift from O'Mahoney to Wallace was offset by Connecticut, which moved from the Vice President to Truman. Kansas, which had cast 21 votes for Wallace on the first ballot, caucused; and both Wallace and Truman made marginal gains in Maine. At this point, the first important shift took place; with the vote at 148 for Wallace to 125 for Truman, Governor Herbert O'Connor of Maryland withdrew, giving his state's 18 votes to Truman. Governor Robert Kerr of Oklahoma followed suit and cast his delegation's 20 votes for Truman. With the Missouri Senator now in the lead, the Wallaceites suffered another blow when a floor poll of the New York delegation demanded by a Wallace supporter resulted in a gain of 5 votes for Truman.[68]

Although the shifts by O'Connor and Kerr are usually considered to have been the turning points on the second ballot, a study of the subsequent voting suggests that this is an oversimplification. After the shifts, Wallace states like Kansas, Michigan, and Minnesota held for the Vice President while Mayor Kelly kept Illinois committed to Lucas. Indeed, both Wallace and Truman showed gains as support for the favorite sons waned. At his peak, the Vice President had 472½ votes to Truman's 477½. Bankhead still held the balance of power on the second ballot, but when his strength in Texas and Mississippi ebbed, the Alabama Senator withdrew and cast his state's 22 votes for Truman. South Carolina followed suit, and the bandwagon was on.[69]

In rapid succession, Frank McHale withdrew the candidacy of Paul McNutt and cast the Indiana delegation's votes for Truman. Bankhead's deep-South following, most of which had supported Byrd over Franklin Roosevelt, quickly switched to Truman. When 19 votes in the New York delegation went from Wallace to Truman and Mayor Kelly brought 54 of Illinois' 58 votes over to the Missouri Senator, the race was over, leaving Ilo Wallace in tears, Hannegan smiling through a big cigar, and a flustered Harry Truman to make the shortest acceptance speech in convention history. The bosses had triumphed over the CIO, James Hagarty would note in the *New York Times* the following morning. In reality, the fragile liberal–labor alliance created by the depression and strengthened by the war had failed to overcome the concurrent majority of the Democratic party—the Southerners and the city and county courthouse machines—and the manipulations of a President who had finally become a prisoner of his own compromises.[70]

In his suite at the Hotel Sherman while the battle raged, Henry Wallace blissfully remained Henry Wallace. Choosing not to go to the convention floor for the balloting, the Vice President had slept through most of the first ballot, awakened, and then listened to the second ballot on the radio. In good humor—some observers even felt that he was relieved—after his defeat, Wallace sent Senator Truman a congratulatory telegram which repeated the message of his seconding speech for Roosevelt the night before: the future of the Democratic party rested with liberalism. Roosevelt, in what may have been an attempt at cynical humor, wrote his congratulations to Hannegan on the management of a Democratic convention that deserved to be called democratic. The new Missouri Compromise, as the *New York Times* quickly dubbed the affair, had been consummated.[71]

IV

Wallace's defeat was greeted with predictable lamentations from the liberal journals, rage at the President for "throwing Wallace to the wolves," and grumblings that Truman's only qualification had been his availability. Still, liberal alienation was fleeting: there was no liberal alternative to Roosevelt. After the convention Roosevelt had seen Ellis Arnall and other disgruntled supporters of Henry Wallace. Had he known the true extent of Wallace's strength, the President said, the outcome would have been different. Prisoners of the Roosevelt personality cult and the New Deal coalition, social liberals could do nothing else but believe the President.[72]

After all the excitement, the convention had betrayed the weaknesses of wartime social liberalism. Marching to Chicago with neither a set strategy nor a clear understanding of the difference between substance and symbol, between consistent action and dramatic gesture, the liberals were personified at the end by Senator Guffy, dashing about in a vain attempt to contact the President in California, hoping for some magic intercession by Roosevelt in Wallace's favor.[73]

In the aftermath of the convention conflict, one could see that Wallace had provided social liberals with the legend of virtue fallen before the machinations of the vested interests. Men, David Lilienthal wrote to the Vice President after the convention, could not despair "because there is one man at least who not only knows that this is a moral universe but acts on that assumption in public as well as in his private life." [74] To wartime liberals, without a coherent ideology to legitimize and gain support for either the world New Deal or the Economic Bill of Rights, the politics of morality and martyrdom were always at hand to serve as a substitute for achievement.

The CIO, one might argue, had achieved something more than the politics of hope or the comfort of martyrdom. Had it not been for the PAC, there would have been no Wallace campaign to speak of, no near victory against long odds, and possibly no activist liberal–labor alliance to thwart the nomination of Jimmy Byrnes and force the choice of a candidate who, by his voting record at least, offered no affront to the New Deal. In that respect the CIO had emerged as Hannegan's ally in the nomination of Truman and had at the same time strengthened its position within the New Deal coalition.[75]

Yet, the convention was primarily an example of Roosevelt's failure to transform the Democratic party into a liberal–labor party. He had failed also to encourage the development of a responsible party system in which leaders would be chosen who represented the party's membership and stood for definite party programs. During the campaign, there had been much speculation that the conflict over the Vice-Presidential nomination really concerned the Presidency (indeed, most of the party leaders boasted after Roosevelt's death that they knew they were nominating a President in Harry Truman). Even with the photographs and newsreels that were later cited as evidence of Roosevelt's failing health, Frank Walker is probably correct in his comment that speculation of this kind had nothing to do with the nomination controversy. Rather, most of the press speculation concerning the conflict over the Vice Presidency saw the decision as reflecting either a final ratification (if Wallace won) or repudiation (if he lost) of the New Deal. If one defines the New Deal as interest-group or Broker State liberalism, then it is possible to argue that the choice of Truman indeed represented the fulfillment of the New Deal. To those with memories of national planning and economic democracy or hopes for the CIO and the Economic Bill of Rights, however, the Truman victory was the nadir of Rooseveltian politics.[76]

Few noticed that the President's acceptance speech to the convention, radioed in from California with all of the clarity of Roosevelt's radiophone messages to the party leaders the previous week, closely followed the outline of the Dr. Win–the–War press conference. After announcing that he would restrict his campaign because of the war crisis, the President described the New Deal as a program of the past. Again, Roosevelt mentioned that the concept of planning would be a major force in the postwar world, but planning, as the President used the term, continued to be so vague as to be meaningless.[77]

The war had given organized labor the strength to gain a certain veto power within the New Deal coalition, but the coalition remained in essence a collection of hostile interest groups united only by the benefits to be gained through attachment to the Roosevelt personality. Although the programs of the Economic Bill of Rights were designed to appeal to the New Deal's working-class constituency, the convention made it appear doubtful that the administration had the command of political institutions, much less the will to carry through that program. According to Eleanor Roosevelt, the President believed that if the Lord had work for him to do, he would be around to do it. If not, the party leaders were entitled to choose his successor.[78]

As was usually the case, Roosevelt had taken the line of least resistance, which in 1944 had meant the choice of a candidate acceptable to all and unknown to many in the name of party and national unity. In a little-known essay in the *Progressive*, Milton Mayer came close to capturing the essence of what had happened at Chicago with the remark that the convention had become a "struggle between Wallace the reformer who failed at politics, and Roosevelt the politician who failed at reform." The subsequent career of Henry Wallace would be a kind of lingering monument to the failures of Franklin Roosevelt.

NOTES

* HAW, Jackson Day Dinner Speech, Washington, January 22, 1944 in *Congressional Record*. 78 Congress, 2 Session, p. A435.

1. In reality, "win the war" had been both the slogan and practice of the administration since Pearl Harbor. Memorandum, FDR to the Attorney General, December 12, 1941, FDR Papers, OF 4226, Box 1.

2. Jerome S. Bruner, "Presenting Postwar Problems to the Public," to Grace Tully, March 15, 1943, FDR Papers, OF 4351, Box 2; Hadley Cantril, "Some Results of a Public Opinion Survey . . .," FDR Papers, PSF, Public Opinion Polls, Box 58; Press Conference, December 28, 1943, FDR Master Speech File, FDR Papers, 1499. A Gallup poll on April 20, 1943, showed that 32 percent of the population considered the Republicans the party of prosperity as against only 27 percent for the Democrats. This general trend toward the Republicans during the war was evident in the polls in the President's Secretary's File.

3. Press Conference, December 28, 1943, FDR Master Speech File, FDR Papers, 1499.

4. Cantril, Confidential Report to FDR, January 4, 1944, FDR Papers, PSF, Public Opinion Polls, Box 58; Memorandum, Rosenman to FDR, January 5, 1944, FDR Papers, Public Opinion Polls, Box 58; for evaluations of the 1942 elections, see Louis Bean to Isadore Lubin and Harry Hopkins, February 4, 1944, FDR Papers, PSF, Public Opinion Polls, Box 58, and David K. Niles to Harry Hopkins, December 16, 1942, Hopkins Papers, FDRL, Box 317; on responses to the NRPB report, see Hadley Cantril and Jerome Bruner, "The NRPB Report and Social Security," April 28, 1943, in Hopkins Papers, Box 320.

5. State of the Union Message, January 11, 1944, FDR Speech File, FDR Papers, 1501, pp. 4, 11, 17.

6. FDR to HAW, January 10, 1944, FDR Papers, PPF 41, HAW Folder.

7. Henry A. Wallace, "America Tomorrow," in Russell Lord, ed., *Democracy Reborn* (New York, 1944), pp. 238–239, 243–245, 240–241. In clearing the speech, Wallace noted that parts of it, especially the sections on labor and race, had "dynamite in them." HAW to Stephen Early, July 15, 1943, FDR Papers, OF 12, Box 1.

8. *New York Times*, July 27, August 1, 1943; James Wechsler in *P.M.*, September 12, 1943; Henry A. Wallace, "What We Fight For," Address, Chicago, September 12, 1943, in the Raymond Clapper Papers, LC, Box 246; Henry A. Wallace, "Transportation," Address, Dallas, October 20, 1943, Clapper Papers, Box 246; Noah Mason (GOP, Ill.), quoted in *Congressional Record*, 78 Congress, 1 Session, p. A4223; for an example of this press interpretation of Wallace's speeches see Lyle Wilson, *Washington Daily News*, September 11, 1943.

9. Henry A. Wallace, "Jackson Day," Address, Washington, January 22, 1944, in *Congressional Record*, 78 Congress, 2 Session, pp. A434–435. Ironically, Senator Harry Truman had the speech read into the *Congressional Record*.

10. For the California speeches, see Lord, ed., *Democracy Reborn*, pp. 17–30. Henry A. Wallace, Address, Milwaukee, February 11, 1944, in *Congressional Record*, 78 Congress, 2 Session, p. A691; Henry A. Wallace, "Regional Economics and the National Economy," Address, Chicago, February 14, 1944, in *Congressional Record*, 78 Congress, 2 Session, pp. A779–82.

11. Wallace made this comment on the Vice-Presidential nomination in San Francisco, in Springfield, Illinois, and upon his return to Washington. See *New York Times*, February 8, 13, 1944, and *New York Herald Tribune*, February 16, 1944; see the *Christian Science Monitor*, February 9, 1944, for the President's response to the charges made about Wallace's Western tour and the *New York Herald Tribune*, February 16, 1944, for Roosevelt's remarks about the Barkley and Rayburn stories.

12. *New York Times*, March 5, 1944; George Creel, "Wallace Rides Again," *Collier's*, CXIII (June 17, 1944), p. 11.

13. Theodore Rosenof, "The Economic Ideas of Henry A. Wallace," *Agricultural History*, XLI (April, 1967), p. 149.

14. Harold Young began to work with Wallace when he was assigned to the latter's 1940 campaign by the Democratic National Committee. The main body of the Wallace papers are full of Marsh's memos on political matters during the war. For example, see Charles E. Marsh to HAW, November 8, 1943, HAW Papers, University of Iowa, Iowa City, Ia.

15. "Will Wallace Be Sacrificed?" *New Republic*, CXI (July 15, 1944), p. 76; "Flower Blessing Scholar," *Newsweek*, CXXIV (August 2, 1944), p. 40.

16. George E. Allen, *Presidents Who Have Known Me* (New York, 1950), p. 119; Ed Pauley, Memorandum, in Frank Walker Papers, Notre Dame University, South Bend, Indiana, Case 22, Shelf IV, Box B; quoted in Jonathan Daniels, *The Man of Independence* (Philadelphia, 1950), p. 306.

17. For examples of both frightened and happy speculations about Wallace's impending political demise, see *P.M.*, February 9, 1943, and Raymond Moley quoted in the *Chicago Tribune*, February 10, 1943; for Byrnes' denial see the *New York News*, June 10, 1943; for a discussion of the post-BEW reports of Byrnes and Rayburn successors to Wallace, see Gould Lincoln in the *Washington Star*, November 11, 1943.

18. *New York Times*, February 4, 25, 1944; George Norris to Owen Grundy, July 29, 1944, George W. Norris Papers, Misc. III, Box 27, LC. Among other minor indignities, the Senate early in the war removed Wallace's control over minor patronage powers associated with the Vice President's duties as president of the Senate. *Raleigh News and Observer*, July 22, 1942.

19. *New York Times*, February 25, June 4, 11, 24, 10, 1944; *Washington Star*, June 25, 1944; *Baltimore Sun*, June 28, 1944; *New York Journal American*, July 8, 1944; *New York Times*, July 14, 1944.

20. Frank Walker Memoir 4, Walker Papers, Case 22, Shelf II, Box 23; Allen, *Presidents Who Have Known Me*, p. 122; *New York Times*, January 12, 1944.

21. Pauley, Memorandum, pp. 1–3, Walker Papers, Case 22, Shelf IV, Box B; George E. Allen is the only figure who supports Pauley's contention, and Allen played a minor role in the affair and was a friend of Pauley. Allen, *Presidents Who Have Known Me*, p. 124.

22. Pauley, Memorandum, p. 5, Walker Papers, Case 22, Shelf IV, Box B; "Fourth Term With Whom?" *New Republic*, CXI (January 31, 1944), p. 134.

23. *New York Times*, January 26, 24, 1944; *Oregon Journal*, February 8, 1944; for a brief biographical sketch of Hannegan, see *United States News*, February 9, 1944.

24. Edward J. Flynn, *You're The Boss* (New York, 1947), p. 181; P. K. Hennessy, Notes of a Conference with Walker, July 26, 1950, Walker Memoir 4, Walker Papers.

25. Interview with Paul Porter, November 25, 1968.

26. *Washington Daily News,* January 15, 1942; Tom Stokes in *New York World Telegram,* January 14, 1943; *Common Sense,* XII (October, 1943), p. 369.

27. Helen Fuller, "Throwing Wallace to the Wolves," *New Republic,* CXI (July 30, 1944), p. 122; I.F. Stone, "Plot Against Wallace," *Nation,* CLIX (July 1, 1944), p. 8; for an account of how Biddle and Corcoran used the Johnson analogy with FDR, see Marquis Childs in the *Washington Post,* July 6, 1944.

28. *Ibid.*

29. Interview with John Abt, January 3, 1969; Interview with C. B. Baldwin, January 9, 1969. For the best general treatment of the CIO–PAC, see Delbert D. Arnold, "The CIO's Role in American Politics, 1936–1948" (Ph.D. thesis, University of Maryland, 1952).

30. Sidney Hillman, "The PAC is Here to Stay," in Philip Murray Papers, A4–9, PAC Folders, Catholic University of America, Washington, D.C.; Arnold, "CIO in Politics," pp. 96, 134–140. For examples of liberal enthusiasm over the victories against the Dies Committee see "Things Are Looking Up," *New Republic,* CX (May 15, 1944), p. 667, and "The Shape of Things," *Nation,* CLVIII (June 10, 1944), p. 666.

31. Interview with Baldwin; Interview with Palmer Weber, February 3, 1969; Interview with Abt; for an account of Lowenthal's supposed role, see Matthew Josephson, *Sidney Hillman, Statesman of Labor* (Garden City, N.Y., 1952), pp. 613–15.

32. "1944," February 13, 1951, interview with Walker, Frank Walker Memoir 4, Walker Papers; *New York Times,* May 24, 1944.

33. James F. Byrnes, *All In One Lifetime* (New York, 1958), p. 219; Interview with Benjamin V. Cohen, December 15, 1968. Jonathan Daniels noted in his diary on June 27, 1944, that FDR remarked that Cardinal Spellman had told the President in 1940 that Byrnes' conversion to Protestantism would cost the party millions of Catholic votes if Byrnes became the Vice-Presidential nominee. Citing a letter from Spellman, Byrnes strongly challenged this contention. See Daniels, *Man of Independence,* p. 243, and Byrnes, *All In One Lifetime,* p. 120.

34. *New York Times,* June 23, 1944; *New York Herald Tribune,* July 7, 1944; *New York Times,* July 8, 1944.

35. Helen Gahagan Douglas to FDR, July 13, 1944, FDR Papers, OF 12, Box 3; John Morton Blum, *From the Morgenthau Diaries* (Boston, 1967), III, p. 281.

36. Samuel Hand, "Samuel I. Rosenman, His Public Career" (Ph.D. thesis, Syracuse University, 1960), pp. 208–214; Admiral William D. Leahy, *I Was There* (New York, 1950), p. 248. See *Washington Daily News,* July 12, 1944, and especially Marquis Childs in the *St. Louis Post-Dispatch,* August 12, 1944, for accounts of the activities of Fortas in California and Ickes in Washington.

37. Carey also remembered that Phil Murray told him that Roosevelt had called Wallace a "yogi man" (Wallace's so-called mysticism is discussed in an appendix to this study). Interview with Carey; Interview with Claude Pepper, February 20, 1969.

38. Interview with Porter.
39. Flynn, Pauley, Allen, Walker, and Mayor Kelly have memoirs of various kinds which cover the meeting. Hague left no memoir. There is, however, Grace Tully's memorandum of a phone conversation with the Jersey City mayor on the morning of July 11 in which he expressed sympathy for Byrnes' candidacy. Hannegan's crucial role must be deduced from the other memoir and interview sources. Grace Tully to FDR, July 11, 1944, FDR Papers, PSF, Box 58.
40. Flynn, *You're The Boss*, p. 181; Walker, "The Meeting at the White House," February 13, 1951, Walker Memoir 4, Walker Papers. Cf. Mayor Kelly's account in the *Chicago Herald American*, May 14, 15, 1947.
41. Ed Pauley tells the celebrated story that he pulled the *Congressional Directory* out of John Boettiger's hands just as the President's son-in-law was about to check Truman's age, quickly changed the subject, and thus saved the Truman nomination. Frank Walker tells the less-dramatic story. See Pauley, Memorandum, p. 7, Walker Papers, and Walker, "The Meeting at the White House," Walker Papers.
42. Byrnes, *All In One Lifetime*, p. 224; Allen, *Presidents Who Have Known Me*, p. 129.
43. Photostats of the handwritten and typed letters are in the Walker Papers, Hannegan Correspondence, Box B; Grace Tully, *FDR, My Boss* (New York, 1949), pp. 276-77; Irma Hannegan to Frank Walker, February 11, 1950, Walker Papers, Hannegan Correspondence, Box B.
44. "The Meeting at the White House," February 13, 1951, in Walker Memoir 4, Walker Papers. For Wallace's response, see Carroll Kilpatrick in the *Chicago Sun*, July 14, 1944.
45. Samuel I. Rosenman, *Working With Roosevelt* (New York, 1952), p. 443; Report from Senator Guffy (delivered to Grace Tully, memo unsigned), July 11, 1944, FDR Papers, PSF, Wallace Folder, Box 63.
46. Interview with Louis Bean, December 1, 1944; Russell Lord, *The Wallaces of Iowa*, p. 529. Lord's account, despite its numerous factual errors, restates the view of the convention that Wallace was later to give the press.
47. *Ibid.*; Rough Draft, FDR to Senator Jackson, undated, FDR Papers, PSF, Democratic National Committee, Box 58.
48. FDR to Senator Jackson, July 14, 1944, FDR Papers, PSF, Democratic National Committee, Box 58.
49. Walker, "The Meeting at the White House," February 13, 1951, in Walker Memoir 4, Walker Papers; Byrnes, *All In One Lifetime*, pp. 221-225.
50. Kelly in *Chicago Herald American*, May 15, 1947; P. K. Hennessy, Notes of a Conference with Mr. Walker, July 26, 1950, Walker Memoir 4, Walker Papers; *Washington Post*, July 18, 1944. C. P. Trussell, in the *New York Times*, July 15, 1944, reported that Senator Guffy and other members of Wallace's board of strategy at the convention were debating when to release the letter, with some in favor of a Monday release. However, the Wallace campaign was disorganized at this point, and there is no evidence that the Vice

President had any plans for the letter. Hannegan's visit to the train and the delivery of the letter by Biffle suggest the opposite.

51. Byrnes, *All In One Lifetime*, pp. 227–28; William F. Cronin, who attended the convention with Walker, supports the view that on the night of July 17 Roosevelt told Crowley to tell Byrnes that his candidacy would need the acceptance of organized labor (thus in practice killing the candidacy). Cronin, Memorandum re: 1944, Walker Papers, Hannegan Correspondence, Box B.

52. Curtis D. MacDougall, *Gideon's Army* (New York, 1965), I, p. 21.

53. Eugene Schmidtlein, "Truman the Senator" (Ph.D. thesis, University of Missouri, 1962), provides ample albeit uncritical background material on Truman.

54. Harry S. Truman, *Memoirs* (Garden City, N.Y., 1955), I, pp. 190–192; Byrnes, *All In One Lifetime*, p. 220; Hennessy Notes, August, 1952, Walker Memoir I, Walker Papers; Interview with Porter.

55. Truman, *Memoirs*, I, pp. 190–192; Josephson, *Sidney Hillman*, p. 662; Freda Kirchwey, "The Battle of Chicago," *Nation*, CLIX (July 29, 1944), p. 118; Tris Coffin, *Missouri Compromise* (Boston, 1947), p. 13.

56. Interview with Baldwin; *Chicago Sun*, July 19, 1944; *Chicago Tribune*, July 19, 1944.

57. Jake More to HAW, July 18, 1944, HAW Papers, University of Iowa; *Chicago Sun*, July 19, 1944; *New York Times*, July 20, 1944; Interviews with Baldwin and Pepper; Francis Biddle, *In Brief Authority* (Garden City, N.Y., 1962), p. 358. After the convention, Ickes wrote to Wallace that "next to the President, you are the strongest man in the Democratic party. Frankly, I had not realized this when I went to Chicago and it was worth the trip to find out. . . ." Harold Ickes to HAW, July 24, 1944, HAW Papers, University of Iowa.

58. *New York Times*, July 21, 1944; Hennessy Notes, July 25, 1950, Walker Memoir 4, Walker Papers; Truman, *Memoirs*, I, p. 192; in a later letter to his press secretary, Charles Ross, Truman maintained that he had remained loyal to Byrnes until "Roosevelt called the Blackstone Hotel on Thursday afternoon and virtually drafted me for the nomination the next day." Truman to Ross, January 22, 1950, in Walker Papers, Hannegan Correspondence, Box B.

59. James Roosevelt and Sidney Shalett, *Affectionately, FDR* (New York, 1959), p. 351; Hennessy Notes, July 26, 1950, Walker Memoir 4, Walker Papers; Truman, *Memoirs*, I, p. 192.

60. *Chicago Tribune*, July 21, 1944; Henry A. Wallace, Address to the Democratic National Convention, July 20, 1944, in *Congressional Record*, 78 Congress, 2 Session, p. A3490.

61. Helen Fuller, "Throwing Wallace to the Wolves," *New Republic*, CXI (July 30, 1944), p. 122; Interview with Pepper. *Official Proceedings of the Democratic National Convention* (Washington, 1944), p. 194; *Chicago News*, July 24, 1944.

62. Pauley, Allen, and Kelly hint at this view, but it is probably a post-facto rationalization. Walker doubted that Wallace would have won that evening. Wallace continued to believe that he might have won had he not made the poll-tax statement and had Hannegan not

tampered with the delegates. See HAW to editor of *This Week* magazine, *This Week*, April 14, 1956.

63. Interview with Baldwin; Interview with Porter.

64. Interviews with Porter, Baldwin, and Carey; *Official Proceedings of . . . Convention*, pp. 197–247.

65. *Ibid.*, pp. 208, 210, 215; Max Lerner to HAW, July 25, 1944, HAW Papers, Box 28, LC.

66. *Official Proceedings of . . . Convention*, pp. 487–557.

67. Ed Pauley, "Why Truman is President, as told to Richard English," pp. 21–29. This later account by Pauley is similar to the Memorandum to Daniels, with the exception that it contains Pauley's story of the floor fight in detail. Professor E.L. Schapsmeier, Illinois State University at Normal, Illinois, was kind enough to let me see his copy.

68. *Official Proceedings of . . . Convention*, pp. 257 ff.

69. Herbert Eaton, *Presidential Timber* (Glencoe, N.Y., 1954), pp. 407–409, repeats the standard view of the O'Connor-Kerr shifts that stemmed from the initial press accounts, *Official Proceedings of . . . Convention*, pp. 262–263.

70. *Ibid.*, pp. 263–265; *New York Times*, July 22, 1944.

71. *Chicago Journal of Commerce*, July 22, 1944; FDR to Hannegan, July 21, 1944, FDR Papers, PSF, Democratic National Committee, Box 52; *New York Times*, July 23, 1944.

72. At his wife's urging, Roosevelt agreed to see Arnall, Mark Ethridge, and Mrs. Mary Bingham, three leading Southern supporters of the Vice President. See Notes on letters . . . FDR Papers, OF 187A, Box 43, and *Washington Post*, September 4, 1944.

73. FDR Papers, OF 12, Box 3, contains letters from anguished liberals pleading with Roosevelt to retain Wallace and save the New Deal.

74. Lilienthal to HAW, July 28, 1944, HAW Papers, Box 28, LC.

75. Of course, it may also be argued that the CIO and the liberal–labor forces in the coalition got little but a stalemate, and that the convention was evidence that the other groups in the coalition could not conceivably unite with them on the issues of an expanded postwar New Deal.

76. The question of whether Roosevelt would serve out a fourth term was a very delicate issue before the nominating convention. Turner Catledge, for example, reported in the *New York Times*, May 28, 1944, that Wallace's opponents felt they were choosing a President rather than a Vice President. In the press, the most common argument was that the President's long service made it more likely that this Vice President, either as Roosevelt's chosen successor, or through some unforeseen circumstance, would reach the Presidency (there was a good deal of speculation about the possibility that Roosevelt might step down before the end of his fourth term and thus permit the Vice President to ascend to the Presidency). See Marquis Childs in the *Washington Post*, July 17, 1944.

77. FDR, Address to the Democratic National Convention, July 20, 1944, FDR Papers, FDR Master Speech File, 1525, pp. 1–3.

78. Eleanor Roosevelt, *Autobiography of Eleanor Roosevelt* (New York, 1961), p. 220.

4

Reconversion and Reaction

I've just heard of the death of our great President. May God bless this nation and the world. I scarcely know what to say. It is as if one of my own family had passed away. If we ever needed men of courage —stout-hearted men, it is now. I simply can't conceal my emotions. How I wish you were at the helm. I know Mr. Truman will rise to the heights of statesmanship so all important in this hour. But, we need you as you have never been needed before.

Hubert H. Humphrey to Henry Wallace
April 12, 1945 *

Even if Dr. Win–the–War had emerged from the 1944 Democratic Convention in a stronger position than Dr. New Deal, Henry Wallace retained his loyalty to Franklin Roosevelt. Raising the banner of the Economic Bill of Rights, Wallace campaigned mightily and successfully to hold his liberal–labor followers for Roosevelt in 1944. He was rewarded after the election with appointment as Secretary of Commerce and prepared to take part in the legislative and administrative struggles to make full employment and the social–welfare goals of the wartime liberal movement into postwar realities.

Roosevelt's death in April, 1945, and Truman's accession to the Presidency ultimately shattered such hopes for Wallace and for most social liberals. Initially confident that political necessity would compel Truman to extend the New Deal, liberals watched with increasing frustration as the President replaced New Dealers with cronies and party hacks, refused to fight the battle for full employment legislation, and alienated everyone with blundering price-control and labor policies. In the embarrassing position of being the last prominent New Dealer in the Truman cabinet in the summer of 1946, Henry Wallace found himself increasingly caught between his duty to the administration and the frustration of his followers as the long night of postwar reaction appeared to be descending from all sides.

I

After Henry Wallace's defeat at the 1944 Democratic National Convention, the *New York Times* congratulated the Vice President for having emerged from the struggle with more honor than his opponents and suggested that he was now free to pursue his plans for world peace without the burdens of public office. Wallace, however, had other ideas. In response to the avalanche of sympathetic mail that followed his defeat, he beseeched liberals to continue to work for the New Deal and Franklin Roosevelt within the Democratic party. Publicly laughing off Republican attempts to portray him as a martyr to Rooseveltian intrigue, Wallace doggedly carried the banner of the Economic Bill of Rights through the campaign, appealing to his liberal–labor constituency in the name of Franklin Roosevelt while the President stressed the win–the–war theme, reminded voters of the Republican record of isolationism, and generally remained silent on domestic issues until his "sixty-million jobs" speech late in the campaign.[1]

In his first public address after the convention, on July 29, Wallace told the Iowa State Democratic Convention at Des Moines that "the liberal cause has not been defeated and will not be defeated. . . . when we battle for full production and equal opportunity we battle for the common man. That cause cannot die no matter what may happen temporarily to certain individuals." Campaigning for the national ticket in August, he made familiar appeals for postwar planning in tours of New England and the South. Bringing his campaign to the Northeast in late September, the Vice President told a Madison Square Garden rally chaired by Orson Welles that a new liberalism, committed to the struggle for full employment and equal rights, was emerging from the war. The Vice President's tours, the press began to note, were turning into a personal triumph when compared with the lackluster performance of Senator Truman.[2]

Wallace's tours were sponsored by the groups of the second popular front, the CIO–PAC and the citizens' committee formed to fight for the reelection of Roosevelt and a progressive Congress. Responding to conservative attempts to use the Smith–Connally Act to restrict the activities of the CIO–PAC, the CIO in June, 1944, created the National Citizens Political Action Committee (NC–PAC) to raise funds for the campaign. After the Democratic convention, NC–PAC expanded its activities greatly, acquired George Norris as its honorary chairman, and sought to organize and coordinate the activities of independent liberal groups working for Roosevelt. Along with the NC–PAC, the Independent Voters Committee of the Arts, Sciences, and Professions (reorganized after the campaign as the Independent Citizens Committee of the Arts, Sciences, and Professions) sought to rally those not reached by CIO–PAC to the President's reelection campaign. Although both organizations contained important administrative officers with close connections to the Communist party, the leading journals of liberal opinion all agreed that the activities of the citizens committees and the CIO–PAC represented the most encouraging development in American politics since the rise of the New Deal.[3]

In mid-October, Wallace began his most important work for the party, an extensive tour of major midde-western states— Illinois, Michigan, Wisconsin, Ohio, Minnesota, and Iowa— where his following was strong and the election was considered close. Repeating his defense of the Economic Bill of Rights, the Vice President warned a Cleveland audience that Dewey

was a front "for big capitalists, monopolists, and cartel builders." Dewey's position on a permanent Fair Employment
Practices Commission, Wallace told a Negro rally in Chicago,
was "doubletalk." As Republicans were attempting to use
reports of hostility between Wallace and Truman for their
own purposes, the Vice President agreed to share the platform
with the much-maligned Missouri Senator at a Liberal party
rally in late October at Madison Square Garden. As a gesture
of unity, the Vice President and his would-be successor walked
down the aisles of the Garden arm-in-arm; the crowd, however,
readily distinguished between the two men, greeting Wallace
with an ovation that dwarfed the polite applause for Truman
and drawing press attention with cries of "Wallace in '48." [4]

Congratulated by the President for his appearance with
Truman, Wallace replied at the end of the campaign by ap-
plauding Roosevelt's call for sixty-million jobs in his Soldiers
Field speech.[5] Rather hopefully, the Vice President wrote to
Roosevelt after the election that the administration now had
the majority to fulfill the promise of full employment after
the war. Unforunately, Wallace understood little about the
conservative coalition's emerging strategy of containment
toward the New Deal.[6]

Conservatives, in spite of a Democratic gain of over twenty
seats in the House that was widely attributed to the CIO–PAC,
retained control of the key committees of Congress. If the
almost hysterical Republican attempts to connect Roosevelt
with "Hillman, Browder, and the CIO Communists" had failed
at the polls, the GOP in particular and conservatives generally
had found in the Communist issue a way to attack the New
Deal's supposed collectivist tendencies without indulging in
suicidal assaults against the social legislation of the 1930s. (That
Roosevelt realized this is evidenced by his order to House
Democratic leaders to eliminate the House Un-American
Activities Committee.) The indifference, if not complicity,
of Sam Rayburn and John McCormack to John Rankin's
maneuver in having HUAC made permanent at the first session
of the Seventy-Ninth Congress in January, 1945, shows the
inability of the administration to control the Democratic

12. A victorious Franklin Roosevelt returns to Washington to pose with a rain-splattered Henry Wallace and Vice President-Elect Harry Truman in November, 1944. (Courtesy of the Franklin D. Roosevelt Library.)

party.[7] After the HUAC debacle, the conservative policy of containment to the postwar New Deal had its most vivid early expression in Henry Wallace's fight for confirmation as Secretary of Commerce.

Hours after Truman's nomination, Roosevelt had wired Wallace that "you made a grand fight and I am very proud of you. Tell Ilo not to leave Washington next January." After he received the telegram on July 22, the Vice President apparently decided to stay with the administration rather than return to private life or accept a position with the proposed Food and Agricultural Organization of the United Nations.[8] Meeting with Wallace for the first time since the Chicago convention on August 29, Roosevelt offered his Vice President the choice of any cabinet post save Secretary of State (a subsequent Wallace for Secretary of State boom, supported by the *New Republic* and Eleanor Roosevelt, angered Cordell Hull and led the President in an election-eve press conference to deny reports that Wallace was being groomed to replace Hull).[9]

With no real background for the Treasury, Justice, and Interior portfolios (all of which were safely held by New Dealers), Wallace also displayed indifference to the pleas of old colleagues that he return to the USDA and lift the department from the lethargy that had settled over it during Claude Wickard's administration. Although it was often rumored that the Vice President might become Secretary of Labor, his strong identification with the CIO was no endorsement for that post, given the bitter rivalry between the CIO and the AFL. (Wallace's appointment would also have been at the expense of Frances Perkins, another of the original New Dealers and a loyal friend.) The Commerce portfolio had none of these handicaps.[10]

First of all, Secretary of Commerce Jesse Jones was Wallace's archenemy within the administration and a hated symbol of reaction to all of the New Dealers. Given the Secretary's power over the government's lending agencies through his control of the RFC and its subsidiaries, the department loomed large in the New Deal's postwar full employment program and appeared to be an ideal stage upon which Wallace could both test his ideas for postwar planning through progressive capitalism and revive his influence within the administration and the party. Although the RFC was scheduled to be separated from the Department of Commerce at the end of the war, it was rumored that Roosevelt might keep Jones' financial empire in the department by executive order (RFC had been joined with Commerce by a 1942 presidential order).[11] After the November elections, Beanie Baldwin had spoken with Harry Hopkins about a possible post for the Vice President, and both had agreed that Commerce was the only logical position for Wallace. Writing to Roosevelt on November 30, the Vice President showed enthusiasm for the coming battle for full employment and noted that in the new administration "my job seems to me to be commerce." [12]

Although Roosevelt was initially committed to the Wallace nomination with retention of the lending agencies by the Department of Commerce, conservative Democrats, James Wechsler reported in early December, 1944, were already searching for ways either to save Jones or at least to prevent Wallace from receiving the fruits of his RFC empire. At a meeting with Roosevelt in late December, Wallace secured the President's pledge to keep the lending agencies in the department. Josiah Bailey, conservative chairman of the Senate Commerce committee, and Senator Tom Connally of Texas asked the President on January 17, 1945, to divest RFC from the Department of Commerce and retain Jones as RFC chairman. The same day, Wallace wrote to Roosevelt that "certain financial people both in this country and south of the Rio Grande . . . are especially interested in your signing Executive Orders one of which would take RFC out of Commerce. If we give in to the financial gang at this time, the people will say that you and I have lost another battle to the reactionaries." [13] In his meeting with Bailey and Connally, Roosevelt showed no sympathy for their proposals and left them with the distinct impression that he would support Wallace's appointment with full control over the lending agencies. Yet the smoldering controversy over the Commerce nomination was only of peripheral interest to the President. Scheduled to leave Washington for the Yalta conference on January 22, Roosevelt handled the Wallace nomination in such a cursory fashion as to doom any chance the former Vice President might have had to retain control over the RFC.[14]

On Inauguration Day the President wrote to Jones that Wallace, because he "displayed the utmost devotion to our cause, traveling almost incessantly and working for the success of the ticket in a great many parts of the country," deserved any post "he thinks he can satisfactorily perform." Attempting to provide Jones with a way to save face, Roosevelt expressed the hope that the Secretary of Commerce "think about a new

13. Henry Wallace, with wife Ilo, leaving the White House after Franklin Roosevelt's last inaugural, January, 1945. (Courtesy of the Franklin D. Roosevelt Library.)

post—there are several ambassadorships vacant. . . ." After a
brief, unsatisfactory meeting with Roosevelt, a bitter Jones released the President's letter and his own angry reply to the press.
Sailing for Yalta the following day, Roosevelt left the country
at the exact moment his appointment of Henry Wallace ex-
ploded into a major public controversy.[15]

The President's carelessly drafted letter provided the enemies
of the New Deal with ammunition to attack the Wallace
nomination. On January 22 William K. Hutchinson of the
International News Service released the story that Wallace,
following his defeat, had received a message from Roosevelt,
"to this effect, 'there will always be room in my household for
you.'" While the press condemned the appointment as a
political payoff, Senator Walter George introduced a bill to
sever the RFC from the Department of Commerce. Senator
Bailey's Commerce Committee quickly agreed to begin hearings on the George bill on January 24, prior to any consideration of Wallace's nomination. In a less than subtle indication
of its sentiments, the committee called Jesse Jones as its first
witness.[16]

Jones' testimony provided the opponents of Wallace with a
field day. In a prepared statement, the outgoing Secretary of
Commerce noted that the RFC had developed under the
leadership of "men experienced in business . . . men who
haven't any ideas about remaking the world." At one point
in the questioning, Chairman Bailey touched on the central
fear of the conservatives by telling Jones that the RFC "might
be used by one in your place to determine the economic direction of the country and affect its whole social and political
structure." Senator Pepper, leader of the pro-administration
minority on the Commerce Committee, was the former Vice
President's only active defender at the hearings.[17]

Wallace's testimony on the following day before the committee—beginning with an elaborate defense of each of the
goals in the President's Economic Bill of Rights message—was
hardly designed to curry favor with the conservatives. Except for a pledge to use the Commerce post to try to expand
foreign trade and a somewhat tongue-in-cheek observation to

Pepper about his own substantial success as a businessman in the hybrid corn field, the former Vice President said little to appeal to the men of the coalition. Testifying against the George bill, Wallace suggested that Congress should appoint a special commission to study the disposition of the RFC, adding that "if it is decided that the RFC should not remain with the Commerce Department, I will carry on the job of Secretary of Commerce until the war ends." At a meeting of the National Businessman's Committee for Wallace in New York a day after his testimony before the Commerce Committee, Wallace learned that the committee had voted to recommend passage of the George bill and to oppose his nomination.[18]

Addressing a testimonial dinner in his honor on January 29, Wallace warned Congress against any "economic Munich or Dunkirque" in the disposition over the lending agencies, but he made clear that his decision to accept the Commerce post would rest on the President's choice of a liberal Federal Loan Administrator rather than upon the fate of the George bill. In the Senate, conservatives moved to both pass the George bill and defeat the Wallace nomination, while Senator Pepper, reflecting the deterioration of the Vice President's position, announced on January 30 that Wallace would be confirmed *after* the George bill was passed. Wallace's Senate supporters now felt that they had to accept the George bill if his nomination were to be salvaged at all.[19]

Although Roosevelt agreed rather testily to send a message to Congress promising to sign the George bill if it were passed, Senator Bailey introduced a resolution on February 1 on the Senate floor to take up the Wallace nomination first and thus defeat the former Vice President before the President's message became known. When the vote on the Bailey motion tied at forty-two to forty-two, Senator Taft, leader of the anti-Wallace Republicans, changed his vote to no in order to put himself in position to move for reconsideration. Aware of the remarkable strength that the conservative coalition had shown on the original vote, Taft had good reason to suspect that he could pick up the additional vote needed to defeat

Wallace. Vice President Truman, however, ignored Taft's attempt to move for reconsideration and recognized Senator Barkley, who moved to call up the George bill, reading President Roosevelt's pledge to sign the bill if it were passed to the assembled Senators. The worst now over, the Senate voted by a margin of seventy-four to twelve to approve the George bill and postponed consideration of the Wallace nomination until March 1, thus giving the House time to consider and approve the bill and the President time to sign the measure. With a great deal of irony and some justice, Truman would cherish the memory that it was he who had saved the Wallace nomination.[20]

14. (Left to right) James F. Byrnes, President Truman, and Secretary of Commerce Henry Wallace at the funeral of F.D.R., April, 1945.

The Right, however, had achieved its "economic Munich," a fact that liberal protest rallies, petitions from CIO unions, and cries of relief when the Senate finally confirmed the former Vice President could not obscure. Although a move by House conservatives to postpone action on the George bill until the Senate voted on the Wallace nomination collapsed in mid-February, observers noted that the bond between the conservatives of both parties had been greatly strengthened by the struggle. The New Dealers, *P.M.* concluded, had little to cheer about. Richard L. Strout (who doubled also as the *New Republic's* TRB) noted in the *Christian Science Monitor* that the successful opposition to giving Wallace control over the lending agencies had really been directed against the "New Economics" of John Maynard Keynes, a fact that boded ill for the postwar New Deal.[21]

Wallace, however, remained optimistic. Responding to his new position with his customary enthusiasm, he recruited New Dealers for the Department of Commerce, made plans to reform the department's data-gathering and planning services and prepared to play a major role in the fight for full employment legislation. As long as Roosevelt was President, he remained confident about his future.

II

For liberals especially, Franklin Roosevelt's death was felt as a deep personal loss. Although they had long criticized his compromises, social liberals saw the President as the most remarkable figure of the age, the architect of the coming victory over Fascism, and the leader of a national movement that had produced more legislation to aid the Common Man than any other in American history. In tributes to the fallen President, however, there emerged a seemingly contradictory theme: Roosevelt, the acknowledged leader of social liberalism, had compelled all liberals to live within the shadow of his person and his party. Tragic in itself, his death would have meaning only if it freed progressives to work with organizations like the PAC to reconstruct American politics. Roosevelt's death,

Freda Kirchwey concluded, "may mean the coming of age of the progressive political forces in America." To Sidney Hertzberg, liberals had for a decade "lived in the debilitating shadow of paternalism." "American Progressives are now free," Hertzberg concluded, "to build a movement that can constitute a really progressive alternative to the chaos which threatens." [22]

The initial response of the liberal journals to Harry Truman reflected a combination of condescension and confidence. Truman, the *New Republic*'s TRB contended, "may or may not be a Roosevelt liberal but I think he is no fool. . . . Will he go conservative? Look at the election returns." In what was perhaps the most typical early judgment of Truman, Margaret Marshall concluded that "whereas a Roosevelt or a Wallace would put forth a bold and comprehensive program . . . Truman is likely to ask for no more than he can get without creating enemies. . . . he will break no new paths, push back no boundaries, and he will tend to equate public opinion with party opinion." [23]

Truman's first sixteen months in office transformed liberal attitudes of confidence and condescension to the President into feelings of bitterness and helplessness toward his administration. "Mediocrity" and "crony" became epithets for the men of the new administration as liberals watched the hopes of 1944 go smash against the unbroken power of the conservative coalition and the President's inept handling of postwar labor and inflation crises. Gradually, liberals came to believe that the President cynically used New Deal slogans while permitting his closest advisors to cripple New Deal programs. As conditions grew steadily worse, liberal disaffection came to be expressed in nostalgia for Franklin Roosevelt, growing fear of a mounting right-wing reaction in the country, and an increasingly pessimistic search for ways to revive the wartime liberal–labor alliance. A brief look at the writings of the *New Republic*'s TRB will help to highlight these trends and put the liberal response to the President in perspective.

Reflecting the common view, TRB portrayed Truman in April, 1945, as a middle-of-the-roader whose first goal would be to keep the Democratic party together and who would be as liberal as conditions would permit. In July the *New Republic* columnist expressed concern that the President's popularity reflected his ability to be all things to all men and that his chief advisors were hostile to the CIO–PAC, still the most admired organization within the liberal–labor alliance. Continuing to stress Truman's personal honesty and good faith, the liberal journalist noted in September that "the mediocrity of some of President Truman's advisors is beginning to show like the mid-day sun." After the President's progressive reconversion message of September 6 fell on deaf congressional ears, TRB expressed concern about the inertia in Washington and especially about the President's privately stated conviction that if Congress refused to act on a given problem, there was little he could do about it. Summing up Truman's first six months in office, the *New Republic* columnist pictured the President in October, 1945, as a moderate "of higher caliber than some feared and of weaker leadership than some hoped." [24]

The collapse of the Economic Bill of Rights as a legislative program and the administration's heavy-handed response to the great postwar strikes led liberals to reconsider their initial attitude about Truman, defending him against any possible Republican alternative while attacking his actions, advisors, and appointments with mounting anger and despair. During the General Motors strike in the winter of 1946, TRB noted that the President's advisors remained antilabor even though they realized that Truman could not be reelected without union support. Initially hopeful that Truman's call to the people in January 1946 to petition Congress in support of full employment legislation was the beginning of new liberal militancy within the administration, TRB commented rather dejectedly in February that the President "is no Franklin Roosevelt but he is the only President we have." [25]

After Franklin Roosevelt, the *New Republic* columnist and liberals found themselves with a far stranger hero, Postmaster-General Hannegan, the architect of Truman's victory at the 1944 Democratic convention. While liberals watched the comic adventures of Ed Pauley, George E. Allen, and Truman's other cronies in high office, Hannegan sought to keep New Dealers like Wilson Wyatt, Paul Porter, and Robert

Nathan in the administration and worked to improve relations between the Democrats and the CIO–PAC. Although liberals were suspicious of Hannegan's background, motives, and style, they respected his actions. Truman's actions had created such frustration by the summer of 1946 that reports of Hannegan's imminent resignation was seen by TRB as further proof of the administration's move to the right.

Commenting on Truman's first year in office in April 1946, TRB could still say that "our Harry's no paragon, but he looks an awful lot better if you've been looking over at the GOP National Committee stable." The President's call for repressive antilabor legislation in the May, 1946, railroad strike made liberals wonder if there were anything positive left in the administration. TRB uttered an involuntary moan when President Truman's request to Congress for powers to draft the railroad workers into the army was broadcast over the radio. Accusing the President of inspiring chaos within the Democratic ranks, the *New Republic* columnist reflected the pessimism of most liberals when, in introducing a column about potential Republican Presidential nominees, he asked, "who will be the Republican lucky man?" [26]

As Truman fell deeper into a morass that was partly of his own making, liberals responded to his troubles with either bitter rage or mocking humor. When Harold Ickes resigned as Secretary of the Interior in February, 1946, in protest over Truman's farcical attempt to appoint Ed Pauley Undersecretary of the Navy, the *Nation* whimsically compared the Ickes–Pauley affair to the American Communist party's purge of Earl Browder, noting that with Truman at least "a Cabinet member is thrown to the wolves and no one speaks of Ickesism." Demanding that the Pauley nomination be withdrawn after Ickes' resignation, the *New Republic* wondered if "President Truman has learned anything by his unfortunate attempts to appoint his friends to top jobs." After the May railroad strike, the tone of liberal criticism became more mordant. When John Snyder, the President's most important conservative advisor, was appointed Secretary of the Treasury, the *Nation* commented that "Mr. Truman is like a mischievous boy who seems to enjoy frightening people with no thought to the consequences." [27]

Sarcasm, like nostalgia for Franklin Roosevelt, was but another measure of liberal defeat. It did little good to mutter "to err is Truman" in a political atmosphere of confusion highlighted by occasional disaster. Social liberals had endured and rationalized Franklin Roosevelt's wartime compromises because of a belief in both the good faith and the leadership gifts of the President and the vision of a better world and a better America represented by the programs of the world New Deal and the Economic Bill of Rights. Both the world New Deal and the Economic Bill of Rights had been smashed to pieces by the summer of 1946. The only serious question facing liberals was what could still be done with the pieces.

III

Among its many other lessons, history, Harry Truman noted in his memoirs, taught him "of the unique problems of Andrew Johnson. . . . when the same thing happened to me, I knew just how Johnson had coped with his problems and I did not make the mistakes he made." [28] Actually, the analogy between Johnson and Truman is useful, as both were chosen as Vice-Presidential candidates in the interest of national unity, became President by accident at the conclusion of great wars, and were expected to produce settlements of the problems that had created the wars. Andrew Johnson, the Jacksonian Democrat uncomfortable with Republicans and contemptuous of Radicals, failed primarily because he could not abandon obsolete principles of states rights and pernicious racial and regional prejudices in order to work with Congress to develop policies for the reconstruction of the South. Harry Truman, the regular Democrat uneasy with New Dealers and reformers, failed because he lacked the understanding, sympathy, and leadership ability to give substance to either the world New Deal or the Economic Bill of Rights.

Truman's view of the Presidency as an instrument of moral

leadership, much like Theodore Roosevelt's "bully pulpit," contributed to his problems with Congress. In spite of his background as a machine politician and reverence for regular Democrats in general and the Senate establishment in particular, Truman had come of age politically in the Progressive Era; his constant oversimplications of everything, legalistic solutions to national and international problems, and tendency to define his enemies in conspiratorial terms all reflected political poses that were better suited to the world of Theodore than Franklin Roosevelt.[29] The Progressive in public as election time neared, Truman was an archetypal standpatter in his relations with Congress, deferring to the conservative establishment until liberal pressure led him to make quixotic gestures that merely hardened his initial defeats.

It is probably fair to say, as Professor Mary Hinchey has noted, that Truman believed that the severe postwar economic crisis predicted by most observers would compel Congress to enact the programs of the Economic Bill of Rights.[30] Although the postwar crisis of deflation and unemployment never developed (Roosevelt, who had failed to reconstruct the party system or develop a public consciousness beyond fear of depression, would have faced the same problem), it must be said that Truman, surrounded by advisors who were hostile to the Economic Bill of Rights, often acted in ways that sabotaged the liberal program and demoralized his social–liberal supporters. Even his progressive reconversion message of September 6, 1945, often cited as the first important link between his policies and the New Deal, came in response to pressure from Claude Pepper and other liberal Senators and represented the first of many ritualistic recitations of the Economic Bill of Rights program. His policy of working with the conservative leadership of Congress, which effectively doomed any hopes for the Economic Bill of Rights, did not change after September, 1945.[31]

In line with this policy, the President supported referral of the Wagner–Murray–Dingell Social Security Bill to Senator George's Ways and Means Committee, where it had no hope of survival. Truman similarly supported the referral of the

Missouri Valley Authority Bill, for which he had little private sympathy and few hopes, to hostile congressional committees. Faced with a severe postwar housing shortage, he failed to provide consistent and effective leadership for the Taft–Wagner–Ellender Housing Bill, even though the act had popular and bipartisan support. Repeatedly, Truman would remark to friends that he had been in the Senate long enough to know that if Congress did not want to do something, there was little that the President could do about it. For his administration, the comment became a self-fulfilling prophecy.[32] His actions in the battle for a meaningful full-employment bill, considered by all to be the core of the Economic Bill of Rights program, constituted the clearest case of his failure to extend the New Deal.

Full employment had been the central point of Henry Wallace's wartime speeches concerning domestic policy, the foundation upon which Alvin Hansen and the left Keynesians based their plans for a postwar compensatory economy. As a slogan, full employment became almost irresistible by the end of the war, surpassing even free enterprise, which had enjoyed a significant revival of its own. Although the Roosevelt administration had prepared a White Paper on Full Employment in the spring of 1944, the train of events leading to the creation of the Full Employment bill began in earnest when James G. Patton, president of the National Farmers Union and a devoted friend and follower of Henry Wallace, proposed an amendment to the Murray–Kilgore Reconversion bill in August, 1944, that called for government studies to ascertain whether public and private expenditures would reach the level believed necessary to maintain full employment. (Patton's proposal provided for authorization to increase public spending and to stimulate private investment through RFC loans to attain full employment.) [33]

In the fall of 1944 Senator Murray assigned his committee counsel, Bertram Gross, who was aided by Louis Bean, to the task of preparing a preliminary draft of a full-employment measure. Wallace, in a speech drafted largely by Gross and Bean, became the first administration figure to endorse the national-budget feature of the proposed full-employment bill in December, 1944. As introduced in January 1945, Murray's bill attempted to win support from moderates by deleting Patton's specific proposals for increased public expenditures under the act; the measure retained, however, the idea of a national full-employment budget that would require the government to estimate the total expenditures necessary to maintain full employment. Along with the federal pledge to sustain employment, the national budget was regarded by friends and foes alike as the heart of the full-employment bill.[34]

Henry Wallace regarded the national budget as a method of analysis, "a procedure that the government will use in guiding and appraising its actions." Wallace dedicated his brief tenure as Secretary of Commerce to transforming the department into a clearinghouse for economic planning and for the creation of a balanced full-employment economy and expanded world trade. "A lasting world peace can be built only on a sound foundation of world trade," he wrote to Truman at the end of 1945 in presenting a series of suggestions for the President's first state-of-the-union message, "our enormous production machine must have world markets if it is to function at its full capacity." [35] Although his private papers and public statements attest to the fact that trade expansion was uppermost in his mind as a departmental project, Wallace placed his special assistant, Philip Hauser, in charge of a program committee for the administrative reform of the department. The committee's report, which Wallace released in September, 1945, called for the reorganization and expansion of the department's informational services and the integration of these services with an expanded National Bureau of Standards. The report also advocated the creation of new offices within the department to work for full employment by stimulating foreign trade, small business enterprise, and cooperative planning between business and government. Public enterprise, the Secretary had written to Senator Wagner in May, 1945, would have assured full production and employment in the depression if government had known how to use fiscal policy to create employment and consumer demand. The national budget, Wallace believed, would provide government with the mechanism to create a full-employment economy. Once the full-employment bill became law, the new statistical services of the department would enable the government to estimate required national economic needs and the public expenditures to fill those needs.[36]

Testifying in August, 1945, before the Senate Banking and Currency Committee, Wallace argued that public expenditures and federal guarantees to maintain production and employment were both "conservative" programs and "a most essential step" in the fulfillment of Franklin Roosevelt's legacy, the Economic Bill of Rights. The Secretary's widely publicized and well-received book, *Sixty Million Jobs* (1945), although it advocated in great detail the Alvin Hansen–National Resources Planning Board program of increased expenditures for social services, was largely a plea for the national budget mechanism of the Full Employment bill. It is little wonder that the minority report of the Banking and Currency Committee condemned the Full Employment bill as a guise for "the so-called compensatory spending theory, advanced by Lord Keynes, Stuart Chase, Sir William Beveridge and Mr. Henry Wallace." [37]

Detailed studies of the full-employment controversy have been made by Stephen K. Bailey and Mary Hinchey. These accounts generally support the contemporary contentions of social liberals that the President's failure to provide strong and consistent leadership for the bill enabled conservatives to modify it greatly. John Snyder displayed the administration's lack of a clear strategy for the bill when, in testifying before the Senate Banking and Currency Committee, he publicly agreed with conservative criticisms of the measure.[38] Although liberals were suspicious of Snyder and unhappy with the Taft amendment, which proscribed federal deficit spending to implement the measure, they were not antagonistic to the Senate bill. In spite of the compromises the bill retained the national budget and the federal guarantee to maintain employment.[39]

For liberals the House bill was a complete disaster. Contributors to the liberal journals began to wonder if the President was really interested in full employment. Truman had initially permitted House Speaker Rayburn to steer the bill to the conservative-dominated Committee on Executive Expenditures rather than the liberal Banking and Currency Committee, where, it was believed, the Senate bill would be retained intact. After the Committee on Executive Expenditures reported out a bill that replaced the national budget with a Council of Economic Advisors and changed the guarantee to maintain employment generally to "high levels of employment," the President, on the advice of Treasury Secretary Vinson, supported the measure and used all of his influence to defeat efforts by House liberals to save the original Senate act. The UDA, a leading group of the liberal–labor lobby for a full-employment bill, was not far wrong when in December, 1945, it accused the President and the House Democratic leadership of betraying full employment.[40]

Henry Wallace, of course, also compromised the cause of full employment when he contacted House rebels and asked them to support the administration. Wallace, informing liberals of the administration's stated intention of restoring the Senate bill in the House–Senate conference committee, continued to press the President for substitutes to the House bill. In early January, the Secretary of Commerce condemned the House bill in an address at St. Paul. As the bill went to the conference committee, Truman fulfilled part of his promise to Wallace and the House liberals with a radio address supporting the original Senate measure and calling upon the people to write their Congressmen in favor of real full-employment legislation. In his State of the Union Address and his formal charge to the leaders of the House–Senate conference committee, the President reiterated his support of the Senate measure. Truman, however, failed to strengthen his verbal commitment to the Senate bill with concrete compromise proposals to the House–Senate conference committee. In part, this reflected the influence of such conservative advisors in the administration as John Snyder, who successfully pigeonholed a suggestion by Vinson that the President recommend a cabinet committee to replace the conservative-backed Council of Eco-

nomic Advisors. (Wallace had suggested such a substitute to
Truman in December, 1945.) [41] Signed by the President on
February 20, 1946, the final bill retained the Council as against
the national budget and made the following pledge on the
question of full employment:

> The Congress hereby declares that it is the continuing
> policy and responsibility of the Federal Government to
> use all practicable means consistent with its means and
> obligations and other considerations of national policy,
> with the assistance and cooperation of industry and agri-
> culture, labor, and state and local government, to co-
> ordinate and utilize all its plans, functions and resources
> for the purpose of creating and maintaining, in a manner
> calculated to foster and promote free competitive enter-
> prise and the general welfare, conditions under which
> there will be afforded useful employment opportunities,
> including self-employment, for those able, willing and
> seeking to work, and to promote maximum employment,
> production and purchasing power.[42]

The struggle for full employment and for the Economic
Bill of Rights had ended, in Bailey's pungent phrase, in "a battle of thesauruses." Contrasting the final measure with the
initial proposals and the Senate bill, the conservative press was
satisfied with the act. Reluctantly asking Truman to sign the
bill now that all hope for serious compromise was gone, liberals expressed faint hopes that the President would salvage
something from the bill through his appointments to the Council of Economic Advisors. For the most part, though, the final
bill was seen by liberals as further evidence of Truman's failure as President. Making the best of the situation, Henry
Wallace noted that "we must take this document at face
value" and continue the fight for full employment, of which
"the Employment Act of 1946 is but a Preamble." [43]

It is true, as Bailey has noted, that many people came to
believe "as time went on that the act was an important step in
the direction of coordinated and responsible economic planning in the federal government." To many others searching
for ways to defend the Truman administration in the age of

containment, the bill was seen as a legitimate commitment to maintain employment and a major achievement of the administration. Edwin G. Nourse, the moderate conservative who became the first Chairman of the Council of Economic Advisors, noted that the final act, designed to "validate free enterprise and representative government," constituted the first time that the United States "explicitly stated a national policy of cooperation between business and government to maximize our national production." [44]

Yet, the powers of the Council of Economic Advisors were not fundamentally different from those of the old National Resources Planning Board: the national budget, one of the planning mechanisms on which the postwar New Deal was to be based, was sacrificed in the final act along with the full-employment pledge. The President might have had both had he fought seriously for the Senate bill. Instead he received an act more in tune with the mood of the Congressional establishment from which he had come and the American business community of the period—an act which mixed liberal and conservative slogans and made a mockery of the effort to create a genuine guarantee for full employment. Conservative containment had triumphed over the Economic Bill of Rights. The inflation and labor crises of 1946 soon transformed domestic containment from a conservative to an administration policy. [45]

IV

Price control had been a major issue of the liberal–labor alliance during the war years. Supporting the OPA against the incessant attacks of conservatives in Congress, liberals watched the New Deal's price–control program work remarkably well in the last two years of the war. [46] The Truman price policies, however, often resembled a Mack Sennett comedy, ended in uncontrolled inflation, and almost shattered the New Deal coalition beyond repair.

Truman, as Allen Matusow has shown, remained in the background of the price controversy, permitting his subordinates to work at cross purposes while the consumer–labor coalition supporting controls slowly disintegrated. Clinton Anderson, for example, worked for the removal of controls and helped to aggravate the meat problem by hinting to a Senate committee in the spring of 1946 that he favored withdrawal of some price restrictions on meat. Although Henry Wallace took to the stump in defense of Chester Bowles (director in turn of the OPA and the Office of Economic Stabilization and the whipping boy for the enemies of price control), Bowles continued to serve as the scapegoat for the administration's failure either to control prices or to end the shortage of consumer goods. Reviving his wartime rhetoric, Wallace in February, 1946, condemned the National Association of Manufacturers' "nefarious fight against OPA" and warned that "the special interest groups and the speculative wolves are hot on Chester Bowles' trail." Bowles, himself, attacked the "pied pipers of profits," but such appeals were drowned in the massive anti-OPA campaign carried on by business and farm groups.[47]

Inflation, by fragmenting the groups of the New Deal coalition, represented a greater threat to Broker State politics than had depression. With inclinations and advisors that were much more conservative than Roosevelt's, Truman in effect aided the mounting opposition to the OPA by failing to coordinate his administration's efforts to achieve noninflationary decontrol. Although a Gallup poll showed that 73 percent of the people favored a strong OPA as late as May, 1946, public opinion increasingly blamed the OPA for the shortages of consumer goods plaguing the country. Bowles, who always considered himself a "lone wolf" in an administration dominated by foes of price control, resigned as director of the stabilization program in June, 1946, leaving OPA director Paul Porter to continue the unpopular and unsuccessful fight for controls.[48]

Porter took hope when Truman in June, 1946, vetoed a very weak bill extending OPA. All of the President's advisors and the Democratic Congressional leadership, the former price director remembered, had advised Truman to sign the measure. Although liberals briefly hailed the President's veto, the "inflationary holiday" that followed the expiration of OPA served only to heighten the price crisis. Truman's acceptance in late July of a new price bill that contained many of the old measure's objectionable features was evidence that his veto had failed to stop the foes of control. OPA, as Matusow has noted, was left in the autumn of 1946 to face "the pale satisfaction of a martyr's end." [49]

Permitting his subordinates to work for contradictory price policies, Truman followed a pattern of drift punctuated by futile action—the general pattern of his domestic and foreign policies. Had he supported Bowles and Porter consistently—or Snyder and Anderson for that matter—he would have had a policy with direction and purpose. Instead, his non-policy encouraged public opinion to blame creeping inflation and food shortages on price controls and to permit conservatives to destroy the OPA and then blame the administration and the Democratic party for the consequences. It may be argued, of course, that Truman's evasions were similar to Roosevelt's and reflect the problems of Broker State politics rather than the merits of an individual president; yet, Roosevelt's rapport with the people, political judgment, and quality of aides and advisors cannot be compared with Truman's. Price control had worked under Roosevelt. It is hard to believe that he would have led his party to the slaughter of the November elections by presiding over such an amateurish and ineffectual price-reconversion policy.[50]

Liberals, of course, had lost faith in the administration well before the July OPA crisis. Truman's labor policies had done much to turn the liberal–labor alliance against the administration and the nation against the liberal–labor alliance.

After V–J day removed the reason for labor's wartime no-strike pledge, Truman called upon workers to adhere to the decisions of the War Labor Board until he convened a Labor-Management Conference to settle wage questions and find alternatives to strikes. In the interim period, the President said he would permit wage increases that did not lead to inflationary price increases, an act that labor interpreted as a further attempt to adhere to the hated wartime "little steel formula" for wage rates. After the President's Labor–Management Conference in November, 1945, which produced nothing more than a set of general statements in favor of voluntary arbitration, cooperation, and industrial peace, the United Auto Workers continued a major strike against General Motors.[51]

The President's initial response to the strike, a suggestion that fact-finding boards deal with the issues of the dispute after the strikers returned to work, was rejected angrily by CIO president Phil Murray. Walter Reuther's contention that corporate profits had to be taken into consideration when determining wage rates made him a hero to liberals, most of whom echoed the *Nation*'s criticism of Truman's "gauche handling" of the strike and "feeble rhetoric" about conciliation and fact-finding boards. Although Truman drew praise from progressives in late December with a statement that successful fact-finding should include an evaluation of corporate profits, the praise was coupled with the uneasy observation that labor could gain more from the administration through defiance than by passive support.[52]

Truman's labor problems did not end after the administration in February, 1946, established an eighteen-and-one-half-cent-an-hour wage increase as a noninflationary model for the resolution of labor disputes. Seeking to emasculate the Wagner Act since its passage, conservatives had taken advantage of John L. Lewis' violation of the wartime no-strike pledge to pass the War Labor Disputes Act in 1943 over Roosevelt's veto. The attempt to enact similar and permanent antilabor legislation for the postwar period was evidenced by the introduction of such anti-union measures as the Ball–Burton–Hatch bill of 1945, which sought to establish machinery for compulsory arbitration. Although the great CIO strikes in the automobile, steel, and electrical industries ended in February and March, the indomitable Lewis once more brought antilabor feelings to the fore when he took his coal miners out on strike on April 1, 1946. After Truman seized the mines in mid-May, Congress, responding to the President's request for legislation to deal with strikes in essential industries, passed the harshly anti-union Case bill. Truman's subsequent veto of the Case measure failed either to curb widespread antilabor feeling or to restore the confidence of the liberal–labor alliance in the administration. What was left of that confidence had been shattered by the President's handling of the national roalroad strike.[53]

The government took responsibility for the operation of the railroads on May 17 after the extension of a strike deadline came to an end. When a compromise agreement between the administration and the eighteen operating railway unions was rejected by the Engineers and the Trainmen, a nationwide rail strike began on May 23. Truman, whose closest connections with labor had always been with the railway unions, told strikers on May 24 to disregard their leaders and return to their jobs, stating that "this is a contest between a small group of men and their government." Three minutes after the strike was formally settled, Truman went before Congress to seek powers to check strikes in essential industries after those industries had been taken over by the government. The President's request for the power to draft strikers into the army drew special fire from the liberal–labor forces. Truman's dramatic announcement at the conclusion of the message that the strike had been settled also led many to believe that the address had been a grandstand play, a cynical and reckless appeal to a public angry with strikes, inflation, and consumer-goods shortages.[54]

A. F. Whitney, president of the Brotherhood of Railway Trainmen, denounced Truman as a political accident, hinted at the formation of a third party, and pledged his entire union treasury to defeat the President in 1948. William Green compared the labor draft proposal with "slave labor under Fascism," and Phil Murray wrote to Truman that the latter's message had as its "sole aim the destruction of the labor movement of this nation." Among some liberals, the strike produced a new wave of nostalgia for Franklin Roosevelt and interest in developing clubs and societies to continue the Roosevelt tradition. Among others, especially in the CIO unions and the groups of the second popular front, third-party talk was widespread.[55]

Wallace had counseled progressives against forming a third

party since his defeat at the 1944 Democratic convention. With great inconsistency, he had argued that he would remain a Democrat as long as the Democratic party upheld the New Deal. When Eleanor Roosevelt suggested in the summer of 1945 that he lead progressives in the creation of a national organization of independent liberals, Wallace replied that he would continue to work for liberalism within the Democratic party.[56] As the featured speaker at NC–PAC and ICCASP rallies, the Secretary of Commerce spoke for the programs of the world New Deal and the Economic Bill of Rights while nominally supporting Truman. Often called the leader of the Democratic party's left by the press, Wallace sought to maintain his paramount position with the groups of the second popular front without hopelessly antagonizing the administration. The interaction of the labor crises and the administration's "get tough" policy with Russia, however, made it increasingly difficult for the Secretary of Commerce to serve both the President and his own followers.

Wallace's relations with the popular-front groups grew more cordial as the cabinet came to be dominated by conservatives. The Secretary frequently saw Hannah Dorner, ICCASP's national director, and he corresponded with Jo Davidson, Harlow Shapley, and other leaders of the citizens' organization. Beanie Baldwin, vice-chairman of NC–PAC, remained Wallace's oldest and closest friend within the second popular front. Openly critical of Truman's foreign and domestic policies, Baldwin, by the winter of 1946, was privately sympathetic to the formation of a third party. Sidney Hillman, however, adamantly opposed any such venture, and his stance enabled Wallace to continue to preach liberal unity within the Democratic party while searching for devices to make the party liberal.[57]

Although he continued to defend the administration, Wallace was not above occasional gestures of independence. In February, 1946, he surprised some supporters by endorsing Johannes Steel, a New York radio broadcaster with far-left connections, against former Congressman Arthur Klein, in a special New York City congressional election. Although Klein had a consistent New Deal voting record, Steel's candidacy, which had both PAC and Communist party support, was seen as an attempt by the organized liberal–labor forces to show their strength to the administration. Steel's narrow defeat was viewed enthusiastically by those on the left who favored militant opposition to Truman.[58]

Wallace's growing frustration about the fate of the New Deal in the Truman administration became apparent in his advocacy of party responsibility. In an address to the National Women's Democratic Club in March, 1946, the Secretary of Commerce argued that Congressmen who opposed major parts of the party program should be punished by the party caucus. In response to a wave of irresponsible criticism that he was advocating party purges and the introduction of totalitarian politics, Wallace elaborated on his notions of party responsibility in an article in *Collier's* in June, 1946. Noting that the programs of the New Deal had been defeated to a great extent by Democrats, the Secretary of Commerce maintained that a system of party responsibility was necessary if Congress was to act on the major issues of the day. After the party caucus had acted, legislators who lost committee assignments and other privileges would still be free to run in the party primaries; the enrolled voters would make the final decision on the qualifications of party mavericks (a stipulation that would probably result in Southern and other anti-New Deal Democrats keeping their party designations and some of their congressional power).[59]

In addresses to liberal rallies in the spring of labor and consumer discontent, Wallace criticized third-party advocates, reminded his audiences of the Republican beast at the gate, and urged independents to take a more active role in reforming party machinery. *P.M.* noted after the railroad strike that labor leaders, looking for an alternative to Truman in 1948, no longer believed that Wallace could be elected President. Indeed, the Secretary's continued defense of Truman was beginning to annoy some of his followers, many of whom suggested that Claude Pepper might prove to be a better opponent for Truman in 1948.[60]

In 1944, PAC pamphlets had hailed Roosevelt and called for

an unceasing struggle to attain postwar full employment and the programs of the Economic Bill of Rights. Ben Shahn's posters showing white and black workers standing together for victory and full employment epitomized the hopes of the liberal–labor alliance for a people's century after the war. Preparing for the 1946 elections, the PAC spoke of inflation and housing shortages and sought to disassociate itself from the administration as much as possible. Liberal admirers warned Wallace that the Democrats faced disaster in the November elections (although no one really grasped the magnitude of the coming defeat). When Wallace told a Political Action Techniques Workshop in June, 1946, that the Democrats were still "ten times" more progressive than the Republicans, Beanie Baldwin, one of the workshop's sponsors, stated publicly that if Truman did not change his ways a third party would come into existence whether Henry Wallace liked it or not. (Wallace shamefacedly agreed in a private conversation with Baldwin afterwards.) [61] With the liberal–labor alliance in disarray, Wallace prepared for an autumn of campaigning for a progressive Congress. Believing that his political power could still be used to influence the administration, the Secretary moved toward an unexpected clash with Truman, a confrontation that would signal his departure from Washington and rapidly be transformed into a command decision on American foreign policy.

It would be simple to compare the failures of Harry Truman with Woodrow Wilson's defeats after World War I. Great strikes, divisions among the functional groups making up the liberal coalition, and widespread public impatience with the manifold problems of reconversion were primary sources of tension in the months after Versailles and Hiroshima. Wilson's errors in the struggle over the League of Nations appear to history to have been much greater than Truman's blunders in the fight for the Economic Bill of Rights. Wilson, however, had only a minority Democratic party and the moral rhetoric of a Progressivism soured by wartime excesses behind him as he sought to create a new international order. Truman had the New Deal's majority coalition and faced a nation molded by depression and war—a nation searching less for the "normalcy" of 1920 (a cynical repudiation of social uplift) than for security and peace. The New Deal had indeed failed to transform the party system or raise the consciousness of the people to participate in the creation of a cooperative society. But few repudiated the sacrifices made in the war and only a bitter conservative minority talked openly of abolishing the programs that had survived the depression. Eventually, a generation of liberal Democrats, the autumn harvest of the New Deal, emerged from the war to improve the quality of the Democratic party in Congress and, ironically, to transform it into much more of an urban liberal–labor party than it had ever been under Franklin Roosevelt.

All this, however, occurred independently of Harry Truman. Unsure of himself and presiding over an administration replete with mediocrities and knaves. Truman failed to deal effectively with either the domestic or foreign problems of the early postwar years. In moving from crisis to crisis he sought only to contain his enemies at home and abroad, but in the process he developed policies that would shape the course of American history for a generation. The Economic Bill of Rights, a summation of the hopes of twentieth-century humanitarian social liberalism, was shattered by Truman's indifference and bungling and then lost sight of as the cold war institutionalized the war economy, stood Keynes on his head, and made Communism into an issue that poisoned the American political climate. Although Truman's failures cannot be separated from the greater failure of New Deal Broker State politics, one must note that he lacked Roosevelt's political skills and vision at a time when America's capacities to achieve abundance at home and lasting peace abroad were greater than at any time in history. Faced with a brawling interest-group coalition, fears of depression, and the programs and personnel of the New Deal, Truman had indeed made the worst of it.

Notes

* Hubert H. Humphrey to HAW, April 12, 1945, HAW Papers, University of Iowa, Iowa City, Iowa.

1. *New York Times,* July 22, 1944; Russell Lord, *The Wallaces of Iowa* (Boston, 1947), p. 538. The Wallace Papers in the Library of Congress are the best source for letters of condolence after the convention. See HAW Papers, Boxes 26 and 28 especially.

2. HAW, Address to the Iowa State Democratic Convention, July 29, 1944, in *Congressional Record,* 78 Congress, 2 Session, p. 3483; *New York Times,* August 25, 30, 1944; *P.M.,* September 22, 1944.

3. Sidney Hillman, "The Truth About PAC," *New Republic,* CXI (August 21, 1944), pp. 209–211; Delbert D. Arnold, "The CIO in American Politics, 1936–1948" (Ph.D. thesis, University of Maryland, 1952), pp. 225–227. For examples of the standard liberal response to the committees, see Bruce Bliven, "The Liberals After Chicago," *New Republic,* CXI (August 7, 1944), p. 154, and Freda Kirchwey, "Campaign Notes," *Nation,* CLIX (September 30, 1944), p. 369.

4. *Detroit Free Press,* October 8, 1944; *Baltimore Sun,* October 14, 30, November 2, 1944.

5. FDR to HAW, November 1, 1944, HAW to FDR, November 7, 1944, FDR Papers, PPF 41, Wallace Folder.

6. HAW to FDR, November 7, 1944, FDR Papers, PPF 41, Wallace Folder.

7. For a summary of attacks against PAC, see Fred Maguire, "The Press Gangup on the PAC," *New Republic,* CXI (October 30, 1944), pp. 558–563. For Rankin's maneuver, see Walter Goodman, *The Committee* (New York, 1968), pp. 168–169.

8. FDR to HAW, July 21, 1944, FDR Papers, PPF 41; for the FAO story see Howard Tolley Interview, *COHC* (this story is told by other Wallace intimates).

9. John M. Blum, ed., *From the Morgenthau Diaries* (Boston, 1967), III, p. 392; "Wallace For Secretary of State," *New Republic,* CXI (November 20, 1944), p. 465; *New York Times,* November 4, 1944. Russell Lord notes that Roosevelt first told Wallace of the cabinet posts open on August 29 and "Wallace chose Commerce." Perhaps Lord, as is true at many points in his work, has confused time and place. My interview with C. B. Baldwin and Wallace's letters to Roosevelt suggest that the Vice President made no clear choice for the Commerce post until after the elections. Lord, *Wallaces of Iowa,* pp. 543–44.

10. *New York Times,* October 28, 1944; HAW, Address to CIO Convention, November 21, 1944, in *Congressional Record,* 78 Congress, 2 Session, p. A4492.

11. Executive Order 9071, February 24, 1942, FDR Papers, OF 3, Commerce Department; to understand liberal feeling against Jones, see Jesse Jones and Edward Angly, *Fifty Billion Dollars* (New York, 1951).

12. HAW to FDR, November 30, 1944, FDR Papers, PSF, Wallace Folder.

13. Wechsler in *P.M.*, December 4, 1944; *New York Times*, December 21, 1944; John Robert Moore, *Senator Josiah William Bailey of North Carolina* (Durham, N.C., 1968), p. 220; HAW to FDR, January 17, 1945, HAW Papers, University of Iowa.

14. Moore, *Senator Josiah William Bailey*, p. 220.

15. FDR to Jesse Jones, January 20, 1945, Jesse Jones to FDR, January 20, 1945, FDR Papers, OF 3, Commerce Department; Jones and Angly, *Fifty Billion Dollars*, p. 279.

16. Hutchinson clipping, Jesse Jones Scrapbooks, Box 311, Jones Papers, LC; *New York Times*, January 23, 24, 1945. The Jones scrapbooks are the best source for press accounts of the confirmation fight, especially the bitter attacks on Wallace.

17. Committee on Commerce, *Hearings on . . . S. 375*, 79 Congress, 1 Session (Washington, January 24, 25, 1945), pp. 25–26, 44–46.

18. *Ibid.*, p. 84; Interview with Claude Pepper, February 20, 1945.

19. HAW, Address to UDA–*New Republic* Testimonial Dinner, January 29, 1945, ADA Papers, Series I, Box 33, Wisconsin State Historical Society (henceforth WSHS), Madison, Wisconsin; *New York Herald Tribune*, January 31, 1945.

20. Memo, Rosenman to FDR, February 2, 1945, FDR Papers, OF 3, Commerce Department; Moore, *Senator Josiah William Bailey*, p. 223; *Philadelphia Record*, February 2, 1945; Harry S. Truman, *Memoirs* (Garden City, N.Y., 1955), I, p. 195.

21. For the sorts of testimonials made at the Wallace confirmation rallies, see Reinhold Niebuhr to Wallace Sponsors, February 17, 1945, ADA Papers, Series I, Box 33, WSHH; *New York Herald Tribune*, February 16, 1945; *P.M.*, February 18, 1945; *Christian Science Monitor*, February 17, 1945.

22. Freda Kirchwey, "End of an Era," *Nation*, CLX (April 21, 1945), p. 430; Sidney Hertzberg, "Politics After Roosevelt," *Common Sense*, XIV (May, 1945), p. 5.

23. "President Truman's Task," *New Republic*, CXII (April 23, 1945), p. 540; Margaret Marshall, "Portrait of Truman," *Nation*, CLX, (April 21, 1945), p. 439.

24. TRB, "The New President," *New Republic*, CXII (April 23, 1945), p. 554; "After the Charter is Ratified," *New Republic*, CXIII (July 23, 1945), p. 102; "Peacetime Miscellany," *New Republic*, CXIII (September 10, 1945), p. 315; TRB, "Back to Normalcy?" *New Republic*, CXIII (October 1, 1945), p. 438; TRB, "Truman's First Six Months," *New Republic*, CXIII (October 15, 1945), p. 498.

25. TRB, "Yuletide Memo," *New Republic*, CXIII (December 24, 1945), p. 867; TRB, "Congress and Truman's Speech," *New Republic*, CXIV (January 14, 1946), p. 51; TRB, "Democrats Have to be Progressive," *New Republic*, CXIV (February 11, 1946), p. 181.

26. *Ibid.*; TRB, "Political Dog Days," *New Republic*, CXIV (August 26, 1946), p. 216; TRB, "Truman's First Year," *New Republic*, CXIV (April 15, 1946), p. 504; TRB, "Putting Labor in Its Place,"

New Republic, CXIV (June 13, 1946), p. 793; TRB, "Good News and Bad," *New Republic*, CXIV (June 24, 1946), p. 888.

27. "The Shape of Things," *Nation*, CLXII (February 23, 1946), p. 211; "A Secretary For Interior," *New Republic*, CXIV (February 25, 1946), p. 268; "The Shape of Things," *Nation*, CLXII (June 15, 1946), p. 705.

28. Truman, *Memoirs*, I, p. 120.

29. For a good general critique of Truman's presidency, see Athan Theoharis, "The Truman Presidency: Trial and Error," paper delivered at the Pacific Historical Association Meeting, Palo Alto, August 28, 1967, at HSTL.

30. Mary Hedge Hinchey, "The Frustration of the New Deal Revival, 1944–1946," (Ph.D. thesis, University of Missouri, 1965), p. 145.

31. *Ibid.*, pp. 107–108; for a good summary of the Economic Bill of Rights program in Congress, see Senator James Murray, "A Plan For America," *New Republic*, CXIV (January 21, 1946), pp. 75–78.

32. Hinchey, "Frustration of the New Deal Revival," pp. 107–108.

33. James G. Patton, "A Plan For America," *New Republic*, CXI (November 6, 1944), pp. 586–587.

34. Stephen K. Bailey, *Congress Makes A Law* (New York, 1950), p. 24, 52, 56; Henry A. Wallace, "Jobs For All," *New Republic*, CXII (January 29, 1945), pp. 138–140; "The Shape of Things," *Nation*, CLX (January 6, 1945), p. 2.

35. HAW, Address to National Marketing Forum, N.Y.C., October 22, 1945, Alfred Schindler Papers, Box 20, HSTL; HAW to HST, December 28, 1945, HAW Papers, University of Iowa.

36. Interview with Philip Hauser, September 26, 1968; Program Committee, "The Future Role of the Department of Commerce," August 10, 1945, released at Press Conference, September 20, 1945, in Schindler Papers, Box 16; HAW to Wagner, May 29, 1945 (released publicly June 11, 1945), Schindler Papers, Box 20; Henry A. Wallace, *Sixty Million Jobs* (New York, 1945), pp. 162–165.

37. HAW, Statement to Senate Committee on Banking and Currency, August 28, 1945, p. 2, Schindler Papers, Box 20; Wallace, *Sixty Million Jobs*, part V; quoted in Bailey, *Congress Makes A Law*, p. 118.

38. Bailey, *Congress Makes A Law*, p. 163; Hinchey, "Frustration of the New Deal Revival," p. 177.

39. "Speed the Murray Bill," *Nation*, CLXI (August 25, 1945), p. 170; "Full Employment—Road to Freedom," *New Republic*, CXIII, (September 24, 1945), pp. 395–415.

40. Bailey, *Congress Makes A Law*, pp. 167–176; *UDA Congressional Newsletter*, December 15, 1945, p. 1, in ADA Papers, Series VII, Box 105.

41. HAW to HST, December 15, 1945, HAW Papers, University of Iowa; HAW Address to AAA Regional Meeting, St. Paul, January 10, 1946, p. 9, Schindler Papers, Box 20; Bailey, *Congress Makes A Law*, pp. 189–222.

42. Barton J. Bernstein and Allen J. Matusow, eds., *The Truman Administration: A Documentary History* (New York, 1966), p. 47.

43. Bailey, *Congress Makes A Law*, p. 224; HAW, Statement of Full Employment Act of 1946, March 4, 1946, p. 2, Schindler Papers, Box 20.
44. Bailey, *Congress Makes A Law*, p. 234; Edwin G. Nourse, *Economics in the Public Service: Administrative Aspects of the Employment Act* (New York, 1953), p. 7.
45. In answer to those who defend the final measure and Truman's handling of the affair, one should note that the Senate bill, which the UDA called a "decent compromise," was passed by an overwhelming vote of seventy-one to ten. It is inconceivable that the conservative coalition in the House could have voted down a similar bill had the President pressed for one. *UDA Newsletter*, December 15, 1945, ADA Papers, Series VII, Box 105.
46. For an excellent account of the difficulties and the triumphs of the wartime OPA, see Chester Bowles, *Promises to Keep: My Years in Public Life* (New York, 1971), pp. 43–125.
47. Allen J. Matusow, *Farm Policies and Politics in the Truman Years* (Cambridge, Mass., 1967), pp. 3, 51–52, 76; HAW, Address, Des Moines, February 16, 1946, p. 1, Schindler Papers, Box 20; Chester Bowles, "The Pied Pipers of Profits," *New Republic*, CXIV (March 4, 1946), p. 306.
48. Henry Hewitt, "OPA and the Elections of 1946," Unpublished Paper, at HSTL; Bowles, *Promises to Keep*, pp. 153–56. Bowles is more sympathetic to Truman in his memoirs than he was reported to be at the time.
49. Interview with Paul Porter, November 25, 26, 1968; Matusow, *Farm Politics*, p. 56.
50. For a defense of the Truman price policies as indicative of the kind of leadership that the people wanted and about all that one could expect, see Allan Harper, "The Policies of the Truman Administration," Comments, Meeting of the Mississippi Valley Historical Association, May 3, 1963, at HSTL.
51. Arthur F. McClure, II, "The Truman Administration and Labor Relations, 1945–1948" (Ph.D. thesis, University of Kansas, 1965), p. 78; Joel Seidman, *American Labor From Defense to Reconversion* (Chicago, 1953), pp. 217–226; Hinchey, "Frustration of the New Deal Revival," p. 197. The "little steel formula" tied wage increases to increases in the cost of living.
52. "Truman and the People," *Nation*, CLXII (January 12, 1946), p. 32; TRB, "Reuther vs. GM," *New Republic*, CXIII (December 29, 1945), p. 724.
53. McClure, "Truman Administration and Labor Relations," p. 87; Seidman, *Labor From Defense to Reconversion*, pp. 229–234.
54. *Ibid.*, p. 237.
55. "Whitney Strikes Back," *Progressive*, X (June 3, 1946), p. 3; Seidman, *Labor From Defense to Reconversion*, p. 237; "Washington Calling," *Progressive*, X (June 10, 1946), p. 1.
56. *P.M.*, November 12, 1944; Eleanor Roosevelt's "My Day" column in *Washington Daily News*, December 31, 1947.

57. HAW to Jo Davidson, January 4, 1945, Jo Davidson Papers, Box 5, LC; Hannah Dorner to HAW, October 22, 1945, in Davidson Papers, Box 5; HAW to Harlow Shapley, March 8, 1945, RG 40, Box 1031, NA; Interview with Baldwin.

58. David A. Shannon, *The Decline of American Communism* (New York, 1959), p. 116; *New York Times*, February 7, 20, 1946; Steel was also supported by former Mayor Fiorello La Guardia.

59. HAW, Address, Women's National Democratic Club, Washington, March 18, 1946, Schindler Papers, Box 21; "Washington Calling," *Progressive*, X (April 1, 1946), pp. 1, 12; Wallace's *Collier's* article in *Congressional Record*, 79 Congress, 2 Session, p. 7367.

60. For an example of these speeches (a complete file is at the Truman Library and the University of Iowa) see HAW, Address, NC-PAC Liberal Voters League of St. Louis, June 14, 1946, Schindler Papers, Box 21; *P.M.*, June 12, 1946.

61. For a sample of PAC's 1946 campaign materials, see Philip Murray Papers, PAC Folders, Box A4-33, Catholic University of America, Washington, D.C.; James Loeb to HAW, February 25, 1946, RG 40, Box 1049; *New York Times*, June 28, 1946; Interview with Baldwin.

5

From Stettin
in the Baltic

*During the past year or so, the significance of peace
has been increased immeasurably by the atom bomb,
guided missiles and airplanes which soon will travel
as fast as sound. Make no mistake about it—another
war will hurt the United States many times as
much as the last war. We cannot rest in the assur-
ance that we invented the atom bomb—and therefore
that this agent of destruction will work best for us.
He who trusts in the atom bomb will sooner or
later perish by the atom bomb—or something worse.
. . . I plead for an America vigorously dedicated
to peace—just as I plead for opportunities for the
next generation throughout the world to enjoy the
abundance which now, more than ever before, is
the birthright of man.*

Henry A. Wallace
Madison Square Garden Speech
September 12, 1946 *

It had been an almost trite assumption among social liberals
during the war that America could not move right while the
rest of the world was moving left without a great explosion.
Yet it had happened, and the fragile liberal–labor alliance nurtured by the war had proved powerless to stop it. Seeking to
bring the Soviet Union into the community of nations and

to both coexist with and channel revolutionary forces in a world moving "left of center," Franklin Roosevelt had made major concessions to Soviet security interests in Eastern Europe in return for Russian support for the United Nations and for American aims in China. Ultimately the success or failure of the President's Grand Design hinged on American capital for Russian reconstruction and Chinese development. Although it is highly doubtful that even Roosevelt could have carried off such an ambitious program in the political climate of 1945, Truman and those around him never tried to continue FDR's conciliatory policies. Instead, the new administration treated the Soviets from the beginning as an enemy rather than as an ally, undermined the hope of cooperation by brandishing America's nuclear monopoly, and sought to win public approval with a highly touted "get tough" policy toward the Russians.

The Russians, of course, did not get out of Eastern Europe, the world did not stop moving left, and American foreign policy under Truman and Byrnes found itself organizing first world opinion and then the world against the Soviet Union. Struggling mightily against these trends in Soviet–American relations, Henry Wallace fought through 1945 and 1946 to gain administration support for a settlement with the Soviets that would insure permanent nuclear disarmament, maintain Allied unity, and thus lay the groundwork for a workable United Nations. Bringing these issues fully into the open in his famous challenge to the Truman–Byrnes "get tough" policy at Madison Square Garden in September, 1946, Wallace compelled the administration to choose between its new foreign policy and the remnant of the world New Deal. Truman's choice intensified the cold war and rang down the curtain on Wallace's thirteen-year career in Washington.

I

Returning from Russia in 1928, American Civil Liberties Union director Roger Baldwin wrote glowingly of the new

Soviet state. Although Russia, Baldwin contended, lacked what the West considered political liberty, the Soviet government's war against poverty and exploitation promised to provide the Russian people with economic liberty. John Dewey, the foremost philosopher of American pragmatism and intellectual beacon for humanitarian social liberals, expressed similar views at the conclusion of the Jazz Age. After a trip to Russia in 1929, Dewey pictured the Soviet Union as a great experiment in the quest for economic security and cultural freedom, "the most interesting experiment going on upon our globe." These complimentary themes of Russia as the bastion of economic democracy (Robert La Follette had used that term as early as 1919) and the world's greatest experiment, became, as Frank Warren has noted, "commonplace" arguments in the popular social liberal defense of the Soviet Union in the 1930s.[1]

Attempting to explain liberal fascination with Russia, Warren has suggested that the comparison between Soviet progress and American complacency and Philistinism in the 1920s, the depression-accentuated view of Russia as the center of social and economic planning and order in the early 1930s, and admiration for the Stalin regime's leadership in the international struggle against Fascism led the majority of American liberals to suspend critical judgment on many of the actions of the Soviet state, a condition that ended abruptly when the Hitler–Stalin pact shattered the popular front.[2] Warren's arguments are well presented and generally support the findings of this study concerning social liberal thought in the 1940s. One may suggest, however, that wartime liberal admiration for Russia, beyond the fact that the bulk of the ground war against Hitler being fought on Russian soil and won with Russian lives made such admiration almost apolitical, was reinforced by Russia's identification with the two great themes of social liberalism—faith in a new society made free by science and technology and belief in the empirical methods of science as the solution to all social problems.

For liberals in the late 1930s, Russia could be seen as a fellow traveler with America on the road to security and abundance.

Maxim Litvinoff, the Soviet ambassador to the United States, had excited the interest of President Roosevelt in 1933 with the remark that Russia and America would share a common destiny in the creation of a just world order.[3] However that view had been damaged by the Hitler–Stalin pact, the pact was of short duration. Hitler's invasion of Russia and the Japanese attack upon Pearl Harbor created a new popular front at home and made support for America's heroic Russian ally quite respectable. While conservatives muted direct criticism of the Russians in the name of wartime unity and films like *Armored Attack* and *Song of Russia* portrayed the Soviets as brave and simple people courageously resisting the Nazi invader, liberals once more suspended judgment on many Russian actions in the hope that postwar Soviet–American cooperation would provide the only realistic alternative to the balance-of-power politics and economic rivalries that had produced the war.[4]

In the early war years, the *Nation* and the *New Republic* rationalized the most brutal Russian acts and accused anti-Soviet critics of undermining Allied unity and inadvertently aiding the machinations of Hitler and Goebbels. *Common Sense*, formerly an isolationist liberal journal, was far less sympathetic to Soviet actions that impinged upon the rights of small nations nominally protected by the Atlantic Charter and thus threatened the foundations of a world New Deal. All liberal journals, however, considered Soviet-American cooperation to be the basis for the world New Deal and the chief barrier against a third world war (the memory of Munich as an attempt to work with Hitler against Russia encouraged these views).[5] Henry Wallace, the leading spokesman for a world New Deal during the war, emerged also as the chief advocate of long range Soviet–American friendship and cooperation, drawing together the sympathetic beliefs that social liberals had held about the Soviet regime since the Bolshevik revolution into a rationale for what another generation would call peaceful coexistence.

Initially, Wallace had had scant sympathy with the Russian revolution. Arguing with a Bryan Democrat who supported the Bolsheviki, he had predicted in the autumn of 1917 that Lenin's government would last but a few years. The inaccuracy of that prediction, coupled with the greed and cynicism that he found in the America of the 1920s, made the embattled farm editor a guarded admirer of the Soviet experiment. Whereas the Western nations had to resort to imperialism to bolster their chaotic economies, Russia, Wallace believed in 1924, was "building a new industrial system out of the wreck that the world war left." [6] Unsympathetic to Red Scare politicians, Wallace felt at times in the 1920s that America could aid Russia through her sophisticated knowledge of modern technology and at the same time reinvigorate her own revolutionary and frontier traditions through contact with the Soviet experiment. His only ambivalence about the regime (apart from opposition to its atheism) stemmed from the threat that it posed to American agricultural exports. Often he argued that the success of the Soviet state, whatever hopes conservatives still held for its collapse, meant that American farmers must abandon their lingering hopes for new markets abroad in favor of realistic programs to control production. [7]

Although a revulsion against Stalin's murderous campaign against the Kulaks, fear for the loss of existing American agricultural markets overseas, and the interesting belief that the Russians would eventually use their growing economic power to disrupt world capitalism led Wallace to oppose American recognition of the Soviet Union in 1933, he continued to express sympathy with aspects of the Soviet experiment. [8] In *Statesmanship and Religion* (1934) he stirred some criticism by comparing Lenin with Martin Luther and John Calvin as a prophet of a new world order. Wallace's close association with Rexford Guy Tugwell, traveler to Russia in the 1920s and leading spokesman for national economic planning in the early New Deal, may also have enhanced his appreciation of Soviet accomplishments. With some justice, James Paul Warburg noted in 1934 that Tugwell and Wallace, of all the New Dealers, had made the most sympathetic references to the Soviet experiment. [9]

In the late 1930s, Wallace's continued advocacy of discipline and sacrifice for the general welfare, along with his increasing tendency to picture the emerging international conflict as a struggle between democracy and Fascism or between freedom and slavery paralleled the central theme of the popular front, the call for all civilized people to commit themselves to the destruction of Fascism.[10] After Pearl Harbor, his passionate defense of a people's century predicated upon a strong United Nations and Soviet–American cooperation made him an ideal leader for the second popular front.

In the Century of the Common Man speech in May, 1942, the Vice President had portrayed the Russian and American revolutions as part of an evolving historical process, "the march of freedom of the past 150 years. . . ." Returning to the social–liberal idea that Soviet Russia was but the extension of a world revolution begun by America, Wallace expanded upon his ideas for the future of Soviet–American relations in an address before a Soviet–American Friendship Congress in November, 1942. Starting with de Tocqueville's assumption that Russia and America were destined to become the dominant powers in the world, the Vice President argued that the two nations had long shared a heritage of internal expansion and contempt for militarism. Through the Russian revolution, Wallace thought, the Soviets had joined the Americans in the quest for mechanisms to provide "for the enduring happiness of the common man." [11]

In the postwar world, the Vice President predicted, America and Russia would be forced to evolve new definitions of democracy. Free from both the rigidities of bureaucratic Communism and the rugged individualism of the Hoover era, the new democracy that Wallace envisioned would provide America with the security to grant her people greater economic and social rights and Russia with the protection to allow her people more political liberties. By uniting to create an international organization to raise living standards and maintain world peace, the two Allies would gradually become more alike, developing one system that would combine the best of political and economic democracy.[12]

Wallace dealt with the problem of Soviet totalitarianism in

an address at Ohio Wesleyan in March, 1943. Picturing Prussianism, Marxism, and Christian Democracy as the three dynamic faiths in conflict in the world, the Vice President conceded that the Communists, like the Fascists, had practiced political terror. The Communists, however, had never advocated racial supremacy or glorified war as the Fascists had; furthermore, the ugly Soviet actions of the previous decade—the purge trials, the pact with Hitler, and the Finnish war—had all stemmed from fear of Germany. Unlike Germany, Wallace argued, Russia did not want to conquer the world. Communism was rooted in poverty, not in Soviet machinations, and it would succeed in the West only to the extent that the Western nations failed to solve the problems of poverty and mass unemployment. If the West failed to overcome its economic problems, Communist agitation would be "inevitable and there is nothing the Russian government or our government or any other government can do to stop it." [13]

Wallace's identification of the foes of Soviet–American cooperation with the enemies of the New Deal grew as his advocacy of a world New Deal made him the favorite target for conservatives. In his speech at Ohio Wesleyan, he touched off a controversy with the contention that World War III would be the result if "we doublecross Russia" or if "fascist interests motivated largely by anti-Russian bias get control of our government." During his national speaking tour in February, 1944, he provoked the anger of conservative newspapers and Congressman Martin Dies by sympathizing with economic and social progress in the Soviet Union and condemning "American Fascists" who wished to divide Russia and America in order to maintain the old system of monopolies and economic imperialism. His visit to Soviet Siberia in the spring of 1944 strengthened his faith in Russian economic democracy. The hydroelectric projects, tractors clearing vast areas of land, and the hardiness and apparent enthusiasm of the people contrasted sharply with the misery and lethargy he found everywhere on his subsequent visit to China.[14]

Returning from his Asian mission, Wallace advocated joint Soviet–American action to assist in the postwar reconstruction and industrialization of China in a speech at Seattle on July 9, 1944. During the presidential campaign, he supported a strong United Nations based on long range Soviet–American cooperation at a time when Republican orators were calling Roosevelt the puppet of a Communist alliance between Sidney Hillman and Earl Browder. After the campaign, the groups of the second popular front provided Wallace with a reliable audience for his speeches in the cause of Soviet–American friendship.[15]

At a testimonial dinner for Marshall Field in December, 1944, Wallace noted that the future would decide whether the "Russians, denying God, should more nearly attain to social justice than we, invoking the name of God." The outline of the future, as he had said through the war, was visible to men of courage and vision. "The people," he concluded with a flourish that captured the best of his wartime oratory and the essence of his wartime message, "are on the march all over the world and there is nothing the reactionary forces in the United States can do to stop it—but we can, if we are sympathetic, channel those revolutionary forces for the constructive welfare of the whole world." [16]

For the world New Deal to function, Soviet–American cooperation was essential. Without such cooperation a workable United Nations was not feasible. Remembering a Munich that still represented Anglo–French attempts to maintain the *cordon sanitaire* by favoring Germany against Russia, Wallace gave faithful and eloquent expression to Roosevelt's somewhat hazy grand design of working with Russia and a reinvigorated China to maintain the peace in Eurasia against the possible revival of German and Japanese militarism and against the machinations of French and English colonialism. It was, Wallace believed, to both America's and Russia's interest to encourage the revolution of order, to coexist and grow together. That this view was naïve, as the politicians and academicians of containment later argued, may be true, although not quite in the way they think.[17] The Roosevelt–Wallace policy was aimed at gaining Soviet support for the new international order under the UN in the *first years* after the war, before the Russians were strong enough to stay outside of the system.

Stalin through the war gave signals that he would sacrifice possible Communist victories in Nazi-occupied Western Europe to Soviet national interests, and Soviet national interests dictated rapid reconstruction from the devastating effects of the war and the creation of a security zone in Eastern Europe. In retrospect, one might suggest that Roosevelt and Wallace understood the Russians more than they understood the Americans.

Economic interdependence and American prosperity through expanded world trade were goals of both the world New Dealers and their enemies. To achieve these ends, two worlds—creating a new *cordon sanitaire* with an America far stronger than Neville Chamberlain's England—had greater shortrange potentialities than one world. The massive reconstruction loans to the Soviet Union upon which the one-world policy had to be based were not politically feasible, given the Congress of 1945 (not to mention its Republican successor). The State Department, which Roosevelt had cheerfully ignored on the question of Soviet–American relations, remained alienated from the President's policies and thought only of making the maximum use of American economic and military power in any settlement with the Russians. Nor had the war been defined to the people in terms that would have enabled the President to exact the postwar sacrifices necessary to make the world New Deal a reality. Wallace after all had seen his own future bartered away by Roosevelt's deviousness at the 1944 Democratic convention, and that same deviousness highlighted the President's foreign policy. In February, 1945, his hopes to play a major part in the reconversion program were dashed by the same conservative coalition that stood ready to cripple the world New Deal. Finally, he would watch as an administration composed of his political enemies drifted into a cold war with the Soviet Union.

II

If Truman had failed to implement the programs of the Economic Bill of Rights, he was completely oblivious to the

implications of the world New Deal and the logic of Soviet–
American cooperation. In his approach to foreign policy
questions he differed mightily from Roosevelt. FDR appears
to have seen his role in foreign policy as one of making and
personally directing major decisions. Wary of State Department hostility to the Soviets, President Roosevelt intervened
personally to see that Lend-Lease aid was transported rapidly
to Russia; and he insisted, over increasing State Department
opposition, that such aid remain unconditional.[18] Although
he yielded at critical points to the State Department, e.g., the
addition of a vague "Declaration on Liberated Europe" to the
Yalta agreement to provide the veneer of self-determination
and Atlantic Charter respectability for a treaty that restored
much of the old Russian empire in Eastern Europe and the Far
East, Roosevelt remained confident of his ability to negotiate
with Stalin. He therefore ignored the anti-Soviet admonitions
of Averill Harriman and the State Department, worked through
Harry Hopkins, and stressed, to the consternation of Harriman
and George Kennan, that Soviet–American points of friction
were minor and would be worked out in time.[19]

Twenty-three years as a county judge and United States
Senator did not prepare Harry Truman either to follow or
to respect the flexibility that had been Roosevelt's approach
in both domestic and international relations. A simple man,
Truman believed that the President's duty was to act as the
moral leader of the nation, state the truth, hope that Congress
would act appropriately, and then enforce the law in a strict
manner. Although he supported wartime Congressional resolutions for an international organization to enforce the peace
and probably shared the same good wishes for the United
Nations that the general public held, there is no evidence that
he ever entertained sympathy for the Soviet experiment, as
Roosevelt had briefly after World War I.[20] Indeed, even as
Roosevelt sought to mobilize congressional support for aid
to Russia after the German invasion, Truman stated publicly
that "if we see that Germany is winning the war we ought to
help Russia; if Russia is winning we ought to help Germany
and that way let them kill as many as possible. . . ."[21]

Truman's angry exchange with Molotov in April, 1945, in

which he demanded that the Russians end their violations of the "Declaration on Liberated Europe" in their occupation of Poland and threatened to begin the San Francisco Conference without Soviet participation, created an atmosphere of hostility that would never lift during his administration. The President's provocation of an international incident in May, 1945, by his signing of an order that abruptly halted Lend-Lease shipments to the Russians, also reflected the administration's general anti-Soviet orientation (the order was drafted by Leo Crowley, who Truman conceded was "anti-Russian"). These acts produced the widespread feeling in government circles that a firmer stand was being taken against the Soviets, a belief that evoked enthusiasm in the State Department.[22]

Gar Alperovitz's contention that the atomic bomb was ultimately responsible for the Truman administration's "get tough" policy toward the Russians is difficult to accept. In spite of the popular conception of a honeymoon period in Soviet–American relations between the Lend-Lease crisis and the Potsdam Conference in July, 1945, Truman's rigid interpretation of the Yalta agreements and unwillingness to take the initiative in establishing programs for the reconstruction of Europe and Russia did not change in that period. Instead, the President's modification of Crowley's Lend-Lease order, Hopkins' last mission to Stalin, joy over the end of the war in Europe, and widespread public optimism over the San Francisco Conference created the false impression of a thaw in Soviet–American relations that briefly obscured the chill that had set in from the first Truman–Molotov talks.[23]

In any analysis of the development of the cold war, the administration's modification of the Munich analogy must receive careful study. Much of Truman's success in legitimizing his foreign policy to the American people can be traced to his use of wartime symbols—national unity in the form of a bipartisan foreign policy, commitment to oppose totalitarian tyranny in order to prevent eventual war. Used to silence opposition to both the "get tough" policy and its rhetorical successor, containment, the Munich analogy ultimately became the higher superstition of the cold war, strengthening the

Truman administration's connection between Stalin and Hitler at a time when the administration needed a surrogate Hitler to focus popular attention away from its domestic failures. Indeed, one should remember that the "get tough" slogan—popularized by the speeches of Byrnes, Arthur Vandenberg, and Walter Bedell Smith—became part of the American lexicon in February and March of 1946, as the administration continued to stumble through the worst labor disturbances in a generation. Stalin's announcement of a new five-year plan with ominous remarks that Russia considered war inherent in the nature of capitalism, Winston Churchill's Iron Curtain speech, and Byrnes' strong note to the Russians demanding Soviet withdrawal from Iran, all occurred during this two-month period. Russia's renewed support for the guerillas in Greece and increased support for the Chinese Communists at this time also heightened Soviet–American tensions and made the "get tough" policy very popular in the country.[24]

The secret of the Munich analogy's success was that it was already deeply established in the American consciousness before Truman used it to develop an anti-Soviet foreign policy. Appealing both to the anti-Fascist memories of the social liberals and the passionate anti-Communism of the right, it was able to disarm effective opposition and win wide support for the administration. In retrospect, the fact that the Truman administration never accepted seriously the view that Soviet security interests had to be considered in determining the governments of Eastern Europe may be attributed to the ease with which the "get tough" policy could gain both elite and mass support in the immediate postwar political climate. The Truman administration was fighting for its life in 1946. In foreign policy, however, its posture of apparent patience with firmness toward the Soviet Union had enormous popular approval.[25]

III

As the war came to an end, social liberals grew more critical of alleged Soviet and American efforts to frustrate a world New

Deal. This criticism, centered on a belief that the old system of power politics was being renewed by the decisions at Yalta, was tempered by the existence of the atomic bomb, growing Soviet–American tensions under the Truman administration, and the fear that the right at home would use the foreign-policy crisis to sow the seeds for a new world war. Increasingly angered by Truman's domestic blundering and confused by much of his foreign policy, liberals grudgingly supported the Truman–Byrnes policy of firmness and patience toward Russia while arguing for greater tolerance of the Soviets and searching constantly for a foreign policy that would be both independent of British Imperialism and Soviet Communism.[26]

The sudden spectre of Hiroshima threatened social–liberal hopes for Soviet–American cooperation and a world New Deal. Calling for prompt internationalization of atomic energy, the *New Republic* angrily denounced President Truman's decision not to share nuclear information with the Soviet Union. Stuart Chase warned that if America did not act quickly, the bomb might produce bitter divisions among the Allies and set the stage for a new world war. Editorials like "Sixty Days to War or Peace" proliferated in the liberal journals, while portrayals of the bomb as representing either a new beginning or an end for mankind became a national cliche in the months after Hiroshima.[27]

The bomb did much to increase liberal distrust of the administration's foreign policy. After Truman took a strong stand in favor of Universal Military Training in the fall of 1945, the *Nation* noted that the administration was "simultaneously and hopelessly attempting to achieve national security through the mutually contradictory methods of unilateral action and international cooperation." Maintaining that the United States could not continue to support a strengthened United Nations while unilaterally provoking Russia, the *New Republic* noted as early as May, 1946, that "the program of American foreign policy is meant to contain Russia." After the deadlock of the May, 1946, Foreign Ministers Council meeting in Paris, the *Nation* wondered if Walter Lippmann's thesis about the need to accept the reality of Soviet "possession" in Eastern Europe might not be more realistic ultimately than Byrnes' continuing attempt to mobilize world opinion against Russian expansion. When Reinhold Niebuhr wrote in September, 1946, that America would do well to emulate Europe's "strategy of patience" toward Russia and "stop the futile efforts to change what cannot be changed in Eastern Europe," he reflected an increasing disenchantment with the "get tough" policy among liberals that would soon gain its most vivid expression in Henry Wallace's Madison Square Garden speech.[28]

As Secretary of Commerce, Wallace renewed his advocacy of increased world purchasing power and expanded world trade as the keys to a lasting peace, portraying a strong United Nations predicated on Soviet–American cooperation as the practical expression of these policies. Writing in the *New Republic* in June, 1945, he repeated his wartime contentions that the United States and the Soviet Union, both committed to the achievement of abundance and equality through the advance of technology, would have to work together to assist in the industrialization of underdeveloped countries. As he would in the years to come, Wallace clung to the wartime belief that America was the only nation with the wealth and the skill to lead in world reconstruction, but that nonimperialist reconstruction through the United Nations required Soviet support.[29]

In view of Russia's long history of attack from the West, Wallace felt that it was imperative for the United States to do everything possible to allay Soviet suspicions of the capitalist countries. After conversations with Department of Commerce observers returning from the San Francisco conference in May, 1945, he began to perceive American hostility to Russia as a major problem within the Truman administration. By June, he was busily reading copies of George Kennan's incoming telegrams from Moscow and requesting copies of Kennan's subsequent dispatches. Two weeks after V–J day, he wrote to Adolph Sabath, a veteran liberal Congressman from Chicago, that "I would place friendship with Russia as number one in our foreign policy." [30]

Wallace still, even after the death of Roosevelt, remained immersed in plans for the reorganization of the Department of Commerce. The atomic bomb, however, which challenged his imagination as a scientist and his conscience as a Christian, served as the stimulus for his early confrontations with the Byrnes–Truman foreign policy.

Unlike President Truman, Wallace's scientific background and wartime experience enabled him to grasp the significance of nuclear energy for the postwar world. Physicist Vannevar Bush, who believed that Wallace was the only high government official able to understand the scientific problems of nuclear energy, had first briefed the Vice President on the progress of uranium research in July, 1941. Bush subsequently met with Wallace and President Roosevelt at the White House in October, 1941 to discuss British and American uranium research. Out of the meeting, a Top Policy Committee, consisting of the President, Wallace, James B. Conant, Secretary of War Stimson, and General Marshall, was created to pass on decisions related to the exchange of nuclear information and facilities between the United States and Britain. Although, as General Groves later noted, Wallace took no part in the Manhattan project, he was kept informed on atomic energy through the committee and, as he remembered, was "in on the whole atomic energy project from 1940 until it reached the military stages." Even though he feared during the war to even inform the British about the technical developments that would one day produce the bomb, his work with the committee, wartime advocacy of an end to German scientific patent monopolies, and close relationship to science and scientists probably created his conviction that scientific information was international and that it would be both dangerous and futile for the United States to refuse to share nuclear information with the Soviet Union after the war.[31]

Retiring Secretary of War Henry L. Stimson proposed to President Truman on September 11, 1945, that the United States make overtures to the Russians about a possible partnership between the two countries in the development and control of nuclear energy. At Truman's suggestion, Stimson's proposal was to be the topic for discussion at the Secretary's final cabinet meeting on September 21.[32] Although this famous meeting has been covered extensively by scholars, hitherto unavailable material from excerpts of the Wallace diaries enables us to get a much fuller view of what impelled the Truman administration to reject Stimson's proposal at this crucial time.

Even before the September 21 meeting, the question of atomic energy had been broached at a cabinet luncheon on September 18 and the lines of disagreement established. Truman himself stated the view that the United States should maintain the secret of the atomic bomb but that the United Nations should be kept informed on questions concerning atomic energy. Secretary of Agriculture Anderson took a stronger view, citing polls that showed that the overwhelming majority of the American people favored a complete American nuclear monopoly. Secretary of the Navy Forrestal strongly supported this position. Stimson and Wallace disagreed. Wallace warned against the "Maginot Line" attitude inherent in the Anderson-Forrestal position and expressed doubt that it was possible "to bottle up scientists the way some people seem to think." [33]

At the September 21 cabinet meeting, Stimson defended his proposal with the argument that a long range American nuclear monopoly was not feasible and that the United States had nothing to lose by offering to cooperate with the Soviet Union to control the bomb and to share information concerning nuclear research. After Dean Acheson, representing the absent Secretary Byrnes, spoke briefly for the proposal, Fred Vinson and Tom Clark made strong dissents, both expressing great distrust of the Russians and questioning Stimson's contention that another nation could develop an atom bomb without American assistance in three to five years. Postmaster General Robert Hannegan also spoke briefly in favor of the proposal, as did Undersecretary of the Interior Abe Fortas, Secretary of Labor Lewis Schwellenbach, and, according to the Wallace diary excerpts, Reconversion director John Snyder. In the midst of the debate, Navy Secretary Forrestal shifted the discussion from the question of sharing information on nuclear research to the irrelevant problem of sharing the bomb itself, arguing that the weapon was "the property of the American people."

The Soviets, Forrestal reasoned, could not be trusted, because "the Russians, like the Japanese, are essentially oriental in their thinking." With crackpot assumptions of Asiatic inscrutability and treachery in the air, Secretary Anderson then repeated his strong objections to the proposal and for good measure denounced Soviet actions in Manchuria and Mongolia. Wallace then spoke briefly but forcefully in favor of the Stimson proposal and drew upon his experiences in Soviet Asia to contend that the Russians were European, not oriental, in their thinking.[34]

Vannevar Bush, whom Stimson had brought to the meeting to advise the cabinet on technical and scientific problems, then answered Forrestal with the comment that the bomb itself had nothing to do with the proposal, for the secret of the bomb's construction lay in the areas of design and technology, not in the general information that Stimson wished to share with the Russians. Seeing that there was great division in regard to the Stimson plan, Truman postponed a decision and asked all of those present to submit their opinions to him in writing. At a subsequent meeting in early October, with Harold Ickes now present and the same general division on the proposal, Truman decided against the Stimson plan. The opposition of Secretary of State Byrnes may have been the crucial factor, although Clinton Anderson now believes that Truman had sympathized with the foes of the proposal from the outset, because they were composed mostly of his cronies. J. Robert Oppenheimer noted to Wallace on October 19 that Byrnes was anti-Soviet, had been provocative in broaching the subject of the atomic bomb to the Russians at Potsdam, and believed that "we could use the bomb as a pistol to get what we wanted in international diplomacy."[35]

The conflict over the Stimson proposal inadvertently served as the background for Wallace's first clash with the administration over atomic energy. Felix Belair, a *New York Times* reporter who had written admiringly of Wallace during the depression, broke the story on September 22 that the Secretary of Commerce had advocated sharing the secrets of the atomic bomb with the Soviet Union. As Belair's account dealt largely with the arguments for and against sharing the bomb with Russia, it is doubtful that Wallace or any supporter of the Stimson proposal leaked the story. (Forrestal, who believe that Wallace wished to give the bomb to the Soviets, and who later told Wallace that the Russians wanted to dominate not only the world but the "solar system," would appear to be a more likely source for the leak.) [36] Truman denied publicly that Wallace had either advocated the giving of the bomb to the Soviets or had played a more important part in the meeting than Stimson had. For his part, Wallace used the furor created by the Belair story to publicly affirm his support for the sharing of nuclear information with the Soviet Union as a prelude to the eventual control of the military uses of atomic energy.[37]

As the conflict over civilian control of atomic energy developed in the fall of 1945 and a coalition of citizen–scientist groups fought to block attempts by the armed services and Congressional conservatives to pass the May–Johnson bill (a bill that would have left the development of nuclear energy largely in military hands), Wallace became the leading administration spokesman for and ally of the advocates of civilian control of atomic energy. When James Newman, special counsel to the McMahon committee (the Senate committee charged with preparing legislation for the peacetime control of atomic energy) and a friend of Wallace, maneuvered in January, 1946, to have President Truman endorse the citizen–scientist-supported McMahon bill, Wallace acted as the "anchor man" among the witnesses testifying for the bill before the McMahon committee.[38]

Wallace's firm advocacy of the McMahon bill and accusation that the May–Johnson measure represented an opportunity for "military domination or dictatorship" gained headlines and gave Newman the impetus he needed to acquire Truman's public commitment to the principles of the McMahon bill and thus assure its passage. When Arthur Vandenberg, the administration's most valued Republican ally on foreign policy matters, added an amendment to the measure in March, 1946, that would have provided for a military review commission to deal with the decisions of the civilian Atomic Energy Commission that affected the military, Wallace denounced the proposal as "having the potentiality of delivering us into military Fascism." Significantly, Wallace's criticisms once more made headlines, helped to revive the citizen–scientist coalition opposed to military control of atomic energy, and led Vandenberg to eventually work out a compromise on the amendment. Although the incident only increased Vandenberg's and the Truman cabinet's hostility to Wallace, its outcome was evidence that the former Vice President's wartime rhetorical style could still mobilize public opinion and influence national policy.[39]

The increased cold-war tensions that followed Churchill's March, 1946, Iron Curtain speech led the Secretary of Commerce to decry the possibility of an arms race between America and Russia that would inevitably produce a new world war. Although initially sympathetic to the April, 1946, Acheson–Lilienthal report for the international control of nuclear energy, Wallace also came to feel by July, 1946, that Bernard Baruch's proposals for nuclear disarmament before the United Nations Atomic Energy Commission distorted the Acheson–Lilienthal recommendations and made Soviet acceptance highly improbable.[40] Believing that an immediate agreement for international control of nuclear energy was the most crucial problem facing the United States, and that the administration's "get tough" policy—through the Baruch plan and its linking of reconstruction aid to its interpretation of the Yalta agreements—made such an agreement less and less likely, Wallace decided in the summer of 1946 to speak out against Byrnes in the hope that he could convince Truman to return to the Roosevelt policies of cooperation and trust with the Soviet Union.[41].

IV

By the spring of 1946, Wallace was the last New Dealer in the Truman cabinet, a distrusted outsider tolerated only, as the

President put it, because "he had a following" and had to be kept in the administration for the sake of the party. Much of this he fully understood, as his conversations with Department of Commerce aides show.[42] Yet he failed to understand how limited his power was in any showdown over foreign policy with Byrnes, and possessed an incredibly naive faith in the good intentions of the President, preferring to see Byrnes as the primary culprit in the creation of the "get tough" policy. Indeed, Truman's method of humoring Wallace—to agree with his general sentiments and ignore his specific proposals—only encouraged the eventually fatal faith that he could change the administration's foreign policy.

Disturbed by the apparent administration sponsorship of Churchill's Iron Curtain speech, which he called "shocking," warlike, and unrepresentative of either British or American opinion, Wallace wrote to Truman on March 14, 1946, arguing that Russian fears of the West, although unfair, were nevertheless understandable considering Russia's "dire economic needs and . . . disturbed sense of security." Since the proposed loan to Russia, which the Secretary had long supported, was at a total impasse because of American insistence that any credits to Russia be tied to an agreement with the Soviets concerning their economic relations with Eastern Europe (the State Department, in what must have been an attempt at humor, claimed to have mislaid the loan proposal from the death of Roosevelt to February of 1946), Wallace advocated a special American trade mission to improve Soviet–American relations by "a new approach along economic and trade lines." Although Wallace was not specific, he was in all likelihood referring to his wartime program of economic assistance for reconstruction and increased trade. After receiving a thank-you note from Truman he replied that he was interested in having the Commerce Department's Office of International Trade press for increased Soviet–American trade. In his memoirs, Truman noted that he ignored Wallace's original letter.[43]

The kind of hostility that existed against Wallace in the cabinet was shown also by a farcical incident in the spring of 1946 involving the Secretary's alleged views concerning American bases in Iceland. After he had given an address at a testimonial dinner to Daisy Harriman, the American ambassador to Norway, Wallace was approached by a Scandinavian journalist who asked him when American troops were going to leave Iceland. Although he had said nothing about Iceland in his speech, Wallace noted off the record that the Americans should leave if the government of Iceland did not want them. A garbled version of this private conversation eventually filtered into the American press, which spread the story that the Secretary of Commerce had called in a speech for American withdrawal from Iceland, stating that the American presence was a provocative gesture toward the Russians. These reports coincided with a political reaction against the bases in Iceland that ruined State Department attempts to renegotiate the base treaty.[44]

Given the predilections of the Truman cabinet, it is little wonder that Wallace was blamed for the entire debacle. At a cabinet meeting from which the Secretary of Commerce was absent, Byrnes grumbled about the affair and declared that he disliked being "shot in the back" by his colleagues. Forrestal noted in his diary that Byrnes should not be "exposed to the violent attacks of his countrymen who follow the party line." Informed of the affair by Byrnes in Paris during the meeting of the Foreign Ministers Council in April, 1946, Senator Vandenberg concurred in the condemnation of Wallace and said of the Soviets "no more Munichs. If it is impossible for us to get along with the Russians, the sooner we know about it the better. America must behave like the Number One World Power she is." As Truman relied more and more on Vandenberg to legitimize his foreign policy for the Republican opposition, that policy came increasingly to resemble Henry Luce's American Century.[45]

Disturbed by the apparently deepening conflict with the Russians in the spring of 1946, Wallace and his staff composed a position paper on Soviet–American relations in the form of an extended letter to the President. Given to Truman on July 23, the letter criticized the technical features of Baruch's nuclear disarmament plan, recited the historical circumstances that had made the Russians perennially suspicious of the West, and defended Russia's legitimate need for a "security zone" in Eastern Europe. Soviet fears of the West, Wallace contended, were rooted in a real history of invasion. America, secure in the Western Hemisphere, feared the Soviet economic system rather than any possible Russian political–military threat.[46]

Truman thanked Wallace for his letter and later claimed to have ignored it, although a copy was forwarded to the Secretary of State. Encouraged by Hannegan, Truman still sought to hold Wallace in the party and use his talents in the 1946 campaign as Roosevelt had done in 1944. Realizing this, Wallace moved to make foreign policy the major issue in his projected autumn speaking tour for the party and thus compel the President to clarify Byrnes' highly touted "get tough" policy toward the Soviet Union.

It is now possible with the aid of unpublished sources and interviews to reconstruct the origins and the development of Wallace's ill-fated Madison Square Garden speech. Initially scheduled for September 18, 1946, the address was to be given at a "Beat Dewey" rally sponsored by the CIO–PAC, the NC–PAC, and the ICCASP to launch the candidacies of Senator James Mead and former Governor Herbert Lehman for the governorship and the United States Senate seat from New York, respectively. After a prize-fight in the Garden forced the rally to be rescheduled for September 12, NC–PAC leader Beanie Baldwin called on Wallace on July 24 and suggested that his speech stress Republican obstructionism in the Seventy-Ninth Congress. Wallace then had his special assistant, Richard Hippelhauser, prepare a draft to present to Baldwin in early August.[47]

Baldwin, who had received a iopy of the July 23 letter, subsequently suggested to Wallace that his speech center on foreign policy, and the Secretary agreed to have Hippelhauser prepare a new draft. When Baldwin wired Wallace on August 27 that the speech would have to be pared down because of the available broadcasting time, Hippelhauser worked with Philip Hauser to make further revisions in the manuscript. After returning from a brief trip to Mexico in early September, Wallace asked Philip Hauser to check the speech carefully for final revisions. Harold Young, Solicitor for the Department of Commerce and still Wallace's political aide, informed Baldwin on September 9 that Wallace personally would clear his speech with Truman the following day. The stage was now set for the fateful appointment that would bring to an end Wallace's eventful thirteen-year career in Washington.[48]

On the basis of evidence now available, one may state with some certainty that Wallace's account of his famous meeting with Truman is substantially true. According to Wallace, he met the President for more than a half hour, brought two copies of the address, and followed the President through the text page by page, occasionally noting key words or phrases. Although Truman, in memoirs that were written in the backwash of McCarthyism, claimed that his meeting with Wallace lasted only fifteen minutes and concerned domestic matters, leaving "no time for me to read the speech, even in part," Wallace's appointments schedule shows that the Secretary was scheduled to see the President at 11:00 A.M. and leave for an appointment with Lawrence Duggan at 12 noon. Joseph E. Davies, who saw Truman immediately before Wallace, notes in his diary that Wallace entered the President's office at 11:15 A.M. Although there is no formal record of when the meeting ended, it appears likely to have been closer to the half hour claimed by Wallace than to Truman's fifteen minutes.[49]

Although Clark Clifford and Presidential press secretary Charles Ross later leaked stories to the press that the meeting had been interrupted a number of times, leaving the President little time to read the speech, there is no evidence to support these contentions. There is, however, evidence that Wallace contacted Louis Bean and Philip Hauser immediately after his meeting with Truman and told them that the President had both read and cleared the speech. Before he gave the address, the Secretary of Commerce made similar comments to Beanie Baldwin and Claude Pepper. As Wallace's conversations with Hauser and the others took place before the speech became a subject of controversy, there was no reason for him to distort what happened at the meeting, as there was for Truman after the controversy broke and again nine years later when he sought to clear himself of the same soft-on-Communism charges that had plagued Henry Wallace. As a matter of fact, Wallace had a star witness to attest to the fact that Truman had read the Madison Square Garden speech. The testimony of that witness on the morning of September 12 set the crisis in motion.[50]

After the President had said at the meeting that he approved the speech, Wallace included that statement in the printed version of the address and had copies distributed to the press on the morning of September 12. In his meeting with Truman, Wallace had read from the speech the statement, "I am neither anti-British nor pro-British—neither anti-Russian nor pro-Russian," and Truman had agreed that that was the policy of his administration.[51] Using this quote and Truman's reply to it, a reporter at the President's September 12 afternoon press conference questioned him about the speech. The transcript of the conference requires no comment:

> Q: In the middle of the speech are these words, "When President Truman read these words he said that they represented the policy of his administration."
> THE PRESIDENT: That is correct.
> Q: My question is, does that apply to just that paragraph, or to the whole speech?
> THE PRESIDENT: I approved the whole speech.
> (later)
> Q: Mr. President, do you regard Wallace's speech as a departure from Byrnes' policy—
> THE PRESIDENT (interjecting): I do not.
> Q (continuing): —toward Russia?
> THE PRESIDENT (continuing): —they are exactly in line.[52]

Needless to say, the reporters at the conference and most of the world the following day had a different view of the speech than President Truman did. On the evening of September 12, Truman was at a stag dinner at the home of Clark Clifford while Charles Ross responded with polite indifference to frantic attempts by Acting Secretary of State Will Clayton and Undersecretary of the Navy John L. O'Sullivan to have him intervene and halt the address. Both Clayton and O'Sullivan, along with Navy Secretary Forrestal, saw the speech as a repudiation of the Truman–Byrnes foreign policy. With great understatement, "Clayton expressed the opinion that Secretary Byrnes will be disappointed in the situation." [53]

The Madison Square Garden speech, itself, struck with simplicity at the simple logic of the "get tough" policy, contending that "the tougher we get, the tougher the Russians will get." Speaking after Claude Pepper had excited the largely pro-Soviet crowd with an impassioned defense of Russia, Wallace, whose speech contained a number of strong anti-Soviet references, was occasionally booed; and he decided to omit some of his more critical allusions to the Soviet Union in order to quiet the crowd. Indeed, the speech as actually given contained a number of interesting variations from the text presented to and reprinted by the press, variations that support superficially the contention of William Appleman Williams and his disciples that the Secretary of Commerce was merely pursuing the world Open Door by a different route than Truman and Byrnes and had no substantive disagreement with the administration's foreign policy. While he specifically opposed any abrogation of American trade rights in the published text, Wallace added in the spoken version that "I'm Secretary of Commerce and I want the biggest market we can get. I want China, I want Eastern Europe, as places where we can trade." At another point, Wallace specifically referred to the maintenance of the Open Door in China and noted in the spoken version that "Mr. Truman read that particular sentence and approved it." The crowd did not, and responded with boos.[54]

After warning his audience that Fascists throughout the world sought to provoke a war between America and Russia and that Britain struggled to save her declining Empire and the balance-of-power foreign policy on which it had rested through American intervention on her behalf, Wallace described the long history of Czarist oppression and military threats from without that had produced the Russian hostility and suspicion which so bedeviled American policy makers. The Russians, however, had real security problems in Eastern Europe, whereas the Americans had no similar problems in the Western Hemisphere. Wallace therefore proposed that each nation respect the other's sphere of influence—America's in the Western Hemisphere, Russia's in Eastern Europe—and that they both work through the United Nations to create the mechanisms of a lasting peace. In essence, Wallace's call for temporary spheres of influence, rather than betraying a shift toward *real-politik* or to what cold-war academicians called realism, actually represented a return to his and Roosevelt's wartime plan for peace through the strength of the great powers and through the creation of regional organizations within a greater international organization.[55]

In Wallace's plan, the United Nations would reign supreme in the areas outside the Russian and American spheres of influence. Significantly, Wallace called for United Nations control of all atomic weapons and all the world's great air bases, thus severely limiting the ability of any nation–state to launch aggressive war. As in the July 23 letter, Wallace believed that a general settlement with the Russians was necessary in order to gain effective international control over atomic energy. Such a settlement, he continued to believe, could come only through the creation of an economic balance of power and through the development of programs to create security and abundance for all nations. In a bow to Jimmy Byrnes' Stuttgart speech of the previous week (which many observers then and afterwards erroneously saw as the occasion for the Madison Square Garden speech), he called for a free and united Germany, but one that would not threaten Russia.[56] Continuing to specifically exclude restrictions of trade rights from the spheres of influence (thus it may be argued that he did not challenge Byrnes' defense of American commercial rights in Eastern Europe at the Foreign Ministers Council meetings), Wallace argued that the degree of freedom allowed in Eastern Europe would ultimately depend upon Soviet–American cooperation for European reconstruction and for the development of the United Nations.

Wallace finished with a reference to his favorite wartime theme regarding the future of Soviet–American relations—a theme that would gain great popularity in academic circles in the 1960s as men searched for an alternative to the cold war. Ultimately, he argued, the Soviet and American spheres would melt away, for the similarities between Russia and America, their common belief in progress and the equality of man, were more important than their political and economic differences. "Under friendly competition," Wallace concluded, "the Russian world and the American world will grow more alike. The Russians will be forced to grant more and more personal freedom; and we shall become more absorbed with the problems of social–economic justice." [57]

Less interested in the speech's philosophy than in its effects on contemporary diplomacy, the press and most radio commentators noted the following day that the address and Truman's endorsement of it put Secretary Byrnes in a difficult position. Byrnes was then restating America's opposition to spheres of influence and strong disapproval of Russian actions in Eastern Europe at the renewed meetings of the Foreign Ministers Council in Paris. Wallace's speech, the press noted, caused great fear in European diplomatic circles that America was returning to her historic policy of isolation and was preparing to abandon Europe to the Russians. On September 14, Truman delivered a statement that "it was my intention to express the thought that I approved of the right of the Secretary of Commerce to deliver the speech. I did not wish to indicate that I approved the speech as an instrument of the foreign policy of this country." [58] American policy, Truman concluded, would be determined by the President and Congress. The comment, however, failed to quell the controversy. As Ben Cohen, who was with Byrnes at the Paris Conference, remembered, the United States delegation was put in an impossible situation, for no one knew what American policy was. [59]

Stung by Truman's endorsement of the Wallace speech, Byrnes remained silent during the early days of the crisis as his colleagues at the Paris conference, Senators Vandenberg and Connally, issued public statements condemning Wallace.

After reiterating his support of Byrnes and the bipartisan foreign policy, Vandenberg placed the resolution of the problem in Truman's hands with the comment, "we can only cooperate with one Secretary of State at a time." Connally, who privately told Byrnes that Wallace should be made to resign, warned "if the United States is to speak with a strong and influential voice in the Peace Conference there must be no division behind the lines." [60]

After the speech, the story circulated that an angry Truman intended to dismiss Wallace, a course of action that James Forrestal strongly advised. As the conflict drifted on without any action by the President, the press and radio turned decisively against Wallace, arguing that the Secretary had grievously compromised the administration at Paris and that unity had to be restored to American foreign policy. Even Walter Lippmann, who had previously expressed great reservations regarding the administration's "get tough" policy toward Russia, suggested on September 16 that events now required that Wallace be "slapped down" by the President. Still confident of his ability to influence the administration, the Secretary of Commerce returned to Washington on that same day and told reporters, "I stand on my New York speech." In the near future, he concluded, he would speak out again on the question of peace. In a letter to Beanie Baldwin on September 17, Wallace reaffirmed his intention to discuss foreign policy in his proposed October campaign tour. On that day, however, he faced a new crisis in the seemingly endless conflict over the speech.[61]

A spokesman for Wallace announced on September 17 that the former Vice President would release his July 23 letter to Truman the following day to prevent Drew Pearson's unauthorized release of the document. While Pearson and Wallace traded charges about how the newspaperman had obtained the letter, Charles Ross noted later on the 17th that the President disapproved of the document's release, but that the administration nevertheless took full responsibility for the affair. As Wallace was scheduled to meet with Truman on September 18, Ross' announcement may have been an attempt to allay the tension resulting from the Madison Square Garden speech. Unfortunately, the letter's release had the opposite effect.[62]

Wallace's attack on the Baruch plan in the letter and his suggestion that groups within the military were contemplating preventive nuclear war against the Soviet Union provoked immediate responses from Baruch and the military. Secretary of War Patterson and Secretary of the Navy Forrestal quickly issued a joint statement denying emphatically that any person in authority in the services had "ever advocated or even suggested a plan of attacking Russia." Baruch, enraged at Wallace's criticisms of his plan for international nuclear control, saw Truman on September 18 and suggested that the President had three alternatives in the crisis: to remove Wallace, to have Wallace print a retraction of his criticisms, or to accept Baruch's resignation as American representative to the United Nations Atomic Energy Commission. Shortly after Baruch's meeting with Truman, Wallace went in to see the President for the first time since the crisis began.[63]

Published accounts of this last Truman–Wallace meeting vary. Truman and his biographers claim that he was firm with Wallace, demanded and received the Secretary's pledge to make no further speeches concerning foreign policy, and then watched with dismay as Wallace broke his word, distorted what had happened at the meeting, and boasted of his deal with the President to his aides in the Department of Commerce. In the Wallace version, Truman had been conciliatory and wished his Secretary to continue to speak for the party on domestic issues, but he (Wallace) had defended his right to discuss foreign-policy questions. The two, according to Wallace, then compromised their differences, agreeing that the Secretary of Commerce would not make any speeches until the end of the Paris Conference. A visibly relieved and smiling Wallace read a brief written statement to this effect to a throng of reporters immediately after his meeting with Truman.[64]

When William Hillman in *Mr. President* (1952) published a bitter Truman diary reference to the meeting that called Wallace a "Pacifist" and "dreamer" who wants to disband our

armed forces, give Russia our atomic secrets, and trust a bunch
of adventurers in the Kremlin Politburo," Wallace threatened
to take legal action and prepared a draft letter that quoted at
length from his own diary notes of the meeting. The hitherto-
unpublished excerpts from the Wallace diary at the very least
support the former Vice President's contention that Truman
had been conciliatory during their discussion. When placed
against the President's own diary reference to the meeting,
which attributed Wallace's support to "the Reds, phonies and
'parlor pinks'. . . . I am afraid that they are a sabotage front
for Uncle Joe Stalin," the Wallace notes suggest either that
Truman was a cynic in saying what Wallace himself had advocated in regard to the Soviets to hold him to the party or
that the conduct of foreign policy at the highest levels of the
administration resembled a Marx Brothers movie.[65]

Defending his right to express his views on the question of
peace, Wallace told Truman that the criticism being leveled
at him for the Madison Square Garden speech reflected the
public's uneasiness over the direction in the country's foreign
policy that he had made public. Peace, he went on, meant more
than armed truce. Truman replied defensively that Byrnes
had been giving him hell, that Byrnes was indeed angrier at
him than at Wallace. In a remarkable statement, the President
then noted that he liked Josef Stalin personally and felt that
the major problems between the United States and Russia
could be resolved if he and Stalin met face-to-face, but he
doubted that the Soviet leader would come to America. Truman
continued by promising to go before Congress and ask for a
Russian loan just as he had requested and received a British loan
after the Soviets signed the peace treaties then being negotiated
at the Foreign Ministers Council meeting in Paris. In an interesting role reversal, Wallace expressed doubt that such a
loan could be put through Congress and suggested as an
alternative a shift to Russia of funds that had been earmarked
for China through the Import–Export Bank. Truman saw this
as a possibility and the two later agreed that Wallace would
refrain from making speeches until the end of the Paris Conference.[66]

Aside from Truman's affection for Stalin (the President,

who had a great deal of experience in these matters, had rather sympathetically compared the Soviet leader at Potsdam to an old-style American political boss), the President's position concerning a summit conference and a reconstruction loan for the Russians mirrored some of Wallace's strongest private views. Truman, it should be noted, had met with Hannegan the day before, and it was reported that the National Chairman, active since the spring in attempts to open up communication with the popular-front groups and hold them to the party, had stressed the need to resolve the conflict without firing Wallace. Truman apparently followed this advice at the September 18 meeting and still hoped that the crisis would somehow fade away.[67]

Events of September 18 made this a remote possibility. In Paris, Wallace's statement was interpreted to mean that he would be free to resume his criticisms of American foreign policy at the conclusion of the conference, thus deepening the confusion over what American policy really was. On the evening of September 18, Byrnes tried to contact Truman for the first time during the crisis. In a teletype message sent to the White House from Paris, the Secretary of State offered to resign if Wallace were not kept from speaking out on foreign-policy matters. Truman read this message the next morning and then, following an unsuccessful attempt to establish trans-Atlantic telephone communication, held a teletype conversation with Byrnes.[68]

Appealing to the wartime themes of national unity and bipartisanship in the face of a foreign enemy, Byrnes told the President that merely curtailing Wallace's statements on foreign policy until the end of the conference would not solve the problem. If Molotov "believed that on October 23 there would be a re-examination of permitting Wallace to again attack your foreign policy, he would derive great comfort. . . ." Again offering to resign if Wallace were offended by his statements, Byrnes concluded, "you and I spent 15 months building a bipartisan foreign policy. We did a fine job convincing the world that it was a policy on which the world could rely. Wallace destroyed it in a day." [69]

Wallace, the President assured Byrnes, had destroyed nothing. Truman then told the Secretary of State that the administration stood behind him and that Wallace had no authority to continue his attacks against American foreign policy after the end of the Paris Conference. The President also pledged to reaffirm his support for Byrnes at his press conference on September 20, but Truman did not promise to dismiss Wallace.[70]

Faced with the pressures that his own ineffectuality and equivocation had helped to produce, Truman now personalized and projected his anger at Wallace (as he would later do against Byrnes and others in his administration). After transcribing in his diary an almost hysterical view of Wallace from their meeting the previous day, as quoted earlier, Truman met with Clark Clifford later on the 19th and attempted to find a solution to the crisis. It is likely that the adverse reaction to the July 23 letter, the added confusion stemming from the September 18 meeting, and the final, decisive pressure from Byrnes convinced Truman that he must fire Wallace. The President called Wallace on September 20 and asked for his resignation, noting with surprise the apparent calm with which the Secretary greeted the news. At his press conference, the President read a statement that praised Byrnes, expressed regret at the necessity of dismissing Wallace, and concluded that "it had become clear that between his [Wallace's] views on foreign policy and those of the administration—the latter being shared by the great majority of the American people—there was fundamental conflict."[71] Firmness, patience and bipartisanship would remain the slogans of American foreign policy as relations with Russia grew progressively worse.

Although Truman received about an equal number of pro and con letters with regard to his decision (testimony to the persistence of Wallace's admirers), domestic reactions to the dismissal from the media and prominent public figures either hailed or accepted the necessity of the President's action. The press, continuing to criticize Truman's handling of the affair, concluded that the dismissal was necessary to restore order and unity to American foreign policy. Wallace's old enemies were, of course, overjoyed. John Rankin praised the Lord. Alf Landon noted, "better late than never." Liberal Democrats in Congress either remained silent about the affair or mouthed the administration and media line that the President's action had been a cruel necessity.[72]

Although liberal journals and newspapers, to Wallace's chagrin, had criticized the use of the spheres-of-influence concept in the Madison Square Garden speech as a surrender to old fashioned power politics, liberals generally expressed bitterness at Wallace's dismissal, paid tribute to the fallen Secretary with attacks on Truman, and wished that Wallace might still be able to serve as a spokesman for liberalism and peace outside the administration.[73]

Abroad, the *New York Times* noted, the reaction to the dismissal was one of relief. C. L. Sulzberger wrote from the Paris Conference that Truman's act was viewed as likely to "reinvigorate" American foreign policy. The American Communist party, after initially condemning the speech for its criticisms of the Soviet Union, made one of its characteristic flip-flops even before Wallace was dismissed. Communist leader William Z. Foster told a party rally on September 19, "our country is being rudely awakened [to the dangers of war and imperialism] by the Wallace speech." Radio Moscow was initially lukewarm to the address, noting quite accurately that "the audience loudly applauded Wallace's condemnation of imperialism but punctuated his remarks against the U.S.S.R. with cries of disapproval." [74] Drew Middleton, however, noted from Moscow the Soviet view that the Democratic party was now in the hands of an anti-Soviet coalition and that the American government was embarked on an anti-Soviet foreign policy. Although some regarded Stalin's conciliatory words in late September as evidence that Truman was correct in his rejection of Wallace's "appeasement," increased Soviet repression in Eastern Europe and the expansion of the Greek conflict were perhaps more accurate indications of Stalin's response to the latest manifestation of the "get tough" policy.[75]

On the day of his dismissal, Wallace reaffirmed his opposition to both Soviet and American imperialism and vowed to continue the fight for peace.[76] Now that he had become a victim of the Truman–Byrnes "get tough" policy (compelling the President to stand with Byrnes against himself and the New

Deal left), Wallace would try to organize the frightened liberals of the old Roosevelt coalition against the Truman foreign policy. A debate on the interlocking questions of Communism and foreign policy broke out among liberals in the wake of Wallace's dismissal. Soon rival organizations, each claiming the mantle of the New Deal, emerged to give the dispute focus. The resolution of the debate would determine the future of social liberalism in the postwar world.

NOTES

* HAW, Septmber 12, 1946, in Alfred Schindler Papers, Box 21, HSTL.
1. Frank A. Warren, *Liberals and Communism* (Bloomington, Ind., 1966), p. 63; quoted in Padriac C. Kennedy, "La Follette and the Russians," *Mid-America*, LXXX (July, 1971), p. 195.
2. *Ibid.*, passim. Cf. James J. Martin, *American Liberalism and World Politics* (New York, 1964), I, 123–160. Martin writes from the perspective of a libertarian conservative.
3. William P. Gerberding, "Franklin Roosevelt's Conception of the Soviet Union in World Politics" (Ph.D. thesis, University of Chicago, 1959), p. 247.
4. Soviet wartime actions, e.g., Stalin's abolition of the Comintern, did much to allay social–liberal fears of revolutionary and terroristic Communism. See articles like "Death of the Comintern," *New Republic*, CVIII (May 31, 1943), p. 718.
5. For *Common Sense*'s criticism of such ritualistic popular-fronters as Max Lerner, see Varian Fry, "The Irresponsibles" *Common Sense*, XIV (July, 1945), p. 5.
6. HAW, "OE" *W.F.*, April 12, 1929, p. 583; "Why Russia Hangs Together," *W.F.*, November 14, 1924.
7. HAW, "OE," *W.F.I.H.*, February 1, 1930; "Collective Farming in Russia," *W.F.I.H.*, April 19, 1930, p. 788; "The Soviet and the Russian Wheat Export," *W.F.*, May 4, 1923, p. 691.
8. Henry A. Wallace, "Henry A. Wallace Tells of His Political Odyssey," *Life*, XL (May 14, 1956), p. 183. As a kind of introduction to his later difficulties with the Communist question, Wallace did write to Cordell Hull that "I have never been one of those reactionaries to be scared by the talk concerning the Red Menace. As a matter of fact, I continually laughed at some of the extreme statements made by certain congressmen; nevertheless the Russian leadership is so utterly without religion, in our sense of the term, and so bitter regarding certain things which we hold dear, that I don't like to place ourselves in their hands by giving them the opportunity to disorganize our markets. . . ." (This in specific opposition to the idea of a developmental loan to a nation like the Soviet Union.) HAW to Cordell Hull, September 29, 1933, HAW Papers, University of Iowa.

9. Henry A. Wallace, *Statesmanship and Religion* (New York, 1934), p. 134; James P. Warburg, *It's Up to Us* (New York, 1934), p. 76.

10. For example, Wallace told a gathering at Baton Rouge, La. in April, 1939, that it "is vital to the peace of us and our children that America turn a strong face to the European dictators who are intent on destroying democracy." *New York Times,* April 8, 1939.

11. HAW, "The Price of Free World Victory," in Russell Lord, ed., *Democracy Reborn* (New York, 1944), p. 192; HAW, Address to Congress of Soviet–American Friendship, November 12, 1942, in *Congressional Record,* 77 Congress, 2 Session, p. A3953.

12. *Ibid.*

13. HAW, "Practical Religion in the World of Tomorrow," in *The Christian Bases of World Order* (Nashville, 1943), pp. 10–20.

14. Wallace's speech coincided with the remarks of America's ambassador to the U.S.S.R., Admiral William Standley, that the Soviet government was deliberately withholding information from its people on the extent of Lend–Lease aid. Although liberals and the foreign press praised Wallace's speech, American politicians generally attacked both speeches for disturbing Soviet–American relations and thus endangering the war effort. *New York Times,* March 12, 14, 1943; Remarks of Martin Dies, February 10, 1944, in *Congressional Record,* 78 Congress, 2 Session, p. 1549; see Henry A. Wallace and Andrew Steiger, *Soviet Asia Mission* (New York, 1946), even though Steiger wrote the book, save the chapter on agriculture, from Wallace's diary notes.

15. *New York Times,* July 10, 1944.

16. HAW, Address to Marshall Field Testimonial Dinner, December 4, 1945, in *Congressional Record,* 78 Congress, 2 Session, p. A4631.

17. For a good summary of cold war historiography, see Norman A. Graebner, "Cold War Origins and the Continuing Debate: A Review of the Recent Literature," *Journal of Conflict Resolutions,* XIII (March, 1969), p. 125 ff.

18. Robert Divine's recent work, although in disagreement with this author, presents a fair summary of Roosevelt's attitude toward Russia. Robert A. Divine, *Roosevelt and World War II* (Baltimore, 1969), pp. 65–98.

19. For a brief presentation of the new revisionist view of Yalta, see Barton J. Bernstein, "American Foreign Policy and the Origins of the Cold War," pp. 21–23, in Barton J. Bernstein, ed., *Politics and Policies of the Truman Administration* (Chicago, 1970). Kennan considered America's wartime policy toward Russia one of "clumsy naïveté." George F. Kennan, *Memoirs, 1925–1950* (New York, 1967), p. 293.

20. In a speech to the popular-front American Youth Congress in February, 1940, FDR, condemning the Soviet government as an absolute dictatorship, remembered that twenty years before he had hoped that the Communists would succeed in making Russia a modern and prosperous state. Divine, *Roosevelt and World War II,* pp. 77–78.

21. Gar Alperovitz, *Atomic Diplomacy: Hiroshima and Potsdam* (New York, 1965), p. 30.

22. For a lucid analysis of the Lend–Lease crisis, see George C. Herring, Jr., "Lend–Lease to Russia and the Origins of the Cold War, 1944–1945," *Journal of American History*, LVI (June, 1969), pp. 105–106; William D. Leahy, *I Was There* (New York, 1950), p. 351; Truman quoted on Crowley in Jonathan Daniels, *Man of Independence* (Philadelphia, 1950), p. 271.

23. Alperovitz argues that Truman's strategy of an immediate showdown with Russia developed between the Lend–Lease crisis and Potsdam, thus creating the illusion of a honeymoon period in Soviet–American relations. It is doubtful, however, that Truman's strategy changed in this period, or even that he had a strategy beyond distrust of all Soviet actions and the wish that those actions would somehow cease if they were resolutely condemned. Alperovitz, *Atomic Diplomacy*, p. 230.

24. Graebner, "Cold War Origins," p. 131; "Enter Morality," *Nation*, CLXII (March 9, 1946), pp. 276–277; TRB, "A New Policy Toward Russia?" *New Republic*, CXIV (March 11, 1946), p. 348; Walter LaFeber, *America, Russia and the Cold War, 1945–1966* (New York, 1967), pp. 28–32.

25. Of course, as George Kennan was to argue so forcefully, Stalin also needed a surrogate Hitler to thwart any postwar movements for liberalization within his regime. To Stalin, Munich represented the desire of the capitalist nations to turn Hitler loose on Russia. This analogy fitted in nicely with Soviet fears of capitalist encirclement, the argument that the Russians used to explain the conflict with the United States.

26. For example, see "Dumbarton Oaks Limited," *Common Sense*, XIV (April, 1945), p. 38, "The New Communism," *New Republic*, CXIII (December 3, 1945), p. 737.

27. "What Does Mr. Truman Mean?" *New Republic*, CXIII (November 5, 1945), pp. 587–589; Stuart Chase, "Atomic Age Balance Sheet," *Common Sense*, XIV (October, 1945), p. 28; "Sixty Days to War or Peace," *New Republic*, CXIII (November 19, 1945), pp. 691–692.

28. "Are We Planning War?" *Nation*, CLXI (November 3, 1945), p. 448; "One Year After," *New Republic*, CXIV (May 20, 1946), p. 716; "Post Mortem in Paris," *Nation*, CLXII (June 11, 1946), p. 644; Reinhold Niebuhr, "Europe, Russia and America," *Nation*, CLXIII (September 14, 1946), p. 289.

29. Henry A. Wallace, "America, Russia and the World," *New Republic*, CXII (June 11, 1945), p. 809.

30. The allusion to the San Francisco Conference appears in HAW, "One World or Two?" Address, March 29, 1950, in the Papers of the Committee to Frame a World Constitution, Box 32, University of Chicago, Chicago, Illinois; Mildred Eaton to Mrs. Noden, June 1, 1945, RG 40, Box 1031, NA; HAW to Representative Adolph J. Sabath, August 21, 1945, RG 40, Box 1038, NA.

31. Richard Hewlett and Oscar E. Anderson, Jr., *The New World, 1939–1946: Volume I, A History of the Atomic Energy Commission* (University Park, Pa., 1962), pp. 45–46, 51, 267. Actually Wallace

participated in only one of the two meetings the committee held, although he remained both interested and informed about the course of atomic energy development. HAW to General Leslie Groves, March 7, 1951, HAW Papers, University of Iowa.

32. For the text of Stimson's memorandum to Truman, see Alperovitz, *Atomic Diplomacy*, Appendix III.

33. Wallace Diary Notes, September 18, 1946, in HAW to Arthur Krock, October 23, 1951, HAW Papers, Krock Folder, University of Iowa.

34. HAW Memorandum, October 15, 1945 (based on diary notes of September 21 meeting) HAW Papers, University of Iowa. Hewlett and Anderson, *New World*, pp. 418–420; Walter Millis and Edward S. Duffield, eds., *From the Forrestal Diaries* (New York, 1951), p. 95.

35. Hewlett and Anderson, *New World*, p. 421; Clinton Anderson to Edward L. Schapsmeier, August 29, 1963, in the private possession of Professor Schapsmeier; Wallace Diary Notes, October 19, 1945, HAW Papers, University of Iowa. Cf. HAW to Brien McMahon, February 4, 1950, HAW Papers, University of Iowa.

36. *The New York Times*, September 21, 1945; HAW to Arthur Krock, October 23, 1951, HAW Papers, Krock Folder, University of Iowa. Acheson believed that Forrestal had leaked the story while Truman apparently suspected Crowley, HAW Diary Notes, October 1 and October 16, respectively, HAW Papers, University of Iowa.

37. *New York Times*, September 24, 1945.

38. Hewlett and Anderson, *New World*, pp. 389–391; James R. Newman and Byron S. Miller, *The Control of Atomic Energy* (New York, 1948), p. 12.

39. *Ibid.*, p. 13; Arthur H. Vandenburg, Jr., and Joe Alex Morris, eds., *The Private Papers of Senator Vandenberg* (Boston, 1952), p. 277; Hewlett and Anderson, *New World*, pp. 505–513.

40. Hewlett and Anderson present a comprehensive treatment of Wallace's quarrel with Baruch, which centered on the former's objection to the role the United States would play under the plan in the stages leading to inspected nuclear disarmament. Philip Hauser, who worked with Wallace in the subsequent negotiations with Baruch over a retraction of his criticism, accepts the Hewlett and Anderson account of the affair. Wallace did not. Looking back on the controversy when the book was published, he wrote to Hauser, "The heart of my personal attitude at the time was that I was certain that if the positions were reversed we would have looked for the hook behind the bait and would have maintained our freedom to go all out after the atom bomb." HAW to Philip Hauser, June 15, 1962, HAW Papers, University of Iowa. Hewlett and Anderson, *New World*, pp. 600–606.

41. For Wallace's growing sense of urgency about the atom bomb, see HAW, Radio Address, March 16, 1946, Schindler Papers, Box 20; for the Soviet attitudes that made the outlawing of the bomb so difficult, see Joseph L. Nogee, *Soviet Policy Towards International Control of Atomic Energy* (South Bend, Ind., 1961), pp. 250–251.

42. Truman, *Memoirs*, I, p. 558; James F. Byrnes, *All in One Lifetime* (New York, 1958), p. 373; Interview with Philip Hauser, September 26, 1968.

43. *New York Times*, March 10, 12, 1946; HAW to HST, reprinted in Truman, *Memoirs*, I, pp. 555–556; HST to HAW, March 20, 1946, HAW to HST, March 21, 1946, HAW Papers, Truman Folder, University of Iowa. Thomas G. Patterson sees the letter as primarily dealing with the Russian loan, a questionable hypothesis, since Wallace made no direct references to the loan negotiations. Thomas G. Patterson, "The Abortive American Loan to Russia and The Origins of the Cold War, 1943–1946," *Journal of American History*, LVI (June, 1969), p. 87.

44. HAW to Ogden Reid, April 1, 1952, HAW Papers, Univesity of Iowa.

45. Arnold A. Rogow, *James Forrestal* (New York, 1963), p. 138; Vandenberg and Morris, eds., *Papers of Senator Vandenberg*, p. 267.

46. HAW to HST, July 23, 1946, text in *New York Times*, September 19, 1946. It is interesting to note that Wallace's aide and speech writer Richard Hippelhauser, in a memo to Philip Hauser, argued that the July 23 letter "devotes too much space to the means for allaying Soviet distrust while slighting the grounds for American distrust of the Russians . . . the letter should advocate a positive program for counteracting the spread of Soviet influence in Western Europe." R. H. Hippelhauser to Philip Hauser, July 17, 1946, in HAW Papers, University of Iowa.

47. Truman, *Memoirs*, I, p. 557; Summary, Telephone Conversations, Baldwin to HAW, HAW to Hippelhauser, July 24, 1946, RG 40, Box 1059, NA.

48. Interview with Baldwin; C. B. Baldwin to HAW, August 27, 1946, RG 40, Box 1051, NA; Memo, Mildred Eaton to Harold Young, undated, Summary, Telephone Conversation, Harold Young to C. B. Baldwin, September 9, 1946, RG 40, Box 1051, NA.

49. Truman, *Memoirs*, I, p. 557; File of Wallace's Callers, Schindler Papers; Diary Journal, September 10, 1946, Joseph E. Davies Papers, Box 24, LC. Wallace's account of the meeting for publication is presented in the Lord Biography. Russell Lord, *The Wallaces of Iowa* (Boston, 1947), p. 576.

50. Ernest Lindley, in *Washington Post*, September 16, 1946, and Marquis Childs in *Washington Daily News*, September 16, 1946; Interviews with Hauser and Baldwin; Interview with Louis Bean, December 1, 1968; Interview with Claude Pepper, February 20, 1969.

51. Years later, Wallace noted to Arthur Hays Sulzberger that "I was enunciating the old Hay Doctrine of the Open Door in China, which had been standard American Policy for more than a half century, and specifically limited President Truman's approval to that sentence." (Actually, the written text disputes this, but China was mentioned in the spoken version in Open Door terms with Truman's approval tacked on.) HAW, draft of letter to Arthur Hays Sulzberger, October 1, 1955, HAW Papers, University of Iowa.

52. Transcript, President's Press Conference, September 12, 1946, in Clark Clifford Papers, Henry Wallace File.

53. Cabell Phillips, *The Truman Presidency* (New York, 1966), pp. 150–151; Millis and Duffield, eds., *From the Forrestal Diaries*, p. 209; Rogow, *Forrestal*, p. 139.

54. HAW, "The Way to Peace," As Delivered, HAW Speeches, Box 10, HAW Papers, University of Iowa.

55. *Ibid.*

56. As Wallace specifically called for a united Germany and opposed any sacrifice of American trade rights in Eastern Europe (which, to say the least, made his conception of a sphere of influence somewhat odd), it can be argued that he was defending the essence of the Truman–Byrnes policy as expressed in Byrnes' September 6, 1946, Stuttgart speech, while condemning the "get tough" tactic as destructive to American interests.

57. Henry A. Wallace, "The Way to Peace," Address, September 12, 1946, Schindler Papers, Box 21. In the spoken version, one finds an interesting variation on this sentence. After Wallace had said, "The Russians will be forced to grant more and more of the personal freedoms," he was booed by the crowd. He replied, "You don't like the word 'forced.' I say that in the process of time they will find it profitable enough and opportune enough to grant more and more of the personal freedoms. . . . That's the course of history . . ." (and, one might add, an expression of the evolutionary positivist faith that buttressed Wallace's ideas of the world). HAW, "The Way to Peace," As Delivered, HAW Speeches, 1946, Box 10, HAW Papers, University of Iowa.

58. For summaries of press and radio comment on the speech, see HST, Papers, Editorial Comment, Box 2; Press Release, September 14, 1946, Clark Clifford Papers, Henry Wallace File.

59. Interview with Benjamin V. Cohen, December 15, 1968.

60. Vandenberg and Morris, eds., *Papers of Senator Vandenberg*, p. 301; Tom Connally, *My Name is Tom Connally* (New York, 1954), p. 302; *A.P.*, Paris, September 14, 1946, in Tom Connally Papers, Box 611A, LC. Vandenberg's criticisms were especially damning, for he played the crucial role of legitimizing the bipartisan foreign policy for the Republican opposition. In the aftermath of the affair and the 1946 elections, Wallace noted privately, "I am certain that Truman whole-heartedly and enthusiastically agreed with my position when he read my speech. What he failed to remember was the extent to which Senator Vandenberg held Secretary Byrnes as hostage." HAW to Lawrence L. Persons, November 12, 1946, HAW Papers, University of Iowa.

61. Rogow, *Forrestal*, p. 139; HST Papers, Editorial Comment, Box 2; Walter Lippmann in *New York Herald Tribune*, September 17, 1946; Wallace's comment in *New York Herald Tribune*, September 17, 1946; HAW to Baldwin, September 17, 1946, RG 40, Box 1068, NA. Wallace received many letters praising his speech. Albert Einstein, for example, wrote that "your courageous intervention deserves the gratitude of all of us who observe the present attitude

of our government with grave concern." Albert Einstein to HAW, September 18, 1946, HAW Papers, University of Iowa.

62. Press Release, September 17, 1946, Schindler Papers, Box 21; Charles Ross, Press Conference, September 18, 1946, Charles Ross Papers, Box 9, HSTL.

63. *New York Times*, September 19, 1946; *Baruch, My Own Story* (New York, 1957), p. 375.

64. *New York Times*, September 19, 1946. Although he repeated it many times over the years, this is substantially the version that Wallace told Philip Hauser. Interview with Hauser.

65. Diary Excerpt in William Hillman, ed., *Mr. President* (New York, 1952), p. 128.

66. Wallace Diary Notes in Draft Letter, HAW to HST, March 15, 1952, HAW Papers, Truman Folder, University of Iowa.

67. The account of the Truman–Hannegan meeting is *National Week*, undated, Democratic National Committee Clipping File, Box 57, HSTL.

68. Byrnes, *All In One Lifetime*, pp. 374.

69. *Ibid.*, pp. 374–376.

70. HST to Byrnes, September 19, 1946, Clifford Papers, Henry Wallace File.

71. David E. Lilienthal, *Journals of David E. Lilienthal* (New York, 1964), II, p. 88; HAW to HST, September 20, 1946, HAW Papers, University of Iowa; *New York Times*, September 21, 1946. Cf. Cabell Phillips, *The Truman Presidency*, p. 153.

72. *New York Times*, September 21, 1946. For public and press opinion, see HST Papers, OF 3, Boxes 18–27 and HST Papers, Editorial Comment, Box 2, respectively.

73. "Washington Calling," *Progressive*, X (September 30, 1946), p. 152; "Wallace–A World Leader," *New Republic*, CXV (September 23, 1946), p. 340. Upset by the criticism from liberals, Wallace stressed that he remained an advocate of one world but that "the question at the moment is a practical one: How much do we have to give up to a power who is dominant in a particular region in order to get real power in certain international fields for the United Nations—I mean power not subject to veto." HAW to Norman Thomas, October 2, 1946, Norman Thomas Papers, Box 50, New York Public Library.

74. *New York Times*, September 20, 21, 24, 1946. *Izvestia* did translate the speech on September 17, with a lead noting Wallace's opposition to the "get tough" policy and Churchill's idea of an Anglo–American alliance. That may explain the American Communist party's flip-flop. Typed Translation of *Izvestia* Story, September 17, 1946, in HAW Papers, 1946, Box 4, University of Iowa.

75. *New York Times*, September 29, 1946.

76. *New York Times*, September 21, 1946. In the wake of the dismissal, temporarily reduced Soviet pressure on Turkey and Stalin's speech on September 23 that the war danger was exaggerated were seen as vindications of the "get tough" policy. "Wallace is Wrong," *Progressive*, X (September 30, 1946), p. 152.

6
A Crisis of the American Spirit

We all know Americans who say they are against Red-baiting except when it is employed against Reds. . . . they reluctantly agree to violation of the Bill of Rights in order to save it, to killing it as far as Communists are concerned in order that Communists may not kill it at some future time. . . . if one agrees that Reds may be properly attacked then one must also agree that their sympathizers may be properly attacked and with the first agreement the gates are open for attacks against all save reactionaries. The only place to make a stand, if we really believe in the Bill of Rights, is on the right of an American to be a Communist—or anything else he wishes to be provided he does not break the law.

Letter to HAW
August 27, 1947

I regard the American communists as foreign agents with whom no liberal organization can be associated without destroying itself and making futile its attempts to lead the American people to progressive political action. Communists only use non-Communist liberals as long as they can use them in promoting their own power and influence while they are serving the changing lines of Russian

foreign policies and their strategy for the promo-
tion of communist power in the United States.

Culbert Olson
(*former governor of California*)
to HAW
March 28, 1947 *

The popular-front left was wholly a creature of the New Deal coalition. However great its organizing talents were, it had worked always for others—for the New Deal's attempts at reform and for the Soviet Union's struggle for survival. When the Truman policies fragmented the New Deal coalition and provoked conflict with the Soviet Union, the popular front was thrown permanently on the defensive. The great Republican election victories of 1946—in themselves a monument to Truman's blundering—led social liberals to abandon the popular front and gradually accept the anti-Communist, anti-Soviet policies of the administration and the mass media. This "cold-war liberal" stance gained its most important expression in the founding of the Americans for Democratic Action in January, 1947. Although hard-core popular fronters had earlier formed the Progressive Citizens of America, they had little hope of checking the "failure of nerve" that largely paralyzed social liberalism after the war and reflected the subservience of social liberals to the Democratic party establishment.

I

Eight days after the Wallace dismissal, a Conference of Progressives met in Chicago to reaffirm the social–liberal commitment to the programs of the Economic Bill of Rights and to organize for the election of a progressive Congress in the fall. At first glance, the gathering appeared to attest to the enduring strength of the second popular front. Harold Ickes, in his last months as chairman of the ICCASP, shared the speakers' platform with Henry Morgenthau, while James Patton, Phil Murray, the NAACP's Walter White, and other prominent leaders of the liberal–labor alliance attended the gathering. Called largely at the behest of the CIO (Beanie Baldwin had been instrumental in gaining Murray's support for the meeting), the conference was publicized as the most extensive gathering of progressives in American history.[1]

The program adopted by the conference—a defense of the Economic Bill of Rights legislation blocked in the Seventy-Ninth Congress and continued support for price control, tax reform, and civil-rights legislation—merely repeated the all but official platform of the wartime liberal movement. In its foreign policy resolutions, the conference came out clearly for the Roosevelt–Wallace commitment to a strong United Nations and to a renewal of cooperation among the wartime allies, specifically endorsing Wallace's spheres-of-influence argument and the former Secretary of Commerce's criticisms of the Baruch plan (although both points raised significant opposition and the latter was expressed in phrases that named neither Wallace nor Baruch).[2]

In a special message to the absent Wallace, the conference called upon him to "carry on with confidence that you have the support of the millions upon millions of Americans who believe in the program of Franklin Roosevelt." When the meeting ended on September 29 amidst rumors that its continuations committee might serve as the starting point for a national liberal organization, there were those who expressed the hope that the long-anticipated goal of national political realignment was approaching fulfillment. For the popular front, however, the Conference of Progressives was an end rather than a beginning.[3]

While those assembled at Chicago spoke of renewed anti-Fascist unity abroad and a revived New Deal at home, the Communist question had surfaced quietly to shatter the popular front. Without CIO support the creation of a national liberal organization along popular-front lines was impossible. In correspondence before the conference, Phil Murray, a devout Catholic whose primary interest was to protect the faction-ridden CIO in a time of mounting anti-Communist and anti-labor feelings, showed that he was unlikely to provide such support. Although all factions of the CIO (and indeed all of organized labor at the time) were deeply alienated from Truman, Murray portrayed the conference exclusively as an attempt to mobilize support for liberal candidates, proscribing third-party considerations and quoting Henry Wallace (before the dismissal) to the effect that the Democrats were still the best hope of the liberal–labor alliance.[4]

In his address to the conference, Murray had departed from his text to announce that "there is no more damn business for an American Communist meddling in our business than there is for any American meddling in the Russian Trade Union Movement." Only pleas from friends that he would divide the liberal–labor alliance over the Communist question convinced Murray to support the conference's foreign-policy resolution. Those close to the CIO leader noted his inner anguish over the Communist issue—an anguish created by the belief that red-baiting was the serpent that would destroy the union movement and by the ever-mounting pressures from his church, through the Association of Catholic Trade Unionists, to enlist him in the struggle against the pro-Communist labor apparatus in the CIO.[5]

Murray played for time, hoping to use the Conference of Progressives as a pawn against Truman while carefully deflating the attempts of those who wished to transform the gathering into the basis for an independent liberal organization and an eventual third party. After a meeting of the conference's continuations committee in mid-October, the CIO leader told the press, "we expect this movement to become in due course the most powerful liberal and progressive organization brought together in the history of the country." When the continuations committee met after the November elections debacle, however, Murray balked at proposals to expand it into a mass organization. Later, he skillfully evaded persistent attempts by Beanie Baldwin to call a second Conference of Progressives.[6]

The sweeping Republican victory in November did nothing to encourage hopes for independent liberal political action. If anything, the disaster had a numbing effect, exposing as nothing else in the period did how dependent the social liberals had been upon Franklin Roosevelt's electoral magic. With the Republicans in control of both houses of Congress and the CIO–PAC having elected only 73 of the 318 congressional candidates it had endorsed, it was obvious that the faith in mass organization and direct political action (almost as ends in themselves) that had waxed strong during the depression and the war had suffered a disastrous defeat.

To a minority who held to the vision of the popular front, Truman and his party were blamed for betraying Roosevelt and the promise of the New Deal; for others, who counseled disengagement from politics, the election merely provided evidence of what the war had done so much to illustrate, that mass organization did not end or necessarily reduce popular ignorance and brutality and that an unthinking faith in the people, or rather the mystique of the people, obscured the complexity of human relationships and social problems. For the disheartened majority, however, the elections encouraged what Sidney Hook in a different context had called a failure of nerve, a wistful desire to adjust as honorably as possible to the mounting anti-Communist passions of the time, uphold the New Deal without abandoning the Democratic party, and proclaim liberal independence from all forms of imperialism and from Communism. This failure of nerve, rather than its restoration, provides one with a starting point on the road to Arthur Schlesinger, Jr.'s enchanted "vital center." [7]

II

The popular front had always rested upon a community of interest between social liberals and Communists rather than on sentimental liberal ideas about the nature of Communism (if anything, Communists appear to have been much more confused about the nature of liberalism). It is true that social liberalism, with its belief in the inevitability of progress through the development of science and technology and its commitment to human action to restructure environment, does have important similarities to Marxism. Though they differ greatly as to the method of historical change, both may be seen as children of the Enlightenment and the bearers of Enlightenment humanism in the modern world. When liberal hopes were at their darkest in the western world in the 1930s, Communists raised the almost irresistible argument of anti-Fascist unity and took the lead in the development of civil-rights groups, labor unions, and organizations to lobby for collective security. At the same time the Soviet Union aided the Spanish Loyalists with advisors and arms and acted as the leading anti-Fascist power until the Hitler–Stalin pact.[8]

The formal popular-front program of the world Communist movement, announced at the Seventh Congress of the Comintern in the summer of 1935, was, in its application by American Communists, an almost complete surrender to liberal means and ends. At times, the new party line was almost comic. A bemused Alf Landon, his sunflower converted into a swastika, was portrayed as a stalking horse for domestic Fascism in the 1936 Presidential campaign. In the late 1930s, Earl Browder counseled his fellow comrades to avoid sounding like "crazy Reds" as the "People's Front" became the "Democratic Front" and the party moved ever closer to the Roosevelt administration.[9] While advocates of proletarian literature went into eclipse, Communists sang the Star Spangled Banner at party meetings, held parades in honor of Mother's Day, and adopted Thomas Jefferson and Abraham Lincoln as hero symbols for the entire left. That the threat of genuine Fascism was largely nonexistent in America, a nation where the right fought state authority and defended the sanctity of private initiative, made the popular-front tactic self-defeating for the Communists in the long run, even though the American party showed a spectacular shortrange gain in membership and in influence.[10]

For the social liberals, also, the popular front represented a self-defeating move to the right, an increasingly uncritical acceptance of the New Deal and a subordination of hopes for structural economic and social reforms to the immediate task of opposing a real Fascism abroad and a fantasy Fascism at home. These mutual frustrations probably explain why the first popular front, in spite of the legend of liberal innocence and Stalinist ruthlessness (a legend that the Communists enjoyed as much as their enemies) actually took place against a background of constant suspicion and unending backstage power struggles.[11]

When the Soviets signed a nonaggression pact with Adolf Hitler, the Communists were compelled to abandon anti-Fascist collective security, and the groups of the first popular front disintegrated, the social liberals walking out to leave the Communists with a remnant of themselves (the party's "isolationist" stance cost it over two thirds of its membership in the Hitler–Stalin pact period). President Roosevelt's public identification of the Soviets with the Nazis as totalitarians, the passage of the Smith Act, and the general identification of isolationism with the right truncated and isolated the Communists and led social liberals to begin a re-examination of the individualist and egalitarian roots of American culture in order to meet the Fascist challenge.[12]

The war revived the community of interest upon which the popular front had been based, permitting the Communists eventually to use their strength in the growing CIO unions (their only notable achievement in the Hitler–Stalin pact period had been to retain this strength) to join in the creation of groups to struggle for the twin programs of wartime social liberalism, the world New Deal and the Economic Bill of Rights.[13]

Although real Communist power was probably greater in the unions and in the federal bureaucracy during the war than it had ever been during the depression, the second popular front was built on the same fragile foundation as the first. Once more, the Communists failed even to try to articulate a socialist position, carrying Roosevelt's Win–the–War slogan to extremes that were laughable. In the unions, the Communists were the most militant supporters of the administration's no–strike pledge, permitting their enemies to picture them as conservatives and losing the respect of many of the younger union organizers. Determined Communist opposition to civil-rights militancy—at a time when the NAACP was increasing its membership five-fold and Blacks were struggling aggressively for equal treatment in the military and in the defense industries—bred hostility that would compromise postwar Communist appeals to the Negroes. Above all, Browder's open support for administration policies that liberals condemned as concessions to the right made the American party something of a joke during the war (the intellectuals, one should note, never returned to an open identification with the Communist party, although many would support the general principles of the second popular front, which were the principles of social liberalism).[14]

Each nation, Gunnar Myrdal once observed, gets the Communists that it deserves. Successfully rebuilding the party's membership during the war, Browder transformed it into the Communist Political Association, strongly supported the Roosevelt–Truman ticket, and even talked about America's need to expand foreign markets after the war to ward off depression. Although their arguments remained couched in Marxist jargon, this could not hide the fact that the Communists under Browder were to the right of the social liberals on immediate policy questions and indistinguishable from them on long range goals. However Roosevelt had failed to prepare the general public to accept the ends of a managed, progressive capitalism at home and cooperation with the Soviets abroad, he and the needs of the Soviet Union had made the American Communists the most dedicated adherents of these goals.[15]

On the surface, Browder did have much to show for his wartime leadership. At the time of the publication of the famous Duclos letter, which signaled his ouster in May, 1945, the Communist Political Association had a membership of about 80,000 and a labor apparatus that either controlled or strongly influenced unions that comprised 20 percent of the CIO's membership. William Z. Foster, the old party stalwart who replaced the purged Browder, revived the doctrinaire rhetoric of the party's Social-Fascist period of the early 1930s and carried out an almost comic purification campaign against Browder's supporters. Social Democracy (which Foster confused with Norman Thomas, David Dubinsky, and Walter

Reuther), Roman Catholicism, and Keynesian economics were also tilted against in the party's crusade to exorcise "Browderism." Browder, Foster announced in February, 1946, had committed the sin of standing with Roosevelt, Truman, and Henry Wallace as an adherent of "the bourgeois liberal reformer Keynes. . . ." [16]

Actually, Browder had really done that, and there was considerable reason for Foster to condemn Catholicism and Keynesianism, for the former struggled mightily to deprive the party of its labor base while the latter dominated the thought of the New Deal left, of which the party was an unacknowledged relation. Still, Foster, in spite of a rhetoric that provided much ammunition to anti-Communist activists, was reluctant to change many of Browder's policies. The Duclos letter, after all, merely brought to America the policy that the Communist parties of Europe were then following, that is, of reconstituting themselves as political parties and co-operating with other left parties in coalition governments. According to Duclos, Browder had erred by blindly accepting all groups within the Roosevelt coalition instead of working to strengthen the New Deal left. Above all, Browder's line of support for long range alliances with progressive capitalists and his transformation of the Communist party into a cross between a New Deal pressure group and an educational association had liquidated the working-class base of the party.[17]

Realistically, Browder's line could not long survive the end of the war. Yet, in spite of the Browder purge, the Communists did not (and could not) abandon the New Deal coalition, for they were wholly creatures of that coalition. Instead, they argued from the outset that it had been Truman who betrayed Roosevelt, while Browder, an early though unwitting exponent of consensus history, took the position that Truman had maintained the Roosevelt policies. In this regard, it is interesting to note that the party's formal resolution condemning Browder declared that "it is imperative that the American people resolutely support every effort of the Truman administration to carry forward the policies of the Roosevelt-Labor-Democratic coalition for Soviet–American friendship, for the economic bill of rights, for collective bargaining, and for the rights of the Negro people." When union hostility to the administration reached its peak a year later in the aftermath of the railroad strike, the Communists, although talking tough, joined with liberals in counseling against any premature third-party venture.[18]

Lacking a program apart from that of the New Deal coalition, Foster acted like a doctrinaire Franklin Roosevelt, creating contradictory policies of support for the creation of new popular-front groups and—very reluctantly—an eventual third party, along with the advocacy of rhetorical left militancy; thus the groups in which the Communists participated were in a constant state of turmoil, divided hopelessly against themselves. Hoping to protect the party's dwindling postwar membership from corrupting contact with the followers of John Maynard Keynes, Foster watched as the CP lost its hard-won gains within the unions, faced growing assaults by the Truman administration, and within a half decade was universally proclaimed as the embodiment of all that was evil and un-American.[19]

Anti-Communism was by no means new in America. In part, the Red Scare of 1919 had rested on the fear that the revolutionary internationalism of Russia had replaced the militarist nationalism of Germany as a threat to democracy and peace. The "Red Fascist" or "Communazi" idea had been a logical response of the old European political center and of the educated middle classes to the rise of Communism and Fascism after World War I. In the early 1930s, Fascism and Communism were portrayed as possible alternatives to capitalism and democracy, with New Dealers boasting that they were saving the country from either and Republicans often arguing that the Roosevelt administration was a hybrid of both. Opponents of the popular front on the left, Norman Thomas Socialists and Trotskyites, stressed the similarities between Stalinist and Fascist methods while the anti-New Deal mass media found it convenient to lump the two ideologies with statism, collectivism, and the administration. The Hitler–Stalin pact unleased these ideas upon the public as nothing had before.[20]

Although the wartime alliance made attacks upon the Soviet

Union unpatriotic and the Communists the purest of super-patriots, the war also made Communism an effective issue for resurgent conservatives, who could thus attack the New Deal without striking at specific administration programs like social security or minimum-wage legislation. As Communist power was based on deference to the New Deal and Communist goals and policies (in spite of the jargon) were not substantively different from those of the social liberals, the rightwing corollary that the liberals were dupes of the Communists did have a certain force, especially when the public was battered by inflation, strikes, and foreign policy crises that it identified with a liberal administration. Also, the issue, having a special appeal to the largest component group within the New Deal coalition, the white working-class Catholics, promised even bigger dividends for the conservatives.[21]

Having given grudging support to the New Deal and to a labor movement to which its parishioners flocked by the millions in the depression, the Catholic Church became a citadel of militant anti-Communism in the 1940s, calling for spiritual regeneration as an alternative to Communist chaos and advocating foreign policy initiatives that would have made even John Foster Dulles tremble. These lessons were not lost on the Wherrys, Jenners, Knowlands and Nixons who staffed the congressional Republican party of the 1940s. After the election debacle of 1946, the Schlesingers, Humphreys, and Paul Douglases would follow suit as the Truman administration made anti-Communism the national politic consensus.[22]

If powerful forces were thus arrayed explicitly against the Communists (and implicitly against the popular front), who stood as their advocates? The qualified answer would be no one. Roosevelt, for example, accepted the support of the popular-front groups in 1944 while publicly repudiating the support of any Fascist or Communist (evidence that the administration's failure to differentiate between Communism and Fascism as ideologies had left the "Red Fascist" idea deeply imbedded in the American consciousness). The groups of the second popular front were based on a tacit understanding that one had to work with Communists to accomplish anything, or, at the very most, that those who sought to deprive Communists of their rights were aping the policies of Hitler and Goebbels. It is little wonder that the Communists, accepted as a necessary evil, sublimated their failure to apply Marxism to American society in a politics of manipulation and conspiracy that only embittered their already suspicious liberal allies.[23]

As the war ended, the popular-front left was as much in need of a surrogate Hitler as the Truman administration. Wartime films like *The Master Race*, which warned of postwar German attempts to sow hatred and division as the pretext for a revival of Fascism and a new world war, were indicative of popular-front fears. In the Dick Powell film *Cornered* (1945), the simple premise of the popular front was expressed in the story of a Canadian ex-serviceman's search for an escaped Fascist war criminal in Argentina. While the serviceman seeks personal vengeance against the Nazi (who works with local rightists for the rebirth of Fascism), a local anti-Fascist warns that discovering the names of those involved in the clandestine Fascist organization is more important than simple retribution. Asked to what organization he belongs, the anti-Fascist replies that there are now only two sides in the world—those who fight for good and those who fight for evil.[24]

The wartime division between freedom and slavery, Fascism and democracy, good and evil was all that the popular front had; this explains perhaps the desperate attempts by popular fronters in the early postwar years to locate the Fascist menace in Spain, Argentina, or China, the courageous and confused attempts both to defend the rights of Communists and yet to be independent of Communism. "We must give the world something better than Communism" was perhaps the most persistent cry of Henry Wallace and the popular-front left in the years leading up to the Progressive Party campaign. What they meant by "something better," of course, was the ghost of the world New Deal. For the main body of liberals, however, it was relatively simple in the long run to substitute Communism for Fascism in the wartime equation and renew wartime unity by presenting a subdued version of the world New Deal, defined in stridently anti-Communist terms, as a rationale for supporting Truman's foreign policy and party.[25]

In spite of the later trauma of the Progressive Party campaign, there was really no great confrontation between popular-front and cold-war liberalism; one merely dissolved opportunistically into the other, the only serious differences between the two pertaining to the rights of Communists and the intentions of the Soviet Union. Both groups fought for the mantle of an ill-defined New Deal. Both would have identified strongly with the America portrayed by playright and New Deal speechwriter Robert Sherwood in the great film of the reconversion period, *The Best Years of Our Lives*— of an America repudiating isolationism and class conflict, of veterans in search of jobs and homes in the country, with easy credit for small businessmen and prefabricated houses in the suburbs. The consolidation of the Truman foreign policy against the background of postwar full employment and economic expansion made the debate between the popular-front and cold-war liberals very academic.[26]

III

Even in the aftermath of the Madison Square Garden speech, Henry Wallace remained a hero to millions. As the Conference of Progressives ended in late September, 1946, UDA leader James Loeb, who had boycotted the meeting, noted in a radio address that the Wallace dismissal had been a great blow to liberals. "For many years," Loeb observed, "American progressives have fought for Henry Wallace and in a very real sense he fought for us." Encouraged by friends to believe that his old following waited for him to continue the struggle for liberalism and peace, Wallace found himself back in private life for the first time in thirteen years.[27]

When Michael Straight, the young publisher of the *New Republic*, met with Wallace shortly after the dismissal to offer him the editorship of the magazine, the former Vice President's only firm offer to that time had been a request to return to *Wallace's Farmer*. After Wallace accepted, James Newman, hero of the McMahon committee's struggle to achieve civilian control of atomic energy, was added to the staff to do most of the day-to-day editorial work. Talented and expensive columnists like Theodore White, fresh from his wartime service in China, were also added to a greatly expanded *New Republic*. Hoping to transform the *New Republic* into the center of liberal criticism in the country, Straight wished to keep Wallace involved in the journal rather than outside politics. The controversy surrounding the dismissal, however, made that a remote possibility.[28]

Before his new position was publicly announced in mid-October of 1946, Wallace accepted a number of invitations from liberal and labor groups to speak for Democratic congressional candidates. Even before the campaign began, he was once more embroiled in controversy. Will Rogers, Jr., the Democratic candidate for the Senate in California, questioned Democratic State Chairman James Roosevelt's decision to invite the former Vice President into the state, and Governors Warren of California and Dewey of New York publicly identified the projected tour in their states with pro-Communists. In California, there were reports that Representative Jerry Voorhis, subjected to savage attacks by Richard Nixon as a follower of Wallace, the CIO, and the Communist line, was worried about the former Vice President's upcoming campaign trip. After *Pravda* announced in late October that Wallace was the only hope of the progressive forces in America, regular Democrats were heard to mutter that the campaign tour spelled disaster for the party.[29]

Launching his tour in California on October 24, Wallace repeated his warnings against those who opposed a genuine peace settlement between the United States and Russia. Speaking to liberal and labor audiences in the Middle West and New York in the last days of the campaign, he teased the administration with hints that the third party would come into existence in 1948 if there were no substantive changes in American foreign policy. America, the former Vice President maintained, must reach an agreement with Russia over the atomic bomb and Soviet security rights in Eastern Europe. The alternative to cooperation with Russia, Wallace continued to argue, was a new cycle of isolationist nationalism, depression, and war.[30]

Wallace ended his campaign tour with the terse comment that the Democratic party would become either progressive or die. After the elections, many believed that the party of the New Deal had indeed died. Liberals had been pessimistic about election prospects since the spring strikes, but few really expected the Republicans to carry both houses of Congress. After the debacle, Truman received the expected condemnation. The President's decision not to campaign, some noted, was one of the few realistic acts of his administration. Truman's national popularity, at a peak of 87 percent in the months after Roosevelt's death, had plummetted to 32 percent on election eve. The widespread use of Franklin Roosevelt's recorded voice by the retreating Democrats was cited as evidence that both the party and the administration were bankrupt. "Conservatism has hit America," TRB mused, in what became a traditional lament. Observing the high number of liberal casualties in the contest, the *Nation* noted that the election showed "that sagging of the spirit in high places and low which marks the end of a great national effort." [31]

The Communist issue did much to spread bitterness in the wake of the campaign. Although the national Republican campaign slogan, "HAD ENOUGH," probably appealed to voters more on the issues of inflation and housing and consumer-goods shortages (the meat shortage was widely regarded as the immediate cause for the administration's defeat), GOP charges of Communist influence in the unions and in the administration proved effective because of the general public hostility to the bungled Truman reconversion policies. Although premature cold-war liberals like Will Rogers, Jr., in California and Howard Costigan in Washington had injected the Communist issue into Democratic primary campaigns and thus provided the Republicans with ammunition, many of the losers in the general elections tended to blame the Communists and what Jerry Voorhis later called the "United Front Liberals" for the debacle.[32]

Robert La Follette, Jr., defeated in the Wisconsin Republican Senate primary by Joseph R. McCarthy (who ran as an advocate of Soviet–American cooperation against La Follette and then as an ardent red-baiter against Democrat Howard McMurray, in the general election), warned liberals to "look out" for Communists in their midst. Observing the carnage in the Far West, Richard Neuberger noted that Washington's Senator Hugh B. Mitchell, leader of the fight for a Columbia River Valley Authority, had been dragged down to defeat by Seattle's leftist Congressman, Hugh DeLacy. A former supporter of the Hitler–Stalin pact, DeLacy had survived a bitter primary battle against Howard Costigan only to lose the election by a landslide in heavily Democratic Seattle. After the elections, the National Planning Committee of the American Veterans Committee, a popular front organization convulsed by factional strife over the Communist issue, declared its opposition to "the entrance into our ranks of members of the Communist party." [33]

At the CIO's annual convention in November, 1946, Phil Murray, still resisting pressure to make substantive moves against the left unions, condemned Communist interference in the CIO. As the convention opened, the Soviet flag hung over the platform along with the other flags of the United Nations. When Murray gave his keynote address, however, the Russian flag was gone, dramatic evidence of the CIO leader's determination to avoid a direct clash over the Communist question and his increasing anger at the Communists.[34]

In this atmosphere, Henry Wallace began his career at the *New Republic* and promptly called upon liberals to remain united in the coming struggle for "jobs, peace and freedom." "If I have importance," Wallace concluded in a premier editorial that sounded much like the narration of a war newsreel, "it is because of the ideas I have come to represent. They are indestructible and on the march." Few liberals were marching in December, 1946, and those that were had begun to listen to different drummer.[35]

IV

Beanie Baldwin, the promoter of the Conference of Progressives, had long dreamed of a national organization to unite all liberals. So had the UDA's James Loeb, although Loeb's organization had specifically barred Communists from membership since its inception in 1941 and had thus provided little competition for the larger, better-organized popular-front groups. Hoping to use George Norris during the war as the unifying symbol upon which to build a national liberal organization, Loeb had seen that plan die because of covert administration opposition.[36] Cultivating Henry Wallace and the issue of full employment in 1945, the UDA leader had watched Wallace identify primarily with the popular-front groups and the full-employment bill turn into a fiasco. After the CIO–PAC, NC–PAC, and the ICCASP formed a joint committee in May, 1946, to work for the election of a liberal Congress, Loeb, fearful that the wrong kind of national liberal organization was in the making, renewed his drive for an expanded UDA.[37]

When the Conference of Progressives was called, Loeb proposed that the UDA convene a Conference of Democratic Progressives for January of the following year (the preliminary meetings were to be held after the November elections). Eleanor Roosevelt, an old UDA patron, implored Phil Murray not to hinder the UDA's expansion plans and received the CIO leader's promise not to prevent his union leaders from affiliating with Loeb's organization. For his part, Loeb publicly condemned the NC–PAC and the ICCASP as Communist-front groups in an effort to block the proposed creation of a national popular-front organization. Because Beanie Baldwin and Hannah Dorner had agreed shortly after the elections to merge the NC–PAC and the ICCASP, rivalry for CIO support and funds grew intense.[38]

In the bitter backwash of the 1946 elections, the Reverend Reinhold Niebuhr, a lapsed Marxist and practicing Protestant theologian, emerged to provide the rationale for the transition from popular-front to cold-war liberalism, reviving and re-defining the wartime rhetoric of freedom as a dynamic faith to fit the changing times. In a letter to prominent liberals asking for attendance at the UDA's expansion meeting, Nie-buhr proposed a "provisional statement of principles" for the gathering, calling for the transformation of liberalism into "a positive, dynamic force, a faith of free men." "A new wave of the future," the minister concluded in an elegant statement of the "Red Fascist" argument, "is being heralded by men to whom democracy is merely a strategic slogan. We are asked to believe that we now face a simple, inexorable choice between imperialist and fascist reaction and communist totalitarianism. We are told that rigid adherence to a one-party line is a necessary discipline to insure economic security, that we must blindly accept the foreign policy of Soviet power or align ourselves with the makers of a new war." [39]

In a sense, one might say that Reinhold Niebuhr's time had come at last (although Niebuhr's view of man and society, consistent in itself, had led him from Social Gospel Christianity, to Marxism, to anti-Communist liberalism). His philosophy, rooted in the "crisis theology" of European Protestant neo-orthodoxy, had stressed both the complexities of life and the persistence of sin—a world where man was neither Prometheus nor the Noble Savage and evil rarely evaporated before the Deweyite slogans of science and democracy. "Believe in the cooperative ideal," Niebuhr had written in an outline to an old sermon that came closest to summing up his general philos-ophy, "Men are selfish. Never trust men." [40]

From a Detroit slum pupit, Niebuhr rejected the optimistic faith of the Social Gospel and secular social liberalism in the 1920s, embracing Marxism and the Socialist party in the depres-sion as the only realistic means to achieve the social control and institutional change necessary to restrain man's evil and pro-mote progress. By the end of the 1930s, however, the Socialists had atrophied, the Communists were discredited, and modern civilization was in the throes of its greatest crisis. As Hitler's armies marched into France in June of 1940, Niebuhr resigned from the Socialist party, cast his first vote for Franklin Roosevelt in the fall, and joined with other ex-socialists and refugees from the popular front to found the UDA in 1941.[41]

The social–liberal revival produced by the war was, as we have seen, anything but Niebuhrian in its aims and its optimism. Occasionally, however, dissenting voices were heard. The "P.M. mind," Granville Hicks wrote in an attack on Max Lerner and other popular-front liberals, always stood ready to condemn those "who ask liberals to think instead of fight." Lionel Trilling, literary critic in the middle of a journey from the left to the center, mocked the "progressive psyche" postulated by neo-Freudian psychologist Karen Horney, portraying the liberal mind as a "kind of New Deal agency which intends to do good but cannot always cope with reactionary forces. . . . Freud had the advantages of suggesting the savage ironies of life."[42] For social liberals during the war, the faith in a world New Deal and an Economic Bill of Rights (both made possible through the "miracle of production" that the war brought) were more real than the "savage ironies of life," the stress upon limits, upon the containment of the messianic drive within man, that Niebuhr so eloquently preached.

While criticizing the "children of light," who naïvely waited for power politics to wither before human reason and righteousness, Niebuhr provided arguments for the wartime popular-fronters as he would later for the cold-war liberals. Rejecting the Communist–Fascist equation with which he and his disciples would be so closely identified after the war, Niebuhr contended that Communism, born in the messianic quest for perfection, had grown morally cynical and brutal when confronted with the failure of the Russian revolution. Fascism, on the other hand, had been morally nihilistic from the outset, rooted in the glorification of racial and national conflict and directed toward an inevitable, limitless war of the nation state against all who resisted its demands. Communism was thus more akin to liberalism, which also possessed a self-defeating universalism, than to Fascism.[43]

When peace was attained, Niebuhr reasoned, the struggle would be between Russian national interest, which would dictate peace and internal reconstruction, and messianic Communism, which would attempt to revive the revolutionary impulse. Although it was later quite fashionable for the minister and his self-proclaimed disciples to denounce "Stalinism" as a substitute for Communism and to equate the Soviet leader with Hitler, Niebuhr during the war praised the Russian dictator as a realist and a nationalist when compared to Leon Trotsky, the apostle of permanent revolution. Always able to provide sophisticated arguments to fit the hopes of his audience, Niebuhr both condemned Soviet actions in Eastern Europe and hinted at the necessity for an accommodation with Soviet power in the months before Henry Wallace's ill-fated Madison Square Garden speech.[44]

Indeed, one might even argue that Wallace, who called for such an accommodation as a step to a genuine peace, was the true Niebuhrian and that Truman and Byrnes, who fought for free elections and free markets in Eastern Europe, were the real children of light. Niebuhr, of course, did not say this, condemning Wallace and the Soviets and providing in his "provisional statement of principles" a preamble for the Americans for Democratic Action.[45]

Young Arthur Schlesinger, Jr., the good soldier of the cold war, would take Niebuhr's emphasis upon the need to accept power and Franklin Roosevelt's "pragmatic" avoidance of ideologically coherent programs and choices to bludgeon all those who disagreed with him and the various factions he attached himself to in the postwar years. As early as 1946, young Schlesinger, fresh from the triumph of the *Age of Jackson*, was exposing the American Communist party in Henry Luce's *Life* magazine, searching for the Niebuhrian mood of toughness and commitment in book reviews and articles (moods and settings were from the outset more important to Schlesinger than ideas, as manipulation and style would be more important than substance to the factions he later served).[46]

In the aftermath of the 1948 elections, Schlesinger would write, in *The Vital Center*, the grand scenario of cold-war liberalism, celebrating the Roosevelt–Truman programs at home and abroad and connecting both with the creation of a

European third force (at first democratic socialism, later anything in a very flexible middle ground between Communism and reaction). Although his influence was very considerable after 1948—when, as Garry Wills has noted, the "Bogart professors," the intellectual bullies who impugned the reason and courage of those who disagreed with them, reigned supreme—Schlesinger merely articulated the final triumph of cold-war liberalism. Neither he nor Niebuhr can justly claim credit for slaying the dragon of the popular-front left. The front, lacking a creative idea to hold it together, had crumbled in the postwar crisis, leaving a remnant to fight a futile, albeit courageous and honorable, rearguard action behind Henry Wallace.[47]

V

The Progressive Citizens of America (PCA) constituted the last major attempt to construct a national popular-front organization in the United States. Although the Progressive Party eventually grew out of the PCA, the widely accepted contention that the organization was formed by the Communists in preparation for a third party has little basis in fact. Indeed, as Curtis MacDougall has noted, the Communists in the ICCASP and the NC–PAC had initially opposed the merger of the two groups into the PCA, contending that independent political action must be based upon working-class strength rather than an amalgam of middle-class groups (later Communist shifts on the third-party question makes any view that puts PCA into a calculated third-party time table ridiculous).[48]

Although Wallace's wish to retain his independence as editor of the *New Republic* barred his formal affiliation with the PCA, he was the featured speaker at the organization's founding conference in late December, 1946. Also, he was accurately referred to in the press as the symbolic leader of the group, as it was almost wholly committed to his views concerning domestic and foreign policy. In his address to the

PCA, Wallace struck at the "enemy" on the right, the conservative press and big business, who threatened the construction of a lasting peace with the Soviet Union. Repudiating both Russophobes and Russophiles in tones reminiscent of the Madison Square Garden speech, Wallace warned the PCA to guard against the "plutocrats and monopolists who will try to brand us as Reds. . . . we are more American than the neo-Fascists who attack us. The more we are attacked, the more likely we are to succeed. I say on with the fight." [49]

The PCA's political-action program, drafted at the organizing convention, pledged the group to continue to fight for the principles of the liberal legislative program that had been buried in Congress since the end of the war. Repeating Wallace's warning, the PCA maintained that "if the Democratic party woos privilege and betrays the people it will die and deserve to die. We cannot therefore rule out the possibility of a new political party." The Communist question provoked little controversy, largely because the avowed anti-Communists did not attend the meeting. In the tradition of earlier popular-front groups, the PCA merely stated its willingness to accept "all progressive men and women in our nation, regardless of race, creed, color, national origin, or political affiliation." Indeed, PCA leaders then and later considered questions of Communist influence in the organization as indicative of reactionary attempts to divide the liberals. As in the past, adherents of the popular front considered the Communists themselves less significant than the problem of red-baiting. When anti-Communist pressure grew, defense of the political rights of Communists became more and more a matter of personal honor for PCA activists. [50]

The Communist question was paramount at the UDA's expansion meeting in early January, 1947. In May, 1946, Loeb had sought to bring the issue out into the open with a letter to the *New Republic* calling for a ban upon Communist membership in liberal organizations and warning that "no united-front organization will long remain united; it will become only a front." Although Loeb's public letter received mixed responses, Reinhold Niebuhr's private invitation to leading liberals to attend the Washington meeting in January drew three times the response that he had initially expected. Even if Phil Murray and A. F. Whitney were chosen as vice chairmen of the PCA, neither they nor other truly prominent national labor leaders had attended the group's founding convention. At the UDA Washington meeting, Walter Reuther, James Carey, CIO director of organization Allen Haywood, and Textile Workers president Emil Rieve (often mentioned as a possible successor to Murray) attended and agreed to serve on the organizing committee for the proposed Americans for Democratic Action.[51]

Walter White of the NAACP and Charles Bolte, founder of the American Veterans Committee, supported the meeting, as did such diverse figures as Stewart Alsop, Sidney Hook, and Mayor Hubert Humphrey of Minneapolis. Of paramount importance, however, was the large number of old New Dealers who attended the meeting. Mrs. Roosevelt, serving as patron saint of the gathering, joined in a testimonial dinner on the eve of the meeting; and Wilson Wyatt, Leon Henderson, Paul Porter and John Kenneth Galbraith were among those present.[52]

Addressing the testimonial dinner on January 3, Chester Bowles prefigured the organizational meeting of the following day by condemning both Republican reaction and Communist totalitarianism. After the UDA formally dissolved at the January 4 meeting, a six-point declaration of principles was adopted and a committee of twenty-five appointed to establish the ADA. Although Mrs. Roosevelt had asked the gathering to work for "a positive program of promoting democracy everywhere" rather than "a negative approach against any country or ideology," ADA's Declaration of Principles gave tacit support to much of the Truman foreign policy. Whereas the PCA had supported Wallace in his controversy with Baruch over the control of atomic energy, the ADA specifically endorsed the Baruch Plan (which was the official American position). Both the ADA and the PCA stressed their support for the United Nations, but the ADA did not raise specific objections to the Truman–Byrnes foreign policy, stating only that "within the general framework of present American foreign policy, steps must be taken to raise standards of living and support civil and political freedom everywhere." [53]

In essence, ADA had connected the general aims of the world New Deal (albeit in a less elaborate form than the PCA) with the Truman–Byrnes foreign policy (which the PCA bitterly opposed). On matters of domestic policy, the ADA's Declaration of Principles was in substantial agreement with the PCA (although the difference again was one of tone, of the lowering of immediate expectations). Instead of the extensive defense of the Economic Bill of Rights that its rival offered, ADA merely stated, "The New Deal program must be expanded to insure decent levels of health, nutrition, shelter and education." Third-party talk at the ADA meeting was almost nonexistent; indeed, many of those present saw the new organization as an attempt to check any potential third-party activity (the overwhelming majority of those present were irrevocably committed to the Democratic party, if not to Harry Truman). Finally, the ADA accepted the Communist–Fascist equation of the mass media and the Truman administration. "We reject any association with Communists or sympathizers with communism in the United States," the Declaration of Principles concluded, "as completely as we reject any association with Fascists or their sympathizers. Both are hostile to the principles of freedom and democracy on which this Republic has grown great." [54]

The liberal journals followed the press in portraying the PCA and the ADA as rivals. As evidence that a lethargic form of cold-war liberalism, born of the disasters of 1946, had already triumphed among social liberals, most writers expressed sympathy with the ADA (the *New Republic*, which, because of its editor's sensitive position, sought a strict neutrality between the two organizations, was the exception). In the *Progressive*, James Wechsler portrayed the PCA as a traditional popular-front group destined, like all of its predecessors, to end in disaster. Robert Bendiner, writing in the *Nation*, agreed with Wechsler and saw in ADA a "revolt of the middle" that promised to revive the liberal movement for the first time since Roosevelt's death. Expressing mild sympathy for the ADA, Freda Kirchwey wanted the new organization to remain free of both pro- and anti-Communist entanglements (a hope that also motivated many of the PCA's founders). As for PCA, Miss Kirchwey doubted that it was possible for the Communists to have any success with a popular-front organization in a period of growing political reaction.[55]

Even Max Lerner, a liberal weathervane who had defended the first popular front and tacitly accepted the second, showed scant sympathy for the PCA. Increasingly critical of the Communists after the November elections, Lerner still retained his friendship with Henry Wallace and his public advocacy of an independent, non-Communist left. ADA's failure to invite Wallace to its Washington meeting, Lerner feared, was evidence that the anti-Communist group was imprisoned by "the very sectarianism which has been the ruin of the left." While noting that the PCA's large initial membership and nominal endorsement by Phil Murray gave it great prospects, Lerner echoed the criticism of the Niebuhrs with the contention that the organization was blighted "by its lack of unity and courage on the issue of disassociation from the Communists . . . disguises, behind the scene influence, remote control by Communists can in the end only destroy the whole progressive movement." [56]

Wallace continued to call for unity among all liberals in a time of trouble. In an effort to defuse any possible conflict between the rival organizations, the *New Republic* editor noted that he was not a member of the PCA and that Mrs. Roosevelt was not a member of the ADA. Loeb replied that Mrs. Roosevelt had not formally joined ADA because of her position at the United Nations, and he accused Wallace of deliberate distortion. Even after the late President's widow issued a public statement reiterating her support for the ADA, the press continued to dramatize the conflict between the two organizations.[57]

Phil Murray, disturbed that he and his colleagues in the CIO leadership were now identified with rival liberal groups, decided in mid-February to withdraw his endorsement from the

PCA and to recommend to the CIO Executive Board that all other CIO leaders withdraw from both organizations. Since a general ban against CIO affiliation with the ADA or the PCA threatened to do much greater damage to the ADA (a comment on the attrition of the popular front), Mrs. Roosevelt pleaded with Murray to change his decision. The CIO leader refused, and the ban went into effect in March before the ADA elected its permanent officers.[58]

Truman's response to the Greek crisis in March, 1947, gave the PCA an issue. Using the Truman Doctrine to mobilize opposition to the administration, the PCA organized protest rallies, established state and local chapters, and entertained hopes for the creation of a grassroots movement throughout the country. "Every day is election day" became a favorite theme for the *Progressive Citizen,* the PCA newsletter, as the smallest precinct victory by a PCA-backed candidate was hailed as evidence that the people were rebelling against the anti-Communist hysteria and the bipartisan foreign policy. PCA leaders, while hinting at an eventual union with the ADA and working with ADA chapters in the few instances where local conditions made this possible, dismissed their liberal competitors as ivory-tower intellectuals without the ability or the will to develop a mass movement. Events soon proved, however, that the PCA, believing its own slogans of direct political action and the common man, was trapped in its own ivory tower.[59]

The deteriorating international situation helped to stimulate a massive press campaign against the PCA, a campaign that, in spite of the popular-front group's countercharge of red-baiting, began to take its toll. By April, 1947, estimated PCA membership had dropped by over 25 percent. Previously, liberals opposed to the Communists but willing to work with them had argued privately that the choice was to have no organization at all or a group constantly threatened by Red influence. In the spring of 1947, however, letters and statements in the liberal journals that Communism and Fascism were enemies of liberalism and indistinguishable from one another became more common than at any time since the Hitler–Stalin pact.

Against this background Henry Wallace prepared to travel to Europe to continue what had become his crusade against the Truman Doctrine.[60] The threat posed by the Doctrine he would see as a crisis of the American spirit. In reality, the crisis had flowed from the failures of the New Deal to the blundering cynicism of the Truman administration to the steady diminution of the wartime liberal–labor alliance. The administration's great departure in foreign policy in the spring and summer of 1947 would now lead the *New Republic* editor on a few final quests for the blasted dream of a world New Deal.

NOTES

* Letter to HAW, August 27, 1947; Culbert Olson to HAW, March 28, 1947, HAW Papers, University of Iowa.

1. Interview with C. B. Baldwin, January 9, 1969; Invitation Call to Progressives, Catholic University of America, Washington, D.C., Box A4-33, Philip Murray Papers.

2. Report of the Conference of Progressives, September 28–29, Murray Papers, Box A4-33.

3. *Ibid.; P.M.,* September 30, 1946.

4. Murray to Norman Cousins, September 13, 1946, Murray Papers, Box A-32; Interview with Baldwin.

5. "The Week in Review," *Progressive,* X (October 7, 1946), p. 3; Curtis D. MacDougall, *Gideon's Army* (New York, 1965), I, pp. 106–107.

6. *P.M.,* October 16, 1946; Baldwin to Murray, February 3, 1947, Murray Papers, Box A-33; Interview with Baldwin.

7. In works like Lionel Trilling's novel, *Middle of the Journey* (New York, 1947), the new pessimism about political action was force-fully expressed. In *The Vital Center,* Arthur Schlesinger, Jr., por-trayed the shift away from the popular front as a vindication of liberalism and a restoration of radical nerve. See Arthur Schlesinger, Jr., *The Vital Center* (Boston, Sentry Edition, 1962), pp. 159–169.

8. While condemning popular-front thinking as superficial and sim-plistic, Frank Warren makes the important point that the wide acceptance of the popular-front idea among liberals reflected not only the practical necessity of opposing Fascism, but also the need to reach out for a wider ideology. Frank Warren, III, *Liberals and Communism* (Bloomington, Ind., 1966), p. 107.

9. Lewis Coser and Irving Howe, *The American Communist Party* (Boston, 1957), p. 340.

10. *Ibid.*

11. For an insightful memoir into the frustrations of the left in the 1930s, see Murray Kempton, *Part of Our Time* (New York, 1955).

12. For an excellent description of the redirection of social–liberal thought in the late 1930s, see Richard Alan Lawson, *The Failure of Independent Liberalism, 1930–1941* (New York, 1971).

13. The institutional strength of American Communism was probably greater during World War II than at any other time in the country's history.

14. For a quick review of the Communists' wartime activities, see Coser and Howe, *Communist Party*, pp. 423–427. (Unfortunately, there is no real secondary literature on American Communism; what passes for such a literature is almost always a polemical recitation of published Communist sources, dubious contemporary accounts, and even more dubious testimony given before congressional committees.)

15. *Ibid.*; Coser and Howe, of course, do not see the Communists as the dupes of liberals.

16. David A. Shannon, *The Decline of American Communism* (New York, 1959), p. 3; Jacques Duclos, "On the Dissolution of the Communist Party of the United States," *Political Affairs*, XXIV (August, 1945), p. 670; William Z. Foster, "Leninism and Some Practical Problems of the Postwar Period," *Political Affairs*, XXV (February, 1946), p. 106.

17. Duclos, "Dissolution of the Communist Party," p. 656.

18. Draft Resolution of the National Board, Communist Party of America, "The Present Situation and the Next Tasks," *Political Affairs*, XXIV (July, 1945), p. 582.

19. See Shannon, *The Decline of American Communism*, pp. 113–248.

20. For a critical look at the Red Fascist idea, see Les K. Adler and Thomas G. Patterson, "Red Fascism: The Merger of Nazi Germany and Soviet Russia in the American Image of Totalitarianism, 1930s–1960s," *American Historical Review*, LXXV (April, 1970), pp. 1046–1064.

21. The role of the Catholic Church in creating the postwar anti-Communist hysteria still needs extensive documentation and analysis, although many studies of McCarthyism have emphasized the specific appeal of the Communist issue to Irish, German, and East European Catholics in America. See Michael Rogin, *The Intellectuals and McCarthy: The Radical Spectre* (Cambridge, Mass., 1967).

22. Popular-front liberals in the 1930s often regarded the Catholic hierarchy as a conspiratorial force working to disrupt the entire left. Many Wallace supporters and Wallace himself, for example, believed that the Church hierarchy was involved in the behind-the-scenes opposition to him at the 1944 Democratic convention. HAW to Francis, Cardinal Spellman, undated (but sometime in the spring or summer of 1948), HAW Papers, University of Iowa.

23. Athan Theoharis, differs from the interpretation of anti-Communism in this study, using public-opinion data to show substantial tolerance of Communists and trust in Soviet–American cooperation as World

War II ended. Theoharis attributes popular anti-Communism to the Truman administration's rationale for its foreign policy. See Athan Theoharis, "The Rhetoric of Politics," pp. 196–241, in Barton Bernstein, ed., *Politics and Policies of the Truman Administration* (Chicago, 1970); and Athan Theoharis, *Seeds of Repression* (Chicago, 1971).

24. Indeed, Hollywood did not sign up for the anti-Communist crusade until 1948, the year that Russia and America confronted each other directly over Berlin, Europe was permanently divided into Soviet and American blocs, and the Progressive party made its futile stand against the cold war. ("The Iron Curtain," a Dana Andrews film based on the atomic espionage revelations of Soviet defector Igor Gouzenko, became the first distinctly anti-Soviet, anti-Communist film of the postwar world.)

25. In effect, this is exactly what the Americans for Democratic Action did and what Arthur Schlesinger, Jr., celebrated in *The Vital Center*.

26. It may be argued, however, that had the popular-front position on the rights of Communists and the intentions of the Soviet Union held after 1945, coexistence with Russia might have become a reality in the late 1940s and the excesses of the McCarthy period might have been avoided. Thus, the differences were significant, even if the lack of a serious division over the ends and the structure of American society assured that the popular-front advocates would fail to articulate these differences before a national audience.

27. James Loeb, Radio Address, September 29, 1946, ADA Papers, Series 7, Box 105, Wisconsin State Historical Society, Madison, Wisconsin (henceforth, WSHS).

28. Straight claims to have stressed from the outset his hope that Wallace would restrict his political activities to the magazine. Interview with Michael Straight, November 25, 1968.

29. *New York Times*, October 12, 22, 23, 26, 28, 1946; Curtis D. MacDougall, *Gideon's Army* (New York, 1965), I, p. 98.

30. *Ibid.; New York Times*, October 28, 1946.

31. *Ibid.*, November 5, 1946; Gallup Poll File, Clark Clifford Papers, Political File, Box 19, HSTL; for press and radio comment on the elections, see HST Papers, Editorial Comment, Box 3, HSTL; TRB, "Forward in Reverse," *New Republic*, CXV (November 11, 1946), p. 615; "Picking Up the Pieces," *Nation*, CLXIII (November 16, 1946), p. 543.

32. "Washington Calling," *Progressive*, X (November 25, 1946), p. 2; Jerry Voorhis, *Confessions of a Congressman* (Garden City, N.Y., 1947), pp. 230, 277.

33. Robert M. La Follette, Jr., "Look Out Liberals," *Progressive*, X (November 14, 1946), p. 2; Richard Neuberger, "The People Spin the Wheel," *Progressive*, X (November 25, 1946), pp. 4 and 11; John S. Atlee, "A.V.C. Sets the Pace," *Nation*, CLXII (June 22, 1946, pp. 740–741.

34. "The CIO Meets," *New Republic*, CXV (December 2, 1946), p. 716.

35. Henry A. Wallace, "Jobs, Peace, Freedom," *New Republic*, CXV (December 16, 1946), p. 789.

36. For an acount of Loeb's attempt to transform UDA into a national liberal organization during the war, see Adam Clymer, "George Norris and Progressive Unity, 1942–1943," undated MS, Franklin D. Roosevelt Library, Hyde Park, N.Y.

37. UDA Minutes, National Board of Directors Meeting, May 22, 1946, Reinhold Niebuhr Papers, Box 10, LC.

38. Memorandum, Proposed Conference of Democratic Progressives, undated, Niebuhr Papers, Box; Alonzo Hamby, "Harry S. Truman and American Liberalism, 1945–1948" (Ph.D. thesis, University of Missouri, 1965), p. 150. When interviewed Beanie Baldwin confirmed reports published at the time that he and Hannah Dorner decided to combine NC–PAC and the ICCASP because of the financial crisis facing both organizations. Harold Ickes, who had been off salary at ICCASP since July because of the crisis, resigned after the elections, thus costing the group its biggest name. In the wake of his resignation, Ickes let the story spread that he quit ICCASP because of Communist influence in the organization, but others believed that financial considerations had more to do with it. Interview with Baldwin, Ickes to Norman Thomas, November 25, 1945, Norman Thomas Papers, Box 50, New York Public Library, and Hannah Dorner to Jo Davidson, Jo Davidson Papers, Box 5, LC.

39. Niebuhr to Oscar Chapman, November 30, 1946, Oscar Chapman Papers, Box 89, ADA Folder, HSTL.

40. Paul Carter, The Decline and Revival of the Social Gospel (Ithaca, N.Y., 1956), p. 156; Reinhold Niebuhr, "The Confusion of Good and Evil," sermon outline, Niebuhr Papers, Box 14.

41. For a brief and well-written summary of Niebuhr's career (although a superficial understanding of his thought), see Arthur Schlesinger, Jr., "Reinhold Niebuhr's Role In American Political Thought and Life" in Charles Kegley and Robert Bretall, eds., Reinhold Niebuhr: His Religious and Social Thought (New York, 1956).

42. Granville Hicks, "The P.M. Mind," New Republic, CXII (April 16, 1945), p. 516; Lionel Trilling, "The Progressive Psyche," Nation, CLV (September 12, 1942), p. 217.

43. For the most succinct statement on Niebuhr's view of power, see Reinhold Niebuhr, The Children of Light and the Children of Darkness (New York, 1944). In a series of lectures at Stanford in January 1944, Niebuhr argued for a middle ground between self-defeating idealism and power politics, contending that only by adopting the wisdom of evil (while rejecting its malice) could the good in life achieve a partial triumph over the bad. Niebuhr was never quite clear about how one could adopt the "wisdom of realpolitik" and yet remain free of power politics; but then, he never believed that power politics, or any particular evil, could be wholly overcome by any universal good.

44. Reinhold Niebuhr, "New Allies, Old Issues," Nation, CLIII (July 19, 1941), pp. 50–52; Reinhold Niebuhr, Letter to the Editor of the Nation, Nation, CLXII (March 30, 1946), p. 383; Reinhold Niebuhr, "Europe, Russia and America," Nation, CLXIII (September 14, 1946, pp. 691–692.

45. Niebuhr to Oscar Chapman, November 30, 1946, Oscar Chapman Papers, Box 89, ADA Folder.

46. See Arthur M. Schlesinger, Jr., *The Age of Jackson* (Boston, 1945); Arthur M. Schlesinger, Jr., "The Communist Party," *Life*, XXI (July 29, 1946), pp. 83–84 ff. Schlesinger himself expressed the frustration and resignation that liberals felt toward the Truman policies before the election. In an article commemorating the first anniversary of the death of Franklin Roosevelt, Schlesinger wrote, "Under Roosevelt or Wallace, the collapse of the New Deal might not have been so complete or pathetic as it has been under Truman, but the fatality of history suggests that there would have been a sudden collapse. . . . ." Arthur Schlesinger, Jr., "His Rendezvous with History," *New Republic*, CXIV (April 15, 1946), p. 554.

47. Schlesinger, *The Vital Center*, pp. 145–147; Garry Wills, *Nixon Agonistes* (Boston, 1970), pp. 573–575.

48. MacDougall, *Gideon's Army*, I, p. 117.

49. Text of Wallace's address reprinted in MacDougall, *Gideon's Army*, I, pp. 114–117.

50. Memorandum, Lillian H. Traugott to PCA State Directors, undated, Progressive Party Papers, University of Iowa, Box 15 (henceforth PP Papers); Program for Political Action, PCA Founding Conference, December 29, 1946, PP Papers, Box 11, Folder 35.

51. James Loeb, Jr., "Letter to the Editor of the *New Republic*" *New Republic*, CXIV (May 13, 1946), p. 699; *New York Times*, January 5, 1947; Interview with Carey.

52. Hamby, "Truman and American Liberalism," pp. 159–161.

53. The text of the ADA declaration and a full list of ADA's organizing committee and committee of the whole, are reprinted in MacDougall, *Gideon's Army*, I, pp. 121–122.

54. *Ibid.*

55. James Wechsler, "Liberals Without Reds," *Progressive*, XI (January 13, 1947), p. 2; Robert Bendiner, "The Revolt of the Middle," *Nation*, CLXIV (January 18, 1947), p. 65; Freda Kirchwey, "Mugwumps in Action," *Nation*, CLXIV (January 18, 1947), p. 62.

56. Lerner in *P.M.*, January 9, 1947.

57. Henry A. Wallace, "The Enemy is Not Each Other," *New Republic*, CXVI (January 27, 1947), p. 22; *New York Times*, January 23, 1947.

58. *New York Times*, February 19, 28, March 7, 1947.

59. *Progressive Citizen*, July, 1947. Lillian Traugott, who was to become Mrs. Beanie Baldwin, presented the most common PCA view about ADA when she suggested, in the spring of 1947, that the latter was an elitist organization which, like its tiny predecessor UDA, "will do little." Lillian Traugott to PCA State Directors, undated, Progressive Party Papers, Box 15.

60. Babbette Deutsch to Jo Davidson, July 9, 1945, Davidson Papers, Box 5. Cf. William Rose Benet to Davidson, undated (but February, 1947), Davidson Papers, Box 8. See Katherine Ann Porter, "Letter to the Editor of the *Nation*," *Nation*, CLXIV (May 24, 1947), p. 640, for an example of the growing hostility to the popular-front idea.

7

Manifest Destiny, 1947: The Triumph of Containment

This is not an imperialistic plan. It covets nothing for America but an honorable peace in a free world of free men. That is not imperialism. I like what Elihu Root once said of our Monroe Doctrine: "It rests upon the right of every sovereign state to protect itself by preventing a condition of affairs in which it will be too late to protect itself." That is not imperialism. That is intelligent self-interest. . . . We point the general direction we propose to go. We do not, we cannot, chart the total course. This plan fits a key, strategic need. Undoubtedly there will be other problems facing other and different needs. For example, our occupational responsibilities in Korea unquestionably will soon demand positive support. It is part of World War II—unless we propose to lose the peace.

*Senator Arthur Vandenberg
on the Truman Doctrine
April 8, 1947 **

As Henry Wallace had left the Truman administration in a dispute over foreign policy, it is not surprising that he returned to the national limelight in the spring of 1947 as a critic of the ever-deepening cold war. After the Truman administration sought congressional approval in March, 1947, for direct aid to civil-war-torn Greece and authoritarian Turkey, Wallace denounced the proposed intervention in major speaking tours in Europe and America. Drawing closer to the Progressive Citizens of America, the former Vice President faced increasingly bitter attacks by the administration and the media as he sought to revive the social–liberal movement to do battle with the Truman doctrine.

When the Truman administration proposed the Marshall Plan for European Recovery in June, 1947, Wallace's cold–war–liberal opponents in the ADA were able to link the containment foreign policy with the general aims of the world New Deal, thus permitting social liberals to draw away from Wallace without abandoning wholly the ideals of the wartime liberal movement. Furthermore, the *New Republic* editor's ambivalent opposition to the Marshall Plan in the fall of 1947 highlighted his growing dependence upon the pro-Communist left in the PCA and hurt him politically. The violent opposition that many of his former supporters expressed to his decision to launch an independent candidacy against Truman in 1948 was in itself evidence of his failure to mobilize an effective opposition to the Truman policies.

I

The conflict in Greece, nurtured by the deterioration of both Soviet–American relations and European economic life, highlighted the failure of the Truman foreign policy. With Soviet acquiescence, Britain had intervened in Greece in October, 1944, to suppress the E.A.M., the Communist-led local resistance movement, and install a rightist authoritarian regime (the Russians received spheres of influence in Rumania and Bulgaria and agreed to share Yugoslavia with the English in the agreement).[1] As Soviet-American rivalry grew in the winter of 1946, Russia began openly though cautiously to champion the E.A.M.'s cause and to encourage the nations within its security zone to arm the guerillas. Unwilling to accept the possibility of an E.A.M. victory in Greece, Truman nevertheless avoided any direct overture to the British about the deepening Greek economic crisis, hoping instead that the American banking community would support the World Bank in making liberal loans to the Greeks and the Turks (whose own dictatorial regime faced a renewal of historic Russian pressures against the Dardanelles after the war).[2]

Although the E.A.M.'s military forces were reduced to poorly armed bands operating out of the northern mountains by the winter of 1946, apparent Soviet support for a revival of the rebellion, coupled with the complete indifference of American bankers, led the Truman administration to contemplate direct American involvement to sustain the British.[3] Working on contingency plans to extend military and economic aid to Greece and Turkey as early as the fall of 1946, the United States moved toward a direct commitment when Truman sent Paul Porter to direct a special American mission to study conditions in Greece in January, 1947. At the same time the United States strongly supported the American-led United Nations Commission of Investigation to study the crisis.[4]

After Great Britain, faced with her own severe recovery problems, informed Washington on February 21, 1947, that she was no longer able to finance the Greek government, the State Department began to prepare a formal request for direct aid to Greece and Turkey.[5]

George Kennan, the department's grey eminence on Soviet affairs and a member of the committee working on the request, expressed his reservations to Dean Acheson over certain sections in the draft message for the President, specifically the wisdom of the section extending aid to Turkey, a nation bordering the Soviet Union and not menaced by internal rebellion. While endorsing the necessity of prompt aid for Greece, Kennan also criticized the "sweeping" nature of the message, especially the ominous possibilities inherent in the statement, "I believe that it must be the policy of the United States to support free peoples who are resisting subjugation by armed minorities or by outside pressure." The statement, however, was to be a highlight of Truman's message to Congress requesting $400 million of American aid to Greece and Turkey.[6]

In conversations with Republican congressional leaders, Truman, Acheson, and General Marshall defended the request as a necessary response to the Soviet and Communist drive for world power. Although the administration made some public gestures to the United Nations, Truman was careful to tell congressional leaders that American aid would be controlled by Americans. Defeated at home and frustrated abroad, the President had moved to meet the Greek crisis with arguments that appealed to the deepest fears of his political enemies and a program that threatened the still-vibrant hopes for a lasting peace through a workable United Nations.[7]

For a time, it appeared that the Truman Doctrine might produce a major revival of the popular front. After the President's message, Freda Kirchwey condemned Truman's version of "manifest destiny, 1947" and warned that the President's policy threatened to substitute unilateral American force for the United Nations as the guarantor of peace. The PCA immediately issued a policy statement that condemned the President for dividing the world into two armed camps and for inaugurating a program of "American imperialism which will take over the policies, methods and failures of the British Empire." Morris Rubin, editor of the bitterly anti-Communist *Progressive*, warned Truman that "Greece will be no more cured by Fascism than by Communism." Walter Lippmann, perhaps the most listened-to critic of the Truman Doctrine, saw the administration's new policy as a potentially dangerous attempt to maintain the status quo through American intervention abroad. Above all, the President's abandonment of the United Nations was the most frightening facet of the Truman Doctrine for Lippmann and for most social liberals who spoke out on the question.[8]

Yet many did not speak out on the question. While the liberal journals closed ranks against the Truman Doctrine, old stalwarts of the liberal–labor alliance sought either to avoid the issues raised by the new foreign policy or to quietly defend the administration. The CIO, beset by bitter divisions over the Communist question, maintained a studied silence regarding the President's proposals. In the ADA, the doctrine became a center of controversy between those who sought independence from the dictates of Communism and imperialism and those who maintained that the administration position had to be sustained in order to prevent the crisis from exploding into a new world war. Elmer Davis, staunchly anti-Communist, nevertheless had strong reservations about any aid to the authoritarian Greek regime; and Charles Bolte, founder of the American Veterans Committee, opposed the doctrine as an exercise in American imperialism. Powerful figures in the organization, however—Wilson Wyatt, Franklin D. Roosevelt, Jr., Hubert Humphrey, Arthur Schlesinger, Jr., and Paul Porter—lobbied for support of the Truman Doctrine. Porter, who would later admit that his involvement in the ADA stemmed from his desire to protect administration policies, was especially influential; his recent trip to Greece and his willingness to criticize the Greek government gave his arguments great force.[9]

The administration's supporters prevailed at the ADA's March 30 meeting, although their victory was far from impressive. By a voice vote, the ADA overwhelmingly passed a lukewarm endorsement of the Truman Doctrine. Reiterating its strong support for the United Nations, the ADA nevertheless resolved that "pending the assumption of full responsibility by the UN, we believe that the United States must take action to achieve conditions in Greece under which free institutions may grow. . . ." In the months ahead, ADA ignored the Truman Doctrine as much as possible. Containment in practice still was difficult even for the paladins of the emerging cold-war liberalism to accept.[10]

A day after Truman's message to Congress, Henry Wallace condemned the Truman Doctrine as a commitment to oppose Russia and Communism all over the world. In a PCA-sponsored radio address, the former Vice President contended that Truman's support for reactionary regimes in Greece and

Turkey made him "the best salesman Communism ever had." The President, Wallace maintained, had abandoned the policies of Franklin Roosevelt for the warlike program of Winston Churchill's Iron Curtain speech. Opposed to any unilateral aid to the Greek dictatorship, Wallace concluded that America "must give the world something better than Communism. . . . this is the time for an all-out world reconstruction program for peace. This is America's opportunity for peace." [11]

In *New Republic* columns and at public meetings, Wallace led the fight against the Truman Doctrine with eloquence. Truman, the former Vice President noted bitterly, had permitted UNRRA to die a year before; now the President argued that the United Nations was unequal to the task of reconstruction. Calling for a general ceasefire and the creation of a coalition government that would include the E.A.M., Wallace condemned the administration's "global Monroe doctrine" and advocated in its place a policy of immediate American support for a Greek reconstruction program suggested previously by the Food and Agricultural Organization of the United Nations. On the question of Turkish aid, Wallace saw the issue privately in terms of American–Soviet rivalry over Middle Eastern oil, markets and trade routes, suggesting that American support for a United Nations initiative to internationalize the Dardanelles offered the best hope for a settlement of the Russo–Turkish conflict.[12]

Trapped in an emerging world conflict that violated everything he had stood for, Wallace revived the rhetoric of wartime social liberalism to do battle with the Truman Doctrine. Denouncing Truman's support of "corrupt and backward looking regimes," Wallace argued that the President had "defaulted our moral position in the world"; moreover, the Truman Doctrine represented a crisis "not of the Greek economy but of the American spirit." In a tone that those who still believed in him considered poignant and those who had stopped listening thought pathetic, Wallace asked a PCA protest rally in Madison Square Garden, "Where are the millions who supported Roosevelt? Where are the inheritors of our great tradition?" [13]

Where were the millions who supported Roosevelt? When it was announced in January, 1947, that Wallace would visit London in the spring as the guest of the *New Statesman and Nation*, organ of the Labor Party left, the *New Leader*, off-shoot of the American Socialist Party's right wing, drafted a petition of protest to British Foreign Minister Ernest Bevin. Signed by an odd collection of seventy self-styled liberals, including Norman Thomas, Henry Luce, Arthur Schlesinger, Jr., and Walter Judd, the petition advised Bevin that "American support for Wallace's position on foreign policy comes from a small minority of Communists, fellow travelers and what we call here totalitarian liberals." A kind of negative United Front of anti-Communist socialists, cold-war liberals, and unabashed reactionaries (similar in composition to the Congress for Cultural Freedom of the 1950s) was already biting at the heels of Henry Wallace.[14]

As opposition to the Truman Doctrine mounted, Wallace accepted invitations to enlarge his English tour to include speaking engagements on the Continent. Communists, Socialists, and various left-of-center parties and organizations that had played a prominent role in the anti-Hitler resistance in Western Europe joined to sponsor the trip. In the United States, the PCA had mixed success in mobilizing support for the tour. Although many of the former Vice President's prominent old supporters signed in April, 1947, a PCA-sponsored scroll wishing him well on his journey, the scroll did not venture far from its noncommittal title, "A Message of Greetings and Friendship to the Progressives of Great Britain from the Progressives of America." Although the aims of the world New Deal were restated in the document, the scroll said nothing directly to challenge the Truman Doctrine. Its silence contrasted in a sharp but increasingly familiar way with the accusatory rhetoric of the *New Leader* petition.[15]

After he arrived in England in early April with Michael Straight and a host of reporters, Wallace found himself the target of bitter attacks in the United States. By contrast, the friendly audiences he found in England, so much like his old lib-lab following in America, were a welcome relief. In an address at London's Central Hall, the former Vice President received his warmest response of the tour when he advocated an American investment of fifty-billion dollars, funded through the International Bank, to achieve reconstruction of the world economy.[16]

In later addresses at Manchester and Liverpool, Wallace resumed his quarrel with the administration. With great bitterness, he struck at the political equation that lay behind the as yet unchristened policy of containment. American decision makers, he noted, "presumably know that 20,000,000 Russians gave their lives to defeat a Fascist dictatorship. Yet, they believe that Fascism and Communism are similar evils." In an address over the BBC, he returned to the anticolonial hopes of the wartime liberal movement and to arguments that the men who had stopped listening to him would see come back to haunt them. "A great national awakening," he concluded, "has occurred in Asia and other parts of the world. This new nationalism will turn into communism and look to the Soviet Union as their [sic] only ally if the United States declares that this is the American Century of Power Politics rather than the Century of the Common Man." [17]

At first, as might have been predicted, the tour was praised by left-Labor British newspapers and attacked by the Tory press. News of strong American disapproval, however, along with the former Vice President's failure to excite any save those who already shared his views, soon produced an unfriendly reaction in unexpected places. The *Manchester Guardian*, initially sympathetic to the tour, noted that "as an apostle of one world, Mr. Wallace is a little clumsy." American ambassador Lewis Douglas, who had maintained a discreet silence during the Wallace visit, made a strong speech in defense of the Truman Doctrine after the *New Republic* editor had left the continent. In late April, a convention of the British Labor Party, standing with Foreign Minister Bevin against the left faction led by Konni Zilliacus, voted overwhelmingly to endorse the Truman Doctrine.[18]

After his arrival in Stockholm on April 19, Wallace was ignored by the American legation. In Sweden, his journey was suddenly enlivened by a report that Winston Churchill had called him a "crypto-Communist." Amused by the story, Wallace noted that his trip to England was no different from Churchill's trip to Fulton a year before. In a comment that did much to sum up the nature of his general philosophy and its limits, the former Vice President stated that he was neither a Communist nor a Socialist but "a Progressive Tory who believes that it is absolutely necessary to have peace and understanding with Russia." [19]

Completing his tour in France, Wallace found himself in the embrace of the Communists. Although a broad spectrum of parties representing the French Center–Left had joined initially to sponsor the trip, all the major sponsors save the Communists had disassociated themselves from the tour by the time the former Vice President reached Paris (a circumstance that Wallace and his supporters attributed to indirect American pressures, but that others saw as a result of negative responses in France to the Communists' militant opposition to the Truman Doctrine). Although he held a cordial private meeting with Wallace, Léon Blum, the most famous of all popular front leaders and the grand old man of French socialism, publicly criticized the former Vice President's speeches. In what was probably the most damning comment a man of the Left could make in France at the time, Blum compared Wallace with Charles de Gaulle as a proponent of negative and futile policies for Europe.[20]

In Paris, Wallace avoided the Communists wherever he could, making his major address before the overseas chapter of the American Veterans Committee. Repeating his familiar argument that capitalism and Communism, given a period of peace, would become more like each other, the former Vice President conceded that "I recognize that conflicts exist between capitalist, Socialist and Communist societies. I assert that the conflicts are not irreconcilable. I answer that these conflicts can be resolved without a resort to war." Shortly before he left Paris for New York, the *New Republic* editor told reporters, "I want to avoid being monopolized by the extreme left who have been so kind to me here in Paris." [21]

The wave of personal abuse that greeted the Wallace tour in America went beyond anything that the former Vice President had experienced in his long and hardly placid career. Capitalizing on the widespread opposition to the trip, the administration maintained a stern silence through the controversy while politicians and the press lambasted Wallace. The prompt and overwhelming passage of the Greek–Turkish Aid bill in April was mockingly attributed by some to the embattled *New Republic* editor's journey.[22] Senator Fulbright announced that one of Wallace's speeches abroad sounded as if it had been written in the Kremlin, while Representative L. Mendell Rivers and others sputtered on about the possibility of denying the *New Republic* editor re-entry into the country or, at the very least, removing his passport. Senator Vandenberg, still the most sacred symbol of the bipartisan nature of the Truman foreign policy, publicly called Wallace an "itinerant saboteur" and privately told David Lilienthal, "The President can have me or Henry, but he can't have us both." For the old isolationist–nationalists, who formed the bulk of the congressional opposition to the Truman Doctrine, the new attacks on Wallace were like a bad dream. One of their number, Representative Howard Buffet of Nebraska, developed a theory about the Wallace trip that showed more insight into the development of cold-war liberalism than it did about Wallace. Noting that the ADA had endorsed the Truman Doctrine, Buffet concluded that the Wallace tour was a ruse to disguise the fact that "95 percent of the leaders of the New Deal Socialist crowd are for the new handout venture." [23]

Although Truman received about an equal number of letters for and against the tour, only a handful of liberals in Congress, Claude Pepper and young Glen Taylor of Idaho among them, rose to defend the embattled editor. Even Wallace's closest supporters, Cabell Phillips noted in the *New York Times* on April 29, believed that the former Vice President had temporarily lost much of his old following. The Gallup poll lent credence to this view. In December, 1946, a poll of Democrats showed that 48 percent favored Truman for the 1948 Democratic nomination against 24 percent for Wallace. During the height of the furor over the European tour, another poll showed that Truman was supported by 79 percent of the Democrats for 1948 as against 9 percent for Wallace. As Ernest Lindley noted, there was "a deep-seated feeling in the country that it is wrong to go abroad and denounce American foreign policy." [24]

During the wave of attacks against Wallace in the spring of 1947 and the passage of the Greek–Turkish Aid bill, few took notice that the cold-war spiral was steadily moving upward. In Hungary, the Soviets hardened their position, ousting the moderate pro-Communist regime of Ferenc Nagy and installing a repressive Stalinist government in its place. In Italy, a similar though bloodless political change occurred, with a new Christian Democratic regime barring the Communists and their United Front allies, the Nenni Socialists, from partnership in the government. In Moscow, *Nation* correspondent Alexander Werth noted that the Soviet government had launched a nationwide propaganda campaign against "American imperialism" and the war danger as a response to the Truman Doctrine. Most disturbing, Werth mentioned, was the nationwide promotion of Konstantin Simonov's "Russian Question," an explicitly anti-American play in which an antifascist, not wholly unlike Henry Wallace, was portrayed as struggling against the forces in the United States ruling class that sought war with the Soviet Union.[25]

At his first press conference after returning from Europe on April 27, Wallace was optimistic about the opposition he had seen to the Truman Doctrine abroad, and he displayed confidence that similar opposition existed in the United States. With this in mind, Beanie Baldwin and Michael Straight, representing a fledgling PCA and a financially embarrassed *New Republic*, respectively, decided in late April to sponsor a nationwide Wallace tour against the Truman Doctrine. The tour, it was hoped, would repair the fortunes of the former Vice President, assist the PCA's membership drive, and increase circulation for the *New Republic*.[26]

Wallace's national tour revived interest in his political future —in himself as much as in the press—and enabled him to recover some of the mass support he had previously lost. Accompanied by Baldwin, Straight, and Harold Young, he launched the tour on May 2 in Cleveland with an attack on Senator Arthur Vandenberg and John Foster Dulles, whom he called the real authors of the Truman Doctrine. Before a labor audience in Minneapolis, Wallace praised Mayor Hubert Humphrey, called for liberal unity in Minnesota and the nation, and advocated a regional program of reconstruction and economic development for Europe. At Ann Arbor on May 15 he called again for a fifty-billion-dollar world reconstruction program to be financed by the United States. The plan now called for the United States, working through the International Bank, to invest five-billion dollars a year for ten years to raise Eastern European and Asian living standards to levels commensurate with prewar Western Europe. Within a matter of weeks, Wallace's enemies in the administration would suggest a somewhat similar, although far less ambitious reconstruction program.[27]

The trip appeared to have been a great success. Both *Newsweek* and *Time*, hardly pro-Wallace journals, admitted that the large crowds, although gathered by the PCA and the pro-Communist labor unions, were made up of non-Communists who were troubled by the course of American foreign policy. Gael Sullivan, Hannegan's stand-in as National Chairman, expressed similar views in a memorandum to the President. Reports to Sullivan from California, Wisconsin, Colorado and Minnesota, all old areas of Wallace strength, showed that the Vice President still had a following among liberal Democrats. Furthermore, it was feared that the funds the PCA gathered at its rallies might be used either to start a third party or to finance a campaign against Truman in the primaries. Significantly, Sullivan suggested that the President's best strategy against Wallace was to go to the people and stress the nonmilitary aspects of the Truman Doctrine. "There is no question," the Acting National Chairman concluded, "that Wallace has captured the imagination of a large segment of the population."[28]

Wallace's columns in the *New Republic* are evidence that

he shared Sullivan's optimism about his political strength. Throughout the journey, as one might have expected, he hailed the rebirth of militant liberalism in all parts of the nation. A closer look at the tour, however, shows that the former Vice President had scant cause for real optimism. First of all, he had failed to pick up support from organized labor for any bid against Truman within the Democratic party. Indeed, his identification with the PCA had grown in the public mind at a time when Phil Murray was seeking to keep the CIO away from either the PCA or the ADA. Moreover, Truman's veto of the Taft–Hartley bill and the announcement of the Marshall Plan in language that revived hopes for a world New Deal were crippling blows to Wallace's attempt to rebuild the shattered liberal–labor alliance. Beanie Baldwin, who had begun the tour believing that a Wallace campaign against Truman in the Democratic primaries was possible, had lost all hope by the time the tour reached California in late May. In Congress, most liberals remained silent about the issues that Wallace was raising while warning against any possible third party. Only Glen Taylor made it a practice to taunt the administration regularly with third-party threats.[29]

Some old New Dealers weren't silent when Wallace entered their districts. Representative Lyndon Johnson of Texas, a moderate New Dealer whom the former Vice President had liked and had sought to aid in the past, announced in the House that the Wallace following was drawn from "the sallow, deluded lunatic fringe that bores and scavenges like termites eating away at the foundations of a strong building." With a rhetorical flourish that united the Munich analogy, the "get tough" policy, and the American frontier, Johnson concluded, "whether Communist or Fascist, or pistol-packing racketeer, the only thing a bully understands is force, and the one thing he respects is courage."[30]

Although liberals were not yet ready to accept fully the simplicities of a Harry Truman or a Lyndon Johnson, they did not embrace Wallace. The social–liberal failure of nerve, expressed in both silence and red-baiting on the Communist question, the fear of leaving the Democratic party, and the declining faith in the old political action philosophy were responsible for the subdued response to Wallace's tour. At the most, liberals expressed guarded sympathy for the tour with the hope that Wallace, by flexing his political muscles, would push Truman to the left (as they had wished during the war that his militancy would move Roosevelt to the left). Even before the national tour had ended, however, the Marshall Plan was on its way to becoming the issue on which Wallace and most social liberals would permanently divide.[31]

II

In one sense, the Truman Doctrine and the Marshall Plan were alike; both had developed out of the interaction between the cold war and the European economic crisis rather than out of any serious attempt by the Truman administration to carry forward the Roosevelt policies. Postwar reconstruction had been among the most talked about of wartime issues under Roosevelt and the most wretchedly handled foreign policy under Truman. By the spring of 1947, Europe was lost in a deepening economic crisis that reflected the Truman administration's evasion and neglect of the reconstruction problem.[32]

Secretary of State Marshall, returning from talks with Molotov and Stalin at the Moscow Foreign Ministers Council meeting in April, believed this lesson was not lost on the Soviets, who were merely biding their time until a general economic collapse in Europe would permit them and the international Communist movement to pick up the pieces. Warning the public of the dangerous conditions in Europe in an April 29 radio address, Marshall deputized the State Department's new policy-planning unit, directed by George Kennan, to make plans for European reconstruction its first assignment. In early May, Undersecretary of State Dean Acheson told an audience in Cleveland, Mississippi, that it was necessary for the United States to aid European reconstruction in order to protect free institutions (Truman was later to call this address the "prologue to the Marshall Plan," even though it specifically barred aid to those nations which could not meet American criteria of freedom). Returning from a continental tour, the State Department's Will Clayton (Jesse Jones' old protégé) composed a memorandum that called for the United States to adopt a plan to send Europe "6 or 7 billion dollars a year for three years." In the spring of 1947, reconstruction plans were in the air, proliferating, and often emanating from the oddest political sources.[33]

Throughout the spring, of course, Henry Wallace had been offering his own world-reconstruction plan as an alternative to the Truman Doctrine. Moreover, the former Vice President's national tour had coincided with public disenchantment with the doctrine. Polls showed that although a majority of Americans supported economic aid to Greece and Turkey, the same majority opposed military assistance. Furthermore, the public by a two-to-one margin supported proposals to bring the problem immediately before the United Nations. It is possible that the disaffection with American foreign policy evidenced in the popular response to the Wallace tour and in the polls convinced Truman to go ahead with the Marshall Plan in spite of expected opposition from the Republican Eightieth Congress.[34]

Presenting his proposal in a Harvard commencement address in early June, Marshall was careful to state that "our policy is directed not against any country or doctrine but against hunger, poverty, desperation and chaos. . . ." The Soviet Union and Eastern Europe were thus not formally excluded from any rehabilitation plan. Although revisionist historians have argued that no one in the State Department wanted Russia to participate in the plan and that the department's demand that the economic records of each involved nation be opened was a device to keep Russia out, this is a highly questionable analysis. The Soviets were invited to the preparatory conference on the Marshall proposal by the governments of England and France (that the specific plan should come from the Europeans themselves was rightly deemed by Americans as crucial to its acceptance and success abroad).[35] Molotov, who represented the Soviet Union at the general

European conference in Paris in early July, argued for separate reconstruction plans for each nation (thus permitting the
Soviets to gain reconstruction funds and block American efforts to use reconstruction as a way to move into Eastern
Europe). After all the Western European nations approved the
Anglo–French proposal for a single European recovery program, the Soviets walked out of the meeting and later put
pressure on Poland and Czechoslovakia not to participate. Indeed, if Russia had entered the plan on the terms of a United
Europe, the Truman–Byrnes position would have triumphed,
as the economic restrictions in Eastern Europe that the Americans had refused to accept from the first Foreign Ministers
Council meeting after the war would have been swept away
along with the possibility of an effective Soviet sphere-of-
influence.[36]

As the United States accelerated its drive to rebuild German
industry in the summer of 1947 and the administration moved
in the direction of selling the Marshall Plan at home as a way
to save Europe from Communism, the Russians grew more
violent in their opposition, awakened anti-Communist hostili-
ties everywhere by creating the Cominform, and prepared for
a world crusade against the European Recovery Program. Had
Stalin been a little shrewder, he might have agreed to participate in the plan, thus leaving Truman and Marshall to the
tender mercies of the Eightieth Congress. As it was, he inadvertently assisted the administration in making the Marshall
Plan the most sophisticated expression of the "get tough"
policy toward the Soviet Union—a policy that made the division of the world into hostile power blocs an irrevocable fact
while appealing to those for whom the dreams of One World
and a world New Deal still had relevance.[37]

For the ADA and the PCA, the Marshall Plan led to a major
role-reversal. In the controversy over the Truman Doctrine,
the PCA had gained funds and new members through strident
attacks against the administration. At a PCA Board of Directors meeting on June 28, the organization gave tentative support to the Marshall Plan as long as it was "consistent with the
principles of the United Nations and the unity of the great

powers." Alluding to the Truman Doctrine, the PCA warned that the Marshall Plan "cannot be isolated from the total policy of which it is but one element, for its character will inevitably be determined by the politics which give it direction." After Molotov walked out of the Paris conference, PCA sought to ignore the Marshall Plan for a time, attacking instead the Truman administration and the Eightieth Congress and speaking in increasingly insistent tones about the possibilities of a third party.[38]

ADA, on the other hand, quickly adopted the Marshall Plan as its own. In mid-July, an ADA petition stated that the proposal was "a conclusive answer to those who decried the negativism of the United States." Throughout the autumn, speakers at ADA dinners stressed support for the Marshall Plan and opposition to any third party. As the movement for a third party neared its climax in December, 1947, ADA issued a foreign-policy position paper reiterating support for the plan as a "constructive alternative" to narrow anti-Communism, an alternative that foreshadowed an "independent Europe" free from Soviet or American imperialism and from "the fatal choice between fascist reaction and communist totalitarianism." Old Wallace friends like Sumner Welles, Herbert Lehman, Eleanor Roosevelt, and Paul Appleby were among the signers of the ADA's foreign policy statement.[39]

Commenting on Wallace's national tour, Gael Sullivan had suggested that if the former Vice President could not be dissuaded from forming a third party, steps should be taken to "pull the rug from under him." In a sense, the Marshall Plan had done exactly that, permitting most social liberals to give their support to an administration they still deeply distrusted in order to protect a program seemingly so similar to everything for which they had fought during the war. Wallace's own struggles with the Marshall Plan reflected the conflict between its attraction for him as a social liberal and mounting pressures from the Communist component of his embattled popular-front constituency.[40]

In the immediate aftermath of Marshall's Harvard speech, Wallace supporters had praised the proposal and rightfully stressed its similarity to the reconstruction program that the former Vice President had long been advocating. In a radio address after the conclusion of the national tour, Wallace gave mild support to the plan, portrayed it as a significant advance over the Truman Doctrine, and concluded that "it looks toward an overall program, which is what I have been advocating all along." Against the background of both growing liberal praise and the PCA's very grudging support, Wallace strengthened his commitment to the Marshall Plan on June 30 with a sharp attack on Ernest Bevin's statement that it was but an extension of the Truman Doctrine. On the other hand, the *New Republic* editor bowed to his popular-front audience by arguing that the recovery program could succeed only if the United States was able to calm Russian fears about capitalist encirclement from the West.[41]

Molotov's withdrawal from the Paris conference made that unlikely. Criticizing the Soviet foreign minister's departure in a *New Republic* article in mid-July, Wallace nevertheless restated the PCA position that there was a "grave danger that without Soviet participation the Marshall Plan may further divide the world." A week later he repeated his criticism of Molotov but noted that the United States would fail to achieve peace if it did not support longrange programs for world reconstruction through the United Nations.[42]

In his July *New Republic* articles, Wallace had constantly repeated the PCA contention that the Truman Doctrine, still the essential foreign policy of the administration, must be resolutely opposed by liberals. Perhaps the first public indication that the former Vice President would oppose the Marshall Plan came on July 20, when in an interview with a reporter from Tanyug, the official Yugoslav news agency, he was quoted as saying that he would oppose the plan if it sought to divide the world into two spheres, or to build up Germany as a bulwark against Russia. (American actions to accelerate German recovery may have troubled Wallace as it embittered the Soviets.) Through August and September, however, the former Vice President said little about the Marshall Plan, following the PCA in attacks on the Truman administration and the

Eightieth Congress and beginning a new round of PCA speaking engagements in September.[43]

The American Communist party had steadily condemned the plan after Molotov's withdrawal from the Paris talks in early July, but the formation of the Cominform was apparently the event that led the Communists in the PCA to push for a stronger stand on the issue. At a secret meeting in Poland in late September, 1947, Andrei Zhdanov, number-two man in the Soviet hierarchy, called for militant opposition by Communists everywhere to the Marshall Plan. After Soviet opposition to the plan thus became final and Communist pressure in the United States grew accordingly, both Wallace and the PCA issued statements in early October opposing the European Recovery Program on the grounds that without Soviet participation the scheme would only increase the danger of war.[44]

Had Wallace decided to restate his general support for the Marshall Plan, he might have carried the PCA rank-and-file with him. After all, he was the group's major asset, and there is little reason to believe that its mass membership did not share his early sympathies for the proposal. Instead, he seized upon a compromise that bordered on the ludicrous and added strength to the contention of his enemies that he and not they had abandoned the heritage of the New Deal. Condemning the divisive effects of the Marshall Plan, the *New Republic* editor nevertheless called upon Congress to appropriate European recovery funds under the program. The problem, he maintained, was to feed Europe rather than to develop rehabilitation programs that might endanger the peace. "I am not in sympathy," he concluded, "with the present political objectives of the Marshall Plan but I am very much in sympathy with hungry people." (After his decision to run for President, Wallace would work this idea into an alternative to the Marshall Plan and present his ideas in testimony before the Senate Foreign Relations Committee.) [45]

Wallace had not irrevocably decided to oppose Truman in 1948, but the collapse of the London Foreign Ministers Conference in September and the formation of the Cominform made it unlikely that the foreign policy he had openly opposed since the Madison Square Garden speech would change in the months ahead. Possessed of a growing fear that the nation was near the edge of a new world war, he came to see himself as the last barrier between the country and chaos and as the instrument by which a new political party—one much like the Republican party of the 1850s—would effect a realignment in national politics and save the Republic from the men who had betrayed the New Deal.[46]

III

Henry Wallace had never been a party man. Nominally a Republican, he had supported Theodore Roosevelt in 1912 and Robert La Follette in 1924. Expressing irregular sympathy for the ideal of a farmer–labor party, he had attacked labor in the early twenties, only to renew support for an alliance of farmers with workers in the McNary–Haugen fight. Angered by the Hoover nomination, he had sought unsuccessfully to convince Frank O. Lowden to direct a third party based on agriculture in 1928. An independent until 1936, he had advocated the transformation of the Democratic party into a farmer–labor–liberal party throughout the depression. In the late thirties, political ambition and the reverses suffered by the New Deal encouraged him to suggest that the Democrats should develop programs to win over small businessmen and the middle classes of the smaller towns. His commitment to a liberal–labor Democratic party, however, grew as his influence in rural America declined and his identification with labor increased.[47]

During the war Wallace continually counseled his followers against forming a third party, warning that such action would inevitably divide the progressive vote and contribute to the election of reactionary Republicans. Yet, his commitment to the Democratic party was always conditional; liberals, he maintained with great consistency, must work within the Democratic party as long as that party retained its allegiance to the New Deal.

Although there was scattered and angry talk for a third party after the railroad strike of 1946, Truman's policies and the resulting debacle of the 1946 elections produced the failure of social–liberal nerve that made bold new ventures unlikely. When the *New Republic* polled liberal leaders on the question of a third party in the aftermath of the 1946 strikes, hostility to Truman was evident in most of the answers, but all of the respondents warned against any premature third party. After third-party talk flared again in September, 1946, with the Wallace dismissal, Freda Kirchwey, defending the fallen Secretary of Commerce against Truman at a meeting in Los Angeles, cautioned her audience against support for an independent liberal party. In the wave of congratulatory letters that the *New Republic* and Wallace himself received from prominent liberals after his editorship was announced in October, 1946, third-party sentiments were conspicuously absent. Indeed, concerned liberals like Helen Gahagan Douglas strongly condemned the divisiveness of third-party speculation. Although Representative Douglas had a greater stake in the Democratic party than most social liberals, her response was typical of American liberals in the last months of 1946.[48]

Wallace had dropped hints of a new political party in the last weeks of the 1946 campaign. Questioned, however, by reporters about his plans for 1948 in the aftermath of the elections, he merely referred to his previous statement that the Democratic party would either become progressive or die, and he noted that he didn't expect the party to die. Although the PCA at its inception had declared, "We cannot ignore the possibility of a new political party, whose fidelity to our goals can be relied upon," third-party interest continued to decline through the winter of 1947 as Phil Murray and the CIO moved away from old associations with the popular-front groups. Declining all PCA speaking invitations in his first months at the *New Republic*, Wallace also deprived third-party enthusiasts of the acknowledged focus of their plans. The Truman Doctrine, however, brought him back into national politics at a time when Communists were preparing to increase their influence in the PCA.[49]

During his national tour, Wallace returned to the strategy

of taunting the administration with threats of a third party. In Bismarck, North Dakota, he told his audience, "If the Democratic party becomes the war party and the party of reaction by 1948, I shall take a Democratic vacation. If the cause of peace shall be helped, I shall do more than take a vacation. The day is coming when labor will agree on a real labor party with forward-looking farmers, businessmen, professional men and scientists." On other occasions he noted simply, "If the Democratic party becomes a war party, a party of reaction and depression, I'll no longer be a Democrat." Of greatest significance in this regard was his comment in Washington's Watergate in mid-June at the end of his tour: "I am convinced by a careful study of the American political scene that a truly liberal party—whether it be the Democratic party or a new party—can elect a useful number of congressmen in 1948." [50] This was to become Wallace's chief answer to charges of vote-splitting in 1948.

Although Wallace later told Curtis MacDougall that he had hoped to work within the Democratic party as late as September, 1947, it is possible that the apparent success of the national tour and growing pressure from his supporters for a third party led him to think seriously about an independent candidacy as early as the summer of 1947. By the summer, a number of left CIO unions had already passed preliminary resolutions expressing sympathy for an independent party in 1948. Hugh Bryson, pro-Communist president of the Marine Cooks and Stewards Union, had taken the first steps toward the creation of a new party for the 1948 elections in California in August 1947.[51]

Returning to the *New Republic* at the conclusion of the national tour, Wallace left the third-party controversy in a state of flux. In the summer, a wave of anti-third-party statements—from Claude Pepper and A. F. Whitney, among others —caused him to waver in September. In an interview with Leland Stowe on September 10, he stated that he still hoped to remain within the Democratic party in 1948. A day later he told a PCA rally at Madison Square Garden, "Unless and until I am definitely proved wrong, I will stay within the

Democratic party." Privately, though, friends remembered that he was quite bitter over the mounting desertions of liberals and labor people—especially over a published report by Henry Morgenthau that Roosevelt had once considered him a mystic (stories of this kind would help set the tone for Wallace's treatment in 1948).[52]

In September third-party pressure abated somewhat as counterpressure from the American Labor party, which was fearful that it would be swallowed up in any third-party movement, compelled Communist and popular-front liberal activists to retreat temporarily from the new party agitation. Previously, the American Communists had followed the "dual policy" of support for both anti-Truman Democrats and third-party proponents. In the unions, the Communists remained on the defensive, accepting CIO resolutions condemning Red influence in the labor movement as long as those resolutions were devoid of punitive action. Although Phil Murray had repudiated the idea of a third party on many occasions between April and September, 1947, the Communists did not and could not make any serious effort to challenge him. At the CIO's annual convention in October, 1947, the issues of the Marshall Plan and a possible third party were thrashed out. On the former, the pro-Communists accepted a compromise resolution which endorsed the principle of aid for Europe without formally mentioning the Marshall Plan. On the latter question, the CIO formally declared its opposition to a third party in 1948. Hoping to continue the alliance with Murray in the CIO, the left-labor leaders minus defections would support the Progressive party only after William Z. Foster and other national Communist leaders had pressed them to do so (indeed, such pressure was needed to mount an opposition to the Marshall Plan, where their position was initially as sympathetic as that of their right brethren).[53]

Communist confusion over the third-party question was evident in the reaction of the Reds to contradictory campaigns in New York and California. After Hugh Bryson began to lay the groundwork for a new party in California, Robert Kenny, national co-chairman of PCA and an opponent of the third-party movement, founded a Democrats-for-Wallace organization both to prepare for the 1948 primaries against Truman and to offset Bryson's activities (there were reports that Communists had attended the first meeting of Kenny's organization). In New York, the Communists joined with the Amalgamated Clothing Workers factions in the American Labor party in opposing any premature third-party venture.[54]

Communist party Secretary Eugene Dennis, in an address that betrayed the Communists' drift toward and hesitancy about a third party, told a Madison Square Garden rally on September 18, 1947, that the party would continue to "promote the trend toward crystallizing a new antiwar and antitrust peoples party in the states and the communities but will not isolate itself unilaterally in a third party without substantial trade union and labor support. . . ." Interviewed in Portland, Oregon, on September 22, William Z. Foster announced that Henry Wallace was the Communist choice for the Presidency in 1948 (it is interesting to note that this announcement came weeks before Zhdanov's celebrated anti-Marshall Plan speech was made public). Yet, Foster couched his endorsement in the same rhetoric that the party had adopted when Browder was purged, that is, verbal support for the left-of-center groups within the Roosevelt coalition. Wallace, the Communist leader told reporters, was the one "upon whom the mantle of Roosevelt had fallen." [55]

Working for a third party with something less than enthusiasm, the Communists in October responded to pressure from abroad and accelerated their campaign to create a new party. When the Cominform was officially announced on October 5, party work for an independent campaign against Truman in 1948 increased. After the CIO's convention in mid-October, major Communist officials met with Michael J. Quill and other left CIO leaders to discuss ways to oppose the Marshall Plan and possibilities for a new party. It was only after the formal announcement of the Zhdanov speech in late October, however, that the Communists began wholeheartedly to press their campaign for a third party. By November, 1947, as the leading student of the Progressive party has noted, Communists everywhere were working for a new party.[56]

Communist action, however, merely facilitated what those close to Wallace, Beanie Baldwin and Lew Frank (Frank had joined Wallace after arranging his Detroit stop on the national tour) had wished for months. Neither Baldwin nor Frank was a Communist, yet both were closely identified with the popular front. Hostile to Truman since the summer of 1945, Baldwin liked to boast that he had supported a third party years before the Communists or Henry Wallace had seriously considered the idea. For Frank, agonizing over the threat of war and incipient fascism, a third party offered the only hope of saving American freedom.[57]

Realizing that the former Vice President had no chance to make a comeback within the Democratic party, Baldwin genuinely believed that the old Wallace following could form the nucleus for a third party. Even the Communists believed that the lower echelons of CIO leaders and important segments of labor's rank-and-file would desert the national leadership and support a third party. Wallace's sympathy for an independent candidacy had blossomed with his national tour. After third-party talk revived in the wake of the tour, the former Vice President never listened seriously to the legion of old friends and supporters who warned him of Communist influence in the new-party movement.

Although his hints that he would remain with the Democrats received a flurry of attention in September, it is perhaps more important to note that he had already committed himself to a new round of speaking and fund-raising for the PCA. At the autumn rallies, Frank Kingdon called again and again for a people's party, a "second party" to save the country from the bipartisan alliance of the Truman administration and the Eightieth Congress. Paul Robeson, whose ideological commitments were less flexible than Kingdon's, regularly addressed the fall meetings with pleas for a third party in 1948 led by Henry Wallace. In late November, Baldwin called a meeting of PCA state directors at which it was determined that a new party could be placed on the ballot in at least forty states.[58]

As had happened so many times before, Wallace continued to leave the day-to-day political decisions to others while he dealt with broad policy matters. After his further commitment to the PCA in the fall, his candidacy became only a question of time. In California, the persistence of Kenny's Democrats-for-Wallace movement made it imperative that the former Vice President announce his candidacy as quickly as possible in order to assure himself a place on the ballot. With this in mind, Baldwin, Frank, and Hannah Dorner met with the former Vice President in Jo Davidson's New York studio on December 2, 1947, to discuss plans for a formal announcement of his candidacy. Wallace gave Baldwin permission to prepare a statement and to arrange for a public declaration of his candidacy. In the following weeks, pro- and anti-third-party advocates fought to influence Wallace, but his decision had already been made.[59]

It is thus false to conclude, as some have, that legions of leftwing delegations, many under Communist party instructions, poured into Wallace's office in the last weeks of December and duped him into launching his campaign.[60] At the most, these delegations reinforced Wallace's belief that his old following would return when it was offered a clear choice. Along with these hopes, his decision to lead a third party was above all a response to the fear that the bitter break with Russia over the Marshall Plan and the tendency of responsible public figures to yield to the anti-Communist crusade at home could only lead to war. It was thus fitting that he announced his candidacy in late December in a speech that echoed all the hopes of the wartime liberal movement that had been so bitterly frustrated under Truman. A "Gideon's Army," a legion of the brave, would be needed, Wallace argued, to "usher in the Century of the Common Man." [61]

But many had deserted Wallace's Gideon's Army even before its creation. In August, Claude Pepper, after a long alliance with the Truman administration, reaffirmed his support for the President and stated publicly that Wallace should keep out of the campaign if he could not support Truman. Noting the timidity of many liberals, Wallace had complained in September, "Some progressives, through an outstanding naïveté and lack of political judgment, are dissipating their power with premature pledges of support for an administration which does not deserve their support." [62]

Active cultivation of cold-war liberals became part of the administration's strategy as the third-party movement entered its final stages. In a forty-three-page memorandum to the President on November 19, 1947, Clark Clifford stressed how important it was for Democrats to adopt a more liberal program for 1948—a program based upon appeals to farmers, workers, consumers, and Negroes—and portrayed Wallace as a mystic with a messiah complex. Although Clifford noted that Wallace was still able to capture the imagination of many people, the presidential aide counseled that the administration pursue a strategy whereby liberals would be used to strengthen the press image that the former Vice President was a dupe of the Communists.

Perhaps, Clifford maintained, Wallace could still be dissuaded from an independent campaign; if not, he had to be defamed. In words that were almost the reverse of the Communist party's dual strategy, Clifford counseled that "every effort must be made *now* jointly and at one and the same time—although of course by different groups—to dissuade him [Wallace] from leading a third party and to isolate him in the public mind with the Communists . . . the Administration must persuade prominent liberals and progressives—*and no one else*—to move publicly into the fray. They must point out that the core of Wallace's backing is made up of Communists and fellow travelers." [63]

While ADA partisans persisted in linking Wallace with the Communists, others battled to convince him to abandon any prospective third-party candidacy. Michael Straight, a critic of both the Truman administration and the new-party movement, was troubled by the growing pressure on Wallace to become a candidate in the fall of 1947. Hoping to get the former Vice President away from his third-party backers, Straight arranged to travel with Wallace to Palestine in late October. Lew Frank and writer Gerold Frank went along, however, and Straight was never really able to speak with his editor. After his return from Palestine, the *New Republic* publisher persuaded Helen Gahagan Douglas and Max Lerner to contact Wallace and warn him against making a third-party campaign. The former Vice President, however, simply noted that these liberals had lost their nerve and were falling victim to the anti-Communist hysteria. When Philip Hauser told him that the Communists were behind the third-party movement, Wallace turned away in sadness and said, "Phil, now you've become a red-baiter, too." [64]

During the national tour, the former Vice President had noted, "I am not afraid of Communism. If I fail to cry out that I am anti-Communist, it is not because I am friendly to Communism but because at this time of growing intolerance I refuse to join even the outer circle of men who stir the steaming cauldron of hatred and fear." Those who sought in the final months to convince Wallace to abandon the new-party movement probably reinforced his decision to run. Convinced of the rightness of his cause and the need to oppose Truman directly over foreign policy and the administration-condoned attack upon civil liberties, Wallace just did not listen to third-party opponents. When Harold Young, after a seven-year association, left New York in early December and did not return to take part in the building of the Progressive party, Wallace hardly noticed. Neither was he especially troubled when Frank Kingdon, seeking the support of the Hague machine in his bid for the Democratic senatorial nomination in New Jersey, opposed the new party, resigned from the PCA, and condemned the entire third-party movement as Communist-inspired. "You won't have a Gideon's army to support you," Kingdon had told Wallace at one of their last meetings in early December, giving the former Vice President the catch phrase for his new movement.[65]

Clark Clifford's strategy of using liberals to destroy Wallace began to work even before the *New Republic* editor's formal announcement of his candidacy. When Michael Straight told a private AVC meeting after the Palestine trip that the formation of a third party was likely, Franklin Roosevelt, Jr., of both the AVC and the ADA, hastily excused himself. The next day Ellis Arnall (perhaps, as Straight believes, at the behest of the White House after it had been contacted by young Roosevelt) repudiated any third-party movement led by Wallace.[66] After the Executive Committee of the PCA had voted in mid-December formally to request Wallace to seek the Presidency on an independent ticket, the ADA's national leadership issued a statement that a third party "would mean a retreat from American responsibility abroad, directly serving the worldwide interests of the Communist party." When the former Vice President officially announced his candidacy on December 29, the attacks on him grew more bitter.[67]

Mrs. Roosevelt, whose initial response to the Wallace candidacy was, "Oh dear," noted in her syndicated column that the former Vice President's approach to Russia was the "same as Chamberlain's with Herr Hitler." The ADA reiterated its charge that the third party was serving the interests of Communism. J. Howard McGrath, the new Democratic National Chairman, joined House minority leader John McCormack in stating that Wallace would help the Democrats by removing the Communist stigma from the party, while Robert Taft and other Republican leaders announced jubilantly that the new party, even without labor support, would be a crushing blow to Truman.[68]

Senator Harley Kilgore, who had stood with Wallace at the 1944 Democratic convention, noted that the former Vice President had "thrown political reality to the winds in a hopeless, misguided venture into political fantasy." Senator Robert Wagner, an old friend, issued a statement affirming his support of the President and the administration's foreign policy. In the campaign, the great mass of Wallace's old following would respond to his calls with either bitterness or pity. Alluding to Franklin Roosevelt, whose political legacy would become the center of the dispute during the campaign, Wagner presaged the mood of 1948 with the comment, "Yes, the angels are weeping and there is a great man and good friend of Henry Wallace who, I am sure, weeps with them." [69]

Wallace entered the campaign seeking an alliance of angels rather than the sympathy of old friends. In spite of the defections, he was confident that workers, Negroes, and independent liberals dissatisfied with the administration's domestic and foreign policies would flock to the new party. Expecting a minimum of four million votes, he would, in discussions with

Lew Frank, often more than double that estimate, believing that the people would respond at last to a simple choice between abundance and peace as against depression and war. Unable, in the face of general prosperity, to use economic arguments to combat the increasing national fear of Communism, Wallace would lead his remnant of the old popular front against the Truman administration and the new cold-war liberals. In the process, the vision of a people's century, clouded by the cold war, would turn into a nightmare of invective and abuse. Neither Wallace nor his cold-war liberal enemies would fully recover from the struggle and its consequences.

NOTES

* Remarks of Senator Vandenberg, April 8, 1947, Congressional Record, 80th Congress, 1st Session, pp. 3195-98.

1. Churchill pushed for the agreement, which the State Department opposed because of its general opposition to spheres of influence. Gaddis Smith, *American Diplomacy During the Second World War, 1941-1945* (New York, 1965), pp. 142-143. Cf. Barton J. Bernstein, "American Foreign Policy and the Origins of the Cold War," pp. 19-21, in Barton J. Bernstein, ed., *Politics and Policies of the Truman Administration* (Chicago, 1970).

2. For a comprehensive treatment of the origins and development of the Greek conflict, see James H. George, "The Background of the Truman Doctrine, April 1945 to March 1947" (Masters thesis, University of Wisconsin, 1966), pp. 3-125.

3. *Ibid.*, pp. 125-131.

4. Interview with Paul Porter, November 26, 1968; Paul Porter "The Pursuit of Peace," *Progressive*, XI (June 23, 1947), pp. 1-2.

5. For administration response to the British note, see Dean Acheson, *Present at the Creation* (New York, 1969), pp. 217-219.

6. George Kennan, *Memoirs, 1925-1950* (Boston, 1967), pp. 313-320. Acheson, who disagreed with Kennan's objections, also claims to have acted to thwart Clark Clifford's attempt to make the message stronger. Acheson, *Present at the Creation*, p. 221.

7. *New York Times*, March 13, 1947; Walter LaFeber, *America, Russia and the Cold War, 1945-1966* (New York, 1967), pp. 44-45. In a statement that summed up the disease theory of Communism that lay behind the containment policy, Acheson noted to congressional leaders, "in the past eighteen months, I said, Soviet pressure on the Straits, on Iran, and on northern Greece had brought the Balkans to the point where a highly possible Soviet breakthrough might open three continents to Soviet penetration. Like apples in a barrel infected by a rotten one, the corruption of Greece would infect

Iran and all to the east. It would also carry infection to Africa, to Asia Minor and Egypt, and to Europe through Italy and France, already threatened by the strongest Communist parties in Western Europe." Acheson, *Present at the Creation*, p. 219.

8. Freda Kirchwey, "Manifest Destiny, 1947," *Nation*, CLXIV (March 22, 1947), pp. 317–319; text of PCA Executive Board's Statement on Truman Doctrine enclosed in Frank Kingdon and Jo Davidson to Vito Marcantonio, March 16, 1947, Vito Marcantonio Papers, Box 7, Progressive Party Folder, New York Public Library; Morria H. Rubin, "The Blind Leading the Broke," *Progressive*, XI (March 27, 1947), p. 1; Walter Lippmann, Address to U.S. Chamber of Commerce, April 29, 1947, in Joseph M. Jones Papers, Box 2, HSTL.

9. Freda Kirchwey, "To the Greeks Bearing Gifts," *Nation*, CLXIV (March 29, 1947), p. 348; Alonzo Hamby, "Harry Truman and American Liberalism, 1945–1948" (Ph.D. thesis, University of Missouri, 1965), p. 173; Charles Bolte, "A Democratic Assembly," *Nation*, CLXIV (April 12, 1947), p. 425.

10. Interview with Porter; *New York Times*, March 31, 1947. Although Elmer Davis strongly criticized the Greek government in his broadcasts and opposed outright endorsement of the Truman Doctrine, he was more sympathetic to the administration's program after the ADA's resolution. Elmer Davis to Forrest K. Davis, April 4, 1947, Elmer Davis Papers, Box 2, LC.

11. HAW Radio Address, March 13, 1947, reprinted in *Congressional Record*, 80 Congress, 1 Session, p. A1329.

12. Henry A. Wallace, "The Way to Help Greece," *New Republic*, CXVI (March 17, 1947), p. 12; Henry A. Wallace, "The Truman Doctrine or a Strong U.N.," *New Republic*, CXVI (March 31, 1947), p. 12; HAW to Jo Davidson, April 2, 1947, Davidson Papers, Box 6, LC.

13. Henry A. Wallace, "The Way to Help Greece," p. 13; Henry A. Wallace, "The Fight For Peace Begins," *New Republic*, CXVI (March 24, 1947), p. 12; HAW, Address, March 31, 1947, reprinted in *Congressional Record*, 80 Congress, 1 Session, p. A1573.

14. *New York Times*, January 23, 1947. In sending a copy of the petition to a London editor, Christopher Emmet was careful to state that the document did not signal "the founding of a new liberal organization to compete with Americans for Democratic Action, which also opposes Wallace." Christopher Emmet to Guy Schofield (editor, *London Evening News*), January 18, 1947, in Elmer Davis Papers, Box 2. For an account of the Congress for Cultural Freedom, see Christopher Lasch, "The Cultural Cold War: A Short History of the Congress for Cultural Freedom," in Barton J. Bernstein, ed., *Towards a New Past: Dissenting Essays in American History* (New York, 1968).

15. *New York Times*, April 8, 1947.

16. Interview with Michael Straight, November 25, 1968; Henry A. Wallace, "Report From Britain," *New Republic*, CXVI (April 28, 1947), pp. 12–16; Mollie Panter-Downes, "Letter From London," *New Yorker*, XXIII (April 26, 1947), pp. 82–85.

17. Curtis D. MacDougall, *Gideon's Army* (New York, 1965), I, pp. 135–137.

18. *New York Times*, April 23, 1947; MacDougall, *Gideon's Army*, I, p. 140.

19. Churchill hastily corrected the report of his statement, claiming that he had said that Wallace "foregathered" with crypto-Communists rather than that Wallace was a crypto-Communist. *New York Times*, April 20, 21, 1947.

20. *New York Times*, April 24, 1947; MacDougall, *Gideon's Army*, I, pp. 141–142. French Communist leader Jacques Duclos (Duclos was second in the French party to Maurice Thorez) wrote to Jo Davidson that he and his colleagues were preparing a great reception for Henry Wallace, "who has taken over the leadership of the progressive movement in the United States." Duclos to Davidson, April 16, 1947, Davidson Papers, Box 6.

21. *New York Times*, April 24, 25, 1947; Henry A. Wallace, "Report on France," *New Republic*, CXVI (May 12, 1947), pp. 12–15.

22. MacDougall, *Gideon's Army*, I, pp. 142–143.

23. *New York Times*, April 26, 1947; Arthur Vandenberg, Jr., and Joe Alex Morris, *The Private Papers of Senator Vandenberg* (Boston, 1952), p. 351; David E. Lilienthal, *The Journals of David E. Lilienthal* (New York, 1964), II, p. 170; Remarks of Howard L. Buffet, April 19, 1947, *Congressional Record*, 80 Congress, 1 Session, pp. A2877–78.

24. For the correspondence concerning the Wallace trip, see HST Papers, OF 1170; *New York Times*, April 29, 1947; Clifford Papers, Political File, Box 19, Gallup Poll Folder; Ernest K. Lindley, "The Strange Case of Henry Wallace," *Newsweek*, XXIX (April 21, 1947), p. 34.

25. "The Peace in Preparation," *Progressive*, XI (June 9, 1947), p. 2; Alexander Werth, "The American Question," *Nation*, CLXIV (May 24, 1947), p. 624.

26. *New York Times*, April 28, 1947; Interview with Straight; Interview with C. B. Baldwin, January 9, 1969.

27. *New York Times*, May 4, 13, 16, 1947.

28. "Old Lochinvar," *Time*, XLIV (June 9, 1947), pp. 25–26; "Maneuvering Around With Wallace," *Newsweek*, XXIX (June 9, 1947), pp. 17–18; "Wha Hae Wi Wallace Bled," *Newsweek*, XXIX (June 30, 1947), p. 17; Gael Sullivan to the President "Re Wallace Situation," June 2, 1947, in Clifford Papers, Henry Wallace File.

29. For an example of Wallace's optimism, see Henry A. Wallace, "Report From the Middle West," *New Republic*, CXVI (May 26, 1947), p. 12; Interviews with Straight and Baldwin. This is Michael Straight's view of Baldwin's response. Baldwin himself was noncommittal when asked if he had entertained serious hopes that Wallace could defeat Truman in the Democratic party primaries before the national tour.

30. For Johnson's remarks, see *Congressional Record*, 80 Congress, 1 Session, p. 4696.

31. Liberal writers did seek to use the excitement of the tour to try

to suggest that Truman would be in difficulty if he did not move to the left. See Richard L. Neuberger, "Wallace Comes to Town," *Progressive*, XI (June 16, 1947), p. 4 and Carey McWilliams, "Wallace in the West," *Nation*, CLXV (July 5, 1947), pp. 6–8.

32. For a summary of Europe's economic problems, see Harry B. Price, *The Marshall Plan and Its Meaning* (Ithaca, N.Y., 1955), p. 31.

33. Kennan, *Memoirs*, pp. 326–329; Truman, *Memoirs*, II, p. 137; Acheson, *Present at the Creation*, pp. 226–230; Memorandum enclosed in Will Clayton to Ellen Clayton Garwood, January 7, 1950, Will Clayton Papers, Box 42, Marshall Plan Memos Folder, HSTL.

34. Polls cited in Joseph Jones, *The Fifteen Weeks* (New York, 1955), p. 179.

35. Acheson, *Present at the Creation*, pp. 232–235; LaFeber, *Cold War*, pp. 48–50.

36. *New York Times*, July 1, 3, 1947. Soviet official responses to the plan were, as Harry Price has shown, very hostile from the outset. On June 25, *Pravda* called the Marshall Plan a device to maintain the economic boom in the U.S. *Tass* on June 29 called the plan a device to foster American imperialism. After Molotov walked out of the Paris conference, the Soviets on July 12 negotiated a series of trade agreements with the Eastern European nations that diverted a large volume of trade that had previously gone to the West. Price, *Marshall Plan*, p. 29.

37. In this regard, it should be noted that the President's Committee on Foreign Aid (chaired by Averill Harriman and comprised primarily of America's corporate elite, with significant university and labor representation), concluded in its report to Truman that "the existence in Europe of a number of strong states committed by tradition and inclination to the democratic concept" was essential to American security. "If these countries do not," the report went on, "by democratic means attain an improvement of their affairs, they may be driven to turn in the opposite direction. Therein lies the strength of the communist tactic; it wins by default when misery and chaos are great enough." Price, *Marshall Plan*, p. 42.

38. MacDougall, *Gideon's Army*, I, pp. 183–184.

39. *Ibid.*, p. 184; ADA Press Release, December 9, 1947, in Records of the Dean of the Maxwell School of Journalism, Syracuse University, RG4.

40. Sullivan to Truman, "Re Wallace Situation," June 2, 1947, Clifford Papers, Wallace File. The Cominform and the anti-Marshall Plan riots through the world inspired fears among liberals that the Communists were returning to the policies of confrontation and terrorism of the early thirties. See "The New Comintern," *Nation*, CLXV (October 18, 1947), p. 398.

41. MacDougall, *Gideon's Army*, I, p. 168; *New York Times*, June 23, 1947; Henry A. Wallace, "Bevin Muddies the Waters," *New Republic*, CXVI (June 30, 1947), p. 12.

42. Henry A. Wallace, "What We Must Do Now," *New Republic*, CXVII (July 14, 1947), p. 13; Henry A. Wallace, "The UN, Our Hope," *New Republic*, CXVII (July 21, 1947), p. 13.

43. *New York Times*, July 21, 1947. For the crucial role of Germany in the Marshall Plan, see Kennan, *Memoirs*, pp. 332–335; for a valuable new analysis of the German question, see Lloyd C. Gardner, "America and the German 'Problem,' 1945–1949," in Barton J. Bernstein, ed., *Politics and Policies of the Truman Administration* (Chicago, 1970).

44. *New York Times*, October 5, 1947.

45. Henry A. Wallace, "Too Little, Too Late," *New Republic*, CXVII (October 6, 1947), p. 12. Wallace's article was probably composed before PCA issued its statement and was completely in line with his occasional comments on the plan through September, that is, that the Truman Doctrine remained the basic policy of the administration and that the plan without Soviet participation might further divide the world. The Zhdanov speech did not become known in the West until weeks after the Wallace and PCA statements.

46. As early as 1932, Wallace, having gone out of the GOP ranks, wrote, "Let's use the progressive leadership either to make a progressive party out of the Democratic party, or, if events prove that impossible, to start a new party." HAW to Roscoe Tertich, December 23, 1932, HAW Papers, Gifts 1967–1970, University of Iowa.

47. Wallace was in the Iowa years an independent Progressive identified with the Republicans—in the Washington years, a New Dealer identified with the Democrats. The movements represented by Progressivism and the New Deal were always more important to him than partisan politics.

48. "Liberals and the Labor Crisis," *New Republic*, CXIV (June 10, 1946), pp. 830–831; Freda Kirchwey, "The Challenge of Henry Wallace," *Nation*, CLXIII (September 28, 1946), pp. 337–339; "Letters to Wallace," *New Republic*, CXV (October 21, 1946), p. 428.

49. *New York Times*, November 12, 1946; MacDougall, *Gideon's Army*, I, p. 120.

50. *Ibid.*, I, pp. 163–164; HAW Address, June 16, 1947, reprinted in *Congressional Record*, 80 Congress, 1 Session, p. A2950.

51. MacDougall, *Gideon's Army*, I, p. 147; "Washington Calling," *Progressive*, XI (September 8, 1947), p. 12.

52. *New York Times*, September 11, October 2, 1947. The attacks by Morgenthau were in the form of excerpts from the Morgenthau diaries that ran in *Collier's* in late September and October. Curtis MacDougall relates that Wallace sat dejectedly in Pittsfield, Connecticut, before one of his speeches, wondering why Morgenthau would do such a thing to him. MacDougall, *Gideon's Army*, I, p. 204.

53. David A. Shannon, *The Decline of American Communism* (New York, 1959), pp. 132–133; "Washington Calling," *Progressive*, XI (September 15, 1947), p. 12; *Washington Post*, October 17, 1947.

54. Robert V. Kenny, Address, Democrats for Wallace, Fresno, July 19, 1947, in Clifford Papers, Political File, Box 19; MacDougall, *Gideon's Army*, I, p. 198; Shannon, Decline of American Communism, p. 131.

55. *New York Times*, September 19, 23, 1947.

56. *New York Times*, October 6, 1947; MacDougall, *Gideon's Army*, I, p. 262.

57. Interview with Baldwin; Interview with Lew Frank, December 25, 1968.

58. Interviews with Baldwin and Frank; *New York Times*, September 2, November 10, 1947.

59. For an extensive account of this meeting, see MacDougall, *Gideon's Army*, I, pp. 124–129.

60. Among the various labor, citizens, and student delegations calling upon Wallace to ask him to run, one finds the Harvard University Committee for Wallace, led by Staughton Lynd. *New York Times*, December 19, 1947.

61. *Ibid.*, December 30, 1947.

62. "Washington Calling," *Progressive*, XI (September 8, 1947), p. 12.

63. Clark Clifford, Confidential Memorandum to the President, November 19, 1947, Clifford Papers, Political File, Box 21, pp. 6, 23.

64. Interview with Straight; Interview with Hauser.

65. MacDougall, *Gideon's Army*, I, pp. 157–158, 235–237.

66. Interview with Straight. Wallace never thought much of FDR, Jr., who, like his brothers, Jimmy and Eliot, had played with the popular-front groups before becoming cold-war liberals and supporters of Truman. Wallace once told Lew Frank that FDR, Jr., was "an evil young man." Interview with Frank.

67. *New York Times*, December 30, 1947.

68. *Washington Post*, January 1–3, 1948; *New York Times*, December 16, December 18, December 30, 1947.

69. *Ibid.*, December 30, 1947; Robert Wagner, Press Release, December 29, 1947, in HST Papers, OF 1170, HSTL.

8
The Last Battle

The fact of the matter is that the Republican party is unwittingly the ally of the Communists. . . . Let us ask ourselves the question: Just why are the Communists backing the third party? They are backing the third party, because they want a Republican victory in November. The Communists feel that by backing the third party they will take away votes from the Democratic ticket and thus elect a Republican President. The Communists want a Republican administration, because they believe its reactionary policies will lead to the confusion and strife upon which Communism thrives. . . . The truth is, the Democratic party has been leading the fight to make democracy effective and to wipe out Communism in the United States. . . . We worked at it every day—and not just before elections. We continue to work at it, and not just before elections.

Harry Truman
September 28, 1948 *

Resigning from his post as editor of the *New Republic*, Henry Wallace threw himself into the struggle to build a third-party opposition to Truman in the winter of 1948. Yet the venture was probably doomed from the outset. Carrying out the strategies suggested by the Clifford memorandum, the ADA and the CIO smeared Wallace from the beginning as a dupe of the Communists and attacked his new party as a Trojan horse for the Republicans and the Soviet Union. Unable to effectively counter these charges, Wallace declined steadily through the campaign as Truman adopted the pose of a populist, reviving the fears of the depression and the hopes represented by the programs of the Economic Bill of Rights to reconstruct the New Deal coalition. The Truman victory, coupled with the Progressive party's disastrous showing, removed the last serious opposition to Truman's domestic and foreign policies from the left. In the aftermath of the election, the road lay open to NATO, Korea, and a man named McCarthy.

I

There was to be a new, anti-Truman party in 1948. At its second annual convention in mid-January 1948, the PCA formally endorsed Wallace's independent candidacy and authorized its chapters to affiliate with the prospective third party. Within weeks a National Wallace for President Committee, composed of hard-core popular fronters and celebrities from the entertainment and academic worlds, was established. "The weak-hearted liberals have left us," Wallace noted, "and we are now ready to rebuild." Defections from the third-party camp, however, grew with the creation of the Wallace for President Committee. "Our whole history," a prominent figure in the Progressive party later noted, "was of people leaving." [1]

After eighteen months as the most vocal liberal critic of the administration's foreign policy, Wallace had completely failed to develop the organized liberal–labor support necessary for any successful third-party venture. The leading journals of liberal opinion were either troubled by or hostile to his candidacy. Formal CIO opposition to the third party was expected by Wallace's campaign managers, and Rexford Guy Tugwell was the only prominent New Dealer to associate himself with the Wallace for President Committee. Senator Glen Taylor of Idaho, a singing cowboy turned politician who had provided colorful criticism of Truman's foreign and domestic policies, agreed against the wishes of his wife and family to become Wallace's Vice-Presidential candidate. Taylor's earthiness and exuberance were to prove welcome contrasts from Wallace's earnest aloofness, providing rank-and-file Progressives with someone they could relate to as a human being while their Presidential candidate, in a campaign that revived memories of the camp meeting and the Broadway road show, preached to them with righteous indignation. Taylor, however, was both a maverick and a relative unknown. He offered the party attention (unsympathetic observers, perhaps realizing his potential appeal, sought to write him off as a clown) rather than increased prestige and new areas of support.[2]

What favorable publicity the Wallace candidacy received in its early months came from the vehicle that was to provide almost half of the new party's votes in the general election, the American Labor party of New York. Leo Isacson, an American Labor party candidate, gained national attention in mid-February of 1948, when he received 56 percent of the vote against Ed Flynn's candidate in a special House election in the Bronx. Since Wallace had campaigned strenuously for Isacson, while Eleanor Roosevelt had joined Mayor William O'Dwyer in speaking tours for the regular Democratic candidate, the Isacson victory was taken by many as evidence of the disaster that awaited Truman in the fall. A closer look at the contest, however, showed that the Progressives had less to celebrate than their enemies imagined. The victory had been achieved by an established party organization which had concentrated its whole city strength in the Bronx district. Outside of New York City, where the PCA had its greatest strength and CIO–PAC was in pro-Communist hands, there was no organization comparable to the American Labor party. The institutional strength of the pro-Communist left, on which so much of the new party was to be based, was negligible outside of a few major metropolitan areas.[3]

The strategies pursued by the Communists during the campaign also increased friction within the new party. Having joined reluctantly in the creation of a popular-front party, the

15. Glen Taylor, The "singing cowboy of Idaho," advocate of the Economic Bill of Rights and postwar peace in the United States Senate, and Henry Wallace's runningmate in 1948. Here, Taylor is outside of Tucson on his cross-country "peace ride" to awaken the people to the dangers of the Truman foreign policy, Autumn, 1947. (Courtesy of Glen Taylor.)

Communists often followed the strategy of united front from below within the party, seeking to control the local organizations instead of deferring to social–liberal leadership and advocating an elite inner party upon which a mass movement would grow. (Besides facilitating Communist control of the new party, this policy produced constant tensions with non-Communist Progressives, who generally shunned the comrades in the flesh while defending their rights in principle and who believed with Henry Wallace in the creation of a broad-based party.) [4]

Communist attacks upon Wallace's Keynesian "progressive capitalism" program, along with boasts of Communist leadership in the creation of the third party, also provided problems for the fledgling Progressives. Indeed, defending party members from corrupting contact with liberals appears to have been a major goal of William Z. Foster throughout the campaign. The Keynesian menace, Foster argued in January, 1948 had as its chief example "the Roosevelt–Wallace movement in the United States." "We Communists," Eugene Dennis told a party National Committee meeting a month later, "resolutely pioneered and used our political influence to help promote a new progressive political alignment. . . ." [5]

Charges of Communist influence in the third party, of course, became the focus for most of the attacks upon Wallace. In one of his few concessions to the postwar anti-Communist hysteria, the candidate himself noted in June, 1948, "If the Communists would have a ticket of their own, the new party would lose 100,000 votes but gain four million." (After the campaign, he would point with pride to this statement, even though he opposed suggestions that he follow it up in the summer of 1948.) Earlier, he had criticized the "excesses of local Communists" in the formation of the party, a problem about which he did little, because organization and purely administrative questions were, as always, of no interest to him. Given the crucial role of the Communists in the creation of the Progressive party, an anti-Communist purge in any case would probably have killed the party in its womb. Such a purge also would have been an abject surrender to the cold-war liberals and would have removed a major reason for the party's existence.[6]

In his public responses to the Communist question, Wallace accepted the classic popular-front argument that the Reds were following his line. If the Communists wished to join in the fight for peace, he maintained in a phrase quoted widely by his enemies, "God bless 'em; let 'em come along." For Wallace and his constituency, the practical effects of red-baiting on American society continued to be far more important than flesh-and-blood American Communists. While making the standard New Deal argument that American Communism was insignificant and could succeed only in times of massive depression, Wallace defended the civil liberties of Communists as essential to the defense of the rights of all Americans and to the maintenance of an atmosphere in which the New Deal could continue to expand. "I have stated elsewhere," Wallace noted in a campaign letter to a UAW leader in May, 1948, that cogently expressed his major ideas on the Communist question, "that red-baiting has paid and is paying great dividends. While masses of people have been distracted by carefully manufactured 'red menaces' the reactionaries have taken control of the government, inflation has continued its spiral upwards, and our major economic and social problems have intensified." [7]

In opposition to the increasing numbers who followed the established political leadership and the media in freely comparing Hitler and Stalin, the Progressive party leader recited passages from a wartime United States Army manual that praised the Soviet dictatorship as peaceloving and progressive and the Nazi state as rooted in the organized degradation of the people and the glorification of war. Invoking constantly the old liberal creed that men had the right to believe whatever they wished, Wallace also decried the type of red-baiting that identified the Communists with every serious reform advocated in the nation. Only the faithful were listening, however, and the candidate's stagnation and eventual decline in the public opinion polls were evidence that Gideon's army remained in the wilderness. [8]

Wallace's early campaign was spent in search of themes to recapture his old constituency. In testimony before the Senate Foreign Relations Committee, he criticized big business and the military for perverting the Marshall Plan into a device to fight

Communism and gain foreign markets.[9] Similarly, he went before Congress to condemn the Mundt–Nixon bill (precursor of the McCarran Internal Security Act) as a crude attempt to punish opposition to the country's adventurous foreign policy, and he took pride in Representative Richard Nixon's attack upon him as a Communist fellow traveler. Since the new party's essential strategy was to appeal to outsider groups whose hopes had been raised by wartime social liberalism—organized workers angry with inflation, Negroes and Jews fighting discrimination at home, and women struggling for equal rights and frightened by the war threat—Wallace pledged in his addresses to restore price controls, fight for the repeal of the Taft–Hartley Act, enact civil rights legislation, protect and support the new Jewish state in Palestine, guarantee the rights of women in economy, and implement a foreign policy to protect the lives of their sons and husbands.

The foreign-policy or peace theme, however, dwarfed all others in Wallace's speeches throughout the campaign. In the spring, Wallace for President Committee pamphlets advocated federal health insurance programs, federal housing quotas to private developers with the proviso that public housing would supplement all unfulfilled quotas, and greatly expanded minimum wage and social security coverage and benefits. While Wallace supported and advocated all of these programs, he de-emphasized them during the campaign in favor of appeals for the election of a "peace party" that could end the cold war through direct negotiations with the Soviet Union.[10]

Sporadic acts of violence against third-party candidates throughout the country, the dismissal of an Indiana theology professor for supporting the third party, and Glen Taylor's arrest by the then-unknown sheriff of Birmingham, Alabama, Bull Connor, for violating local segregation laws provided the new party with much publicity but little new support in the early campaign. Industrial workers, many from anti-Communist Roman Catholic backgrounds, seemed to follow enthusiastically the anti-third-party pronouncements of their leaders; even in some of the pro-popular-front unions, worker opposition compelled the leadership to limit its contributions to the third party. The Czechoslovak and Berlin crises in the first half of 1948 brought anti-Soviet feeling in the country to new heights and further isolated the third party before its national convention in July. Wallace was the only certain candidate embarked on a national campaign in the spring of 1948, and he found himself invariably on the defensive on the interlocking questions of foreign policy and Communism.[11]

The Czech coup did much to undermine Wallace's contention that longrange cooperation was possible with the Soviet Union. For Americans of all political views the February, 1948, Czech putsch revived memories of Munich, and Munich represented the alliance of tyranny and cowardice to subdue freedom. Wallace's initial response that "the Czechoslovakia story will repeat itself as long as our gun and dollar policies in Greece, in China, and elsewhere on Russia's doorstep are continued," did not satisfy most liberals.[12]

Czechoslovakia, the *Nation* noted bitterly, was not to be compared to Poland or Rumania, where Soviet power had been arrayed against viciously reactionary dictatorships. Bénes and Masaryk had stood for democratic socialism, for the new Europe that liberals hoped would emerge from the war. Indeed, Czechoslovakia's relationship with the Soviet Union since 1945, that is, Czech acceptance of Soviet preeminence in foreign-policy matters in exchange for Soviet acknowledgement of Czech local autonomy, conformed closely to the model of Soviet–American detente in Eastern Europe that Wallace had proposed in the Madison Square Garden speech.[13]

In March, Wallace told reporters that the Czech coup fulfilled his earlier predictions that American intransigence toward the Soviet Union would produce an inevitable Russian reaction. After Jan Masaryk's supposed suicide, the Progressive leader accepted the Communist version that the coup had thwarted a planned seizure of power by rightists and told a news conference that American ambassador Laurence Steinhardt had issued statements during the crisis that were designed to aid the rightists. Following Steinhardt's heated denial of those charges—Wallace's comments referred to remarks by Steinhardt that Czechoslovakia might still join the Marshall

Plan—the controversy died down, although Wallace was often met at his rallies throughout the campaign with skeptical questions about Czechoslovakia from ADA liberals and other opponents of the third party. Even within the new party, as Curtis MacDougall notes, there were many who regarded Wallace's stand on the Czech question as detrimental to the party's future.[14]

The Wallace spring campaign was largely a continuation of the PCA tours of the preceding year: carefully staged fund-raising rallies that were well attended by the faithful but provided no real basis for a successful third party. More conscious of the uses of mass media than any of their opponents, the Progressives sought to publicize their case with clever party pamphlets, question-and-answer radio programs, and ersatz folk songs. The press, however, continued to be the new party's worst enemy. Newspapermen often made it appear that Wallace was the captive of a leftist "palace guard" that wrote his speeches and controlled his actions. During the press conference at which he denounced Steinhardt, for example, *New York Times* reporter Warren Moscow indulged in cloak-and-dagger hypothesizing by making a major point of the fact that the conference broke up when "an aide slipped a note to Mr. Wallace, contents unknown." (The aide was merely informing Wallace that if he didn't hurry, he would miss a train.) [15] After the former Vice President's staff had wrestled with the idea of an Open Letter to Stalin on the peace issue as a device to gain public attention (Anita McCormick Blaine, an octogenarian Chicago heiress and the leading financial angel of the party had conceived of the Open Letter idea), the release of the letter over a nationwide hookup in early May was scooped by the publication of an exchange between Soviet Foreign Minister Molotov and American Ambassador Walter Bedell Smith in Moscow that hinted at the possibility of Soviet–American negotiations to end the cold war.[16]

Although Truman backed away from any concrete commitment to negotiate with the Russians, and Stalin (whom the President would again call a likable prisoner of the Politburo

16. Wallace addressing a Progressive Party campaign rally in Nashua, New Hampshire, 1948. (Courtesy of the University of Iowa.)

during the campaign) praised the Wallace letter as a major advance over the Smith–Molotov exchange, the Open Letter was either minimized or cited as evidence that the Wallace candidacy had its origins in the Kremlin. After the Berlin Crisis began in earnest in June, 1948, the pro-Communist, pro-Soviet image of the new party was greatly increased.

Foreign policy frightened Americans, and Wallace was the only candidate who continued to discuss foreign policy above all else. Czechoslovakia, Berlin, even Tito's defection from the Cominform, all tended to confirm the administration's argument that the cold war was a quarrel, not between the United States and the Soviet Union, but between the Soviet Union and the world. By the time of the Progressive party's Philadelphia convention in July, 1948, the Wallace candidacy had declined to the point that it no longer represented a serious challenge to the Truman administration.[17]

Truman's decision to ignore Wallace, although in keeping with the strategies suggested in the Clifford memorandum, was probably the result of the new party's failures rather than of any prearranged plan. At the conclusion of the Wallace national tour in June, 1947, Gallup had reported that 13 percent of the electorate was prepared to support a Wallace-led independent party (the high point of reported third-party strength). In the first polls taken after Wallace's formal announcement in December, 1947, third-party strength was down to 7 percent. After six months of active campaigning, Wallace had declined to 6 percent. On the eve of the Progressive party convention in late July, 1948, his strength had ebbed to 5 percent. With this in mind, Truman refrained from direct attacks against the new party while permitting the ADA, the CIO–PAC and the newly constituted Research Division of the Democratic National Committee to continue the successful campaign against the Progressives.[18]

Truman, however, had gained little from the Wallace decline. Instead, his own general standing in the polls and strength against the eventual Republican nominee, Thomas E. Dewey, had dropped sharply in the same period when Wallace's strength was ebbing. Dewey, saying little and stressing national unity as his high-power organization rolled over such diverse opponents as Harold Stassen and Robert A. Taft on the road to the GOP nomination, was becoming the chief beneficiary of the Democratic and independent defections that had hurt both Truman and Wallace.[19] With the South in rebellion against the administration in the aftermath of the Democratic

National Convention and the President a definite underdog in the polls, there was little that Truman could do but follow the direction of the Clifford memorandum and wave the bloody social-security card, revive the antagonisms of the depression, and hope to win back the Northern liberal–labor coalition that the Progressives had failed to capture. William Batt, a prominent ADA leader who was chosen to direct the National Committee's new Research Division, pressed for this strategy throughout the campaign, writing to Clark Clifford shortly after the Progressive party convention that the Democrats should "present the President as a crusader rallying the people to save the tremendous social gains made under the New Deal and carried forward by his administration." [20]

After a few off-the-cuff assaults upon "Henry Wallace and his Communists," in March, 1948, Truman fell silent and permitted the ADA and the CIO–PAC to carry the brunt of the campaign against the new party. The cold-war liberal strategy was simple and devastating: portray Wallace as peculiar and pathetic, picture his party as a sorry front for Communism, and accuse him of acting to split the liberal vote and thus insure the election of a reactionary President and Congress and the destruction of the New Deal. The ADA, for example, ran newspaper ads "exposing" the front-group connections of prominent Wallace backers throughout the country while writing to "PCA friends" who might still be saved from supporting the third party.[21]

After Wallace unthinkingly told reporters that he would follow in Roosevelt's footsteps in his response to the Communist question (in practice, he was attempting to), the ADA advertised the late President's repudiation of Communist support in 1944 and continued to taunt the third-party candidate with this point throughout the campaign. In the spring, ADA reprinted articles by Frank Kingdon that the new party was Communist-inspired. When Transport Workers Union president Michael J. Quill broke with the Wallace for President Committee and made similar charges about the Communist origins of the third party, the ADA cooperated with the CIO–PAC in disseminating Quill's allegations. Along with the CIO–

PAC, the United Auto Workers, the Liberal party of New York, and the Socialist-supported National Education Committee for a New Party, the ADA sought to rationalize its opposition to Wallace and distaste for Truman with hints that a new, independent, anti-Communist third party would rise eventually on the ashes of the Progressive party. After Truman's nomination, this theme was muted, only to be repudiated fully in the McCarthy era.[22]

The Wallace campaign, ADA's James Loeb warned, had as its purpose the destruction of the Marshall Plan and was thus a blow "against the hopes and the very life of all European socialists." The ADA's most important assault upon the early Wallace campaign came in the form of a report, "Henry A. Wallace: The First Three Months," which published distorted charges that Wallace had condoned segregation while Secretary of Commerce, suppressed a report on the condition of Southern tenant farmers while he was Secretary of Agriculture, and refused while he was Vice President to listen to a delegation pleading for the life of Odell Waller, a Negro sharecropper condemned to death in Virginia. Mary McLeod Bethune and other prominent Negro leaders who were out of sympathy with Wallace's Presidential bid but who could have testified to the distortions involved in the ADA's allegations refused to heed the requests of the Progressive party officials that they come forward and give detailed explanations of the events in question. The stories spread by the ADA thus helped to give substance to the contentions of the NAACP's Walter White and the CIO's Phil Murray that Wallace had really done nothing for the Negroes or for organized labor during his long career in Washington.

Scanning Communist party literature, the ADA also strung together the quotes of Communist party leaders to produce the wild scenario that the Progressive party had its origins with the Duclos letter. Although the ADA generally held to its theme that Wallace was a confused victim of the Communists, descriptions like "disciplined puppet," which was reminiscent of the anti-Communist melodrama that regularly graced the Hearst newspapers, appeared occasionally in ADA campaign literature. On the campus, the ADA, especially fearful that the third party would appeal to the young, fought the Progressives with constant references to the supposed Communist background of the new party's youth leaders. In retrospect, one may conclude that the ADA acted throughout the campaign to keep the third party off-balance and demoralized, compelling the Progressives to engage in a defensive, self-defeating debate on the question of Communism before the very audience that should have been the nucleus for their party.[23]

While the ADA battled Wallace for his old middle-class liberal constituency, the CIO–PAC fought to deprive him of the mass labor support that both Communists and non-Communist Progressives saw as decisive to the success of the new party. Centering their appeals to workers on hard economic issues, that is, pledges to improve minimum-wage and maximum-hour legislation, curb inflation, and repeal the Taft–Hartley Act, the Progressives were often met with physical assaults and eggings from anti-Communist locals. Although Progressive party leaders were mildly disappointed when A. F. Whitney, president of the Brotherhood of Railroad Trainmen, resigned his vice presidency in the PCA and strongly denounced the new party, they had never really expected his active support. The AFL Executive Council's bitter attack against the Wallace candidacy in February, 1948, caused no feeling of surprise among the new party's leaders. Similarly Phil Murray's long-standing opposition to any third party was well known. Yet, the new party's managers had high hopes of protecting the rights of small, pro-Communist unions within the CIO to support Wallace while making use of trained CIO–PAC people, compelled to resign their positions in order to join the Progressive party campaign, to appeal to the workers over the heads of their union leadership. Besides being based on a serious miscalculation of potential third-party sympathies among the workers, this strategy grossly underestimated the lengths to which Murray was willing to go in order to fight the new party.[24]

After Wallace announced his candidacy, Murray wired all

CIO affiliates to refrain from endorsements of Presidential candidates prior to the CIO's Executive Board meeting in late January. At the Executive Board meeting, the CIO leader was successful in committing his organization to support the Marshall Plan and oppose the third party in a resolution warning that "It would be politically unwise to inject a third party into the political scene . . . a third party would weaken the possibility of electing a progressive Congress." The most the left unions could accomplish was to secure a concession from Murray that the resolution was not binding on member unions.[25]

When some of the left unions defied the Executive Board by endorsing Wallace, Murray wrote to all of the CIO's industrial-union councils and regional directors and strongly suggested compliance with the board's anti-third-party resolution. After Harry Bridges was ousted as CIO regional director for Northern California for failing to retract his endorsement of Wallace, John Brophy, an old colleague of Murray's from the United Mine Workers, the CIO's director of councils, and an ardent anti-Communist, issued a circular letter to all state and local councils stating that "The CIO does have the power, under the rules adopted by its convention, to secure compliance with its national policies by its chartered councils. . . . No evasion or compromise on this score is possible." [26]

The Brophy letter was the basis for the limited anti-Wallace purges conducted by the CIO during the campaign. In New York, Los Angeles, and San Francisco, cities in which pro-Wallace CIO metropolitan councils ignored this letter, the CIO assisted in the creation of rival councils composed of anti-third-party unions. After the withdrawal of third-party supporters from the CIO–PAC, that organization flooded union members with pamphlets denouncing the Progressive party as a creature of Communism and a boon to the Presidential aspirations of Thomas E. Dewey.[27]

"We see the strange combination," a typical PAC radio spot went, "of the Communist-dominated third party teamed up with notorious reactionaries, with the single purpose of defeating any semblance of real liberal government." Endorsing Truman without enthusiasm after the July conventions, the CIO threw itself wholeheartedly into the campaign against Wallace. The fact that intraunion purges were not widespread during the campaign was probably less a result of Murray's tolerance for the left than his fear of potential third-party strength. After the Progressives' disastrous electoral showing, the purges eventually became a torrent. By October, 1948, the Gallop poll reported that the Progressive party had the support of only 3½ percent of the CIO's members, which was, ironically enough, approximately half of the party's estimated following among the AFL rank-and-file and a stark commentary on its failure to gain a constituency among organized workers.[28]

II

Among cold-war liberals, opposition to Wallace was rivaled only by contempt for the candidate of containment, Harry Truman. Even "realists" like Arthur Schlesinger, Jr., were convinced that the President whose foreign policy they had so loyally supported was doomed. Along with major leaders of the ADA and the CIO, Schlesinger participated in 1948 in a strange boom for Dwight David Eisenhower, a general turned university president whose views on most public issues were unknown but whose chances of victory were considered certain. A minority of ADA leaders and much of the organization's rank-and-file expressed sympathy for a presidential bid by Supreme Court Justice William O. Douglas. Commenting on the Douglas and Eisenhower booms of the spring, the *New Republic* noted, "From the sidelines, we'll admit any stop-Truman movement looks good to us." [29]

The Eisenhower boom was by far the more serious of the two. After the General had issued a statement in January, 1948, renouncing the support of delegates pledged to him in the New Hampshire Republican primary, prominent Democrats and disgruntled New Dealers began to look fondly upon him as a successor to Truman. Torn by the third-party controversy and contemptuous of Truman since the 1946 strikes, Phil Murray slowly heeded the advice of Jim Carey and other CIO leaders in turning to Eisenhower as the candidate best suited to save the Democratic party and the New Deal. After seeing Milton Eisenhower, Murray arranged for an appointment with the General only to be told by Eisenhower that he would run for the Presidency if the CIO could guarantee him the nominations of both major parties. He did not, it seemed, want his campaign to become a partisan issue. Following this setback, the Eisenhower boom revived in the last weeks before the convention as party bosses Jake Arvey of Chicago and Mayor William O'Dwyer of New York joined the Liberal party in endorsing the General; and ADA, pledged to fight Truman to the last, organized its delegates to struggle for an open convention at which either Eisenhower or Douglas might be drafted.[30]

President Truman, believing rightly that his nomination was safe, showed little interest in the movements to unseat him. Paul Porter, who represented the President's interests in ADA, remembered a White House discussion regarding plans to thwart the Douglas and Eisenhower booms at the ADA's spring Pittsburgh convention. Truman advised Porter to do what he could to prevent an outright endorsement of alternative candidates but remarked that any incumbent President who could not secure his own renomination did not belong in office. Even Herbert Hoover, the President noted wryly, had been renominated, and he was in far better shape in 1948 than Hoover had been in 1932.[31]

In early July the ADA acted out the final scenes in its peculiar passion play for Dwight Eisenhower. James Roosevelt, who supported the draft-Eisenhower movement, sponsored a telegram to all of the prospective delegates to the convention, calling for an "open and free Democratic convention." In an obvious reference to Eisenhower, the signers of the telegram stated, "it is our belief that no man in these critical days can refuse the call of duty and leadership implicit in the nomination and virtual election to the Presidency of the United States." When Democratic leaders went on to offer their support, Eisenhower officially ended the boom with a letter to Claude Pepper warning that he would not run even if nominated. Although the liberal journals continued to call to the very last for "anyone but Truman," no liberal alternative to the President emerged. (Pepper quickly launched and just as quickly killed his own unsupported candidacy.) Ironically, Southern conservatives, standing behind the candidacy of Senator Richard Russell of Georgia, comprised the only serious opposition to Truman at the convention.[32]

Although liberals hailed the successful fight for the civil-rights plank at the convention, the Truman–Barkley ticket evoked little enthusiasm. In the aftermath of the conventions, the *Progressive* endorsed Norman Thomas for the Presidency. The *Nation*, although it criticized Wallace throughout the campaign for failing to take a clear stand on the Communist question, refused to endorse any of the candidates, advising its readers on election eve to vote for someone other than Dewey. While the *New Republic* continued to be the most bitter critic of the Truman policies long after Wallace had resigned as editor, Michael Straight, moving toward a reconciliation with the ADA during the campaign, finally decided to support the President as the least of the available evils. Straight, however, was hardly optimistic about the election. On election eve, the young publisher was busily contacting prominent progressives to attend a *New Republic* symposium on the problems of American liberalism in the Dewey administration.[33]

Although it still held some wistful hopes of Wallace gaining the Democratic nomination for the Presidency, the *New Republic* openly rejected the popular-front idea in May, 1948, when it accused its former editor of being blind to the fact that "the tactics, the principles, the techniques, the loyalties and the ultimate aims of Communists and Progressives are not the same." Similar arguments were repeated by the *Nation* and the *Progressive* in the ensuing months of the campaign. Stories reflecting the ADA's charge that the Soviets were using Wallace to elect Dewey also appeared in the liberal journals.[34] However suspicious they remained of Truman, the liberal magazines stood with the ADA and the CIO–PAC in the new two-front war against Dewey and Wallace.

III

The Progressive party's July convention proved to be a monument to the failure of the arts of publicity—at least to the curious mixture of dramatic indignation and socially conscious folk music that had punctuated popular-front rallies since the late thirties. Amid the televised shouting and singing of the party's young delegates, the floor fights over such burning questions as Macedonian independence, and the carefully staged convention finale—the candidates' acceptance speeches at an evening rally in Shibe Park—the party failed either to solve its serious structural problems or to overcome its Communist-front image. With the aid of a press that saw what it wanted to see, the convention did much to extend that image.

Most accounts of the Progressive party's nominating convention accept uncritically the charges of Communist domination made by James Loeb before the party's platform committee and later expanded and used widely by the ADA, Norman Thomas, and other enemies of the third party. These accounts all agree that the major decisions concerning the party's platform and organizational structure were made by Communists and near-Communists, producing party machinery designed to permit a Communist minority to achieve eventual control and a platform so worded as to be subservient to the interests of the Communist party and the Soviet Union. Despite their predominance, these views distort much more than they explain about the workings of the Progressive party.[35]

Although "pro-Communists" held key positions in the management of the convention—Pressman on the platform committee, Abt and Marcantonio on the rules committee—their policy stands were, as Karl Schmidt and Curtis MacDougall have shown, often diametrically opposed to what the press declared them to be. Pro-Communist influence at the convention, as John Cotton Brown, a student of Rexford Guy Tugwell who was given special access to the private hearings of the platform committee has noted, represented a "common left-wing system of beliefs" that made the "behavior of Communists and non-Communist left-wingers indistinguishable." Both Communists and non-Communists were committed to a strategy of direct appeals to industrial workers and minority groups; both groups sought to identify the new party with the Roosevelt heritage and to condemn the Truman foreign policy and the growth of domestic anti-Communism as cause and effect; and both saw depression and war as the logical outcome of the course then followed by the administration.[36]

Even though non-Communists in the Progressive ranks tended to view the new party as an American version of the British Labor party and pro-Communists were generally more interested in a small, highly disciplined balance-of-power party, this division, which engendered destructive factional disputes at the local level during the campaign, was not a factor in the creation of the party's national institutions. When the Wallace for President Committee met in April, 1948, to prepare for the new party's nominating convention, it agreed to organize the national committee on the basis of population rather than geography (each state was permitted to add a member for every five electors it possessed above ten). The decision to follow British Labor party precedent and hold an annual convention also had wide support as a device to assure continuity within the party. Given the unwieldy size of the national committee, the Rules Committee's decision to create a smaller executive committee to manage the monthly affairs of the party was not seriously challenged before the general sessions of the convention began, even though a committee of this kind had enabled the pro-Communists to exercise their inordinate influence in the PCA.[37]

On the point of party organization that was to create the greatest stir at the convention, the pro-Communist left initially pursued a course very different from that claimed by the press. Both Rules Committee Chairman Vito Marcantonio and

John Abt (who did most of the real work for Marcantonio) were unsympathetic to suggestions to organize the national committee on the basis of the functional groups of the party (women, labor, youth, etc.), again after the fashion of the British Labor party. Marcantonio finally accepted a compromise by which the functional groups were permitted to choose forty new members for the national committee. Although dissidents on the convention floor criticized the Rules Committee report as discriminating against the smaller states and, in accepting the functional groups, creating a situation analogous to Fascist Italy's corporate state, objections to the proposal were defeated by a show of hands.[38]

In retrospect, the organizational structure of the Progressive Party, while containing many features that made it clearly more democratic and representative in principle than its major party rivals, was far closer to the administrative chaos of the New Deal than to the centralized party machine usually associated with the Communists. Failing to provide leadership, Wallace fell back on the same faith in decentralized authority, mediated somehow by multiple committees, that had characterized the early Agricultural Adjustment Administration. Without a workable central authority to deal with mounting factional strife and party fragmentation, the most the candidate and his managers could do was to dispatch troubleshooters in futile efforts to compose local differences over party organization and tactics.[39]

Although the party's platform was far less important than its organizational structure, the document received wide coverage both during and after the convention as an abject surrender by the Progressives to the Communist line. Immediately, the press picked up James Loeb's statement, given in testimony before the open hearings of the platform committee, that "the presence of Mr. Wallace does not alter the fact that the real authority of your party is vested in the hands of men and women, many of whom followed the dictates of totalitarianism in the period of the Nazi–Soviet pact." The supposed conflict between committee chairman Rexford Guy Tugwell and committee secretary Lee Pressman was also stressed by anti-third-party commentators; and after the convention stories were spread that Tugwell, rebelling against the Communists, had abandoned the party in disgust. The ADA made much of these contentions in later assaults against the Progressives; and Norman Thomas, attacking Wallace with the same fury that third-party advocates reserved for the Truman administration, made Communist control of the Progressive convention his major anti-Wallace campaign theme.[40]

Confusion and occasional comedy rather than conspiracy were largely responsible for the final draft of the Progressive party platform. In the preconvention period, Lee Pressman authorized Wallace's New York research staff, in which Communists Tabitha Petran and David Ramsey played the important roles, to prepare a draft platform. Under Tugwell's direction, Richard T. Watt, a law professor at the University of Chicago, began to work on a second draft. To complicate matters, Paul Sweezy and Leo Huberman, two non-Communist Marxists in the party, presented a third-party platform that they had prepared the previous year, and Scott Buchanan, a party leader from Massachusetts, had his own preamble. After Tugwell met with Pressman and the legion of would-be platform writers in New York on July 17, a compromise was worked out between the major New York and Chicago drafts (which, press reports to the contrary, differed more in style than in substance).[41]

Perturbed at the problem of having to negotiate with pro-Communists, Tugwell sulked during the Platform Committee sessions and made no real effort to exercise the authority his great prestige gave him in dealing with the clever and resourceful Pressman. Only on the question of Puerto Rican independence, where his own reputation as a former governor of the island was involved, did Tugwell act against the committee majority and prevail upon Wallace to intervene personally to block an independence plank. Neither Tugwell nor the majority of the committee showed any interest in a proposed anti-Communist plank. Tugwell was also unsuccessful in blocking a plank that called for the widespread nationalization of basic industries—a proposal that critics attributed to the

Communists even though the pro-Commmunist "New York draft" had not called for nationalization and Pressman had accepted the proposal reluctantly.[42]

As the candidates to be selected were known in advance, excitement at the convention focused on an attempt by Vermont delegates to offer from the floor an amendment to the platform which declared, "Although we are critical of the present foreign policy of the United States, it is not our intention to give blanket endorsement to the foreign policy of any nation." Initially proposed at the platform committee meetings, the Vermont Resolution failed to gain much support. After the platform sessions, however, Frederick L. Schuman had succeeded in gaining Wallace's approval for a resolution criticizing both America's military and corporate leaders and the Soviet Union's policy of "aggrandizement and power politics" for the threat to peace. Although Pressman was hostile to this resolution, he yielded to Wallace, and the Schuman statement was inserted into the platform and read to the convention.

After the Vermont Resolution was introduced on the convention floor, both Tugwell and Pressman opposed it on the ground that its substance had already been covered in the platform (although it was lost sight of at the time, the Schuman addition was a clearer and more forceful indictment of the Soviets than the Vermont Resolution). A free and spirited debate then commenced on the convention floor, concluding with a voice vote by which the resolution was narrowly defeated.[43] In spite of the defeat, most of the party delegates returned home in high spirits, committed to both Henry Wallace and the cause of peace. The increasingly hostile climate of opinion fomented by the media and powerful interest groups against the third party and the old difficulties of working with doctrinaire Communists, however, soon produced the defections and the crippling decline in morale that characterized the last months of the Wallace campaign.

After the party had been placed on the ballot in all but a handful of states, the Wallaceites sought to use their new machinery to reach a mass audience.[44] That machinery, how-

ever, remained essentially the old PCA with the addition of
the Communists, activists from other popular-front groups,
and young recruits who remained with the party throughout
the campaign. The Progressives, if anything, had followed
the New Deal model too well in the creation of the party.
Just as the New Deal evolved eventually into a personality cult
for Franklin Roosevelt, so the Progressive party from the
outset based its entire existence on Henry Wallace. In competing with the administration for the support of the liberal
elements of the New Deal coalition, however, the Progressives
faced enormous obstacles.

Although the Wallaceites offered organized labor the hope
of a host of reforms to achieve permanent security and abundance, these promises could hardly compete with the existing
high wages and high levels of employment produced by the
explosion of postwar consumer demand, the administration's
renewed opposition to both the Taft–Hartley Act and uncontrolled inflation, and the stigma of Communism so assidu-
ously attached to the new party by most of organized labor's
political machinery. Roman Catholics, who represented perhaps the majority of the organized industrial workers in the
North, were especially susceptible to the latter appeal, a fact
that the Clifford memorandum noted with the comment that
"the controlling element in this group [the Catholics] is fear
of Communism." [45]

Among black voters, a crucial targeted group for the New
Party, the Dixiecrat rebellion did much to enhance the advice
of NAACP leaders and regular Negro Democratic politicians
against any support for the third party. The Progressives'
choice of Charles Howard, a black attorney from Des Moines,
to keynote their national convention and persistent attempts
by third-party activists throughout the country to recruit
Negro candidates and campaign workers and to register black
voters were ultimately to prove unsuccessful for the new
party (less than ten percent of the black vote went to Henry
Wallace). The strength of existing Democratic party machines
in urban areas where the Negro vote was considered crucial,
the militant campaign of unions like the UAW against the third

party, and the President's own actions to advance the cause of civil rights all contributed to Wallace's dismal showing among the blacks.[46]

Still, it was Wallace who did the most to popularize the race issue during the campaign, winning the grudging admiration of ADA opponents by his tour through the South in late August and early September. The heroic voter-registration drive put on by the Progressives in the South has also never received the credit it deserves as an important step forward in the struggle to attain black voting rights. Refusing to countenance segregated meetings or facilities, Wallace braved the assaults of egg-throwing racists to argue that the suffering of the Negro was but a symptom of the backwardness of the South and that the Progressive party's stand against both racial segregation and Northern monopoly capitalism represented the only hope for a new South.[47]

While Wallace campaigned in the South, Truman followed the advice of the Clifford memorandum in bringing black voters back to the Democratic party. Although Truman's private feelings about Negroes betrayed the prejudices of a border-state background and his actions were often very ambivalent, he did, when one remembers the times, take more advanced positions on civil rights than any ever publicly taken by Roosevelt. If he specifically neglected to include the anti-segregation recommendations of his own Civil Rights Committee in his February, 1948, message to Congress, his call for legislation to support the Committee's other recommendations set an important precedent. He accepted the liberal civil-rights plank and the ensuing rebellion of the Deep South at the convention, even though he and party chairman McGrath had fought to retain the conservative 1944 plank in order to placate the Southerners. His July civil-rights executive orders, which immediately followed the Progressive party convention, may have been a response to "the combined threat of Dewey and Wallace," as William Berman has argued. Those orders nevertheless created fair-employment-practices boards in each department of the government and provided machinery to eliminate discrimination (although not segregation) from the armed forces. They were the most important examples of White House action in the field of civil rights since Roosevelt's famed 1941 executive order prohibiting discrimination in the war-production industries. Aided by the Dixiecrats and the liberal–labor alliance, the President eventually polled over two-thirds of the Negro vote, a percentage higher than had ever been attained by Franklin Roosevelt.[48]

In the emerging Truman campaign the Eightieth Congress played the role that Republican leaders had assigned to the South during Reconstruction. Truman pictured the Congress as attempting to overturn the gains made under Roosevelt and restore the old Hoover regime of special privilege for the few and unemployment for the many. In a supposedly nonpolitical trip to the Pacific Coast in June, 1948, the President began to pick up his campaign style, combining earthy anecdotes about small-town life in Missouri with a studied defense of the programs of the Economic Bill of Rights and a staccato attack upon the Republican-controlled Congress. After the Democratic convention, Truman called Congress back for a special session and demanded rent and price controls to curb inflation, prompt enactment of the Taft–Wagner–Ellender Housing bill, and extended minimum-wage and social-security benefits. Following Senator Taft's advice to give the President nothing, the Republicans responded with an investigation of Communism in government, an act that earned Truman's scorn and probably did more damage to the Progressives than to the Democrats.[49]

Assured of solid union support, Truman began his official campaign on Labor Day in Detroit's Cadillac Square with a blistering attack on the Eightieth Congress and a warning that workers would deserve the disasters in store for them if they elected Dewey. Picturing the Republicans at home (like the Communists abroad) as conspirators against the security of the common man, Truman warned Iowa farmers that the grain storage crisis in the Middle West was a result of the Eightieth Congress' surrender to speculation and greed and the "first step" in a Republican campaign to destroy the price-support program. In what was perhaps the supreme irony of the campaign, Truman, whose administration had seen the de facto death of the Economic Bill of Rights, ran as a cross between a Populist and a New Dealer; clearly further to the left in his public statements than any other major party candidate in the twentieth century, he was able to combine militant support for a host of reform proposals (including national health insurance) with the fears spawned by the depression and the bitter memories of corporate greed and Wall Street manipulation that lived on in the America of the towns and the farmsteads. Dewey's carefully prepared denials, filled with the proper mixture of contempt for and indifference to the President, were politically ineffective replies.[50]

Truman's campaign rhetoric succeeded in reactivating latent party loyalties and in reinforcing existing loyalties, two of the classic functions of political propaganda. As the Democrats were already the majority party, the President, unlike both Dewey and Wallace, did not have to convert new voters. By appealing simultaneously to men's hopes and fears, Truman could recapture many small town and farm voters and, as Samuel Lubell has noted, Coughlinite urban Democrats who had abandoned the New Deal while holding enough of Roosevelt's 1944 support to win the election.[51] In this the President was aided by the ineptitude of his major opponents.

Harold Ickes' terse comment at the end of the campaign about "Thomas Elusive Dewey, the candidate in sneakers" did much to sum up both the Republican challenger's strategy and his problem. Trying to alienate no one and thus benefit from Democratic defections to Wallace and the Dixiecrats, Dewey ran as the smiling advance agent of efficiency and national unity, blurring issues in such a way that one might assume he was the incumbent President. Ultimately, Dewey's themes of efficiency, and unity would be much more important in post-1948 politics than Truman's pose as the tribune of the common people. But this did the Republican candidate little good. Dull and insipid in speech and resembling, many chuckled, the groom on the wedding cake in demeanor, Dewey failed to appeal positively to any major group within the New Deal coalition, quite literally dodging his way to defeat.[52]

If Dewey's problem was elusiveness, Wallace's was invisibility. The fall campaign merely repeated the futile quest of the spring, as the rallies became more stale, the candidate's oratory more strident, and the attendance and campaign funds more limited. Nothing went right. The lack of labor support became poignantly clear when even the pro-Communist-led United Electrical Workers Union, responding to pressure from both the CIO's national leadership and its own rank-and-file, gave Wallace an ovation but no endorsement at its annual convention in early September. When Harry Dexter White died of a heart attack after testifying before a congressional committee in August about charges of his involvement in Communist espionage activities, Wallace hailed his friend and fellow New Dealer as a martyr to the witch hunters. But the candidate's increasingly angry defense of civil liberties and his contention that there were many kinds of Communists won him no new support.[53]

The worsening Berlin crisis and the autumn drama of the Berlin airlift further hurt the Progressives. Wallace's attack upon the airlift as an attempt to obscure a foreign policy designed to rearm German Fascism for a new war against the Soviet Union appealed only to his ritualistically pro-Soviet followers. To most voters, it probably heightened the Progressive party's identification with the interests of a hostile foreign power.[54]

When Beanie Baldwin announced on September 21 that the Progressives, following a course developed during the spring and summer at the local level, were withdrawing their candidates against Hubert Humphrey, Helen Gahagan Douglas, Chester Bowles, and other prominent liberal Democrats, critics jibed that this too was but another example of the third party's decline. In October, the President's brief sponsorship of a proposed peace mission to Moscow by Supreme Court Justice Fred Vinson was leaked to the press after it had been abandoned in the face of State Department opposition. Although it came to nothing, the peace mission won a flurry of attention in liberal circles, encouraging those, one might argue, who were looking for reasons to vote for Truman and further undercutting the Progressives' position.[55]

Acknowledging the failure of their barnstorming tours, Wallace's campaign managers shifted in mid-October to their own version of the fireside chat, a series of national radio addresses that exhausted funds and failed to halt the party's decline in the polls. Although the campaign of the final weeks sounded almost like a dirge for a lost America where men yet believed in progress and democracy, Wallace still fulfilled his familiar role as prophet with frenzied attacks upon what such different men as C. Wright Mills and Dwight Eisenhower would later see as a military-industrial complex. The alliance of the generals with the "men of monopoly," Wallace argued, was at the heart of the bipartisan foreign policy. "The old parties," the candidate maintained at the conclusion of the campaign, "are run basically by Wall Street and the Pentagon who are backing the killing of thousands of people abroad. . . ." [56]

The cold-war liberals, of course, had triumphed over the Progressives before the contest began. Their victory had been sealed by the domestic defeats of 1946 and the international conflicts of 1947. Reinhold Niebuhr, whose circular letter in the aftermath of the 1946 elections had set the stage for the founding of the ADA, drafted an Appeal to Liberals in October, 1948, that represented cold-war liberalism's final, triumphant thrust against the Progressive party. Paul Appleby, Herbert Lehman, and other old friends of the former Vice President were among the signers of a document that defended containment as a national duty and fully accepted the use of the Munich analogy against the Soviet Union.

Whereas Wallace still maintained that cooperation with the Soviet Union was the true legacy of Roosevelt's foreign policy, Niebuhr argued that it was "a slur upon a great statesman and patriot" to suggest that Roosevelt would not have stood "firmly against Communist encroachments." Wallace's own foreign policy ideas were condemned as a "betrayal of free people throughout the world," the Wallace movement as "a corruption of liberalism . . . a fundamental challenge to the liberals of America—to their sense of responsibility." [57] A free world was once more in arms against a slave world in a new postwar political consensus in which men increasingly argued over means rather than ends, in which the new liberals of containment were soon to answer "Europe first" to conservative cries of "Asia first," support limited wars against massive retaliation, and wonder eventually how the ideology of the vital center had been twisted to lead their country into a crusade for freedom in the jungles of Southeast Asia.

IV

Politicians rarely admit defeat, and Wallace was no exception. Congratulating Truman after the campaign, the Progressive candidate suggested that the President's victory allowed him to "cut loose from the advice of the military and the reactionaries from the South and from Wall Street." In a post-election address to the party faithful, Wallace argued that the Progressives had really won the contest by compelling Truman to move to the left. Few people, however, bothered to look at the Progressives after the campaign except as curiosity pieces. The peddlers of the anti-Communist hysteria, capitalizing on Republican frustration and the liberal commitment to the Truman policies, went after bigger game. Rexford Guy Tugwell's almost pathetic post-election letter to Charles Ross, asking the administration to welcome errant Progressives back into the fold, was symbolic of the hopelessness of the third party's position.[58]

By any standard, the Wallace showing was a complete disaster. Although Progressive party leaders had fiercely disputed election-eve polls that their candidate would receive as little as 4 percent of the vote, the Wallace–Taylor ticket garnered only 2.37 percent of the total ballots. The four million votes that Wallace initially saw as the minimum for victory turned into an ignominious 1,157,140, less even than the number received by Dixiecrat candidate Strom Thurmond. The Wallaceites failed to receive more than 4 percent of the vote in any state other than New York or California, and even in those states the totals were well below what the polls predicted. Although Wallace probably cost Truman New York, Maryland, and Michigan, the President had won the election behind a new Democratic Congress that many saw as the most liberal since the 1930s. The only serious challenge to the Truman foreign policy from the left had been removed.[59]

The liberal journals greeted the Truman victory with the reserve one usually finds at a religious revival. The election, the *New Republic* thundered, was the most important event for the cause of peace since the establishment of the United Nations Charter. The *Nation*, adopting the President as its own, counseled Truman to remove Snyder and Forrestal as a gesture to his progressive friends. "Conservatism in America," the *Progressive* exulted, "is as dead as William McKinley." Even the *Progressive*'s candidate, Norman Thomas, who had the distinction of running behind the third party in the last of his Presidential campaigns, had the dubious satisfaction of being told by John Roche, a supporter from Cornell, "We done our best—and kept the intellectuals away from Henry Wallace." [60]

The intellectuals were through with Henry Wallace as a man; the ideas he had come to represent during the war, however, the impersonal revolution of technology and the growing together of the Soviet and American worlds, would return in the fifties and sixties under the headings of modernization and coexistence. Liberals of the Kennedy era and Wallace himself would then express these ideas in narrowly anti-Communist terms. It could be said with justice that Wallace had been the wrong man at the wrong time to lead a political movement. James Wechsler was correct when he pictured Wallace at campaign's end as "an inarticulate, awkward 60-year-old man, taking a terrible beating . . . to resurrect the shattered dream of the Popular Front." [61]

Yet, for the Progressives to have offered no opposition to Truman in 1948 would have meant to accept complete political isolation or co-optation by the administration. In spite of the enormity of their failure, the Progressives had faced the real questions confronting postwar America. They had sought the political alignment that all social liberals believed in and that was necessary to save and fulfill what was worthwhile in the New Deal heritage. They had realized that a democracy is only as strong as its treatment of dissenters and that religious and class unity obtained in the name of a mindless anti-Communism would ultimately tear the country apart or erode it from within. They had struck at those who held real power in the country—the corporations and the military. They had called for a foreign policy that recognized what the Soviet Union had suffered in the war and what both Russia and America must do to live together in the years ahead. Truman and his supporters had linked the domestic policies of the Economic Bill of Rights with the foreign policy of containment, leaving in the aftermath of the elections the Achesons to indulge their geopolitical fantasies and the McCarthys to usurp the banner of the common man. Henry Wallace, spending his final years in virtual exile at his South Salem farm, would observe the ensuing foibles and dilemmas of the cold-war liberals with faint interest, preferring instead to return to God, strawberry planting, and a celebration of the eternal verities of rural life.

NOTES

* HST, address on the Communist Question, Oklahoma City, September 28, 1948 in *Public Papers of the Presidents: Harry S. Truman, 1948* (Washington, 1964), 215.

1. *Washington Post*, January 19, 1948; Henry A. Wallace, "Third Parties and the American Tradition," *New Republic*, CXVIII (January 19, 1948), p. 14; Curtis D. MacDougall, *Gideon's Army* (New York, 1965), III, p. 628.

2. This was also true of the non-Communist left abroad. In both instances, sympathy for the Marshall Plan and fear that the Progressive party would only disrupt it were the principal stated reasons for the early opposition. (Americans, of course, connected this with the election of a reactionary Republican administration and the destruction of the New Deal.) See "Foreign Comment on Wallace," *Nation*, CLXVI (January 17, 1948), p. 74; in retrospect, Taylor claims to have recognized from the outset that an alliance with the third party would "end my political career." The struggle for civil

rights and for coexistence with Russia, he claimed as of 1963, was worth the effort. Glen Taylor to Edward L. Schapsmeier, September 20, 1963, in the private possession of Professor Schapsmeier, Illinois State University, Normal, Illinois.

3. Max Lerner in *P.M.*, February 19, 1948; typical Isacson campaign pamphlets stressed support for a Jewish state in Palestine along with advocacy of low-cost housing, increased social security benefits, and anti-discrimination legislation. See especially "Let My People Go" and "The Modern House," Progressive Party Papers, Box 10, Folder 29, University of Iowa (henceforth, PP Papers).

4. In states like Colorado, where the Progressives had significant early support from disaffected liberal Democrats, Communist steamroller tactics virtually destroyed the party. "Split in Colorado," *New Republic*, CXIX (August 30, 1948), p. 8.

5. William Z. Foster, "The Political Significance of Keynesianism," *Political Affairs*, XXVII (July, 1948), p. 29; Eugene Dennis, "The Role of the Communist Party in the Present Situation," *Political Affairs*, XXVII (March, 1948), p. 208.

6. Wallace's declaration at Center Sandwich, New Hampshire, in June, 1948, received virtually no coverage by the press. Although he returned to the statement as an example of his anti-Communism many times after 1948, Wallace wrote to a supporter who had read of the address, "I was thinking out loud and talking extemporaneously at Center Sandwich. . . . On reflection I see that they [the remarks] can be interpreted as red-baiting and that the enemy can use them in a way which will lead, sooner or later, to the denial of civil liberties and the declaration of war against Russia." HAW to Dr. John G. Rideout, July 12, 1948, HAW Papers, University of Iowa. For Wallace's defense of the statement, see HAW to Curtis D. MacDougall, September 1, 1952, HAW Papers, University of Iowa.

7. *New York Times*, May 22, 1948; HAW to J. G. Couser, May 11, 1948, HAW Papers, University of Iowa.

8. Wallace even sent excerpts of the army manual account to those who wrote him for information on his stand on the Communist question. As for Russia, he maintained that "communism is not practiced in Russia today. . . . Stalin, a good many times, has said that Russia is building a socialist state as a step on the road to eventual communism." HAW to Mr. A. E. Drake, July 14, 1948, HAW Papers, University of Iowa.

9. Although Wallace's testimony was largely prepared by pro-Communists Victor Perlo and David Ramsey, they used liberal rather than Marxist arguments in their critique. See Victor Perlo and David Ramsey, "Europe and American Aid," *New Republic*, CXVIII (January 12, 1948), pp. 15–20, and Earl Latham, *The Communist Controversy in Washington* (Cambridge, Mass., 1966), pp. 113–116, 145, for subsequent espionage allegations against Perlo.

10. Henry A. Wallace, "The Tyrant's Doctrine," *New Republic*, CXVIII (May 24, 1948), p. 11; "Fact Sheet on Housing," June 24,

1948, PP Papers, Box 18, Folder 61; "Fact Sheet on Social Security," undated, PP Papers, Box 18, Folder 61; Interview with Lew Frank, December 25, 1968.

11. MacDougall, *Gideon's Army*, II, pp. 390–391; Taylor to Schapsmeier, September 20, 1963.

12. HAW, Address, Minneapolis, February 27, 1948, p. 2, PP Papers, Box 20, Folder 73.

13. "The Shape of Things," *Nation*, CLXVI (February 28, 1948), pp. 225–228.

14. Freda Kirchwey, "Masaryk," *Nation*, CLXVI (March 20, 1948), p. 317; HAW to Arthur Hays Sulzberger, March 24, 1948, HAW Papers, University of Iowa; MacDougall, *Gideon's Army*, II, pp. 334–356.

15. HAW to Arthur Hays Sulzberger, March 24, 1948, HAW Papers, University of Iowa.

16. Smith, in the notes he used in his discussions with Molotov, had used the phrase "the door is always wide open for full discussions and composing our differences," a phrase similar to that which the President had used at the conclusion of his March 17 message to Congress announcing a three-point program of Universal Military Training, temporary re-enactment of the Selective Service law, and completion of the congressional mandate for the Marshall Plan. *New York Herald Tribune*, March 18, 1948. Walter Bedell Smith, *My Three Years in Moscow* (New York, 1950), Chapter VIII.

17. *Ibid*. Commenting on his talks with Molotov, Smith made the observation that his remarks were largely a response to Wallace's criticisms of American foreign policy and a warning to the Russians that America was united behind the administration and that the administration was still committed to its policy of firm opposition to aggression.

18. For an account of Wallace's decline in the polls, see HST Papers, OF 505, Gallup Poll Folder.

19. *Ibid*.

20. Batt to Clifford, August 11, 1948, Clark Clifford Papers, Political File, Box 20, HSTL. The Research Division, as Irwin Ross points out, became more of an adjunct to the White House staff directly involved in strategy formulation than an arm of the National Committee. (Under Batt's direction, the division was staffed by ADAers.) Irwin Ross, *The Loneliest Campaign* (New York, 1968), p. 79.

21. Truman's comments came in a St. Patrick's Day address to the Loyal Sons of St. Patrick in New York City. After Cardinal Spellman had stirred the crowd by calling for a total struggle against world Communism, the President departed from his text and announced, "I do not want and I will not accept the support of Henry Wallace and his Communists. If joining them or permitting them to join me is the price of victory, I recommend defeat." *New York Times*, March 18, 19, 1948. For a brief summary of ADA campaign activities, see *ADA World*, November 10, 1948.

22. *Ibid.;* Clark Foreman to Vito Marcantonio, August 2, 1948, Vito Marcantonio Papers, Box 7, New York Public Library; Norman Thomas, "The Broken Party System," *Progressive,* XII (October, 1948), pp. 15–16.

23. James Loeb, Jr., to Professor Albert Sprague Coolidge, June 22, 1948, ADA Papers, Box 94, Series 2, Wisconsin State Historical Society, Madison, Wisconsin (henceforth, WSHS); ADA, "Henry A. Wallace: The First Three Months" (Washington, 1948), p. 2; MacDougall, *Gideon's Army,* III, p. 657; ADA, "The First Three Months," p. 1; ADA, "Batboy for Reaction" (Washington, 1948), p. 1.

24. A. F. Whitney to Rexford Guy Tugwell, June 18, 1948, in HST Papers, OF 1170; Interview with Baldwin; Interview with John Abt, January 3, 1969.

25. "The Shape of Things," *Nation,* CLXVI (January 31, 1948), pp. 113–115; Press Release, CIO Executive Board Meeting, Washington, January 22, 1948, p. 4, Philip Murray Papers, Box A4-45, Catholic University of America, Washington, D.C.

26. James Wechsler in *New York Post,* January 24, 1948; Oral History interview with John Brophy, December 23, 1963, pp. 946–949, in John Brophy Papers, Box A5-38, Catholic University of America, Washington, D.C.; MacDougall, *Gideon's Army,* II, p. 320.

27. *Ibid.,* pp. 320–322.

28. CIO–PAC Recording, undated, in Murray Papers, Box A4-56; Executive Officer Recommendations to the CIO Executive Board, August 30–31, 1948, p. 5, in Clifford Papers, Political File, Box 20; Milton Edelman, "The Labor Vote in '48; An Analysis," *Nation,* CLXVII (October 23, 1948), p. 465.

29. Interview with Arthur Schlesinger, Jr., November 18, 1968; "The Man Nobody Knows," *New Republic,* CXVIII (April 12, 1948), p. 5.

30. Interview with James Carey, February 18, 1948. To some the possibility of an Eisenhower candidacy was a useful ploy to keep the Republicans from nominating an ultraconservative candidate like Robert Taft. Elmer Davis to Milton Eisenhower, May 4, 1948, Elmer Davis Papers, Box 2, LC.

31. Interview with Paul Porter, November 25, 1968. At the ADA Pittsburgh convention, sixteen of the forty-seven chapters represented announced for Eisenhower, fourteen for Douglas, and two for Truman (under the circumstances, Porter considered the convention's decision not to endorse anyone the best that could be done for Truman). Batt to Clifford, April 15, 1948, Clifford Papers, Political File, Box 20.

32. *ADA World,* June 5, 1948; *New York Times,* July 4, 8, 11, 1948.

33. "The Choice For President," *Progressive,* XII (August, 1948), pp. 5–8; "How Do You Separate Them, Mr. Wallace?" *Nation,* CLXVII (September 4, 1948), p. 246; "Your Mandate," *Nation,* CLXII (October 30, 1948), p. 479; Interview with Michael Straight, November 25, 1968; Straight to Oscar Chapman, November 2, 1948, Oscar Chapman Papers, Box 85, HSTL.

34. "If Not Truman, Who?" *New Republic*, CXVIII (May 17, 1948), p. 27; Percy Winner, "Russia Has A Candidate," *New Republic*, CXIX (October 4, 1948), pp. 17–21; William B. Hesseltine, "The Perversion of Progressivism," *Progressive*, XII (September, 1948), pp. 5–8.

35. For an account of the party convention that presents in concise form that Communist-front view held by most of the press at the time and by most scholars afterwards, see Sumner Welles in *Washington Post*, August 17, 1948.

36. MacDougall, *Gideon's Army*, II, pp. 506–586; Karl M. Schmidt, *Henry A. Wallace: Quixotic Crusade, 1948* (Syracuse, 1960), pp. 180–201; quoted in *ibid.*, p. 256.

37. Helen Fuller, "The New Party Meets," *New Republic*, CXVIII (April 19, 1948), p. 10; MacDougall, *Gideon's Army*, II, p. 521; Interview with Baldwin.

38. Interview with Abt; MacDougall, *Gideon's Army*, II, pp. 521–523.

39. Lew Frank occasionally served in this troubleshooter role. Interview with Frank.

40. *New York Times*, July 23, 1948; *Washington Post*, August 28, 1948; Norman Thomas, "The Progressive Party," September 19, 1948, Copy in HAW Papers, University of Iowa. Tugwell eventually voted for Truman, although he never repudiated the Progressive Party. Interview with Baldwin.

41. In addition to the Brown dissertation, the tangled history of the platform drafts is most fully presented in MacDougall, *Gideon's Army*, II, 534–562.

42. *Ibid.*, 546, 556–561. Cf. David A. Shannon, *The Decline of American Communism* (New York, 1959), pp. 164–182.

43. MacDougall, Gideon's Army, II, pp. 570–579. On the eve of the convention, a Gallup poll showed that 51 percent of the people believed that the new party was "run by Communists," 21 percent did not, and 28 percent had no opinion. *Washington Post*, July 21, 1948.

44. Wallace failed to get on the ballot in Nebraska, Oklahoma, and Illinois (the Illinois case was finally decided against the Progressives by the Supreme Court). In Ohio, Wallace electors were permitted to run on the ballot without any party label, compelling third-party voters to mark their ballots for twenty-one separate electors. Given Truman's narrow victories in Ohio and Illinois, it is possible that the Progressives, had they been fully on the ballot in those states, might have denied him the Presidency.

45. Schmidt, *Henry A. Wallace*, pp. 245–246; Ross, *Loneliest Campaign*, p. 254; Clifford Memorandum, November 19, 1947, Clifford Papers, Political File, Box 21.

46. Schmidt, *Henry A. Wallace*, pp. 245–246.

47. For an example of Wallace's speeches in the South, see HAW, Address, Norfork, Va., August 29, 1948, PP Papers, Box 21, Folder 80.

48. See Barton J. Bernstein, "The Ambiguous Legacy: The Truman Administration and Civil Rights" pp. 281–292, in Barton J. Bernstein, ed., *Politics and Policies of the Truman Administration* (Chicago, 1970); William C. Berman, "The Politics of Civil Rights in the

Truman Administration" (Ph.D. thesis, Ohio State University, 1963), pp. 107–111. Wallace said of Truman's executive order that it "says nothing, promises nothing, does nothing, and leaves segregation intact." *Ibid.,* p. 112.

49. Harry S. Truman, *Memoirs* (Garden City, 1956), II, pp. 211–212; R. Alton Lee, "The Turnip Session of the Do Nothing Congress: Presidential Campaign Strategy," *Southwestern Social Science Quarterly,* XLIV (December, 1963), pp. 256–257.

50. *Washington Post,* September 7, 1948; Ross, *Loneliest Campaign,* pp. 183, 199–200. As the Assistant Publicity Director of the Democratic National Committee remembered, everything was done to portray Truman as the champion of the people against Dewey, the calculating politician. When Dewey, whose fits of temper were well-known to the reporters who followed him, gained some unfavorable publicity with some nasty comments about his train engineer, Truman went out of his way to say some nice things about train engineers. Interview with Samuel C. Brightman, December 7, 1966, TLOHC, HSTL.

51. These definitions of the role of political propaganda in an election campaign are taken from Paul F. Lazarsfeld, et al., "The People's Choice," pp. 148–164, in William Peterson, ed., *American Social Patterns* (Garden City, N.Y., 1956); Samuel Lubell, *The Future of American Politics* (Third Edition, New York, 1965), p. 203.

52. Harold Ickes, Press Release of Radio Speech, October 17, 1948, in Clifford Papers, Political File, Box 19.

53. HAW, Address, United Electrical Workers Convention, September 6, 1948, PP Papers, Box 2, Folder 74; HAW Address, Bridgeport, Connecticut, August 21, 1948, PP Papers, Box 20, Folder 74. Mrs. White wrote to Wallace that "Harry felt so badly because he could be of no use to you in your campaign" but that his death had made him of use to the party. Mrs. Harry Dexter White to HAW, September 14, 1948, HAW Papers, University of Iowa.

54. HAW, Address, Newark, N.J., October 24, 1948, PP Papers, Box 21, Folder 80. Although it was occasionally noted during the campaign that Wallace, in private discussions with small groups, took a more moderate position than he did in his speeches (a fact generally cited as evidence that he was the prisoner of the Communists), his principal speechwriter remembered that he considered the final foreign policy statements *too mild* and had to be restrained from further attacks on the administration. Interview with Frank.

55. "New Party's New Policy," *Nation,* CLXVII (October 2, 1948), p. 359; Interview with Baldwin; Ross, *Loneliest Campaign,* pp. 212–215.

56. HAW, Radio Address, "Peace and the U.N.," October 24, 1948, p. 4, Box 20, Folder 74; HAW, Address, Newark, N.J., October 24, 1948, p. 5, PP Papers, Box 21, Folder 80.

57. Loeb to Leon Henderson, September 21, 1948, ADA Papers, Series 2, Box 94; "Appeal to the Liberals of America," enclosed in Harold Ickes to Oscar Chapman, October 14, 1948, Chapman Papers, Box 85.

58. HAW to HST, November 5, 1948, HST Papers, PPF 1917, Folder

537; HAW, Address, November 13, 1948, p. 1, PP Papers, Box 21, Folder 76; Tugwell to Ross, November 15, 1948, HST Papers, OF 1072, Folder 394. In an angry reply to a *New York Herald Tribune* post-election editorial denouncing him as a "well-labelled prisoner" of the Communists, Wallace argued that the Progressives had used the peace issue to slow down the bipartisan war policy and had compelled Truman "to don the mantle of Roosevelt and promise the American people a return to the New Deal." HAW to *New York Herald Tribune*, November 8, 1948, copy in HAW Papers, University of Iowa.

59. Schmidt, *Henry A. Wallace*, pp. 233, 329, 334–335. Samuel Lubell's analysis of the third party's electoral failure is very valuable even though his bitter animosity toward the Progressives shows through. See Lubell, *Future of American Politics*, pp. 196–204.

60. "The Ruhr Is Labor Business," *New Republic*, CXIX (December 6, 1948), p. 5; "The Reconstruction," *Nation*, CLXVII (November 20, 1948), p. 564; "The Meaning of the Month," *Progressive*, XII (December, 1948), p. 3; Roche to Thomas, undated, Thomas Papers, Box 57, New York Public Library.

61. James A. Wechsler, "My Ten Months With Wallace," *Progressive*, XII (November, 1948), p. 4.

9

The Twenty-First Century

First we must remember that the Democrats inherited Viet Nam from the Republicans who in turn had inherited their policy from Truman. Truman and Dulles took the steps which will make the USA bleed from every pore.

HAW to James Pappathanasi
July 4, 1965 *

After 1948, as America's leaders more fully prepared the citizenry for a longrange struggle against the people's revolution, Henry Wallace slowly adjusted himself to the anti-Communism of the men who had vanquished him. Leaving the Progressive party after the outbreak of the Korean War, he soon denounced the American Communists, condemned the Soviet Union, and by the end of the 1950s warned almost hysterically of the racial and political threat of Communist China. Even though he remained committed to a program of peace through progressive capitalism, Wallace's final years underscored the tragic consequences of the social–liberal attempt to combine private enterprise with humanitarian reform. The leaders of the America he left at his death in the fall of 1965 were in the early stages of an armed struggle against the Com-

mon Man at home and abroad, a struggle that made prophetic
a warning he had given the nation in 1943: "Our feeling of responsibility must match our economic power or the very
magnitude of that power will rot us inside." [1]

I

Defeat for the Progressives was total. Although Wallace
had asserted in the last days of the campaign that Truman
would be "the worst-beaten candidate in history," election
night returns quickly belied this prediction. Bitterly disappointed, tired and numb, Wallace muttered to his colleagues,
"that lying son of a bitch," as a triumphant Truman greeted
the television cameras. In response to an election-eve report
that he would abandon the Communists and repudiate the
Progressive party within six months, the third-party leader
told friends, "I couldn't even if I wanted to." [2]

"We have gained time in which to gather strength against
the breeders of insecurity and war . . . ," Wallace wrote to
Jo Davidson weeks after the election, but time was now working against the Progressives. Truman's pledge in his inaugural
address to fulfill the program of the Economic Bill of Rights
under the new slogan of the Fair Deal coincided with the
administration's successful struggle to obtain congressional
approval for the capstone of its foreign policy, the North Atlantic Treaty Organization. For most of the remaining Progressives, the anti-Soviet collective security system created by
the NATO treaty constituted a conscious and complete rejection of the United Nations, a return to the law of the
jungle.[3]

At peace rallies throughout the country in the spring of
1949, Wallace condemned the NATO pact as a harbinger of
military Fascism and world war, a perversion of everything
for which the war had been fought. "The symbols of collective security," he noted bitterly, "are being used to build collective aggression, the unity of the great nations against fascism
is becoming a unity of the nations against communism, the

ideals of the defeated have been taken over by the victors." [4]

In defeat, Wallace began to wallow in a kind of paralytic nostalgia, to assume the pose of a dishonored prophet. Testifying before the Senate Foreign Relations Committee in May, 1949, against the NATO pact, he remembered that "two years ago when President Truman announced the Truman Doctrine of containing Russia and Communism at every point, I predicted that it would cause us to bleed from every pore." [5]

Retreating to his farm at South Salem, Wallace listened impassively to his wife's denunciations of the Progressive party, and he greatly limited his participation in political activities. After Robert Wagner retired from the Senate in 1949, he refused to enter the New York senatorial contest between Herbert Lehman and John Foster Dulles. Vito Marcantonio's candidacy in the 1949 New York mayoralty race received a pro forma endorsement rather than active support. Wallace, the *New York Post* noted, felt increasingly isolated in the third party and remained in it only out of a sense of loyalty to the surviving non-Communist Progressives.[6]

In the years following the Madison Square Garden speech, Wallace had constantly asked, "Where are the great liberal voices who rallied to Roosevelt's and Willkie's one world at peace with Russia. . . ?" After Truman's victory, he could no longer delude himself about where his old constituency had gone. Liberals, he told a Progressive party audience, were "acquiescing in an arms program as though the arming of Europe were a new WPA with guns . . . underwriting reaction in foreign policy and waiting for the promised crumb of domestic reform that cannot be delivered. . . . They have lost the right to speak for the conscience of America." [7]

Liberal identification with Truman and the Democrats, Wallace believed, had produced the NATO disaster. The Democrats, he argued in October, 1949, were lost in "a fool's paradise of temporary business prosperity. . . ." Whereas the Progressives remained the true heirs of the New Deal and disciples of a welfare state, "the Democrats who claim that they have already created a welfare state have fooled themselves. What they have done is to use their damnable foreign policy based on fear and hate to scare Congress into deficit financing of a huge foreign aid program." [8]

Wallace thus grasped the problems posed by containment, but he offered few solutions save New Deal clichés, old liberal nationalism, and a continued faith that the country could find an independent course between doctrinaire ideologies and authoritarian systems. For a progressive, he told a Philadelphia rally in October, 1949, "final authority must be in his sense of the unfolding future." The vision of a world New Deal, "the concept of old-fashioned Americanism moving to bring about a sense of responsibility for the whole world," still loomed large in his speeches as a sensible alternative to the closed systems in competition for international hegemony, that is, monopoly capitalism, British colonialism, Roman Catholicism, and Russian Communism. Marxist analyses of history, the Progressive party leader said with increasing irritation, were irrelevant to the American experience.[9]

Wallace pointed out to Paul Sweezy and other Marxists in the Progressive party that Roosevelt had been too intelligent to use self-defeating terms like right, left, class struggle, and mass action to define his program. Rather, he had been satisfied to call himself a liberal. Although the Progressive leader was willing to admit that the New Deal had failed to achieve recovery short of war, he continued to express his criticism of Roosevelt in Keynesian rather than Marxist terms, maintaining that a comprehensive use of public investment rather than the elimination of private investment held the key to prosperity. (In 1949, also, he began to doubt the predictions of Progressive party economists that a depression was imminent—a prediction that probably represented the only hope for the party's revival.) America, he told a Chicago meeting in November, 1949, would never accept Socialism or Communism; at the most, Americans would turn in times of depression to extensive business–government cooperation and, failing that, to the creation of a welfare state. Without an "outraged peasantry . . . ready for the kill" or a proletariat prepared to seize the state, ideas of imminent revolution in America were nonsense.[10]

Wallace's last attempt to reshape the Progressive party high-lighted the party's decay following the 1948 elections and his own growing bitterness over the role of the Communists in the party. "If people can say with considerable justification," he wrote to New Jersey Progressive party leader James Imbrie in December, 1949, "that we are a Communist front, we are through. The trouble is that we here in the U.S. are being made a tail to the struggle which is going on in Europe." [11]

When the Progressive party held its second annual convention in February, 1950, Wallace pressed for a stronger stand on the Communist issue, even though fewer than half of the delegates who had attended the original nominating convention were present and the party had failed to strike roots anywhere in the nation. In his keynote address to the convention, Wallace decried the party's failure to adopt the Vermont Resolution in 1948, emphasized the Progressives' need to convince the people that their membership was predominantly non-Communist, and called upon Communists within the party to serve American rather than Soviet interests. Although the party's leadership—probably reflecting Communist influence to a much greater degree than had been true during the Presidential campaign—generally accepted Wallace's recommendations, few took notice except ADA which, out of habit perhaps, issued a statement condemning the Progressive party as a Communist-front group. Speculation continued as to when Wallace would leave the party.[12]

Wallace was probably wondering about the same thing. Later, he would remember that Soviet terrorism against old liberals and socialists in Czechoslovakia in 1949 had led him to begin to realize that the Russians were seeking to export their system by force rather than responding to threats from the West. Although these statements may have been hasty, post-facto rationalizations of his separate peace with the advocates of containment, he did note in 1949 that the Truman foreign policy, if not checked, might become a self-fulfilling prophecy, transforming "the Russians and the Communists into the preachers of hate that their [the administration's] propaganda has so long proclaimed." Through 1949 and early

1950, his correspondence with party leaders and friends displayed a search for some way to disengage from the Communists. After Claude Pepper fell before the red-baiting attacks of George Smathers in the 1950 Florida Democratic senatorial primary, Wallace sent his condolences, reminding his old friend that "you and I want nothing to do with totalitarianism of either the right or the left." [13]

When the call of party militants in 1949 for mass mobilization to protect Progressive rallies led to clashes with veterans groups protesting Paul Robeson's right to hold a meeting at Peekskill, New York, Wallace expressed private scorn for the "Peekskill boys" who countenanced the use of force to achieve their ends. After Fulton Lewis, Jr., told his radio audience that General Leslie Groves had accused Wallace in secret testimony before the House Committee on Un-American Activities of advocating the shipment of uranium oxide and uranium nitrate to the Soviet Union during the war, the former Vice President engaged a lawyer, wrote to Albert Einstein and others in an effort to obtain evidence to clear his name, and strongly denied Lewis' allegations in testimony before the committee. Dining with Michael Straight in early 1950, Wallace suddenly blurted out that he did not want to live in America anymore. The type of treatment he was being subjected to was hardly what a citizen, much less a former Vice President, should expect.[14]

Except for some old friends from the Department of Agriculture, he had become an unperson to the New Dealers who had stood with him during the Roosevelt years. His sacrifice moreover was productive of nothing. When F. O. Matthiessen, the renowned literary historian and a Progressive party member, committed suicide in the spring of 1950, he symbolized the plight of the party in the face of its own contradictions and the anti-Communist hysteria. Among his effects, the press reported, Matthiessen had left a note saying that he had been a Christian and a socialist and was deeply troubled by events in the world. Wallace was also a devout Christian, but he had never been a socialist, and his defense of the world New Deal and the social–welfare state in the utilitarian terms of prosperity and stability was no real alternative to a cold war that

successfully provided prosperity and stability. Holding on to
the ruins of the old social–liberal ideology, Wallace was completely exhausted by the spring of 1950.[15]

When the United Nations Security Council responded to
the outbreak of fighting in Korea in June, 1950, with a condemnation of North Korea as the aggressor and a call for
armed resistance against its incursions into South Korea, it
paved the way for Wallace to make his peace with the containment foreign policy. Convinced that the North Korean
attack had occurred at the behest of the Soviet Union, the
former Vice President was now able to do what his cold-war
liberal antagonists had begun to do four years before, to transfer the wartime ideals he had done so much to popularize—
resistance to external aggression and support for the United
Nations—to the struggle between Russia and America.[16] The
Korean crisis permitted him to directly challenge the Communists within the party over an issue of foreign policy.

At an emergency meeting of the Progressive party's executive committee on July 6, 1950, a rift developed between
Wallace and the rest of the committee because the former Vice
President objected to a resolution criticizing the Security
Council's call for armed resistance to the North Koreans and
opposing any UN action until Russia returned to the Council
and China was ousted in favor of the new Communist regime
on the mainland. When another meeting on July 8 failed to
compose these differences, Lillian Helman moved that a special
subcommittee be established to revise the party's Korea resolution in consultation with Wallace. The former Vice President
gave his tentative approval to a revised draft after the subcommittee met with him on July 10, but he called Beanie Baldwin
the following morning and demanded that the resolution omit
any criticism of Truman's action in sealing off Formosa, call
for a prompt return by the Soviets to the Security Council,
and support the Council's actions in Korea pending the return
of the Russians. When the executive committee rejected these
revisions, Wallace informed Baldwin that he would issue a
separate statement on the Korean question.[17]

Released on July 15, 1950, along with the Progressive party's official resolution, Wallace's statement upheld the United Nations' condemnation of North Korea as an aggressor and contended, "Undoubtedly the Russians could have prevented the attack and undoubtedly they could now stop the attack any time they wanted." In a final comment on the crisis that provided an apt introduction to the political climate of the 1950s, the former Vice President concluded, "the time has passed for trying to find out who is to blame." [18]

After the release of his Korean statement, Wallace received a torrent of letters from rank-and-file Progressives in support of his position, but emergency meetings of the state party organizations, controlled largely by the pro-Communist left, endorsed the stand of the national committee. In a letter to Anita McCormick Blaine, he conceded, "I do hate war with all my heart but when my country gets into war and that war is sanctioned by the United Nations, I have to support my country and the U. N. I am afraid the Progressive party people will not go along with me." When it became obvious in August that the Progressives' national leadership would not go along with him, Wallace resigned from the party. Many of the remaining non-Communist leaders joined him, as did Lee Pressman, whose desertion was indicative of how little was left of the party.[19]

Not known for their sentimentality, the Communists did Wallace the one favor of savagely condemning his stand on Korea. In October, 1950 the *Moscow Literary Gazette* listed the former Vice President among the "enemies of humanity" and concluded that no one had been more anxious "at the most convenient and advantageous moment to throw off their masks than the political businessman, Henry Wallace. . . . " [20] Wallace had not thrown off a mask; rather, the ideas that he had come to represent had failed to gain a viable constituency in the political wars of the 1940s. Seeking somehow to retain the program he had put forth in the Century of the Common Man speech, realizing perhaps that it was his one hope of historical vindication, Wallace now sought to accommodate a truncated version of the world New Deal to the exigencies of cold-war politics and popular anti-Communism.

II

The common man had failed. The new social machinery had not been perfected. The cooperative commonwealth (the secular expression of the Kingdom of God on Earth) had not flowed freely from the hearts of the people. The hope for unity between American enterprise and the aspirations of oppressed peoples everywhere now stood naked in a bipolar world. Hostile to limitless military expenditures, believing still that the world faced a choice between a "century of blood or milk," Wallace began to modify his ideas to conform to the national temper.[21]

The politicians appealed to both the smug and the pietistic with attacks against Communism as Godless. As a scion of evangelical Protestantism, Wallace found it relatively easy to enlist the Diety as an ally in the cold war. The politicians also equated Communism with slavery, a theme which brought back memories of the Century of the Common Man speech, but one which could be recruited for the struggle against Stalin if one accepted the Communist–Fascist equation of the mass media, the Truman administration, and the cold-war liberals. The politicians, of course, had no need to say anything about the people's revolution or the common man. (In the early 1950s films like "It's a Big Country," the common man in the ethnic and religious guise of his choice, became the bearer of Americanism against Communism, the hero of a spiritually armed melting pot.) Seeking to develop a rationale for peace through progressive capitalism in the 1950s, Wallace was compelled largely to repudiate both the people's revolution and the common man.

This is not to say that Wallace ever again played a really active role in public life. Although he remained keenly interested and involved in activities designed to raise agricultural productivity in the underdeveloped world, most of his time was spent at his South Salem farm, where he carried out experiments in the crossbreeding of different strains of chickens and various types of strawberries or in travels related to those experiments. His occasional addresses were made before church audiences, scientific groups, and business and social clubs. His search for respectability in a nation embarked upon a crusade to maintain the status quo against a hated ideology became something of a half-hearted burlesque of the political rhetoric in the Truman-McCarthy era. In some respects, one can argue that his occasional quotations from the geopolitician Sir Halford MacKinder and renewed interest in the cyclical theories of history espoused by Sir Flinders Petrie and Oswald Spengler were logical expressions of the balance-of-power sophistry that was then so much in vogue in the government and the universities, providing a kind of higher superstition for those who told the people that they fought to defend freedom and the West.[22] Even his nightmarish resurrection of the Yellow Peril carried to a logical extreme the policy of men who considered it a matter of national honor to ignore the existence of the legitimate government of one-fifth of mankind.

Gradually, Wallace became an example of what he had dimly seen and hopelessly fought against in the desperate years after Roosevelt's death, the triumph of the American Century in the shadows of the anti-Communist crusade. In an address to a church audience in New York City in November, 1950, he conceded that Communism was "far more dangerous than fascism," that it had led the common man on a march of destruction, but that it must be fought with economic and psychological rather than military weapons. Although he still advocated negotiations with the Russians, Wallace, in an obvious and painful allusion to the Century of the Common Man speech, proclaimed his conviction that the United States, in spite of the McCarran Internal Security Act, constituted a free world and the Soviet Union, whatever her social advances, represented a slave world.[23]

Confessions came more easily after that. In December, 1950, Wallace was quoted as saying that he believed the Soviets were out to dominate the world. He wrote articles bearing such titles as "Where I Was Wrong" and "How I'd Stop the March of Stalin" to justify his actions after Roosevelt's death as an attempt to reach an accommodation with Russia before the Soviets grew strong enough to challenge the United States. Anxious to defend what remained of his reputation, he testified before the McCarran Committee when it investigated the Institute of Pacific Relations in 1952 and saddened many of his old admirers by defending his 1944 mission to China in anti-Communist terms and implicitly repudiating the sympathy he had previously shown for the Chinese revolution.[24]

When Truman's notorious diary entry for September 19, 1946, was published in William Hillman's *Mr. President* in 1952, Wallace threatened to sue the President if the references to him as a pacificist and a Communist dupe were not retracted. After the *Saturday Evening Post* published reports of Communist activity in the Department of Agriculture in the thirties, Wallace wrote an indignant letter to the editor denying that Communists had played any role in policy-making. In a letter to Presidential assistant Joseph Short in April, 1952, he noted, "to the best of my knowledge I never met Harold Ware [the leader of the Communist cell in the department]. . . . A USDA man told me last week that in 1934 Ware was very anti-New Deal and said that AAA was working to postpone some sort of uprising among negroes and sharecroppers." [25]

Negroes and sharecroppers were no longer the custodians of the people's century. Communism, Wallace argued throughout the fifties, "brutalizing the souls of its adherents, now directed the common man of color" in its war against the developed nations. As early as 1942, he told a Boston church group in March, 1953, Roosevelt had "feared that the common man of Asia might march against the white man." Now combining the program of the people's century with the vision of Henry Luce, he advocated the use of American capital through the United Nations to detach China from the Soviet orbit and to create a world economic community that would thwart the forces of Communist revolution. In the tradition of the cold-war liberals who followed the hounds of containment, Wallace warned that if the underdeveloped nations "do not learn from us, they will learn from the Communists." [26]

The ADA, condemned as "pink" in the McCarthy years, was saying much the same thing. Preaching the gospel of containment, the Reverend Reinhold Niebuhr praised the Western nations for their supposed ability "to correct the injustices of their earlier industrialization and to perfect the balance-of-power in both their political and economic life to such a degree that they have attained a measure of health which could serve as an antidote to the Communist poison." Much like John Foster Dulles, a more highly placed theologian of the time and a political enemy, Niebuhr called for the creation of a dynamic faith with which to fight Communism.[27]

Attempting in his own way to attain that faith, Wallace came to place increasing trust in the mid-1950s in the public pronouncements of President Eisenhower as a partisan of peace. Eisenhower's identification with summit diplomacy and atoms for peace, variants of Wallace ideas that had been called treasonous in the late 1940s, may help to explain this sympathy for the Republican President. Writing to an old Progressive party supporter in 1955, he noted, "I have been impressed with Eisenhower's sincere desire for peace. And strangely enough, I have been impressed with the similarity of his ideas . . . to my own." [28]

Although he admired and remained friendly with Adlai Stevenson, whom he remembered from the AAA's legal division, Wallace publicly supported Eisenhower in 1956. His endorsement, however, meant little, and his only reported involvement in the campaign merely highlighted the extent of his isolation from political life. Standing against a lamppost near the hotel where both men were staying, Wallace, the press reported, saw Adlai Stevenson begin to approach him. Caught in an awkward situation, the Democratic candidate was apparently willing to chat with the man for whom he had worked in 1933. A campaign aide then purportedly intervened and advised the candidate against such a precipitous act. Although he shortly wrote Wallace a warm letter of apology and offered to get together soon, Stevenson walked away from the former Vice President that day, as most of his followers had begun to do a decade before. Without bitterness, Wallace told reporters that he respected Stevenson and that he was quite happy to be out of political life.[29]

As his faith in the people's revolution eroded, Wallace expressed mild support for one of the more discredited "scientific" reforms of the Progressive era, eugenics. Commenting on a scientific paper delivered at the Smithsonian Institution in January, 1959, he called upon government to keep careful genetic records of all people just as it noted births and deaths. Although he made it a point to clearly differentiate his proposals from those of a "genetic Hitler"—young people would choose voluntarily whether or not to use the records in finding prospective mates—his plan was evidence perhaps of a search for a rationale to defend the new faith in elites that waxed strong throughout the 1950s in politics and academia. In another sense, these ideas were a culmination in caricature of the tradition of administrative reform that he had advocated for so long in government—another informational service, a clearing house provided by the state to strengthen the populace against a world revolution directed by the common man of color.[30]

Eventually, Wallace's new fear of the common man was transformed into a feverish prophecy of the "Chinese century" to come if America failed to use her wealth to defeat the revolution of destruction in the underdeveloped countries. China had always fascinated Wallace. At Ames, a schoolmate remembered his prediction that the Chinese empire would ultimately provide the greatest threat to the United States. During the 1920s, however, he stressed the need to develop a more conciliatory attitude to the Chinese in order to preserve the Middle Kingdom as a market. As Vice President, he served as President Roosevelt's personal emissary to Chiang Kai-shek and pictured China in rosy, progressive capitalist terms as a vehicle for responsible, nonimperialist investment and for future Soviet–American cooperation in the creation of an interdependent world economy. During the *New Republic* and Progressive Party periods, he strongly criticized the Truman administration's limited support for Chiang Kai-shek in the Chinese civil war and advocated American acceptance of the Communist regime after the Generalissimo abandoned the mainland in December, 1949.[31]

Although Wallace withdrew his support for the immediate seating of the Mao Tse-tung regime in the United Nations after China entered the Korean war, he continued during the early 1950s to advocate American initiatives to wean China away from the Soviets. Continued American support for reactionary regimes in the Orient, he warned, would provide Russia with "the affection, admiration, and increasingly the trade of Asia." Chinese civilization, he believed, was too old, too close to the soil, to accept Russian Communism permanently. Yet, he claimed as early as 1952 that the Chinese were professing loyalty to Moscow in order to drive the "White men" of the world into war. By the late 1950s, the racial theme in Wallace's condemnation of the Chinese dwarfed all else. The latter were now seen as the potential barbarian hordes of the twenty-first century, and the ghosts of MacKinder and Brooks Adams were conjured up to support the prophecy of an eventual Soviet–American alliance to stop the sons of the Middle Kingdom.[32]

By the early 1960s, Wallace was arguing that Soviet attempts to foment revolution in the poor countries only played into "Chinese hands." Projecting his own racialist fears upon his victims, he argued that the Chinese possessed a racial arrogance and inhuman discipline greater than Hitler's Germany; moving "glacierlike" against the Soviets, they sought to provoke a nuclear war that would destroy the developed world. Variants of these ideas were certainly in evidence through the 1960s, both in the United States and among the Soviet leadership. For Wallace, however, such notions reflected the souring of a lifelong fascination with East Asia's culture, religion, and future in a One World community. Thus did a progressive capitalism, spurned in its vision of a world New Deal, become in the mind of its leading advocate a moral and racial nightmare. It was almost as if John Foster Dulles had joined hands with John Maynard Keynes in Wallace's thought.[33]

Wallace's final years were a curious mixture of old fears and lingering hopes. Labor, he argued in rather cranky fashion, had grown too strong and selfish in the postwar period, gaining at the expense of business and agriculture. Inflation and crime increasingly began to worry him, and he feared that a major financial crisis was in the offing for the mid-1960s. Beatnik culture offended him, and he looked at the apostasy of the young from the vantage point of the old agrarian: corrupting prosperity, withdrawal from the soil, the inevitable cycle of rise and decline within civilization were responsible for the deterioration of public morals. Perhaps, he wrote to his most recent biographer, Sir Flinders Petrie and Oswald Spengler had been correct after all. The problem of modern society was how to exist with abundance without surrender to its "rotting effect." [34]

Labor, of course, had broken his heart in 1948, as had the young and the minority groups whose involvement in crime he occasionally alluded to. The rise of John Kennedy troubled him. As Kennedy's nomination appeared more imminent, Wallace expressed concern to Henry C. Taylor that "the Catholics [are] plopping 90 percent for Kennedy." Although he refrained from formally endorsing either Kennedy or Nixon during the campaign, Wallace apparently voted for Nixon and issued a statement in late October strongly condemning Kennedy's farm proposals as inflationary and praising Nixon's by comparison. These remarks gained the somewhat flustered praise of Republican spokesmen, who with embarrassment noted that Henry Wallace, whatever else he had been, was a distinguished authority on agricultural matters.[35]

In some respects, though, Wallace had not come out of the 1950s that badly. When he received a questionnaire from the Democratic National Committee in 1960 on issues that the party should support, he did not check proposals to increase spending for defense purposes or to continue to press for freedom for the captive nations. In spite of his ambivalent feelings toward Kennedy, Wallace moved haltingly back into the society that had ostracized him during the Kennedy years. In a generous gesture, the young President invited him to the inauguration. In an ironical one, Eleanor Roosevelt and William O. Douglas invited him to attend an anniversary dinner for Walter Reuther. When Secretary of Agriculture Orville Freeman was threatened by the Billy Sol Estes scandal in 1962,

Gladys Baker and other Wallace admirers in the USDA convinced the former Vice President to write to President Kennedy in Freeman's defense. Wallace even expressed a certain sympathy for the Kennedy administration in an address comparing the aspirations of the New Frontier with those of the early New Deal.[36]

The Kennedy years also served as the backdrop for Wallace's first return to the USDA since his retirement from public life. With great reluctance, he agreed to take part with other former Secretaries of Agriculture in a forum in November, 1961, at the Agriculture building on the past history of the department. Gladys Baker remembered his dread before the speech. Would the old accusations of Communist be whispered? Had he said enough and paid enough since Korea? As it was, Wallace, reminiscing about the New Deal, returned briefly to the warm, idealistic rhetoric that had captured the hearts of another generation and held spellbound an audience composed of young USDA workers. His comment, "I hope that along with its scientific work the Department will do such a skillful job in cooperation with the farmers and the State Department that farm income will be increased and peace preserved in the hungry parts of the world," reflected the hopeful mood of the Kennedy administration as much as it did the hopes that had hardened into the containment policy.[37]

Containment, traditional politics at home, and power politics abroad still stood behind the glitter of the Kennedy administration. The New Deal had collapsed in egalitarian rhetoric, Keynesian fiscal manipulation, an unwieldy political coalition, and a personality cult. The New Frontier began and ended with a personality cult, spewed forth the high priests of modernization and systems analysis, and expanded the budgets and the influence of the military. Perhaps Wallace was right to be unimpressed. When friends attempted with some justice to see in the Peace Corps the culmination of ideals for which he had stood during the war, he was quietly amused. After the Bay of Pigs fiasco, he wrote to Henry C. Taylor, "at the Machiavellian game we are not a world cham-

*17. An aged Henry Wallace speaking at the Centennial of the
United States Department of Agriculture, Washington, 1961.
(Courtesy of United States Department of Agriculture.)*

pion." Alluding to Franklin Roosevelt's legendary way of choosing among tyrants, Wallace expressed beautifully the problem of containment in the New Frontier with the question, "Do we have schizophrenia as we try to find out which dictatorships are our S.O.B.'s?" [38]

Wallace had done much to make his peace with the liberals of containment. Although he maintained friendly albeit distant relations with Beanie Baldwin and Lew Frank and never publicly repudiated the Progressive campaign nor questioned the motives of the party's members, he was willing to admit privately that he and others had been used by the Communists. (In the early 1950s, he came to blame the Communists for having kept millions of liberals out of the party.) When he visited the Dominican Republic during a political upheaval in October 1963, he even paid a lefthanded compliment to his old antagonists (and to the politics of the last Truman years, when the champions of Arthur Schlesinger, Jr.'s "vital center" became Joseph McCarthy's favorite Communists) with the remark that Juan Bosch "is about the same kind of communist as Dave Dubinski [sic] and Norman Thomas and Bob Hutchins and Bill Douglas." [39]

The high point of Wallace's accommodation with cold-war liberalism occurred in 1962 at a Washington dinner honoring the twenty-first anniversary of the wartime Truman committee. With Truman on the dais, Wallace played the role of Henry IV at Canossa or Winston Smith in the final pages of Orwell's *Nineteen Eighty-Four*, telling the former President, "I am glad you were the man who was appointed head of the Truman Committee and I am glad you fired me when you did." When the Republican party in 1964 nominated the sentimental hero of the unreconstructed right and thus threatened in a negative sense the calculus of Keynes and containment that had served as national policy in postwar America, Wallace made his first campaign appearances since 1949, taking the stump in Iowa for the Johnson–Humphrey ticket. Johnson and Humphrey, he wrote to Gladys Baker during the campaign, "are what the country needs right now. Both men are levelheaded." [40]

This was perhaps the least valid of his prophecies. As he

neared the end of his life Wallace returned to the faith in the eternal verities of a rural civilization that had been a central belief in the Iowa of his youth. In an article published in the *Washington Daily News* in February, 1962, he warned against the threats a mechanized society posed to human values that had developed through contact with the soil. Writing to Gladys Baker, he maintained as he had in the twenties that an identity with the land had served as the basis for the spiritual growth of civilization and that urbanization "can cause psychic, aesthetic and spiritual losses as well as material gains." Returning to the vision of industrial decentralization that had intrigued New Deal planners, Wallace portrayed his last commonwealth as "a civilization which is neither urban nor rural but one designed to serve all people in abundance against a background of earth and trees with continuous and full awareness of the growth processes and the seasons." [41] As America moved into the Great Society, Henry Wallace prepared to face a crisis out of which there were no middle paths or new frontiers to seek.

Although his political enemies had always poked cruel fun at his experimental diets and exercises, Wallace had outlived most of his detractors. At seventy-six, he remained strong and vigorous. While climbing an ancient pyramid in Guatemala in 1964, he felt some pain in his leg but he attributed this to exertion. The pain continued to plague him when he returned to the United States. Diagnosticians at the Mayo Clinic, Danbury Hospital and Columbia Medical determined eventually that his condition was amyotrophic lateral sclerosis, the rare and fatal disease of the nervous system that had claimed the life of New York Yankee star Lou Gehrig. Refusing to yield to approaching death, Wallace traveled to Germany in February, 1965, for an operation and finally entered the National Institute of Health (the nation's leading institution dedicated to the study and treatment of rare diseases) at Bethesda, Maryland, where his condition was diagnosed beyond any reasonable doubt. [42]

As his life ebbed, Wallace remained optimistic, keeping a record of the progress of the disease and hoping until the final weeks that science would cure his malady and that the work the doctors were doing with him would contribute to the cure. Refurbishing his reputation as a prophet, he noted in July, 1965, "I see enough trouble ahead so that I feel there is even a chance of the Republicans gaining the Presidency in 1968. They will not change our foreign policy and in a short time will be in worse trouble than Johnson now is." [43]

As the disease entered the final stages, Wallace lost the power to speak, to coordinate his arm and leg muscles, and to swallow freely, communicating with friends via a slate. The news that Henry Wallace was dying brought a flow of friends from the many avenues of his life to his bedside. The old friends from Agriculture came, as did Beanie Baldwin. Lew Frank contacted Harold Young, who contacted Wallace after a seventeen-year silence. He died at Danbury Hospital on November 18, 1965. Six months before his death, he wrote pessimistically to a friend about the coming harvest of containment, "As I see the future, you and I should feel very fortunate in living at the time we have lived." [44]

The customary eulogies followed from politicians. Sending John Gardner with a wreath to represent the administration at the funeral at St. Stephens Church in Ridgefield, Connecticut, Lyndon Johnson said of Wallace, "His views may not always have been popular, but they were always sincere." Harry Truman said simply that Wallace had been "an asset" to the nation. Hubert Humphrey, alluding to the struggles of the early Truman years, remarked, "we had our political differences but to me this never diminished the fact that he was a great public servant and one of the greatest friends American agriculture has had." As a postscript to the affair, James Farley, who had earlier called Wallace one of the finest men he had ever known, was the only prominent figure of the Roosevelt administration reported to have attended the funeral. Among the tributes, the fairest came from Thomas E. Dewey, who had shared with Wallace the disappointments of 1948. "Henry Wallace," Dewey noted, "was a man of good will who led many a brave fight for the social advances made in his lifetime." [45]

III

In his will, Henry Wallace called upon his heirs to keep the corn companies strong, maintain a proper sense of responsibility for their employees, and remember always that "there are values higher than monetary values." [46] In retrospect, these were the admonitions of a Christian and a progressive capitalist, a sober, responsible representative of twentieth-century American civilization. This was the image that Wallace sought to develop in the long years after Korea. To this image, one must add the increasingly popular one, that of a tragic, misplaced figure, an object of pity for the mellowing cold-war liberals who, in the late 1960s, defected from Lyndon Johnson's version of their own foreign policy while retaining for the most part their sentimental attachment for Harry Truman (an object of scorn for the ADA in 1947 and 1948, Truman became something of a folk hero to the cold warriors in the 1960s). Finally, there is the image that Wallace and his followers revered most during his years of influence, that of an Old Testament prophet leading the people in the ways of righteousness, waiting for the future to vindicate his judgments. All of these images continue to cluster around the memory of Henry Wallace, coexisting with the less attractive popular impressions of a mystic and a Communist dupe. None present a just view of Wallace or of his place in American history.

Such a view of course will derive from the work of future historians and social scientists. As primary materials concerning national politics and foreign policy in the 1940s become more available, as scholars free themselves from the intellectual prisons created by an unquestioning adherence to such concepts as collective security and the balance of power, they will hopefully begin to rediscover and reassess the liberal tradition in America and to reinterpret the role of Henry Wallace as a political thinker and leader. This study, limited by the available source materials, is but an introduction to that reassessment.

Yet, there are some tentative conclusions that one may draw

from the course of liberal thought and the career of Henry Wallace in the 1940s. Going well beyond the frustration and confusion of the 1930s, American social liberals had turned during World War II to the ideas of a world New Deal and an American social-welfare state, to the goal of rational planning for economic growth and social welfare in a world beset by war and revolution. Combining the evolutionary positivist faith in the advance of society through the development of science and technology with an evangelical Protestant fervor that filled men's need to identify with something greater than themselves, Wallace provided wartime social liberals with a spokesman and a symbol at the same time as the CIO appeared to provide the vehicle for the postwar reconstruction of American politics and the fulfillment of the world New Deal and the Economic Bill of Rights.

The Keynesian cooperative commonwealth, however, the One World coming after the war with black and white and Russia and America together, with jobs, peace, and freedom for all, turned out to be a heap of loose sand. This was not because Henry Wallace and those who followed him were Open Door imperialists of another color, as William Appleman Williams, Walter LaFeber, and Ronald Radosh have charged.[47] Rather, the war both created the program of the people's century and brought businessmen back into government while strengthening greatly the conservative coalition in Congress and the urban machine bosses and moderate congressional leadership within the Democratic party. Social liberals were in fact prisoners of New Deal broker-state politics and the Roosevelt personality cult. Their creation of a countercult around Henry Wallace was both an example of what New Deal politics had become and a futile attempt to bargain with a President who already had their allegiance and submerged their interests within a larger political coalition.

The revival during the war of the popular front, creating through the CIO–PAC and the independent committees political institutions around which liberals could organize to attain Franklin Roosevelt's one enduring legacy, the Economic Bill of Rights, was, like the New Deal itself, a utilitarian stopgap, an attempt to deal with complex problems through a combination of intelligence and good will. Unwilling to turn planning and economic democracy into anything more than slogans (for to do otherwise would have meant to challenge seriously the economic system it sacrificed all to save), the New Deal could not solve the problem of employment short of war and then could not survive as a movement of social–liberal reform after the end of mass unemployment had eliminated the major reason for its existence. The popular front, blithely ignoring the images of atheism and collectivism that made Communism an anathema to the general population, could not long survive the death of Adolf Hitler.

Believing that the world New Deal and the Economic Bill of Rights were interdependent and connected directly to the creation of a One World Community based on a workable United Nations and Soviet–American cooperation, Henry Wallace and his ever-decreasing band of followers refused to invert the wartime anti-Hitler rhetoric against the Soviet Union. Yet, because they too were New Deal siblings, they were unable to provide an alternative to the inversion of that rhetoric by the Truman administration and the liberals of containment. Their message and criticism of the Truman policies were perhaps best summed up in a scrawled postscript to a letter Henry Wallace wrote in the last months of his life: "Hungry people = Communist Opportunity. . . . Too little–too late." [48]

The "new liberalism" of containment, as Palmer Wright has effectively shown, rebelled eventually against the optimism of both the New Deal and the popular front and stressed a "stoic discipline," a systematic belief in the viability of lesser evils. Whereas the advocates of the popular front had failed to define the Communist question to the people (as the New Deal had not defined the war in anti-Fascist terms to the people), the cold-war liberals accepted the conservative commitment to oppose Communism by force throughout the world, veiling that commitment behind what Arthur Schlesinger, Jr., called "not right, not left, but a vital center." [49] The leading scholar–politician of the postwar or pre-Kissinger period, Schlesinger would become the caricature of the cold-war liberal, leaving the rarified world of Reinhold Niebuhr for the Kennedy entourage and for a celebration of political history as the story of great men.

The cult of the hero, which had done so much to isolate and destroy Henry Wallace, and its opposite, the revulsion against political action and social engineering, became the two faces of the postwar liberal movement. These two traditions, the one representing manipulative social action through the Leader Cult, the other an antiparty, antipolitics morality and a desire for independence, met in the late 1960s in the forms of Robert Kennedy and Eugene McCarthy, respectively. Yet, neither man offered anything beyond the utilitarian use of power and a sophisticated revulsion against power's use. Henry Wallace had sought to unite both traditions in his lifetime—as he had sought to subsume most of the great contradictions of life—in the vision of a people's century, a vision that had crumbled before the containment policy of the armed Keynesians.

Henry Wallace remains a compelling figure because the problems he struggled with, the problems emerging from the collapse of colonialism after the war and the relations of the developed nations with each other and with the underdeveloped areas in an age of atomic energy and nationalist and socialist revolutions, have yet to be solved. The program of a people's century, expressed in terms of liberation rather than containment, of a world New Deal rather than a brutalizing international posture against Communism, remains a challenge to the energies of the American people. Yet, before Americans can cooperate in the freeing of others, they must free themselves. Although a genuine welfare state remains the most reasoned immediate response to the domestic social problems that were largely lost sight of in the years between the Truman Doctrine and the Vietnam war, it is doubtful that the progressive capitalism of Henry Wallace could give Americans either security or freedom.

Thirty years ago Henry Wallace and most American social liberals committed themselves to a program their enemies called milk for Hottentots. Their opponents, the liberals of containment, accepted eventually an internationalism based on guns for Hottentots. The Hottentots, the poor and oppressed in America and the world, have seen the program of the triumphant American century and responded to the violence behind it with their own violence. The program of the people's century, as we have seen, was never seriously tried. Within the context of modern American capitalism, it was nothing more than a fascinating and courageous false consciousness. In a democratic socialist America, the America that John Dewey finally saw as the only way to redeem both the nation and the liberal tradition, it would have meaning. As Americans force their way out of the political strait jacket created by containment and move toward the possibilities of democratic socialist reconstruction, they may rediscover and vindicate their country's idea of freedom and the Century of the Common Man.

NOTES

* HAW to James Pappathanasi, July 4, 1965, Gifts, 1960–1965, University of Iowa.
  1943), p. 96.
1. Russell Lord, ed., *The Century of the Common Man* (New York,
2. MacDougall, *Gideon's Army*, III, p. 883.
3. HAW to Davidson, December 22, 1948, Jo Davidson Papers, Box 6, LC; Interview with John Abt, January 3, 1969.
4. HAW, Address, Progressive Party Caucus For Peace, April 4, 1949, Progressive Party Papers (henceforth PP Papers), Box 4, Folder 4, University of Iowa.
5. HAW, Testimony Before Senate Foreign Relations Committee, May 5, 1949, p. 1, PP Papers, Box 2, Folder 1.
6. *New York Post*, September 16, 1949.
7. HAW, Address, New York City, April 27, 1949, p. 4, PP Papers, Box 2, Folder 1; HAW, Address, Philadelphia, October 27, 1949, p. 6, PP Papers, Box 2, Folder 1.
8. *Ibid.*
9. *Ibid.*, p. 2; HAW, Address, March 27, 1949, p. 7, PP Papers, Box 2, Folder 4.
10. HAW, "Cooperation For the General Welfare," pp. 1–3, in Committee to Frame a World Constitution Papers, Box 32, Folder 1, University of Chicago, Chicago, Illinois; HAW, Address, Chicago, November 18, 1949, p. 3, PP Papers, Box 2, Folder 1.

11. HAW to James Imbrie, December 3, 1949, HAW Papers, University of Iowa.

12. HAW, Address, Chicago, February 24, 1950, pp. 5–7, PP Papers, Box 2, Folder 1; Press Release, Charles M. La Follette, ADA National Director, February 26, 1950, in PP Papers, Box 3, Folder 7; Karl M. Schmidt, *Henry A. Wallace: Quixotic Crusade, 1948* (Syracuse, 1960), pp. 298–302.

13. See Henry A. Wallace, "Where I Was Wrong," in *This Week,* September 7, 1952; HAW, Radio Address, April 28, 1949, p. 4, PP Papers, Box 2, Folder 1; HAW to Pepper, May 5, 1950, HAW Papers, Gifts, 1967–1970, University of Iowa.

14. Schmidt, *Henry A. Wallace,* pp. 294–297; HAW to Albert Einstein, January 30, 1950, HAW Papers; HAW, Draft of Statement on Fulton Lewis, Jr.'s charges, undated, PP Papers, Box 2, Folder 1; Interview with Michael Straight, November 25, 1968. Wallace hired a lawyer in an attempt to clear himself of the charges. For his account of the affair see HAW to General Leslie Groves, March 7, 1951, and HAW to Walter Freedman, February 13, 1951, HAW Papers, University of Iowa.

15. *New York Times,* April 2, 1950; Schmidt, *Henry A. Wallace,* p. 303.

16. *Ibid.*

17. Minutes of the Meetings of the Executive Committee, Progressive Party, on Korea, PP Papers, Box 3, Folder 4. Wallace also suggested to Baldwin that the party send a telegram to Stalin asking him to send his representatives back to the UN Security Council. HAW to Baldwin, July 13, 1950, HAW Papers, University of Iowa.

18. HAW, Statement on the Korean Situation, July 15, 1950, pp. 1–2, PP Papers, Box 3, Folder 4.

19. Schmidt, *Henry A. Wallace,* p. 306; HAW to Anita McCormick Blaine, July 18, 1950, Anita McCormick Blaine Papers, Box 743, WSHS; HAW to Baldwin, August 8, 1950, HAW Papers, Gifts, 1967–1970, University of Iowa.

20. Quoted in the *New York Times,* October 3, 1950.

21. HAW, Address, "A Century of Blood or Milk?" Community Church, NYC, November 12, 1950, PP Papers, Box 2, Folder 1.

22. Wallace used MacKinder and Brooks Adams as evidence that the struggle between Slavs and Anglo-Saxons, between Russian and American empires, preceded the rise of Communism, even though Communism gave the conflict a new dimension. In the early sixties, Wallace tended to deliver a set speech in which geopolitical references were mixed with denunciations of the Chinese and continued advocacy of American action to strengthen the United Nations and provide aid for underdeveloped countries. See HAW, Address, Taylor Hibbard Club, March 21, 1961, in Henry C. Taylor Papers, Box 23, WSHS.

23. HAW, Address, "A Century of Blood or Milk?" p. 9.

24. See Henry A. Wallace, "Where I Was Wrong," *This Week,* September 7, 1952, and Henry A. Wallace, "How I'd Stop the March of Stalin," *Coronet,* November, 1950, copies in PP Papers, Box 51; Senate Committee on the Judiciary, *Hearings on . . . The Institute of Pacific*

Relations, U.S. Senate, 82 Congress, 2 Session (Washington, 1952), pp. 1298–1303.

25. *Chicago Sun Times*, March 18, 1952; HAW to Joseph Short, April 14, 1952, HST Papers, OF 1170, HSTL.

26. HAW, Address, "March of the Common Man, Constructive or Destructive?" Boston Community Church, January 21, 1951, p. 1, PP Papers, Box 2, Folder 1; HAW, "Hatred, Love and Faith in a World of Force," Boston Community Church, March 29, 1953, p. 7, PP Papers, Box 2, Folder 1.

27. For example, an ADA radio program noted in 1953, "We cannot merely give relief alone for a better world. What we need in Asia as well as in Europe are stable satisfied allies." ADA Radio Script, "The Offensive Against Communism," July 1, 1953, p. 6, ADA Papers, Series 2, Box 94. WSHS; Reinhold Niebuhr, "American Spiritual Resources For International Cooperation," undated, p. 7, Reinhold Niebuhr Papers, Box 16, LC.

28. Enclosed in "J" to Curtis MacDougall, August 3, 1955, PP Papers, Box 10. Wallace wrote to Henry C. Taylor, "I am for Eisenhower running again because I think he has the best position to further the cause of peace. . . . Peace is so important that I overlook the other issues." HAW to Taylor, October 25, 1955, Taylor Papers, Box 23.

29. For accounts of the Stevenson–Wallace encounter, see *New York Times*, September 29, 1956, and *Chicago Sun Times*, September 29, 1956. Stevenson wrote to Wallace before the campaign ended, "I was distressed to find after I left St. Louis that we had been staying at the same hotel. I hope that you will let me know the next time because I would enjoy seeing you again—and who knows—perhaps we could contrive a game of tennis." Stevenson to HAW, October 9, 1956, HAW Papers, Adlai Stevenson Folder.

30. HAW, Comments on Dr. George Beadle's Papers on Molecules, Viruses, and Heredity, Resources For the Future Forum, Smithsonian Institution, January 8, 1959, p. 8, in Taylor Papers, Box 23. For press handling of the address, see *Kansas City Times*, January 9, 1959.

31. "American Wheat and the Chinese Farmer," *W.F.*, April 1930, p. 788; "America and China," *W.F.*, March 11, 1927, p. 382; For Wallace's hope of a new China after the war, see Henry A. Wallace, *Our Job in the Pacific* (Washington, 1944). After the proclamation of the Peoples Republic of China, Wallace told a church audience that "communism was necessary in Russia and China in order to overthrow ancient feudalistic regimes full of corrupt practices." *Washington Post*, November 28, 1949.

32. HAW, Address, "A Century of Blood or Milk?" p. 5; Henry A. Wallace, "Where I Was Wrong," *This Week*, September 7, 1952; *Kansas City Times*, May 8, June 12, 1958.

33. Wallace repeated these ideas and catch-phrases in the speech that he usually gave through the early 1960s. See HAW, Address, "Looking Ahead," Food Forum, Boston, March 27, 1960, HAW Folders, United States Department of Agriculture (henceforth USDA).

These views also dominated his private correspondence about China. Writing to Henry C. Taylor, he noted that America, to meet the coming crises of the 1960s, would have to expand the United Nations or assume greater leadership of the West. "I hope the former," he said, "because I believe that the menace of China . . . is such that it is essential to have Russia in with the other white peoples. The Common Man of Color is on the march in a really big way." HAW to Taylor, March 31, 1960, Taylor Papers, Box 23, WSHS.

34. HAW, Address, "Equality of Bargaining Power and the General Welfare," Madison, Wisconsin, March 28, 1961, p. 8, Taylor Papers, Box 23, WSHS; HAW to Gladys Baker, April 21, 1961, April 15, 1962, in the private possession of Miss Baker, Washington, D.C.; HAW to Edward L. Schapsmeier, January 12, 1961, in the private possession of Professor Schapsmeier, Illinois State University, Normal, Illinois.

35. HAW to Taylor, April 2, 1960, Taylor Papers, Box 23, WSHS; *New York Times*, October 27, 28, 1960; *Des Moines Register*, October 30, 1964, quotes Wallace that he voted for Nixon.

36. Copy of questionnaire enclosed in HAW to James Pappathanasi, July 9, 1960, HAW Papers, Gifts, 1960–1965, University of Iowa; Cabell Phillips in *New York Times*, October 6, 1963; Eleanor Roosevelt and William O. Douglas to HAW, May 8, 1961, HAW Papers, Important Correspondence Folder, University of Iowa; HAW to JFK, May 20, 1962, HAW Files, USDA; Henry A. Wallace, "A New Dealer Looks at the New Frontier," *Journal of Farm Economics*, XLIV (May, 1962), pp. 463–475. Wallace even received an invitation to attend a fund-raising dinner celebrating the first anniversary of the Kennedy inauguration at which the President was scheduled to speak. Matthew McCloskey to HAW, December 29, 1961, HAW Papers, University of Iowa.

37. Interview with Gladys L. Baker, December 16, 1968; HAW, Address, "The Department as I Have Known It," November 1, 1961, p. 14, HAW Files, USDA. Also in Wayne D. Rasmussen, ed., *Growth Through Agricultural Progress* (Washington, 1961).

38. Interview with Baker; HAW to Taylor, April 28, 1961, Taylor Papers, Box 23, WSHS.

39. Interviews with Baldwin and Frank; HAW to Taylor, October 9, 1963, Taylor Papers, Box 23, WSHS. Through the early 1950s especially, Wallace expressed great bitterness against the Communists and wrote countless letters to public figures in an effort to defend himself from the blows against his reputation. See, for example, HAW to Herbert Brownell, October 24, 1954, HAW Papers, University of Iowa.

40. The dinner took place in the Mayflower Hotel in Washington on February 13, 1962. *Danbury (Conn.) News*, November 19, 1965; HAW to Gladys Baker, October 10, 1964, in the private possession of Miss Baker.

41. *Washington Daily News*, February 27, 1962; HAW to Gladys Baker, April 15, 1962, in the private possession of Miss Baker.

42. Wallace had his tonsils and sinuses removed in Munich in February, 1965, recuperating in Vevey, Switzerland, before returning to America and launching his last trip abroad to the Dominican Republic in the spring. HAW to Dr. Joseph Belsky (Danbury Hospital), March 23, 1965, HAW Papers, Gifts, 1960–1965. For Wallace's own account of his condition, see HAW to James Pappathanasi, July 4, 1965, HAW Papers, University of Iowa.

43. *Ibid.*

44. Interviews with Gladys Baker, Louis Bean, C. B. Baldwin, Mordecai Ezekiel, and Lew Frank; HAW to James Pappathanasi, May 9, 1965, HAW Papers, University of Iowa.

45. *New York Times*, November 19, 1965; *UPI*, November 19, 1965; *Des Moines Register*, November 19, 22, 1965.

46. Text of will in *Des Moines Register*, December 8, 1965.

47. For a recent expression of the Williams school's view, see Ronald Radosh and Leonard Liggio, "Henry A. Wallace and the Open Door," in Thomas G. Patterson, ed., *Cold War Critics* (Chicago, 1971). Wallace's commitment to capitalism as a system ultimately made him ineffective. To say that it made him indistinguishable from those who crushed him is to make a mockery of history.

48. HAW to James Pappathanasi, May 9, 1965, HAW Papers, University of Iowa.

49. Palmer Winslow Wright, "The 'New Liberalism' of the Fifties: Reinhold Niebuhr, David Riesman, Lionel Trilling, and the American Intellectuals" (Ph.D. thesis, University of Michigan, 1966), pp. 1–14.

Appendix: The Mysticism Legend

Throughout his long public career, Henry Wallace was haunted by gossip in high places and low that he was some species of mystic. Friendly colleagues remembered that he would sometimes sleep through meetings, casual acquaintances were put off by his blank and distant stare, and strangers often equated his shyness with oddness. Hostile reporters and political opponents of course took advantage of these rumors to insinuate that Wallace was as strange as his ideas (indeed, his personal eccentricity was perceived as *prima facie* evidence for his ideological peculiarity). Thus, derogatory references to the Secretary of Agriculture's experimental diets were occasionally made, and his more serious work in encouraging nutritional research was ignored. Vague references to his interest in the sciences of the occult were sometimes cited, and a reporter for *Time* even hinted that there was something strange and sinister about the fact that the Secretary of Agriculture liked to throw boomerangs. During and especially after the war, there were even cartoons that portrayed him as a swami, staring into a crystal ball.[1]

In 1948, Hearst columnist Westbrook Pegler gave these innuendoes more credence than ever before by publishing alleged mystical letters that Wallace had written to Nicholas Roerich, a refugee Russian artist, while he was Secretary of Agriculture. Because Pegler was probably the most notorious rightwing journalist in the country, few doubted that his story of the letters was a deliberate attempt to smear the Wallace presidential candidacy. Given, as will be shown later, the complicated nature of his involvement with Roerich, Wallace refused to answer Pegler's charges and thus gave his old conservative and new liberal enemies more ammunition with which to attack him (even though overt references to the "mysticism" letters played no significant part in his crushing defeat in 1948, just as covert references to the same letters had little to do with his defeat for renomination in 1944).[2]

As Pegler and Wallace's other enemies in the media used everything they could to attack him, as they used everything they could to attack the New Deal, it would be pointless to hold them to account. However, when an historian of the reputation of Arthur Schlesinger, Jr., in a work as popular and prestigious as *The Coming of the New Deal* writes that "neither mysticism nor rhetoric could abolish the fissure, the emptiness at the core of his [Wallace's] own personality" he can and must be called to account. Schlesinger's further contention that Wallace's opposition to recognition of the Soviet Union in 1933 may have stemmed from his involvement with Roerich is also patently ridiculous (see Chapter 5). Finally, his comment that the Secretary of Agriculture's peculiarities led to the cultivation of "revolting diets of rutabaga, soybeans or cottonseed meal" is indicative of the kind of professional character assassination that Wallace regularly faced from less pretentious journalists.[3]

Of course, Wallace was the opposite of the Hail-Fellow-Well-Met type, that American politics compels so many of its practitioners to become. He was interested in the occult and did speak with and correspond with various representatives of mystical groups in an effort to learn about their philosophies (evidence for this comes almost exclusively from the 1920s and early 1930s).[4] Yet there is really no evidence that he ever committed himself to any set of ideas that would be commonly considered occult, save those of Christianity. Memoir sources often allude to his seemingly eccentric personality and occasionally connect this to mysticism gossip. In response to such an allusion in Alben Barkley's memoirs, Wallace made two replies, which when taken together, provide the most effective answer to the mysticism allegations: "Mysticism did not enter into the picture in the slightest degree, unless you wish to call the doctrine of Christ mysticism. . . . Folks who hated me used the word 'mysticism' to smear me." [5] Although his religious views have been looked at earlier (see Chapter 1), they nevertheless provide the point of departure for any understanding of the so-called Guru letters.

I

Henry Wallace's religious faith has been wondered at and mocked but rarely interpreted as an integral part of his faith in a new society freed from the cruelties of competition and exploitation. In the sense that mysticism implies a rejection of this world and an attempt to achieve individual religious exaltation through direct union with God, Wallace's faith was not primarily mystical. Instead, his lifelong fascination with the religions of the Orient and with practices commonly considered occult can be understood better as an extension of the strong social gospel strain in his thought and of his quest to find a unifying principle that would bring order and peace to this world. Science, Wallace believed, must ultimately embrace spiritual values if it was to become the servant rather than the master of man. In his pursuit of a new science, Wallace, as his old colleagues from the Department of Agriculture Louis Bean and M. L. Wilson remembered, maintained that all hypotheses must be tested, however hostile opinion might be to the specific ideas involved. Shortly after Wallace became Secretary of Agriculture, Felix Belair mentioned that he recently surprised scientists by testing some folk superstitions about agriculture and discovering that many were valid. Louis Bean, who shared many of Wallace's spiritual interests, remembered that Wallace was always quick to abandon something when it was shown to be false, as he had done with numerology in the 1920s and in his relations with Dr. Nicholas Roerich, whose adventures in Central Asia in the mid-1930s introduced the least understood and most bizarre incident in Wallace's long public career.[6]

The truth about the "Guru" letters is stranger in many respects than the twisted accounts privately bandied about by anti-New Deal reporters and publishers in the late 1930s and early 1940s and later publicized by Westbrook Pegler and Arthur Schlesinger, Jr. Roerich, to begin with, was not the wild White Russian cultist of the Pegler–Schlesinger fable but an internationally known artist driven out of Russia by the Bolshevik Revolution. He first came to America in 1920, spent the greater part of the ensuing decade leading an expedition to Central Asia to gather Asian art objects, acquired a strong taste for Oriental mysticism that was expressed in his paintings and poetry, and returned to New York at the end of the 1920s to found a museum on Riverside Drive to house his Asian art treasures. In the late 1920s and early 1930s, Roerich traveled in the best of circles, gave addresses before exclusive Eastern girls' schools, and devoted his energies and the energies of his museum staff to lobbying for the passage of an international treaty to protect national monuments and art treasures in time of war. In 1929, he was nominated for the Nobel Peace Prize.

The movement for what became popularly known as the Roerich Pact (a Pan-American treaty embodying Roerich's ideas was signed in 1935) took as its rallying symbol the Banner of Peace, a flag composed of three circles representing both the trinity and diversity within a greater circle representing unity. Although the Banner of Peace was in reality a medieval mystical symbol and stories were later spread that Roerich used the banner as the basis for a cult that considered him to be God, Miss Frances Grant, Secretary of the Roerich Museum and a long-time activist in groups seeking to promote Pan-Americanism and the extension of democracy throughout the Western Hemisphere, has hotly denied this. Since Miss Grant both introduced Henry Wallace to Nicholas Roerich and was a recipient of some of the letters that Wallace was supposed to have sent Roerich, her account of the "Guru" letters is the key to any understanding of the strange and tangled affair.[7]

Wallace, Miss Grant remembered, had initially become interested in the work of Roerich and his son George because of the Secretary of Agriculture's curiosity about Central Asian agriculture. Miss Grant, who was to be instrumental in encouraging Wallace's interest in Latin America, visited the Secretary of Agriculture on numerous occasions in 1933 to lobby for the Banner of Peace treaty, of which Wallace was the leading advocate in the cabinet. In the process, she incited the hostility of Paul Appleby and other Wallace aides, who feared that Roerich's reputation as a mystic would adversely affect the department. Wallace further antagonized his colleagues in 1934 by sending Roerich and his son on a mission to Inner Mongolia to study drought-resistant grasses. As Roerich had traveled extensively in the area before and was familiar with the languages, the mission was by no means as peculiar as critics later contended, especially in view of the course of the drought then in progress in the United States. Hostility in the department to the mission, however, soon gave way to wild stories of Central Asian intrigue and Roerich's search for Shangri-la among the Mongols. Newspaper accounts of the mission tended to lend credence to such stories.[8]

The Roerich mission was blighted from the beginning. In Japan the artist and his entourage were quickly sent on their way by a government that remembered his White Russian past. When the expedition reached China, there were reports that Roerich had added twelve former Cossack officers to his party and had asked the American legation at Tientsin for supplies, including twelve army rifles. When Howard MacMillan and James L. Stevens, two botanists assigned to the expedition, sent dispatches back to the department complaining of Roerich's activities, Dr. Knowles Ryerson, director of the Department's Bureau of Plant Industry and an opponent of the Roerich mission, took the criticisms to the Secretary. After a bitter quarrel over the expedition, Wallace stood by Roerich and dismissed Ryerson. Meanwhile, as accounts spread in the press that Roerich was holding Banner of Peace prayer meetings among the Mongols, American consuls in North China began to notify the State Department that the artist's political activities were strongly frowned upon by the Russians and the Japanese (one should remember that North China in 1935 was a cockpit of Sino–Soviet–Japanese rivalries). A Treasury Department investigation of Roerich's tax delinquencies also contributed to the Secretary of Agriculture's growing estrangement from the Russian artist. Finally, Louis Horch, an official of the Department of Agriculture who was also involved in the management of the Roerich Museum, turned against the painter. Wallace responded to the adverse publicity and governmental and private pressures by severing his connections with Roerich, recalling the mission, and eventually apologizing to Ryerson.[9]

Roerich's stay in the United States after his return was brief; the Treasury Department's attempt to prosecute him for back taxes led to his departure for the Kulu Valley in the Himalayas in 1936, where he was to spend the rest of his life at the institute he had founded in 1930. Louis Horch then sought to gain control of the museum, whose location made it a very valuable piece of property. In the protracted legal struggle between Horch and the Roerich forces, Wallace strongly rejected the entreaties of Miss Grant and others that he aid the Roerich family. Eventually, the Horch faction gained control of the museum (which is still in existence). In the process, a series of letters that Wallace had written to Miss Grant and to the Roerich family about the Roerich Pact fell into the hands of anti-New Deal newspaper publisher Paul Block, who had gained some notoriety in anti-administration circles in 1937 after his papers had exposed Hugo Black's membership in the Ku Klux Klan. Although Miss Grant is not entirely sure how Block got the letters, she believes that the attorney for the museum during the litigation with Horch, who had received the letters along with other museum files to help prepare his case, might have made copies of the letters and then sold them. The original letters are still in Miss Grant's possession.[10]

Some of these letters begin with the salutation, "Dear Guru," as the Pegler reproductions and the Schlesinger account maintained. None is mystical in the sense that mysticism

implies membership in any cult or adherence to any philosophy. Rather the letters are cryptic, drawn partly from
Arthur M. Hopkins' allegory, *The Glory Road*, which had
initially been sent to Wallace to read by Franklin Roosevelt!
The references to Cordell Hull as the Sour One and to Franklin
Roosevelt alternately as the Flaming One and the Mediocre
One, although reflecting the administration's procrastination
over the treaty and hardly complimentary to the President
and his cabinet, had little to do with mysticism (if Miss Grant's
account is accurate).[11]

Many of the letters published by Westbrook Pegler in the
Hearst newspapers in March, 1948, are quite innocent, others
reflect extensive interpolations, and some are apparently complete forgeries. To a reader unaware of their origins and
specific context, the letters would appear quite damaging to
Wallace. Certainly Harry Hopkins, who received copies of
the letters in 1940 (whether these copies were wholly or partly
accurate, one cannot say) from his and the New Deal's friends
among the press, was very upset when told by Paul Appleby
that it was "very plausible" that Wallace had written the letters,
and he asked if there were any way to remove Wallace from
the national ticket.[12] President Roosevelt was supposedly
angered by the letters to the point that he talked privately
about the possibility of eliminating Wallace from the ticket,
but the President's wrath was probably stirred more by the
insulting references in the letters than by Wallace's alleged
mysticism.[13] Late in the campaign, Paul Block invited a number of publishers and Republican leaders to a meeting at the
Waldorf-Astoria Hotel in New York to decide what to do
about the letters. Republican National Chairman Joseph Martin,
fearful that the letters, perhaps like last-minute Republican
attacks against social security in 1936, might somehow re-
bound in Roosevelt's favor, decided against publication. On
election eve, Verne Marshall, an extreme isolationist publisher,
commented in the *Cedar Rapids Gazette* that he and other
publishers had possessed letters from Henry Wallace calling
the President the Wavering One, the Flaming One, and the
Mediocre One and that these letters would have been pub-

lished had it not been for the pressure from the "bigger and more important newspaper men." The controversy was not ended by Wallace's election to the Vice-Presidency.[14]

During the war, references in the press to Wallace as a mystic and private talk in Washington circles about the letters were common. In the most famous, albeit apocryphal, story of the period, Roosevelt, worried that the American public would never understand the Vice President's letters to a lady on occult matters, supposedly said to Anna Rosenberg, "Hell, couldn't we prove that Henry slept with the woman?" In the early stages of Wallace's 1944 renomination fight, Charles Michelson, no friend of the Vice President, published a very brief account of the letters in his memoir, *The Ghost Talks*. Although these revelations were not intended to do Wallace any good, Michelson stated that Harry Hopkins had told him that the letters were probably forgeries. Even Dwight Mac-Donald, commenting on the supposed "Zenda" letters in his anti-Wallace tirade, *Henry Wallace: The Man and the Myth* (1948), noted that handwriting experts were divided with regard to the authenticity of the letters, some of which were handwritten, others typed, some on Department of Agriculture stationery, and some unsigned.[15] Although there were scattered references to Wallace's mysticism in the early Truman and *New Republic* years, publishers, fearful of lawsuits, did not print the letters, which apparently grew in number and peculiarity over the years as different publishers received new and bogus copies.

When Westbrook Pegler published his potpourri of dubious and twisted truth in March, 1948, Nicholas Roerich (inaccurately seen as the sole recipient of the letters) had been dead for three months and Wallace, embarked on a presidential campaign, was hardly in a position to sue. Wallace wisely decided to ignore the charges. When he confronted Pegler at a press conference, the Progressive party leader made clear his contempt for the Hearst columnist, saying only that the whole affair would be cleared up after the campaign.[16] Miss Grant, still believing that Wallace had wronged Roerich in the conflict over the museum and fearful that any publicity would further damage the late artist's reputation, remained silent. Under the circumstances, Wallace would have appeared like a fool rather than a mystic had he sought to tell the truth about the Pegler letters. As it was, the letters were of no importance in the campaign. Wallace's enemies had far more effective images of conspiracy to use against him than the vision of poor Roerich among the Mongols. To the liberals of containment, the letters only reinforced the already prevalent belief that the once-heralded heir of the New Deal was a strange and pathetic figure. For Arthur Schlesinger, Jr., who in *The Coming of the New Deal* told Pegler's story with greater skill and less forthrightness than the Hearst columnist, the letters served as a weapon to further denigrate Wallace long after he had fallen from the New Deal pantheon.

In retrospect, one can find in Wallace's writings evidence that Roerich and the Banner of Peace was but another expression of his lifelong search to find a grand mechanism that would reconcile order with freedom and science with religion and would allow the new world of peace and cooperation to be born. For men to see the future, Wallace wrote in 1934, they must return to a symbol from the ancient past, perhaps to "the design used by Nicholas Roerich for the Banner of Peace." For Wallace, the Banner became for a while the vehicle through which diverse groups would "unite their economic, social and cultural endeavors under this imagined circle of unifying freedom." Eventually, the unity for which Wallace always searched would be achieved by the gurus of containment in the name of a mystical anti-Communism far more destructive than Nicholas Roerich and the Banner of Peace.[17]

NOTES

1. "Stranger," *Time*, XXXVI (July 29, 1940), p. 13.
2. See Pegler in The *New York Journal American*, March, 1948.
3. Arthur Schlesinger, Jr., *The Coming of the New Deal* (New York, 1959), pp. 31, 54. For Wallace and nutritional research, see Russell Lord, *The Wallaces of Iowa* (Boston, 1947), pp. 386–387.

4. See the HAW Papers, University of Iowa, for the late 1920s and early 1930s. There is a fascinating and colorful correspondence between Wallace and California mystics along with a great deal of material pertaining to the Roerich expedition.

5. Quoted in Edward L. and Frederick H. Schapsmeier, *Henry A. Wallace of Iowa: The Agrarian Years, 1920–1940* (Ames, Iowa, 1968), p. 275.

6. Interviews with M. L. Wilson, November 25, 1968, and Louis Bean, December 1, 1968; Felix Belair in *New York Times*, April 2, 1933.

7. Interviews with Frances Grant, January 6, 1969. The New York Public Library contains a large collection of Roerich's poetry and reproductions of his paintings, which were published by the Roerich Museum press in the 1930s.

8. *Ibid.*; Paul Appleby, Howard Tolley and James LeCron Interviews, *COHC*. For an example of the stories that floated around the department about the mission, see Calvin Hoover, *Memoirs of Capitalism, Communism and Nazism* (Durham, N.C., 1965), p. 156.

9. *New York Times*, April 18, 1935.

10. Interview with Miss Grant. Block, the publisher of the *Toledo Blade* and *Pittsburgh-Post Gazette*, died in 1941. For a summary of the early history of the letters, see Curtis D. MacDougall, *Gideon's Army* (New York, 1965), II, pp. 500–502.

11. Although it is clear from the letter that Wallace was merely citing phrases from an allegory that Roosevelt had asked him to read, Schlesinger ignored this point and used it as evidence of Wallace's mysticism. Cf. HAW to FDR, October 27, 1933, FDR Papers, PPF 827, and Arthur Schlesinger, Jr., *The Coming of the New Deal* (New York, 1959), p. 32.

12. See Record of the Dean of the Maxwell School of Journalism, RG 13, Box 1, Syracuse University.

13. For an account of Roosevelt's private feelings about the affair, see Raymond Clapper, Memo, October 28, 1940, Raymond Clapper Papers, Box 9, LC.

14. Joe Martin, *My First Fifty Years in Politics* (New York, 1960), p. 117; *Cedar Rapids (Ia.) Gazette*, November 4, 1940.

15. Quoted in Dwight MacDonald, *Henry Wallace: The Man and the Myth* (New York, 1948), p. 123; Charles Michelson, *The Ghost Talks* (New York, 1944), p. 197; MacDonald, *Henry Wallace*, p. 120.

16. See Pegler in *New York Journal-American*, March 8, 15, 22, 1948. For an account of the Pegler–Wallace confrontation, see MacDougall, *Gideon's Army*, II, 497–498.

17. Henry A. Wallace, *New Frontiers* (New Lork, 1934), p. 279.

Postscript: Since the writing of this book, alleged photostatic copies of the mysticism letters were opened up in the Rosenman papers, Franklin D. Roosevelt Library. Rosenman received these copies in 1949–1950 from Paul Appleby and from the attorney for the Roerichs in the museum litigation. If they are authentic, they would lend credence to Westbrook Pegler's reproductions although not necessarily to his interpretations. With this in mind, I fully accept responsibility for any errors in the appendix.

Select Bibliographical Essay

Unpublished Sources

Manuscripts

The main body of the Henry A. Wallace Papers, University of Iowa, Iowa City, Iowa, is now available to scholars, as are the Henry A. Wallace Papers, Franklin D. Roosevelt Library, Hyde Park, New York (henceforth referred to as FDRL). The Wallace diaries at Iowa City remain closed until 1975. It is expected that the family will open all of the Wallace Papers at Iowa City upon the publication of excerpts of the Wallace diaries, which are currently in the hands of the Houghton Mifflin Company.

The Henry Wallace (Uncle Henry) Papers, University of Iowa, and the Henry C. Wallace Papers, University of Iowa, are essential sources for an understanding of Henry A. Wallace in his formative years. The Henry A. Wallace Folders, Iowa State Historical Collections, Iowa State University, Ames, Iowa, contain interviews with former teachers and fellow students of the future Vice President as well as a few Wallace letters of interest. Wallace's career as a farm editor and lobbyist for the McNary–Haugen bill in the 1920s led him into close contact with other farm leaders. The George Peek Papers, Western Historical Collections, University of Missouri, Columbia, Missouri (henceforth cited as WHC), contain valuable Wallace correspondence from this period, as do the

Frank O. Lowden Papers, University of Chicago Library, University of Chicago, Chicago, Illinois. The Chester C. Davis Papers, WHC, while generally disappointing, should also be consulted for the 1920s and early 1930s. The Henry C. Taylor Papers, Wisconsin State Historical Society, Madison, Wisconsin (henceforth cited as WSHS), are useful for the 1920s; but the greatest value of the Taylor Papers is the extensive and illuminating Wallace–Taylor correspondence of the 1950s and 1960s. For the events leading up to Wallace's nomination as Secretary of Agriculture, Rexford Guy Tugwell, Notes for a New Deal Diary, Tugwell Papers, FDRL, is a significant source.

The William D. Hirth Papers, WHC, and the Xenophon Caverno Papers, WHC, contain some Wallace correspondence with fellow farm editors in the early 1930s. Wallace's changing ideas about agriculture within the national economy in the late 1930s are covered in the John D. Black Papers, WSHS. The Paul Appleby Papers, Carnegie Library, Syracuse University, Syracuse, N.Y., although consisting of only one transfer case, contain important material concerning Wallace's career as Secretary of Agriculture and his entrance into national Democratic party politics. The Addresses of the Secretary of Agriculture, Record Group 16, National Archives (henceforth cited as RG –, NA) present the complete account of Wallace's public statements and speeches as Secretary of Agriculture. The Records of the Agricultural Adjustment Administration, RG 145, NA, include Wallace's statements and addresses in 1939 and 1940.

The Franklin D. Roosevelt Papers, FDRL, constitute a major source for the study through 1945. The Henry A. Wallace Papers, Library of Congress (henceforth cited as LC), although disappointing because of the omission of most of Wallace's important private correspondence, contain the Vice President's general correspondence for the early war years and valuable material concerning the BEW affair and the struggle over the Vice-Presidential nomination. The Raymond Clapper Papers, LC, contain Wallace speech materials for the war and correspondence related to his Vice Presidency. The Jesse Jones Papers, LC, present another view of the BEW controversy and the Commerce appointment. Although one must receive State Department clearance to consult the Records of the Foreign Economic Administration (in which the full BEW records are subsumed), the Records of the Bureau of the Budget, RG 51, NA, contain the unpublished government history of the BEW and vital primary materials concerning the Board's conflicts with the Departments of State and Commerce. The Frank Walker Papers, University Archives, Notre Dame University, South Bend, Indiana, are of great value in understanding the forces behind Wallace's defeat at the 1944 Democratic convention. The George Norris Papers, LC, also contain some noteworthy items concerning the convention struggle, as well as important insights into the hopes of the wartime liberal movement.

For material concerning Wallace's career as Secretary of Commerce, one should begin with the General Correspondence File of the Secretary of Commerce, RG 40, F. 104251, NA, which includes vital interoffice correspondence along with the more general material. The Alfred Schindler Papers, Harry S. Truman Library, Independence, Missouri (henceforth cited as HSTL), contain a complete record of Wallace's public speeches and statements while Secretary and copies of the plans for departmental reorganization and of the reports concerning the economy that Wallace used to brief himself for cabinet meetings. Budget Director Harold Smith's diary, in Harold D. Smith Papers, FDRL, contains interesting insights into the early Truman administration. The Harry S. Truman Papers, HSTL, are especially good for the President's public statements and the summaries of public and mass media opinion concerning the many points of conflict between Wallace and Truman from the Madison Square Garden speech through the 1948 presidential campaign. The Arthur Vandenberg Papers, William L. Clements Library, University of Michigan, Ann Arbor, Michigan, contain important material related to the formation of postwar American foreign policy (one should especially note Vandenberg's San Francisco Conference Diary and the Vandenberg–John Foster Dulles correspondence). The Tom Connally Papers, LC, and the Robert Wagner Papers, Georgetown University, Washington, D.C., although generally quite disappointing, contain scattered materials of some value concerning postwar Democratic party politics and the Truman–Wallace struggles.

The Clark Clifford Papers, HSTL, are very valuable for an understanding of Democratic party politics and the Truman–Wallace relationship as seen from the perspective of the administration. The Charles Ross Papers, HSTL, contain useful material concerning the Madison Square Garden speech controversy and the administration's dealings with the mass media. The Ellen Clayton Garwood Papers, HSTL, contain valuable interviews and correspondence about the Marshall Plan. The Democratic National Committee Records, HSTL, are useful for summaries of media response to the Progressive party and materials related to the third-party movement and campaign.

The major collections that enable one to analyze the struggle between popular-front and containment liberalism are the Americans for Democratic Action Papers, WSHS, and the Progressive Party Papers, University of Iowa, the most important source for both the PCA and the third party. The Stuart Chase Papers, LC, are helpful for the hopes of wartime liberalism. The Joseph E. Davies Papers, LC, especially Davies' diaries, are useful as a gauge of pro-Soviet thinking during and after World War II. The Reinhold Niebuhr Papers, LC, although very scanty in personal correspondence, contain invaluable material concerning the UDA, the ADA, and the minister's philosophical differences with the wartime popular front and the later Progressive party.

The Harry Hopkins Papers, FDRL, provide interesting insights into the New Deal at war and the administration's search for a postwar program. For the postwar period, the Eric Severeid Papers, LC, and the Elmer Davis Papers, LC, include revealing correspondence concerning liberal disenchantment with the administration and conflict over questions of foreign policy and domestic Communism. The Philip Murray Papers, Catholic University of America, Washington, D.C., contain valuable material concerning the CIO's postwar estrangement from popular-front liberalism. The Jo Davidson Papers, LC, are useful for information on the groups of the second popular front, and the Norman Thomas Papers, New York

City Public Library, have a wealth of material concerning the ideological conflicts that convulsed the American Left between Pearl Harbor and NATO. The Vito Marcantonio Papers, New York City Public Library, have some PCA and Progressive party material, although surprisingly little in the way of manuscripts about the third-party movement. The American Labor Party Papers, Rutgers University, New Brunswick, N.J., should also be consulted. ADA materials of value may be found in the Oscar Chapman Papers, HSTL, a collection that is also useful for the wartime period, and the Records of the Dean of the Maxwell School of Journalism, Syracuse University.

Along with the collections previously mentioned, the Minnesota Progressive Party Papers, LC, have useful information concerning the Progressive party convention and the uneasiness among party members over the Communist question. The Committee to Frame a World Constitution Papers, University of Chicago, contain interesting Wallace correspondence with G. A. and Elizabeth Borgese and copies of Wallace's speeches and articles in the last years of the Progressive party. The Anita McCormick Blaine Papers, WSHS, are valuable for the Progressive party period. The Henry A. Wallace Files, United States Department of Agriculture, include a collection of Wallace addresses in the last years of his life, as well as some interesting material concerning the 1920s. The Henry A. Wallace correspondence with Gladys L. Baker, in the private possession of Miss Baker, and the Wallace materials in the private possession of Professor Edward L. Schapsmeier are of great value for understanding Wallace's final years.

Interview and Oral Histories

The memoirs of the Columbia Oral History Collection (COHC) and the Truman Library Oral History Collection (TLOHC) greatly enrich this study. The most valuable memoirs in the COHC pertained to Wallace's career in the Department of Agriculture, but the Norman Thomas and Rexford Guy Tugwell Memoirs contained brief but interesting references to Wallace's activities in the 1940s. The Memoirs of

Louis Bean, COHC, Mordecai Ezekiel, COHC, and James LeCron, COHC, provided great insight into Wallace's personality and into the functioning of the Department of Agriculture in the 1930s; the Memoirs of Samuel Bledsoe, COHC, Fred Henshaw, COHC, and Howard Tolley, COHC, helped to round out the picture of Wallace and provided interesting fragments concerning the Vice President's career in the early war years. The Paul Appleby Memoir, COHC, is invaluable for its insights into the Wallace personality and its information concerning the 1940 Democratic convention. The Henry A. Wallace Memoir, COHC, is closed until 1975 (or upon the discretion of the family).

The John Brophy Memoir, COHC, had fragmentary information about Brophy's struggle against the Communists within the CIO. The Will Alexander Memoir, COHC, presented a colorful negative portrait of Wallace as a weak and vacillating administrator. The TLOHC project, now in its early stage, includes useful materials in the Memoirs of William Batt, speechwriter John Franklin Carter, Democratic National Committee deputy publicity director Samuel C. Brightman, and General Harry Vaughan.

Were it not for the gracious assistance of those who granted me interviews, this study would have suffered greatly. The following shared their past with me: John Abt, Gladys Baker, C. B. Baldwin, Louis Bean, James Carey, Benjamin V. Cohen, Mordecai Ezekiel, Lewis Frank, Jr., Frances R. Grant, Philip Hauser, Claude Pepper, Paul R. Porter, Arthur Schlesinger, Jr., I. F. Stone, Michael Straight, Palmer Weber, and M. L. Wilson. James Loeb, Jr., Donald Murphy, and Harold Young answered my questions by correspondence.

PRIMARY SOURCES

Periodicals

The *New Republic*, *Nation*, *Progressive*, and *Common Sense* are the leading periodical sources studied systematically for an understanding of liberal thought in the 1940s. *Political Affairs*, the theoretical journal of the Communist party of the

United States, was valuable for the period 1945–1948. The *Iowa Agriculturalist*, a student publication of Iowa State University at Ames, includes contributions from Henry Wallace for the period 1906–1910. The *Congressional Record* for the period 1941–1948 was a valuable source for Wallace's speeches and for Congressional comment concerning the vital issues of the period. Pamphlets in serial form, for example, the *University of Chicago Roundtable* and the *Town Meeting of the Air*, were useful as gauges of liberal thought during and after the war.

Newspapers

Newspaper sources were especially valuable for the 1944 Democratic convention. The *New York Times* was an essential source for the entire period. *Wallace's Farmer* was valuable for Wallace's early years, for the period 1910–1921, and especially for the period of Henry A. Wallace's editorship, 1921–1933. *P.M.* was useful for topics involving Wallace for the period 1941–1948. *ADA World* and the *CIO News* were helpful for specific topics involving the third-party movement in the period 1947–1948.

Scrapbooks and clipping files were the sources for many other newspaper references used in this study. For Wallace in the 1930s and the early 1940s, special mention should be made of the Henry Wallace Scrapbooks in the HAW Papers, LC. The extensive though disorganized newspaper clippings in the HAW Papers, LC, are invaluable for an understanding of the events surrounding the 1944 Democratic convention. The Frank Walker Scrapbooks are useful for regular Democratic party politics in the early 1940s. For Wallace's relations with the Truman administration from the Madison Square Garden speech through the 1948 Presidential campaign, the Democratic National Committee Clipping Files, HSTL, are very helpful, as is the Wallace File in the ADA Papers, WSHS. The most important source of newspaper materials concerning the PCA, the Progressive Party, and Wallace's career in the early 1950s is to be found in the extensive though disorganized clipping material in the Progressive Party Papers, University of Iowa.

A compilation of Wallace obituary materials and newspaper accounts of his last years may be found in the HAW Folders, Iowa State Historical Collections, Iowa State University, and the HAW Files, United States Department of Agriculture.

Hearings and Reports

The *Report of the Secretary of Agriculture . . .* (Washington, 1933–1940) is a useful source for understanding departmental policies in the 1930s. The *Yearbook of Agriculture . . .* (Washington, 1936–1940) is helpful in understanding the goals of the department in the late 1930s. Committee on Agriculture, *Hearings on . . . HR 8,* 75 Congress, United States House of Representatives, 1 Session (Washington, 1937) and *Report of the Special Committee of Farm Tenancy* (Washington, 1937) are useful for Wallace's views on the problem of farm tenancy. The National Resources Planning Board, *Plan For 1943 . . .* (Washington, 1943) is very helpful for an understanding of wartime hopes to build a genuine welfare state in America. Committee for Economic Development, *First Year's Report* (Washington, 1943) is valuable for gaining insight into the goals of the new welfare capitalism that emerged from the war.

Democratic National Committee, *Official Proceedings of the Democratic National Convention* (Washington, 1944) is invaluable for the convention. Committee on Commerce, *Hearings on . . . S.375,* 79 Congress, United States Senate, 1 Session (Washington, 1945) is an essential source for any evaluation of the controversy surrounding Wallace's appointment as Secretary of Commerce. Committee on the Judiciary, *Hearings on . . . The Institute of Pacific Relations,* 82 Congress, United States Senate, 2 Session (Washington, 1952) is useful for an understanding of both Wallace's 1944 mission to China and for the nightmarish political persecutions of the McCarthy era.

Memoirs and Diaries

For an understanding of the world that produced Henry A. Wallace, one should begin with Henry Wallace, *Uncle Henry's*

Own Story (Des Moines, 1917), 3 vols. Among the memoirs and diaries of fellow New Dealers, Frances Perkins' *The Roosevelt I Knew* (New York, 1946) contains cogent observations of the Roosevelt–Wallace relationship. Eleanor Roosevelt's *This I Remember* (New York, 1949) and *The Autobiography of Eleanor Roosevelt* (1961) also provide significant insights into the Roosevelt–Wallace relationship. Samuel I. Rosenman, *Working With Roosevelt* (New York, 1950) is especially helpful for the 1940 and 1944 Democratic conventions. Harold L. Ickes, *The Secret Diaries of Harold L. Ickes* (New York, 1954), 3 vols., although unfortunately omitting the war and postwar years, contains the author's jaundiced observations of Henry Wallace and the rest of the world. John M. Blum, ed., *From the Morgenthau Diaries* (Boston, 1967), 3 vols., contains useful observations concerning Wallace's career by a not-so-friendly New Dealer. David E. Lilienthal, *The Journals of David E. Lilienthal* (New York, 1964), 2 vols., has valuable comments about the career of Henry Wallace in the 1940s and vivid insights into the problems of the New Dealers in the postwar world.

Cordell Hull, *The Memoirs of Cordell Hull* (New York, 1948), 2 vols., gives one an appreciation of State Department opposition to Wallace and a world New Deal. Jesse Jones and Edward Angly, *Fifty Billion Dollars* (New York, 1951) presents the Texan's account of his struggles with Henry Wallace. Memoirs related to the 1944 fight over the Vice Presidency are plentiful, although often contradictory. Of special interest in this regard are George E. Allen, *Presidents Who Have Known Me* (New York, 1950), a combination of fancy and underestimated fact by a Truman crony; Edward J. Flynn, *You're the Boss* (New York, 1947), the reminiscences of a key participant in the preconvention struggle; Grace Tully, *F.D.R., My Boss* (New York, 1949), which contains the story of the "Douglas or Truman" letter; and Francis Biddle, *In Brief Authority* (Garden City, N.Y., 1962), a view of the convention by a leading supporter of Supreme Court Justice William O. Douglas. Alben Barkley, *That Reminds Me* (Garden City, N.Y., 1954), contains interesting anecdotes concerning the

1944 convention, as does James Roosevelt and Sidney Shalett, *Affectionately, F.D.R.* (New York, 1959). Harry S. Truman, *Memoirs* (Garden City, N.Y., 1955), 2 vols., although vague and often highly inaccurate, must be consulted for an understanding of the convention struggle and of the subsequent Truman–Wallace controversies.

Although really significant memoirs of the Truman period are few, one should note that James F. Byrnes in *Speaking Frankly* (New York, 1947) and especially in *All In One Lifetime* (New York, 1958) is indispensable for the political and diplomatic events of the war and early cold-war period. Chester Bowles, *Promises to Keep* (New York, 1971) contains valuable material on the OPA controversy. George F. Kennan, *Memoirs, 1925–1950* (Boston, 1967) contains vital information concerning the origins of the cold war, the Truman Doctrine, and the Marshall Plan. William D. Leahy, *I Was There* (New York, 1950) presents the views of a major advisor to President Truman on foreign policy matters. Walter Millis and Edward S. Duffield, eds., *From the Forrestal Diaries* (New York, 1951) contains revealing although perhaps questionable references to administration attitudes concerning Wallace and the cold war. Bernard Baruch, *Baruch, My Own Story* (New York, 1957) and *The Public Years* (New York, 1960) present the financier's observations of the Madison Square Garden speech and the Baruch–Wallace controversy concerning the atomic bomb. E. G. Nourse, *Economics in the Public Service* . . . (New York, 1953) is a useful account of the workings of the Employment Act of 1946 by the first chairman of the Council of Economic Advisors. Arthur Vandenberg, Jr., and Joe Alex Morris, eds., *The Private Papers of Senator Vandenberg* (Boston, 1952) contains valuable insights into the thinking of the leading Republican internationalist. Walter Bedell Smith, *My Three Years in Moscow* (Philadelphia, 1950) includes the background for the Smith–Molotov exchange and its relation to the Wallace Presidential campaign. Jerry Voorhis, *Confessions of a Congressman* (Garden City, N.Y., 1947) presents a portrait of a New Dealer in the process of becoming a cold-war liberal. Dean Acheson, *Present at the*

Creation (New York, 1969) is a sophisticated and eloquent defense of the kind of thinking that Wallace fought in the government.

Primary Books

To understand the difference in moods between the old liberalism and the new, one might begin by contrasting John Dewey, *Liberalism and Social Action* (New York, 1935) with Reinhold Niebuhr, *The Children of Light and The Children of Darkness* (New York, 1944). For a vivid indication of the shift from the wartime hopes for a world New Deal to the postwar concept of containment, one would be wise to see Michael Straight, *Make This the Last War* (New York, 1943) and Arthur Schlesinger, Jr., *The Vital Center* (New York, 1949). The changing concept of commitment within American liberalism can be seen by comparing Charles Merriam, *On the Agenda of Democracy* (Cambridge, Mass., 1941), the hopeful vision of a scholar who had stood with both Theodore and Franklin Roosevelt, and Daniel Bell, *The End of Ideology* (New York, 1962), a bittersweet defense by an ex-"socialist" of pragmatic reform, containment of Communism, and the rejection by intellectuals of mass ideologies and movements.

Henry Wallace, *Trusts and How to Deal With Them* (Des Moines, 1899), a work that prefigures Uncle Henry's later commitment to Theodore Roosevelt and the first Progressive party, and Henry C. Wallace, *Our Debt and Duty to the Farmer* (New York, 1925), a mixture of rural nostalgia and hard-headed farm politics, are both essential to an understanding of Wallace's background. Of Henry A. Wallace's many published works, *New Frontiers* (New York, 1934) is the broadest statement of the ideas that he brought with him to the New Deal. Henry A. Wallace, *Agricultural Prices* (Des Moines, 1920) presents the influence of Veblen upon the early Wallace. Henry A. Wallace, *America Must Choose* (New York, 1934), an influential work, includes the Secretary of Agriculture's call for a moderate foreign economic policy to combat the depression. Henry A. Wallace, *Whose Constitu-*

tion? (New York, 1936) shows the Secretary as an amateur historian and opponent of the Supreme Court's assault upon the New Deal. Henry A. Wallace, *Technology, Corporations, and the General Welfare* (Chapel Hill, 1937) portrays Wallace's wrestling with the old problems of regulated competition, controlled monopoly, and a planned economy on the eve of the recession of 1937 and 1938. Henry A. Wallace, *Statesmanship and Religion* (New York, 1934) is the Secretary's most important statement of his religious views; and *Pathways to Plenty* (Washington, 1938) provides a general statement of his philosophy of abundance and a defense of the New Deal's farm program. Henry A. Wallace, *The American Choice* (New York, 1940) is especially useful for its ideas on Pan-American relations and the problems caused by the war in Europe.

Russell Lord, ed., *The Century of the Common Man* (New York, 1943), a compilation of the Vice President's important early wartime speeches, and Russell Lord, ed., *Democracy Reborn* (New York, 1944), which presents Wallace's most significant public statements for the period 1933 to 1944, are especially useful for World War II. Henry A. Wallace and Andrew S. Steiger, *Soviet Asia Mission* (New York, 1946) contains Wallace's account of his wartime Siberian excursion, even though he later noted that Steiger had written the work (save the chapter on Soviet agriculture) from the Vice President's diaries. Henry A. Wallace, *Toward World Peace* (New York, 1948) presents in a very simplified form Wallace's ideas concerning foreign policy after 1945 and his quarrels with the Truman administration concerning relations with the Soviet Union and nuclear disarmament.

SECONDARY SOURCES

Liberal Thought

Studies of the liberal mind in America are plentiful, although they often tend to recapitulate the vagueness of their subject. Sidney Fine, *Laissez Faire and the General–Welfare State*

(Ann Arbor, 1956), a comprehensive study of the development among social scientists in the late nineteenth century of rationales for state intervention in the economy, places the thought of the later Progressive era in historical perspective. Louis Hartz, *The Liberal Tradition in America* (New York, 1955) presents a stimulating thesis about the role of liberal ideology in American society. Morton White, *Social Thought in America* (Boston, 1966) contains in the later edition a useful treatment of the conflict between Dewey and Niebuhr. David W. Noble, *The Paradox of Progressive Thought* (Minneapolis, 1958) includes valuable insights into the Progressive mind but often permits its thesis of the Progressive paradox to obscure the historical context of Progressivism. Robert Wiebe, *The Search For Order* (New York, 1967) is a stimulating though perhaps exaggerated treatment of the growth of bureaucratic thought in the early twentieth century and its relationship to the Progressive era. James Weinstein, *The Corporate Ideal in the Liberal State* (Boston, 1968) attempts to apply Martin Sklar's challenging conception of corporate liberalism to the development of the National Civic Federation. Clarke A. Chambers, *Seedtime of Reform* (Minneapolis, 1963) portrays the broadening and deepening of social-work ideals in the adverse climate of the 1920s. Although Henry May, "Shifting Perspectives on the 1920s," *Mississippi Valley Historical Review*, XLIII (December, 1956), pp. 405–27, provides a stimulating introduction to the intellectual history of the 1920s, no one has yet produced a comprehensive study of intellectual currents in the decade.

Richard Alan Lawson, *The Failure of Independent Liberalism, 1930–1941* (New York, 1971) is a valuable analysis of liberal attempts to find a middle path between Marxism and the New Deal in the 1930s. Theodore Lowi, *The End of Liberalism* (New York, 1969) is a scathing and brilliant critique of interest-group liberalism by a political scientist. Frank Warren, III, *Liberals and Communism* (Bloomington, Ind., 1966) challenges the "Red Decade" interpretation of American intellectuals in the depression and presents a penetrating interpretation of liberal responses to Communism and the Soviet Union.

Although nothing of real consequence has yet been done on American liberalism during the Second World War, Alonzo L. Hamby, "Harry S. Truman and American Liberalism, 1945–1948" (Ph.D. thesis, University of Missouri, 1965) contains useful material concerning the wartime liberal movement. Hamby's study also contains important material concerning the founding of the ADA, much more so than Clifton Brock, *Americans For Democratic Action* (Washington, 1962), a poorly conceived and often highly inaccurate work. A real history of Americans for Democratic Action is sorely needed. Concerning the new liberalism of the postwar era, Palmer W. Wright, "The 'New Liberalism' of the Fifties; Reinhold Niebuhr, David Riesman, Lionel Trilling and the American Intellectual" (Ph.D. thesis, University of Michigan, 1966) analyzes containment liberalism in terms of modern European intellectual history.

General Works

Ellis W. Hawley, *The New Deal and The Problem of Monopoly* (Princeton, N.J., 1966) is the most penetrating historical analysis of the New Deal's failure to deal with either the immediate problems created by the depression or the longrange problem of the relation of governmental power to concentrations of private economic power. Herbert Stein, *The Fiscal Revolution* (Chicago, 1969) is a fine study of the development of economic thought in recent American history. Richard S. Kirkendall, *Social Scientists and Farm Politics in the Age of Roosevelt* (Columbia, Mo., 1966) is a cogent account of the achievements of planners and reformers in the Department of Agriculture. Sidney Baldwin, *Poverty and Politics* (Chapel Hill, N.C., 1968) paints a vivid picture of the deficiencies of a broker state at war in its chronicle of the rise and fall of the Farm Security Administration.

The war period itself greatly needs serious study. Richard Polenberg, *War and Society* (Philadelphia, 1972) is scholarly, comprehensive, and largely unimaginative. Roland A. Young, *Congressional Politics in the Second World War* (New York,

1956) is a superficial account of domestic politics by a political scientist. Richard R. Lingeman, *Don't You Know There's a War On* (New York, 1970) is a colorful, but skin-deep survey of the home front. Rhoda D. Edwards, "The Seventy-Eighth Congress on the Home Front: Domestic Economic Legislation" (Ph.D. thesis, Rutgers University, 1967) is poorly researched and badly thought out. Mary Hedge Hinchey, "The Frustration of the New Deal Revival, 1944–1946" (Ph.D. thesis, University of Missouri, 1965) is a valuable study of the transition from Roosevelt to Truman, even though it too suffers from a paucity of really useful manuscript sources. For Truman's pre-presidential career, Eugene F. Schmidtlein, "Truman the Senator" (Ph.D. thesis, University of Missouri, 1962) contains important material, even though Schmidtlein tends to be uncritical about his subject and defensive concerning the Truman–Pendergast relationship. Lyle W. Dorsett, *The Pendergast Machine* (New York, 1968) puts that relationship in a clearer perspective.

An interesting and insightful treatment of New Deal diplomacy, especially for the war, can be found in Lloyd C. Gardner, *Economic Aspects of New Deal Diplomacy* (Madison, Wis., 1964). Herbert Feis, *Churchill–Roosevelt–Stalin* (Princeton, N.J., 1957), is a detailed analysis of wartime diplomacy, and Robert A. Divine, *Roosevelt and World War II* (Baltimore, 1969) is a well-argued interpretation of Roosevelt's changing approach to international relations. William P. Gerberding, "Franklin Roosevelt's Conception of the Soviet Union in World Politics" (Ph.D. thesis, University of Chicago, 1959) contains a great deal of useful information concerning Roosevelt's attitude toward the Soviet Union during the war.

Among the studies of the cold war, David Rees, *The Age of Containment* (New York, 1967) contains a succinct defense of postwar American foreign policy in terms of the struggle between West and East, freedom and Communism; Louis J. Halle, *The Cold War As History* (New York, 1967) is the ablest presentation of the "realist" argument that the cold war arose from the modifications of the balance of power created by both world wars; and Walter LaFeber, *America,*

Russia and the Cold War (New York, 1967) is a useful revisionist synthesis that applies William Appleman Williams' thesis of the world open door to American–Soviet rivalries over Eastern Europe. Elting Morrison, *Turmoil and Tradition: A Study of the Life and Times of Henry L. Stimson* (Boston, 1960), Arnold A. Rogow, *James A. Forrestal* (New York, 1963), and Raymond G. Hewlett and Oscar E. Anderson, *The New World, Vol. 1, A History of the United States Atomic Energy Commission* (University Park, Pa., 1962) are especially helpful for Wallace's involvement in the conflict over foreign policy within the Truman administration. Norman A. Graebner, "Cold War Origins and the Continuing Debate: A Review of the Recent Literature," *Journal of Conflict/Resolutions,* XIII (March, 1969), pp. 123–132 is a fine treatment of the historiographical conflicts concerning the cold war.

Allen J. Matusow, *Farm Policies and Politics in the Truman Years* (Cambridge, Mass., 1967) is a lively and insightful study that is especially good in its treatment of the OPA controversy. Barton Bernstein, ed., *Politics and Policies of the Truman Administration* (Chicago, 1969) is a useful collection of recent scholarship on the Truman period. Of the studies portraying Truman's domestic policies, the best are William C. Berman, *The Politics of Civil Rights in the Truman Administration* (Columbus, Ohio, 1970); Susan M. Hartmann, *Truman and the 80th Congress* (Columbia, Mo., 1971); Richard O. Davies, *Housing Reform During the Truman Administration* (Columbia, Mo., 1966); and Arthur F. McClure, *The Truman Administration and the Problems of Postwar Labor, 1945–1948* (Rutherford, N.J., 1969). Delbert D. Arnold, "The CIO's Role in American Politics, 1936–1948" (Ph.D. thesis, University of Maryland, 1952), is an excellent account of the CIO in politics. David A. Shannon, *The Decline of American Communism* (New York, 1959), although often degenerating into polemics, contains useful material concerning the Communist party's problems after 1945.

Curtis D. MacDougall, *Gideon's Army* (New York, 1965), 3 vols., is, in spite of its poor organization and lack of discrimination among sources, the most important work yet published on the Progressive party campaign. Karl M. Schmidt, *Henry A. Wallace: Quixote Crusade, 1948* (Syracuse, N.Y., 1960) is a scanty, although useful analysis of the third party. John Cotton Brown, "The 1948 Progressive Campaign: A Scientific Approach" (Ph.D. thesis, University of Chicago, 1949) is valuable chiefly for its account of the party convention and platform committee hearings. Irwin Ross, *The Loneliest Campaign* (New York, 1968), although lacking imagination, employs important manuscript and interview material hitherto not used in depicting Truman's role in the campaign. Athan Theoharis, *Seeds of Repression* (Chicago, 1971) is a stimulating study relating the Truman policies to the rise of Joseph McCarthy. Michael Paul Rogin, *The Intellectuals and McCarthy: The Radical Specter* (Cambridge, Mass., 1967) is as valuable for its insights into the intellectual history of the 1950s as it is for its analysis of the social composition of McCarthy's following.

Henry Wallace

A really satisfactory comprehensive biography of Wallace has yet to be done. Russell Lord, *The Wallaces of Iowa* (Boston, 1947), a warm, rambling account of the three Henry Wallaces by a farm reporter and Wallace associate from the USDA, remains the best general study, despite numerous historical errors. Frank Kingdon, *An Uncommon Man, Henry Wallace and 60,000,000 Jobs* (New York, 1945) glorifies Wallace in a simplistic manner, while Dwight MacDonald, *Henry Wallace: The Man and the Myth* (New York, 1948) vilifies its subject by a colorful recitation of most of the anti-Wallace stories of the 1930s and early 1940s. Edward L. Schapsmeier and Frederick H. Schapsmeier's two-volume study, *Henry A. Wallace of Iowa: The Agrarian Years, 1910–1940* (Ames, Ia., 1968) and *Prophet in Politics: Henry A. Wallace and the War Years, 1940–1965* (Ames, Ia., 1970), goes beyond the Lord biography in its use of manuscript material, if not necessarily in its insight into Wallace's personality. Ronald Radosh, "The Economic and Political Thought of Henry A. Wallace"

(Masters thesis, University of Iowa, 1960) portrays Wallace's faith in an expanding American capitalism in ways that conform to the thinking of William Appleman Williams and his disciples. Ronald Radosh and Leonard Liggio, "Henry A. Wallace and the Open Door," in Thomas G. Patterson, ed., *Cold War Critics* (Chicago, 1971), take up these ideas and critically analyze Wallace's post-1945 foreign-policy positions.

A number of articles concerning Wallace are also especially valuable. Mordecai Ezekiel, "Henry Wallace, Agricultural Economist," *Journal of Farm Economics*, XLVIII (November, 1966), pp. 789–802, is quite good for Wallace's early career. Theodore Rosenof, "The Economic Ideas of Henry A. Wallace, 1933–1948," *Agricultural History*, XLI (April, 1967), pp. 143–153, and Alonzo L. Hamby, "Henry A. Wallace, the Liberals, and Soviet–American Relations," *Review of Politics*, XXX (April, 1968), pp. 153–169, are helpful for an understanding of Wallace in the 1930s and 1940s, although the criticism of Wallace by both authors for lacking New Deal flexibility represents an uncritical acceptance of Arthur Schlesinger, Jr.'s celebration of New Deal "pragmatism."

Index